Haynes

Classic Car Bodywork

Repair manual

The complete, illustrated step-by-step guide **4th Edition**

Lindsay Porter

First published as *Car Bodywork Repair Manual* by G. T. Foulis & Co in 1985
Reprinted 1985, 1986, 1987 (thrice), 1989 (twice) and 1990
Second edition 1991
Reprinted 1991, 1993, 1996 (twice) and 1997
Third edition published by Haynes Publishing in 2000
Reprinted 2001, 2002 (twice), 2003, 2006 and 2007
Updated and reprinted as *Classic Car Bodywork Restoration Manual* in 2010
Reprinted 2010

British Library cataloguing-in-publication data:
A catalogue record for this book is available from the British Library

ISBN 978 1 84425 829 1

Library of Congress Catalog Card Number 2009936968

Published by Haynes Publishing,
Sparkford, Yeovil, Somerset BA22 7JJ, UK

Tel: 01963 442030 Fax: 01963 440001
Int. tel: +44 1963 442030 Fax: +44 1963 440001
E-mail: sales@haynes.co.uk
Website: www.haynes.co.uk

Haynes North America Inc,
861 Lawrence Drive, Newbury Park,
California 91320, USA

Printed in the USA

**Jurisdictions which have strict emission control laws may consider any
modifications to a vehicle to be an infringement of those laws. You
are advised to check with the appropriate body or authority whether
your proposed modification complies fully with the law. The author
and publishers accept no liability in this regard.**

**While every effort is taken to ensure the accuracy of the information
given in this book, no liability can be accepted by the author or
publishers for any loss, damage or injury caused by errors in, or
omissions from the information given.**

I'd like to dedicate this book to my wife, Shan.
Most of the jobs covered here were carried out in
our workshop, next to our house, and since the
book has taken several years to prepare, she has
put up with a lot!
  She also checked and typed the original
manuscript and took many of the photographs,
and so there's a lot of her in here.

Contents

Body language

Cars old and new have some strange names for their body parts. Some of them date back to the days of horse-drawn coaches but other names seem obscure just to make life difficult. To add to the problems, many British terms are not the same as those in the USA so this section will start off with a glossary.

British	American
Aerial	Antenna
Alternator	Generator (AC)
Battery	Energizer
Bodywork	Sheet metal
Bonnet	Hood
Boot	Trunk
Bulkhead	Firewall
Cellulose (paint)	Enamel
Chassis	Frame
Dynamo	Generator (DC)
Earth	Ground
Engine bay	Motor compartment
Filler	Bond
Handbrake	Parking brake
Hood	Soft top
Indicator	Turn signal
Locks	Latches
Number plate	License plate
Paraffin	Kerosene
Petrol tank	Gas tank
Propeller shaft	Driveshaft
Quarter light	Quarter window
Saloon	Sedan
Seized	Frozen
Self-grip wrench	Locking pliers
Sidelight	Parking light
Sill	Rocker panel
Spanner	Wrench
Stopper	Glazing putty
Tailgate	Liftgate
Unitary/monocoque	Unitized body
Van	Panel wagon/van
Wheel arch	Wheelhouse
White spirit	Stoddard solvent
Windscreen	Windshield

In the olden times, a car's bodywork and its frame or chassis were two separate units. The chassis provided the car with its basic strength while the bodywork, which bolted to it, contributed little. Since the 1960s, almost all cars have been built along 'unitary' or 'monocoque' lines, where the chassis has become part of the floorpan of the car, the surrounding panels being welded or bolted to the base structure and contributing greatly to its overall strength. These more modern construction techniques take advantage of high-stress steels and the chassis has often disappeared altogether, the shape of the whole car making up its strength. A very small number of cars have been built with glass-fibre bodywork or GRP – see the chapter on working with GRP – and others (but a small number) have aluminium bodywork. Some body panels, such as most cars' bumpers and some bonnets, are made of plastic. Aluminium is difficult to work with but is covered briefly in the chapter on 'Welding'. A very small number of cars, mainly pre-1940, were fitted with fabric bodies but work on this type of body is of course, beyond the scope of this book.

BODY EVOLUTION

▼ *Figure BL1. This is a very typical completely conventional 'Three Box' saloon, with a central passenger compartment with four doors, an engine bay area at the front and a luggage bay area at the rear. Outer panels are bolted or welded on, depending on their position, and add to the strength of the floorpan. (Courtesy FIAT Auto UK)*

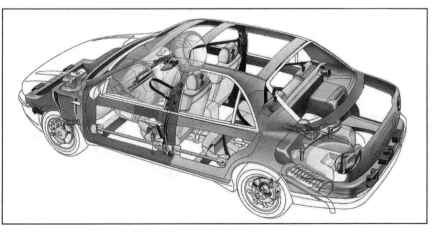

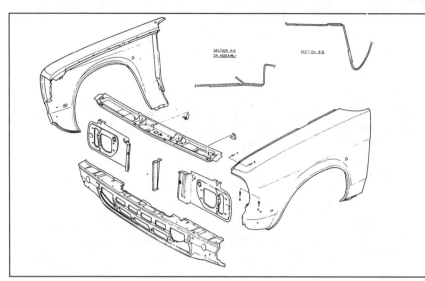

◀ Figure BL2. These external panels form the front-end outer sub-assembly and are the sorts of panels which the skilled DIY-er could consider replacing. Note from sections A-A and B-B that every panel is joined to another by an overlap. These laps would have been spot-welded together during assembly but it is not always possible for the home repairer to gain access to duplicate these spot welds. Use the alternative welding techniques outlined in this manual. (Courtesy Austin-Rover)

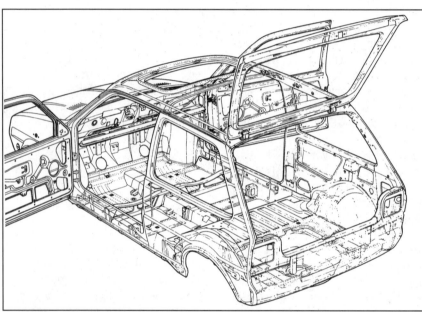

◀ Figure BL3. 'Hatchback' styling makes maximum use of passenger space. Two door construction adds greatly to the shell's stiffness. (Courtesy Austin-Rover)

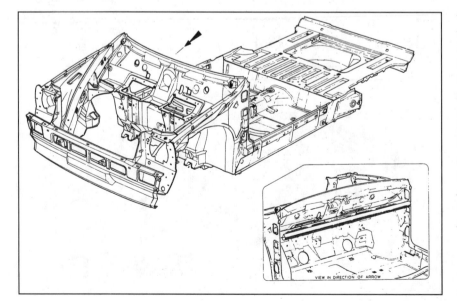

◀ Figure BL4. This time there is virtually no trace of the old chassis rails. Two important components missing from this drawing are the front subframe, which carries almost all of the front-end mechanical components and also the rear subframe. Similar, basic floorpan/bulkhead structures are used by manufacturers to produce several apparently different models of car. An example is the VW Golf, 'New' Beetle, Audi A4 and Skoda Felicia, all based on the same floorpan structure. (Courtesy Austin-Rover)

▶ *Figure BL5. Even with the addition of subframes, the floor pan in Figure BL4 looks barely rigid enough and indeed it takes the addition of these complete-looking body sides to give the shell much of its strength. Repair panels are available from the manufacturers and from specialist panel makers to repair parts of these assemblies; it is not necessary to go out and buy the whole thing! (Courtesy Austin-Rover)*

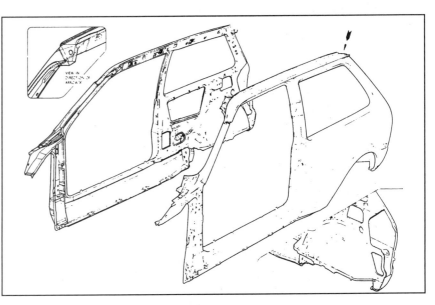

▶ *Figure BL6. This shows how the strength of a whole modern car is crucially dependent upon the bits and pieces it is made from, especially in high-stress areas such as seat-belt mounting points. When repairing panels like this, it is important that all the minor components are refitted correctly. MIG welding is preferable to oxy-acetylene because many of the panels are of high-grade steel which is weakened by the application of too much heat. (Courtesy Austin-Rover)*

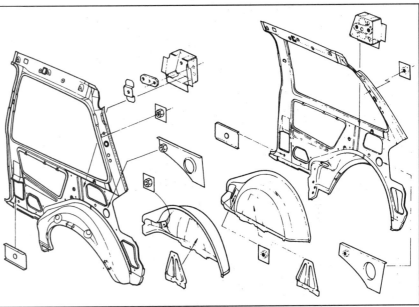

Tools and equipment

This section shows some of the tools and equipment that the author has used while working on the many projects that have gone towards making up this book.

COLLECTING THE SET

You will never have a complete set of tools; there will always be something else that you need! But over the years, if you buy equipment a little at a time, as you need it, you will accumulate a surprisingly large range of items. I still use some of the same tools that were bought for me as Christmas and birthday presents when I was a teenager and, now that I'm middle-aged, I give the same advice that I was given then always buy the best tools you can afford.

Actually, having said that, times have changed and it certainly pays to shop around. Tools that you won't need to use regularly, such as an impact screwdriver or a rubbing block for use with abrasive paper can be picked up for a song and will usually have been made in China. In general, British, German and American hand tools are better made and last longer than Far-Eastern tools, although most power tools seem to be built there: just look for a reputable maker.

When it comes to large and expensive items, such as a compressor or welder, it again pays to stick to a known maker rather than to take a chance with an apparently cheap tool whose manufacturer you may never have heard of.

▶ T&E1. Although this book is about bodywork, there is often a need to remove mechanical items to enable you to get at the part to be repaired. In the worst cases, you may have to take an engine out, which is where this Clarke engine hoist comes into its own.

▶ T&E2. The Clarke Strong-Arm engine hoist has the advantage of being able to be folded into a really small space for storage.

▶ T&E3. For the serious home restorer or home repairer (and you have to be serious to go this far!) the Autec Car Lift from Holden Vintage & Classic brings professional standards of access to the home workshop. If you have ever tried welding under the car's floor while lying on your back on the ground, and you've got a lot of repair or restoration work to do, you'll think this was made in heaven, rather than in an engineering workshop!

▶ T&E4. Where access beneath the car needs to be totally unimpeded, or for extra support when fitting and aligning sills or floorpans, Holden can also supply these extra-tall but very stable support stands, capable of supporting the whole vehicle off the ground while you wheel the Autec Car Lift out of the way.

▲ T&E7. The least expensive, but the least versatile type of welding set is an arc welder. It's not really suitable for light-weight bodywork repairs but you could probably use one for welding the chassis on something quite heavy duty, such as a Jeep or Land Rover.

▼ T&E8. The cleanest, neatest welds of all can be carried out by a spot-welder, and if you are serious about carrying out lots of car bodywork repairs, you ought to think about obtaining one. Manufacturers such as Clarke also offer a range of extension arms which enable you to get round all sorts of obstructions.

▲ T&E5. For serious bodywork repairs, you won't be able to get far without the use of a welder of some sort. The type of welding that gives you the best quality while being the easiest to learn how to use (always provided that you carry out preparation immaculately) is a MIG welder. Among their vast range of workshop tools, Clarke offer many different sizes of MIG welder, most of which will handle almost any car bodywork repairs that you are likely to encounter.

▲ T&E6. The most versatile type of welder – although it does have certain drawbacks which are described in Chapter 1, Welding and cutting – is an oxy-acetylene gas welding set. This is the BOC Portapack set which is capable of carrying out the smallest welding or brazing job as well as quite heavy-duty cutting through thick steel. They are available through commercial welding centres and are compact enough to be stored by the enthusiastic home mechanic.

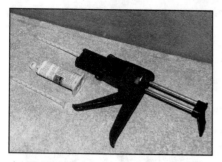

▲ T&E9. Why, you might ask, is this 3M glue gun and two-pack epoxy resin kit shown next to the welding section? The reason is quite simple. For certain repairs, it is possible to use adhesive instead of welding and, if you doubt that it would be strong enough, remember that the entire structure of the Jaguar XJ220 Supercar, capable of 220mph, was fixed together almost exclusively with such adhesives. And we haven't heard of any falling apart yet! (See later in this manual for more details on adhesives.)

▲ T&E10. Before welding steel, you will have to cut it. If you have a lot of cutting out to do, these Sykes-Pickavant cutting tools will slice through steel like nobody's business and can also cut gentle curves. For smaller amounts of cutting, regular tin snips are fine.

▶ T&E11. This is another Sykes-Pickavant tool, one that is invaluable if you have to cut out and replace sections of rusty steel. It pulls the edge of the sheet along between two rollers which form a shoulder on the edge of the steel. This allows you to join two flat pieces of metal with all the smoothness of a butt joint but with the strength and ease of a welded lap-joint. Wonderful!

▲ T&E12. Most home mechanics will find this a little out of their price bracket but the Sykes-Pickavant folder is the best way by far to create perfectly formed bends in sheet steel. Bear in mind that you can buy ready-folded strips of steel from most bodywork parts suppliers.

◀ T&E13. Another tool that you can scarcely do without is a compressor. At the bottom end of the range, both in terms of price and performance, is a compressor such as the Clarke Monza. This tiny compressor will power a spray gun sufficiently for 'blowing-in' a panel and you'll also be able to use it to inflate tyres and carry out all sorts of other lightweight jobs.

▲ T&E14. A medium-sized compressor such as the Clarke Warrior Air 25 is capable of running most air tools. The downside is that you may have to wait now and again for the compressor to recharge the reservoir, and tools which consume large quantities of air, such as a random orbit sander or fully professional spray gun, will definitely leave it a little breathless!

▲ T&E15. The Clarke Raider 120 is a V-twin mobile compressor, which produces plenty of air for spraying, inflating and air tools. Mine has performed well for a good few years now with only the most basic maintenance.

▲ T&E16. As you develop your spraying skills, you will undoubtedly wish to invest in a better gun and you will find them far easier to use into the bargain! There is a huge range available but you must make sure that your compressor is capable of coping with the gun you choose, and for the DIY sprayer, the dearest equipment may not be necessary.

▼ T&E17. The Clarke Air Kit 400 provides a very useful and remarkably low-cost set of air tools capable of being powered by even the smaller compressors.

◀ T&E18. Another use to which you will be able to put your compressor is spraying cavity protection wax. This Würth injection gun is dual-purpose. It takes throw-away Würth screw-on canisters and also has its own large separate canisters for injecting any protection wax that you may want to use 'loose'. You may feel that this is an expensive piece of equipment but, in terms of protecting your vehicle against rust, it's actually very cheap! Hand-powered, cheap and cheerful injectors simply don't atomise the protection wax or blast it far enough into nooks and crannies for it to be effective and then the whole exercise will have been a waste of time and money.

▲ T&E19. The Clarke random orbit sander boasts a far lower air consumption than most professional models. It is an essential tool if you have large areas of filler to sand because it doesn't leave scratch marks or furrows. I used to use a sanding pad which took stick-on sanding discs, but the surface of this type of pad is forever becoming contaminated with dust, turning them into 'fly-off' discs! The 3M Hookit system uses a Velcro-type of adhesion between the back of the sanding disc and the front of the sanding pad. Problem solved!

▲ T&E20. For hand sanding, 3M also produce a wide range of sanding blocks and papers, all using the same Hookit system. You will definitely need a hand block for sanding large areas of filler to prevent the surface from coming out wavy. 3M also produce small, disposable pads for fine finishing and their hand blocks and sheets have the facility for dust extraction equipment to be added (such as from an old vacuum cleaner) to keep potentially dangerous dust out of the air, and out of your, and other people's, lungs.

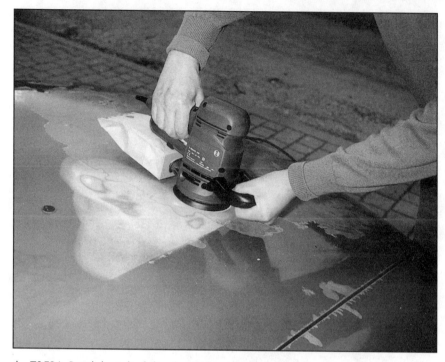

▲ T&E21. Bosch have had the clever idea of a random orbit sander which can be used on vehicles but which is also perfectly suitable for use around the home. The Bosch Multi Sander has a dust collection bag and is powered by electricity rather than air so you don't need to worry about owning a sufficiently large compressor, and as you can see here, it is perfectly capable of dealing with all types of car bodywork.

▲ T&E24. Another invaluable tool is an angle grinder. This is the Bosch PWS 7-115. A beautifully built piece of kit which is perfect for using with grinding and cutting discs but, when used with this twisted-wire brush (available from any bodyshop supplier), scours paint and rust off steel in seconds. Always wear goggles when using an angle grinder.

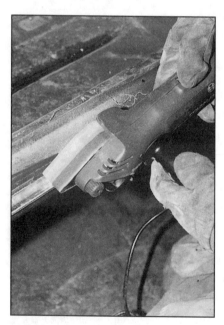

▲ T&E22. This Bosch Compact Belt Sander was produced primarily for use on wood but, with the correct type of blue belts, can be used for car bodywork and is handy for getting into small spaces, for enlarging slots and even for sharpening tools such as cold chisels and the like.

▲ T&E23. At the other end of the sanding scale is this Dremel Multi tool. It's like an electric drill but it's not! It runs at variable speeds, right up to far higher speeds than are reached by electric drills and it takes a wide range of small attachments, including this sanding head. It can be used for drilling, grinding, polishing, and almost anything else you can think of. So, if you need to remove the head from a pop rivet in a confined space, grind out rust from a recessed area or clean out a crack in plastic ready for repairing it, this is your man!

▲ T&E25. A rechargeable inspection lamp, such as this hands-free, high-power, LED lamp from Ring Automotive, gives hours of energy-efficient light, a cool bulb that will never burn or cause a fire, and great resistance to breakage, plus a complete absence of potentially dangerous trailing wires.

▲ T&E28. Another invaluable Makita tool is the BTD140Z 18V LXT Lithium-Ion Impact Driver. It produces 145Nm maximum torque, has both forward and reverse action and, once again, there's an integral job light. If you've never used an impact driver for dismantling and reassembly, you wouldn't believe how much time you can save. The BTD140Z shares its batteries with the BHP452RFE drill.

Note: LXT Lithium-Ion provides longer run time and a self-discharge rate that is five times lower than conventional batteries. The 45-minute charger and battery communicate throughout the charging process, using the built-in chip in the battery and built-in CPU chip in the charger. Clever stuff!

▲ T&E26. Another power tool that has a lot of domestic applications, as well as being almost indispensable when carrying out restoration work, is a power washer. Beware that cheaper washers don't use corrosion-resistant components, and often fail once they have been used and left standing for a while. The Kranzle 1150 power washer shown here is, like all its stablemates, made from highest quality materials, and will still be working when you want to pressure-wash the waterfront drive next year or the year after.

▲ T&E29. If your budget – or your workshop space – won't run to a stand-alone pillar drill, the Clarke CDS1 Drill Stand will turn your mains-powered drill into a perfectly adequate home-user version. Clarke also offer a hand vice which is an essential piece of equipment for gripping small workpieces.

▲ T&E27. At the top of the 'must-have' scale comes a cordless electric drill. These days, Makita li-ion drills are widely regarded as the best in the business. They are light in weight, but extremely strong. Their li-ion batteries can be recharged without damage, regardless of their state of discharge (ordinary rechargeable batteries should be fully discharged before charging, otherwise they lose efficiency). And the built-in light of the BHP452RFE 18-volt LXT Lithium-Ion Combi Drill/Driver enables you to locate the business end of the drill accurately against centre-punch marks, spot-welds and in the darkest of nooks and crannies. This fine drill has two mechanical gears, plus a variable-speed trigger and an electronic brake. The charging time is amazingly quick at about 22 minutes.

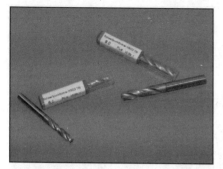

▲ T&E30. You'll do a much cleaner job of removing old spot-welded body panels by using a spot-weld drill bit. Suitable for use in any standard drill, the Würth HSCO Spot Weld Drill Bit gives a longer life than a standard spot-weld bit, though all of them will last longer if you make sure that you lubricate the drill tip and don't run the drill faster than the recommended maximum speed – in this case 1200rpm for the 6mm bit, and 950rpm for the 8mm bit.

▲ T&E32. The tote tray from the Space Maker Chest with a selection of Sykes-Pickavant tools. It is almost impossible to carry out high quality work without high quality tools.

▲ T&E31. There is a wide range of tool boxes and chests sold by Sykes-Pickavant. They're made of tough, heavy gauge steel, are lockable, and contain separate filing cabinet-type drawers for tool storage. Some of the units are stackable.

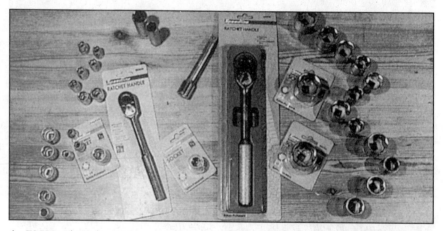

▲ T&E33. The Sykes-Pickavant 3/8in drive socket set is so well built that it's easily tough enough for most jobs yet it is lighter, easier to handle and less expensive than its 1/2in drive counterparts. Buy sockets in sets or individually bubble-packed as shown. Sykes-Pickavant surface-drive sockets work by bearing on the flat of the nut rather than its points, making it far less likely to round off the nut. The disadvantage is that the socket always feels loose on the nut, which means you have to hold it in place more firmly and it can take a bit of getting used to.

▶ *T&E34. Now we buy combination sets like the Speedline spanners pictured in the background. The extension set, pictured right, has a wonderful semi-universal joint end on each one; a boon in awkward spaces.*

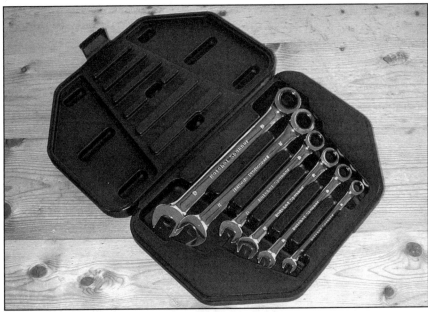

▲ *T&E35. This ratchet ring-spanner set from Halfords has taken over as my 'go-to' basic spanner set. The open-end is conventional, but the ratchet-end can save you ages when removing nuts and bolts. Nicely made, too.*

▲ *T&E36. Regard the purchase of a top-quality workshop fire extinguisher as an essential investment! When you buy the fire extinguisher, be sure to explain fully the use for which you want it. There are several different types and some can be dangerous in certain circumstances. For instance, a water-based extinguisher should never be used for a fire where there are live electric cables, for a fat fire and under other specific circumstances. Different parts of the world have different colour coding systems, so check that you understand what these are and that you obtain the right type of extinguisher for your workshop.*

Safety sense

Professional motor mechanics are trained in safe working procedures, whereas the onus is on you, the home mechanic, to find them out for yourself and act upon them. However enthusiastic you may be about getting on with the job in hand, do take the time to ensure that your safety is not put at risk. A moment's lack of attention can result in an accident, as can failure to observe certain elementary precautions.

There will always be new ways of having accidents, and the following points do not pretend to be a comprehensive list of all dangers; they are intended rather to make you aware of the risks and to encourage a safety-conscious approach to all work you carry out on your vehicle.

Be sure to consult the suppliers of any materials and equipment you may use, and to obtain and read carefully operating and health and safety instructions that they may supply.

ESSENTIAL DOS AND DON'TS

DON'T rely on a single jack when working underneath the vehicle. Always use reliable additional means of support, such as axle stands, securely placed under a part of the vehicle that you know will not give way.

DON'T attempt to loosen or tighten high-torque nuts (eg, wheel hub nuts) while the vehicle is on a jack, it may be pulled off.

DON'T start the engine without first ascertaining that the transmission is in neutral (or 'Park' where applicable) and the parking brake applied.

DON'T suddenly remove the filler cap from a hot cooling system – cover it with a cloth and release the pressure gradually first, or you may get scalded by escaping coolant.

DON'T attempt to drain oil, automatic transmission fluid, or coolant until you are sure it has cooled sufficiently to avoid scalding you.

DON'T grasp any part of the engine, exhaust or catalytic converter without first ascertaining that it is sufficiently cool to avoid burning you.

DON'T allow brake fluid or antifreeze to contact vehicle paintwork.

DON'T syphon toxic liquids such as fuel, brake fluid or antifreeze by mouth, or allow them to remain on your skin.

DON'T inhale dust – it may be injurious to health (see Asbestos below).

DON'T allow any spilt oil or grease to remain on the floor – wipe it up straight away, before someone slips on it.

DON'T use ill-fitting spanners or other tools which may slip and cause injury.

DON'T attempt to lift a heavy component which may be beyond your capability – get assistance.

DON'T rush to finish a job, or take unverified short cuts.

DON'T allow children or animals in or around an unattended vehicle.

DON'T park vehicles with catalytic converters over combustible materials such as dry grass, oily rags, etc, if the engine has recently been run. As catalytic converters reach extremely high temperatures, any such materials in close proximity may ignite.

DON'T run vehicles equipped with catalytic converters without the exhaust system heat shields fitted.

DO wear eye protection when using power tools such as an electric drill, sander, bench grinder, etc, and when working under the vehicle.

DO use a barrier cream on your hands prior to undertaking dirty jobs – it will protect your skin from infection as well as making the dirt easier to remove afterwards; but make sure your hands aren't left slippery. Note that long-term contact with used engine oil can be a health hazard.

DO keep loose clothing (cuffs, tie, etc) and long hair well out of the way of moving mechanical parts.

DO remove rings, wristwatch, etc, before working on the vehicle – especially the electrical system.

DO ensure that any lifting tackle used has a safe working load rating adequate for the job, and is used precisely as recommended by the manufacturer.

DO keep your work area tidy – it is only too easy to fall over articles left lying around.

DO get someone to check periodically that all is well, when working alone on the vehicle.

DO carry out work in a logical sequence and check that everything is correctly assembled and tightened afterwards.

DO remember that your vehicle's safety affects that of yourself and others. If in doubt on any point, get specialist advice. IF, in spite of following these precautions, you are unfortunate enough to injure yourself, seek medical attention as soon as possible.

FIRE

Remember at all times that petrol (gasoline) is highly flammable. Never smoke, or have any kind of naked flame around, when working on the vehicle. But the risk does not end here – a spark caused by an electrical short-circuit, by two metal surfaces contacting each other, by a central heating boiler in the garage firing up, or even by static electricity built up in your body under certain conditions, can ignite petrol vapour, which in a confined space is highly explosive.

Always disconnect the battery earth (ground) terminal before working on any part of the fuel system, and never risk spilling fuel on to a hot engine or exhaust.

It is recommended that a fire extinguisher of a type suitable for fuel and electrical fires is kept handy in the garage or workplace at all times. Never try to extinguish a fuel or electrical fire with water.

FUMES
Certain fumes are highly toxic and can quickly cause unconsciousness and even death if inhaled to any extent. Petrol (gasoline) vapour comes into this category, as do the vapours from certain solvents such as trichloroethylene and those from many adhesives. Any draining or pouring of such volatile fluids should be done in a well-ventilated area.

When using cleaning fluids and solvents, read the instructions carefully. Never use any materials from unmarked containers – they may give off poisonous vapours.

Never run the engine of a motor vehicle in an enclosed space such as a garage. Exhaust fumes contain carbon monoxide which is extremely poisonous. If you need to run the engine, always do so in the open air or at least have the rear of the vehicle outside the workplace.

If you are fortunate enough to have the use of an inspection pit, never drain or pour petrol, and never run the engine, while the vehicle is standing over it; the fumes, being heavier than air, will concentrate in the pit with possibly lethal results.

THE BATTERY
Never cause a spark, or allow a naked light, near the vehicle battery. It will normally be giving off a certain amount of hydrogen gas, which is highly explosive.

Always disconnect the battery earth (ground) terminal before working on the fuel or electrical systems.

If possible, loosen the filler plugs or cover when charging the battery from an external source. Do not charge at an excessive rate or the battery may burst.

Take care when topping up and when carrying the battery. The acid electrolyte, even when diluted, is very corrosive and should not be allowed to contact the eyes or skin.

If you ever need to prepare electrolyte yourself, always add the acid slowly to the water, and never the other way round. Protect against splashes by wearing rubber gloves and goggles.

MAINS ELECTRICITY
When using an electric power tool, inspection light, etc, which works from the mains, always ensure that the appliance is correctly connected to its plug and that, where necessary, it is properly earthed (grounded). Do not use such appliances in damp conditions and, again, beware of creating a spark or applying excessive heat in the vicinity of fuel or fuel vapour.

Also, before using any mains powered electrical equipment, take one more simple precaution – use an RCD (Residual Current Device) circuit breaker. Then, if there is a short, the RCD circuit breaker minimises the risk of electrocution by instantly cutting the power supply. Buy from any electrical store or DIY centre. RCDs fit simply into your electrical socket before plugging in your electrical equipment.

IGNITION HT VOLTAGE
A severe electric shock can result from touching certain parts of the ignition system, such as the HT leads, when the engine is running or being cranked, particularly if components are damp or the insulation is defective. Where an electronic ignition system is fitted, the HT voltage is much higher and could prove fatal. Consult your handbook or main dealer if in any doubt. Risk of injury while working on running engines, eg adjusting the timing, can arise if the operator touches a high voltage lead and pulls his hand away on to a projection or revolving part.

WELDING AND BODYWORK REPAIRS
It is so useful to be able to weld when carrying out restoration work, and yet there is a good deal that could go

dangerously wrong for the uninformed – in fact more than could be covered here. For safety's sake you are strongly recommended to seek tuition, in whatever branch of welding you wish to use, from your local evening institute or adult education classes. In addition, all of the information and instructional material produced by the suppliers of materials and equipment you will be using must be studied carefully. You may have to ask your stockist for some of this printed material if it is not made available at the time of purchase.

COMPRESSED GAS CYLINDERS
There are serious hazards associated with the storage and handling of gas cylinders and fittings, and standard precautions should be strictly observed in dealing with them. Ensure that cylinders are stored in safe conditions, properly maintained and always handled with special care and make constant efforts to eliminate the possibilities of leakage, fire and explosion.

The cylinder gases that are commonly used are oxygen, acetylene and liquid petroleum gas (LPG). Safety requirements for all three gases are: Cylinders must be stored in a fire resistant, dry and well-ventilated space, away from any source of heat or ignition and protected from ice, snow or direct sunlight. Valves of cylinders in store must always be kept uppermost and closed, even when the cylinder is empty. Cylinders should be handled with care and only by personnel who are reliable, adequately informed and fully aware of all associated hazards. Damaged or leaking cylinders should be immediately taken outside into the open air, and the supplier and fire authorities should be notified immediately. No one should approach a gas cylinder store with a naked light or cigarette. Care should be taken to avoid striking or dropping cylinders, or knocking them together. Cylinders should never be used as rollers. One cylinder should never be filled from another. Every care must be taken to avoid accidental damage to cylinder valves. Valves must be operated without haste, never fully opened hard back against the back stop (so that other users know the valve is open) and never wrenched shut but turned just securely enough to stop the gas. Before removing or loosening any outlet connections, caps or plugs, a check should be made that the valves are closed. When changing cylinders, close all valves and appliance taps, and extinguish naked flames, including pilot jets, before disconnecting them. When reconnecting ensure that all connections and washers are clean and in good condition and do not overtighten them. Immediately a cylinder becomes empty, close its valve.

Safety requirements for acetylene: Cylinders must always be stored and used in the upright position. If a cylinder becomes heated accidentally or becomes hot because of excessive backfiring, immediately shut the valve, detach the regulator, take the cylinder out of doors well away from the building, immerse it in or continuously spray it with water, open the valve and allow the gas to escape until the cylinder is empty. If necessary, notify the emergency fire service without delay.

Safety requirements for oxygen are: No oil or grease should be used on valves or fittings. Cylinders with convex bases should be used in a stand or held securely to a wall.

Safety requirements for LPG are: The store must be kept free of combustible material, corrosive material and cylinders of oxygen.

Cylinders should only ever be carried upright, securely strapped down, preferably in an open vehicle or with windows open. Carry the suppliers safety data with you. In the event of an accident, notify the Police and Fire Services and hand the safety data to them.

DANGEROUS LIQUIDS AND GASES

Because of flammable gas given off by batteries when on charge, care should be taken to avoid sparking by switching off the power supply before charger leads are connected or disconnected. Battery terminals should be shielded, since a battery contains energy and a spark can be caused by any conductor which touches its terminals or exposed connecting straps.

When internal combustion engines are operated inside buildings the exhaust

fumes must be properly discharged to the open air. Petroleum spirit or mixture must be contained in metal cans which should be kept in a store. In any area where battery charging or the testing of fuel injection systems is carried out there must be good ventilation, and no sources of ignition. Inspection pits often present serious hazards. They should be of adequate length to allow safe access and exit while a car is in position. If there is an inspection pit, petrol may enter it. Since petrol vapour is heavier than air it will remain there and be a hazard if there is any source of ignition. All sources of ignition must therefore be excluded.

LIFTING EQUIPMENT

Special care should be taken when any type of lifting equipment is used. Lifting jacks are for raising vehicles; they should never be used as supports while work is in progress. Jacks must be replaced by adequate rigid supports before any work is begun on the vehicle. Risk of injury while working on running engines, eg adjusting the timing, can arise if the operator touches a high voltage lead and pulls his hand away on to a projection or revolving part. On some vehicles the voltage used in the ignition system is so high as to cause injury or death by electrocution.

Consult your handbook or main dealer if in any doubt.

WORK WITH PLASTICS

Work with plastic materials brings additional hazards into workshops. Many of the materials used (polymers, resins, adhesives and materials acting as catalysts and accelerators) readily produce very dangerous situations in the form of poisonous fumes, skin irritants, risk of fire and explosions. Do not allow resin or 2-pack adhesive hardener, or that supplied with filler or 2-pack stopper to come into contact with skin or eyes. Read carefully the safety notes supplied on the tin, tube or packaging.

JACKS AND AXLE STANDS

Special care should be taken when any type of lifting equipment is used. Any jack is made for lifting the car, not for supporting it. NEVER even consider working under your

car using only a jack to support the weight of it. Jacks are only for raising vehicles, and must be replaced by adequate supports before any work is begun on the vehicle; axle stands are available from many discount stores, and all auto parts stores. These stands are absolutely essential if you plan to work under your car. Simple triangular stands (fixed or adjustable) will suit almost all of your working situations. Drive-on ramps are very limiting because of their design and size.

When jacking the car from the front, leave the gearbox in neutral and the brake off until you have placed the axle stands under the frame. Make sure that the car is on level ground first! Then put the car into gear and/or engage the handbrake and lower the jack. Obviously DO NOT put the car in gear if you plan to turn over the engine! Leaving the brake on, or leaving the car in gear while jacking the front of the car will necessarily cause the jack to tip (unless a good quality trolley jack with wheels is being used). This is unavoidable when jacking the car on one side, and the use of the handbrake in this case is recommended.

If the car is older and if it shows signs of weakening at the jack tubes while using the factory jack, it is best to purchase a good scissors jack or hydraulic jack – preferably trolley-type (depending on your budget).

WORKSHOP SAFETY – SUMMARY

1 Always have a fire extinguisher at arm's length whenever welding or when working on the fuel system – under the car, or under the bonnet.
2 NEVER use a naked flame near the petrol tank.
3 Keep your inspection lamp FAR AWAY from any source of dripping petrol (gasoline); for example, while removing the fuel pump.
4 NEVER use petrol (gasoline) to clean parts. Use paraffin (kerosene) or white (mineral) spirits.
5 NO SMOKING!

If you do have a fire, DON'T PANIC. Use the extinguisher effectively by directing it at the base of the fire.

PAINT SPRAYING

NEVER use 2-pack, isocyanate-based paints in the home environment or home workshop. Ask your supplier if you are not sure which is which. If you have use of a professional booth, wear an air-fed mask. Wear a charcoal face mask when spraying other paints and maintain ventilation to the spray area. Concentrated fumes are dangerous!

Spray fumes, thinners and paint are highly flammable. Keep away from naked flames or sparks.

FLUOROELASTOMERS
Most important! Please read this section!

Many synthetic rubber-like materials used in motor cars contain a substance called fluorine. These substances are known as fluoroelastomers and are commonly used for oil seals, wiring and cabling, bearing surfaces, gaskets, diaphragms, hoses and 'O' rings. If they are subjected to temperatures greater than 315°C, they will decompose and can be potentially hazardous. Fluoroelastomer materials will show physical signs of decomposition under such conditions in the form of charring of black sticky masses. Some decomposition may occur at temperatures above 200°C, and it is obvious that when a car has been in a fire or has been dismantled with the assistance of a cutting torch or blow torch, the fluoroelastomers can decompose in the manner indicated above. In the presence of any water or humidity, including atmospheric moisture, the by-products caused by the fluoroelastomers being heated can be extremely dangerous. According to the Health and Safety Executive, 'Skin contact with this liquid or decomposition residues can cause painful and penetrating burns. Permanent irreversible skin and tissue damage can occur'. Damage can also be caused to eyes or by the inhalation of fumes created as fluoroelastomers are burned or heated. If you are in the vicinity of a vehicle fire or a place where a vehicle is being cut up with cutting equipment, the Health and Safety Executive recommend the following action:

1 Assume unless you know otherwise that seals, gaskets and 'O' rings, hoses, wiring and cabling, bearing surfaces and diaphragms are fluoroelastomers.
2 Inform firefighters of the presence of fluoroelastomers and toxic and corrosive fume hazards when they arrive.
3 All personnel not wearing breathing apparatus must leave the immediate area of a fire.

After fires or exposure to high temperatures:
1 Do not touch blackened or charred seals or equipment.
2 Allow all burnt or decomposed fluoroelastomer materials to cool down before inspection, investigation, tear-down or removal.
3 Preferably, don't handle parts containing decomposed fluoroelastomers, but if you must, wear goggles and PVC (polyvinyl chloride) or neoprene protective gloves whilst doing so. Never handle such parts unless they are completely cool.
4 Contaminated parts, residues, materials and clothing, including protective clothing and gloves, should be disposed of by an approved contractor to landfill or by incineration according to national or local regulations. Original seals, gaskets and 'O' rings, along with contaminated material, must not be burned locally.

Symptoms and clinical findings of exposure:
A Skin/eye contact:
Symptoms may be apparent immediately, soon after contact or there may be considerable delay after exposure. Do not assume that there has been no damage from a lack of immediate symptoms; delays of minutes in treatment can have severe consequences:
1 Dull throbbing ache.
2 Severe and persistent pain.
3 Black discolouration under nails (skin contact).
4 Severe, persistent and penetrating burns.
5 Skin swelling and redness.
6 Blistering.
7 Sometimes pain without visible change.

B Inhalation (breathing): – immediate
1 Coughing.
2 Choking.
3 Chills lasting one to two hours after exposure.
4 Irritation.

C Inhalation (breathing) – delays of one to two days or more:
1 Fever.
2 Cough.
3 Chest tightness.
4 Pulmonary oedema (congestion).
5 Bronchial pneumonia.

FIRST AID

A Skin contact:
1 Remove contaminated clothing immediately.
2 Irrigate affected skin with copious amounts of cold water or lime water (saturated calcium hydroxide solution) for 15 to 60 minutes. Obtain medical assistance urgently.

B Inhalation
Remove to fresh air and obtain medical supportive treatment immediately. Treat for pulmonary oedema.

C Eye contact
Wash/irrigate eyes immediately with water followed by normal saline for 30 to 60 minutes. Obtain immediate medical attention.

Chapter 1

Welding and cutting

Large numbers of people are doing their own welding nowadays. From old-car enthusiasts to DIY car-repairers – including those who make useful pocket money out of their hobby – there's a realisation that if you are going to get serious about car bodywork repairs, you really have to start welding. We'll take a look at four kinds of welding here, all of them suitable for car bodywork repairs, looking first into the whys and then into a few of the hows. Then, because all kinds of welding are pretty complicated when you start taking them seriously, we will take each of them apart a little bit, and look at the sort of information you will need to know if you're going to take your welding past the beginner's stage.

To understand how welding works, all you have to remember is that any metal will melt if you make it hot enough. Then remember those plastic model kits that most youngsters seem to build. They are held together with a special kind of cement that melts the surfaces of the plastic being joined together so that when they are held tight against one another and the plastic re-sets itself, the two surfaces have flowed into one another so that there is a welded joint as opposed to two entirely separate pieces of plastic. Apart from the fact that plastic 'welding' of this sort is carried out with a plastic solvent while metal welding is carried out with heat, the principles involved are much the same. The two bits of metal being welded together are melted around a joint (and more often than not, some extra metal is flowed in to help strengthen the joint) and as soon as the metal cools below its 'freezing'

point, you have got a joint which consists of a more-or-less continuous piece of metal, rather than two separate pieces stuck together with some kind of super-glue. Outside the hi-tech world of lasers and ultrasound there are only two practical ways of getting sufficient heat into the metal: one is by using a high burning temperature bottled gas; the other is electricity.

BRAZING
It would really be wrong to go any further without mentioning brazing or 'braze welding' as it is sometimes called. Brazing has the great advantage that it is one of the easiest ways of holding two pieces of steel together, with beginners usually getting it right within a very short time. Just as in fusion welding, two pieces of steel are held close together and heated up but this time, instead of extra steel being flowed into the joint, a rod of bronze alloy is pushed into the heat of the flame and this adheres to both pieces of metal. It actually 'slicks' extraordinarily well because there is molecular bonding between the braze and the steel, which gives, in effect, something in between a glue and the total fusion you get from a welded joint. Brazing rod is often given the slang name of 'bronze' or 'brass' because it contains the same basic constituents of copper with tin and/or zinc. Strange though it may seem, brazing can be carried out not only with gas welding equipment but also with electric welding gear by using a special adaptor. The disadvantages of brazing are mainly that it is relatively expensive to carry out (the cost of rods is the main reason) and that

it is nowhere near as strong as a full welded joint, so it is not suitable for use with main structural components such as chassis or even sills on most cars. In fact, in the UK, brazing is not accepted at MoT-testing stations on structural components.

TYPES OF WELDING

ARC WELDING
Electric arc welding is the easiest to set up and also the cheapest to buy but unfortunately for car bodyworkers, it's just not suitable for welding thin steel, although it can be adapted to carry out brazing. Another snag is that it takes a bit of practice to get it right. The equipment consists of a welding machine, or transformer, which takes the ordinary household current and transforms it into the type of current suitable for safely welding steel. Leading from the machine are two heavy-duty cables; one, the 'earth' cable, has a clamp on the end which must be clipped onto the workpiece, and the other has a special handgrip and welding rod holder on the end of it. A steel welding rod with a special flux coating is gripped by the holder/handgrip and, when the power is on, the end of the rod is touched onto the workpiece at the place where welding is to be carried out. This completes the electrical circuit and the low-voltage-with-high-amperage current pushed out by the transformer causes a bright electric arc to jump between welding rod and

workpiece. This melts the steel at the point near the end of the rod and it also melts the end of the rod, too, the molten metal being thrown in liquid droplets into the weld pool. The melting process is pretty well instantaneous so it is a great system for cutting down on heat distortion – in other words the metal is less likely to kink when welded than with some other systems – but it's pretty fierce and it's almost impossible to avoid burning right through thin steel. You can usually arc weld old fashioned chassis, and even some more modern box-sections when you become more skilful, and bumper brackets and general workshop construction welding is fine with arc welding, but if you want to use the arc welder with thin panels, you have to go over to brazing with a carbon-arc attachment. It is worth pointing out that you can buy a more expensive type of arc welder, one that gives out direct current, which is much less prone to burning through sheet steel.

CARBON-ARC BRAZING

Here a special adaptor is used on the end of the cable which would normally carry the welding rod grip. This consists of two rods of carbon, one of which is fixed and the other is on a slide arrangement. The two rods are held close together and then moved near the workpiece. As the arc is formed, the two rods, in effect, burn against each other which forms a flame. This is used to heat up the workpiece sufficiently for a brazing rod to be fed in and melted. The torch has to be moved, the carbon rods have to be slid close together, and the rod has to be moved and fed in at the same time. Once you have mastered all those simultaneous movements, patting your head and rubbing your stomach at the same time seem child's play although, once mastered, you will wonder why the skills seemed so tricky!

OXY-ACETYLENE WELDING

Traditionally, this type of welding has been the staple of every car body repairer and garage, although it has been held back from the DIY market, almost deliberately it seems. With this kind of welding, a special torch is used which mixes oxygen and acetylene in just the right proportions to produce a very hot flame indeed. The gas is fed through tubes from cylinders of the gases being used. The small, hot flame is played onto the steel being welded and when a molten puddle begins to form, a thin rod of steel is fed in. The rod melts and helps build up a good thickness of metal round the joint. Because the torch has to be moved around and the rod has to be fed in and along at the same time, it can take a little while to become proficient at this kind of welding although it is very versatile indeed. In addition, there are many DIY gas welding kits of varying kinds on the market nowadays, a number of which use a substitute gas instead of acetylene. One of the UK's leading gas suppliers, BOC, promotes the use of small oxygen and acetylene bottles along with professional-standard hardware. Gas welding is very good for brazing, of course, and it can be controlled so that it doesn't burn through car body panels. There is, however, one big snag: transference of heat from the gas flame to the workpiece is inefficient, thus the time taken to raise the weld area to melting point is relatively long. By the time a molten puddle forms, a great deal of the heat energy has gone into the air and much has dissipated through the surrounding steel. The latter aspect causes big problems as a later section on 'Distortion' shows.

MIG WELDING

This is the crown prince of car bodywork welding, containing the main advantages of other systems with none of the disadvantages, except that it can't be used for brazing and, compared with gas welding, it is not so versatile and can't be used for cutting metal or freeing stubborn bolts: it just welds, but it does it really well!

MIG welding is based on the idea of arc welding but with very significant modifications. Instead of a fixed length of rod which is clamped to the holder then thrown away when reduced to a stub and replaced by a new rod, the MIG welder has a long coil of welding wire inside the machine casing and a tube which runs out to the welder's handgrip. Also in the machine casing is an electric motor, so when the welder wants to start welding, he presses a button on the handgrip and wire is fed out of the end of the gun on the handgrip. Just as in ordinary arc welding, there is an earth lead clamped to the workpiece and, in the same way, as the wire touches the workpiece the arc is completed and welding takes place. All of this makes the MIG welder very easy to control indeed because all the operator has to do is set the machine controls up correctly, press the button and move the gun at a slow 'n' steady pace. The MIG has another ace up its sleeve, however. The MIG welder does not only push welding wire along the supply pipe to the welding gun (or 'handset' if you want to be absolutely correct), it also feeds an inert gas (ie one that does not react in any way with the weld) such as Argon, Argon/CO_2 or even just CO_2 (Carbon Dioxide) along the pipe, through the gun and invisibly around the weld as it takes place. This helps cooling and cuts distortion even further, which means that you are far less likely to end up with rippled panelwork, trim does not have to be stripped out except around the weld area itself, and paintwork only burns back a little way. The only snag with MIG is that, being a little princely, it does insist upon having clean metal to work on, too much rust or paint contamination causing it to cough and splutter in a most un-royal way!

TIG WELDING

This is a highly specialised arc-welding process but one which is finding its way into some body shops, especially those where a good deal of aluminium is welded, so it will be briefly examined later.

Plasma cutting is the quickest and cleanest method of cutting sheet steel. Because electrical contact is needed an area of paint-free steel is required to start cutting. Another bonus with this type of cutting is the total absence of distortion as the machine is connected to a supply of compressed air to cool the torch and cutting area.

SELECTING YOUR WELDING GEAR

These thumbnail sketches of the various types of welding equipment are not intended to be anything like a thorough grounding in the subject, but they should give an idea of what each system is about. So which one is best for the home body repairer? Well, it all depends how much you want to spend and what sort of work you intend to carry out. Here are a few possible 'user profiles': see which one you most closely resemble, then look at the system I think would be best for you.

1. You have a few repairs to carry out on your car's body, including structural parts, and you may want to do a little similar welding at some time in the future.

The best choice for you could be one of the really cheap gas welding kits on the market. They can be fiddly to use and are harder to learn with than a more professional kit, but if time is no real problem, so what? They also cost a lot to use because their small gas cylinders need replenishing fairly often and they would work out *very* expensive if you had to use them on a full-time basis. They are widely advertised in the DIY-type journals, but do try to see one before you buy it. Make certain you get one that works from Mapp gas. Anything else is too cool to allow you to weld. Note that none of these kits use acetylene because bottling and handling it is hugely expensive, and risky unless properly controlled. *Recommended supplier*: The Welding Centre, Glasgow who sell kits which are slightly more expensive than some but all of which come with a superb welding torch.

2. You want a welding system that will allow you to patch rust holes in your car and carry out 101 other welding jobs around the home, such as repairing the gate, making a sledge for winter and so forth. If your car needs major structural welding you'll take it into the garage anyway.

There's no doubt that an arc welder with a carbon-arc brazing attachment will do everything you want! You will be able to braze repair patches to your car's bodywork or on the lawnmower's grass catcher and the arc welder itself will prove invaluable if you're a keen oddjobber. It's also handy for making lifting brackets, mending tools and constructing one-off special tools in the workshop, although of course any other system could be used for this, but only arc and MIG welding are at all quick where thicker metal is involved.

3. You find repairing cars a fascinating hobby. Perhaps you like restoring old cars, or maybe you buy a succession of bangers, tidy them up and sell them on. Maybe you even do the odd job for your friends and neighbours. Or perhaps you just take your hobby very seriously and insist that if you're going to do something at all, you must do it absolutely properly.

You may wish to use more than one welding system, so here are two suggested packages which complement each other well. Neither package comes cheaply but both will do just about every job you could conceivably want in a home workshop.

Package A: A cheap arc welder (for those medium-thickness steel odd jobs) and a good quality gas welding set. The Welding Centre's most expensive offering just about comes into this category but the best DIY gas welding system is the Portapack. Here, a full professional Murex Sapphire welding gun with full kit of accessories including cutting gear and a portable cylinder trolley/stand goes with a pair of Portapack cylinders (oxygen and acetylene) rented out by BOC Ltd from their nationwide distribution system. There is absolutely no difference between the finest welding kits you will find in a professional workshop and this set-up, except that the bottles are smaller and therefore more portable and easier to store, although of course they run out faster and give around 10 or 20 hours of

welding burn time per pair, depending upon the type rented. The bad news is that, in the UK, the bottle rental has to be paid all of *seven* years in advance, which can be a rather hefty amount. *Recommended Supplier*: SIP (Industrial Products) Ltd for a less expensive arc welder. Murex Ltd for a really top-of-the-range oil-cooled DC arc welder (although this is really more a medium duty industrial piece of equipment). Murex Ltd/BOC Ltd for the complete Portapack hardware/gas or The Welding Centre for something a little less expensive but less professional.

Package B: (This would be my favourite!) A really cheap gas welding set for the few occasions where brazing is necessary. Could also do a little crude cutting, by turning the oxygen up high and would be useful for freeing stubborn nuts and bolts. And a small MIG set, which gives the best quality welds of any system with very little or no distortion. Can also be used on quite thick plate for a few minutes at a time so there are no practical limitations there. In addition, if a lot of welding is anticipated MIG has to be just about cheapest in terms of materials consumption. *Recommended Supplier*: SIP (Industrial Products) Ltd for MIG, plus the cheapest supplier you can find offering a usable kit for gas welding (**NB** *not* acetylene).

WELDING CONCEPTS AND PRINCIPLES

Without becoming at all technical, there are one or two basic concepts involved in all kinds of welding that need to be considered. Briefly, they are as follows:

COMPATIBILITY

Obviously, you can't weld just any two materials together; the materials being welded together need to be compatible with each other as does the filler or rod being used. You can't weld aluminium to steel but that apart, as a car bodywork repairer, you don't have to worry about the problem of materials. When buying sheet steel or (in rare cases) sheet aluminium for repairing the panelwork of your car, make sure that your supplier knows what you are going to be using the sheet for and so supplies you with the correct material. Similarly, when buying welding rods or welding wire (for a MIG welder), explain to your supplier what you are welding.

DISTORTION

As everyone knows, when you heat metal up it expands, and when you let it cool down, it contracts again. In an ideal world, the two would cancel each other out and cooled metal would be exactly the same shape and size as the original. Unfortunately, when you cut and shape pieces of metal, then weld them together, they experience pushes and pulls in all sorts of directions as they are heated up and that's why car body panels are prone to distortion when they are welded. The two main conditions when excessive distortion is likely to occur are when, (i) a great deal of heat is put into the panel, such as with gas welding and (ii) the panel is a large, relatively flat area such as a door skin or bonnet (hood) panel. On a very large flat area, even MIG welding, which is known for being the least distortion-prone of all systems, can cause ripples in the surface of the panel and so can lead-loading a large flat panel or soldering something on to it. The trick when welding is to clamp panels together at close intervals and to tack-weld them together at regular intervals too, before carrying out the welding proper. (Tack welding is explained in later sections, but it is essentially a process of putting little blobs of weld across the joint to hold both pieces together temporarily, the tacks being lost later in the main weld.) Then, avoid welding from one end of the seam to the other in one go. Instead, weld from one end for a little way, stop to allow the panel to cool. Then weld in the centre, cooling the panel after each weld, and then fill in the gaps. This helps to equalise the stresses in the panel and prevents too much heat from building

up. When soldering, surround the area with wet rags, so that they draw the excess heat out of the panel rather than allowing it to spread. If distortion does take place and you are left with a 'bump' in the panel, don't despair! Turn to the section on shrinking a panel, which shows how to get rid of the excess metal, this time turning heat and expansion to your advantage. If a panel is left very slightly rippled, you can get rid of it with a thin spread of plastic body filler or even, in very mild cases, with a high-build spray filler.

IMPURITIES

The more impurities there are in a weld, the weaker it will be – that much speaks for itself. It is important to weld with metal that is substantially free of paint, rust, grease or any other contamination because, although much of it is burned off, the residue gets into the weld, weakens it and makes the weld look lumpy and generally scruffy. Any welding involving an electric arc creates its own impurities unless the air is excluded for the duration of the weld. In MIG and TIG welding a shield is provided by blowing an inert (or 'dead') gas over the weld, while straightforward arc welders use coated welding rods. The coating melts with the rod, floats over the weld and protects it from the air. It then goes hard and has to be chipped away later. Both brazing and soldering require a flux to be applied to the metal, otherwise the oxides formed prevent the solder or braze from combining with the workpiece. Only oxy-acetylene welding requires no shielding of any kind, but it is still important to start off with fairly clean metal.

Protection
All kinds of welding give off a great deal of heat, a lot of bright light and some give off fumes that can be dangerous in certain circumstances.

Take careful note of the 'Safety'

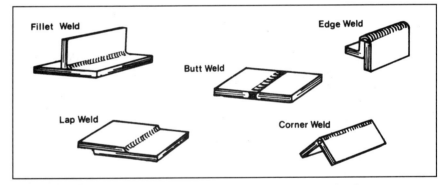

▲ *Figure W1. Basic weld types. (Courtesy SIP (Industrial Products) Ltd)*

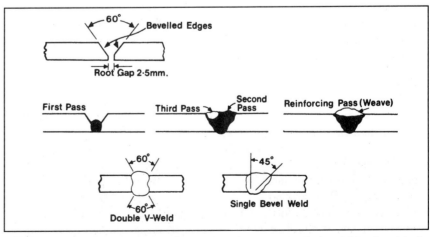

▲ *Figure W2. Multiple-pass welding method. (Courtesy SIP (Industrial Products) Ltd)*

section of each welding system described and refer to the 'Safety' section at the beginning of this book for general safety information.

WELDED JOINT TYPES

The illustrations in Figure W1 show some of the most common types of welded joint for sheet steel. Each has its own use according to the job in hand. Before you try a new type of joint, it should be practised on pieces of scrap metal. When butt welding thicker plates together, especially with arc or MIG welding, it is best to use the technique where a first pass is made from one side of the joint and then a second pass is made from the other side, with a slightly higher setting used to encourage the second weld to fuse with the first. Alternatively, use the method shown in Figure W2. Here the plates have been bevelled and are welded together using a series of runs as shown. This method is of course most suitable when access can only be gained from one side of the workpiece.

WELDING TECHNIQUES

There's only one way of becoming really proficient at welding – and that is by getting out there and doing it. This section takes each of the main types of welding and shows how to tackle them, right from first principles. Each section shows how to weld on small pieces of metal rather than full panels, because that's the best way to start. Then you can work at a height that is comfortable to you and arrange the pieces in such a way that you can weld them easily. You'll have plenty of opportunity to weld above your head whilst lying on your back later on, when you have mastered the basics!

ARC WELDING

As already explained, arc welding is the fusing together of two (or more) pieces of metal by means of the heat generated by an electric arc. Figure W3 shows how the process takes place.

SAFETY

The greatest danger when arc welding comes from the extremely bright light given off during the process. Not only is it so bright that it will damage the eyes if looked at directly, the light also contains a good deal of ultraviolet light which can cause direct and permanent damage to the eyes. *Always* use the full face shield provided when arc-welding and resist the temptation to peek round the edge 'just to start off with'. Since UV light can cause skin damage too, always wear gloves and button-down sleeves. Red hot sparks are thrown off as arc welding takes place, so wear shoes and overalls that prevent a red-hot droplet of metal going down inside your shoe, and for the same reason, keep the overalls buttoned at the neck. When welding overhead, keep the sleeves closed at the wrists. Don't weld in very enclosed spaces without ventilation because the fumes can be harmful. Wear cotton overalls; nylon can quite easily catch fire with disastrous consequences. Take very

▲ W1. This is one of SIP's basic arc welding kits and, like most kits of its type, includes everything that is necessary to get going.

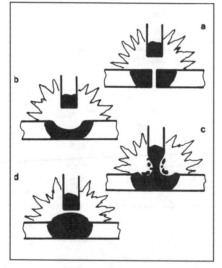

▲ Figure W3. Arc welding process. (Courtesy SIP (Industrial Products) Ltd)

(a) Both edges of the metal are heated by the arc until ...
(b) ... they almost immediately melt and flow together forming one piece.
(c) Simultaneously more molten metal and flux is added from the rod.
(d) This fills the crater with weld and covers the top of the weld with protective slag.

great care when handling hot metal and keep children and pets right out of the work area so that they can be neither burned, nor affected by the UV rays. Make sure that there is nothing flammable near the area where you are working. When working on car bodywork, strip out all flammable materials from the inside of the car around the area in which you are welding and *never* weld near the fuel tank, or near plastic fuel or brake lines. Always have a fire extinguisher of the correct type available, for when things get really out of hand, and have a washing-up liquid bottle full of water to douse local outbreaks. *Don't*, whatever you do, allow water to come into contact with mains electricity equipment because of the high risk of electric shocks. When cleaning the weld, clear goggles should be worn because the brittle slag can 'fly' as it is chipped off the weld. If you accidentally look at the weld taking place, you can develop 'flash' or 'arc eye' within twelve hours or so. You will know if this happens because the feeling is akin to having a handful of gravel beneath each eyelid. In severe cases hospital treatment may be necessary and it is always advisable to consult a doctor.

If this incredibly long list of safety notes seems daunting; it needn't be. Every one of the points mentioned is of great importance but if you proceed with care and with a sense of involvement, it will all quickly become second nature.

THE FIRST WELD

Set up the equipment to the right settings for the thickness of steel being welded. The rod selected should, as a guide, match the thickness of the material being welded. As a starting guide, set the machine in accordance with the following table, but be prepared to modify it according to the results you get.

Electrode diameter	swg	Current required (amps)
1.60mm (1/16in)	16	25–50
2.00mm (5/64in)	14	50–80
2.50mm (3/32in)	12	80–110
3.25mm (1/8in)	10	110–150
4.00mm (5/32in)	8	140–200
5.00mm (3/16in)	6	200–260
6.00mm (1/4in)	4	220–340

Make certain that your earth clamp is clamped to the workpiece at a point where a good contact is made and where the metal is clean, otherwise the weld quality will suffer. Find a comfortable position and support the cable to the electrode holder, perhaps by draping it over the arm supporting the electrode holder.

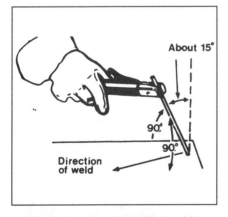

▲ Figure W4. The electrode should be presented to the workpiece at an angle of 15° to the vertical, leaning in the direction of the weld. Practise with the machine switched off until you have the feel of it with your eyes closed – because that's in effect what you will start off by doing! (Courtesy SIP (Industrial Products) Ltd)

▲ W2. When you feel ready to start, switch on, hold the face shield in the other hand to your welding hand, hold the electrode a couple of inches away from the workpiece, pull the shield in front of your face and strike an arc. The main difficulty is in getting the current to flow and the weld buzzing nicely while avoiding the initial momentary tendency for the electrode to stick to the workpiece. There are two ways of preventing sticking: one is to tap the end of the electrode against the place where you want to start welding, allowing it to bounce off again each time until the welding current starts to flow, and the other method is to scratch the electrode across the workpiece, the movement helping to prevent the end of the electrode from sticking. If the end of the electrode should hold fast to the workpiece, try twisting it off, otherwise, simply depressing the lever on the electrode holder will release it instantly. Even if you are using the screw-up type of electrode holder, a quick twist should do the trick and release the electrode. If you still get tied up in knots, just turn around to the machine and quickly turn it off or take the earth clamp off the workpiece. The electrode might be glowing red or almost red hot by now, so pull it off the workpiece when it has cooled down. If a lump of flux has broken away from the end of the electrode, starting up will be even harder. 'Burn' the bare steel back to where the flux is complete by taking a piece of scrap sheet and connecting it up to the earth. Hold the faceshield in place and scrape the electrode rapidly across the scrap steel until enough steel has been thrown off as sparks (watch out for them!) for you to have reached flux covered electrode again.

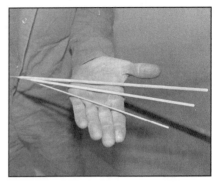

▲ W3. Choose the size of rod (electrode) according to the thickness of metal you are welding. Rod thickness (not including flux coating) should, as near as possible, equal the thickness of the metal being welded. If the flux on the rods has become damp, you will find great difficulty in welding with them. If necessary dry them out before use. Electrodes should be stored in a dry place when not in use. If damp, they can be gently dried out in a domestic oven. If they have suffered to the point where flux is cracked and flaky when dry, throw them away.

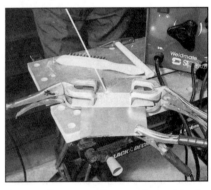

▲ W4. Some practice may be required before an arc is struck successfully but if you don't seem to be making any progress at all, check that the earth connection is a good one, then try turning the power up, a notch at a time, until you can get started – then if you 'blow' right through the steel, turn it down again. Once you get going, the idea is to move the rod grip down as the rod burns away and also to move it along the workpiece. Try moving the end of the rod right into the weld puddle so that the weld 'splutters' then try to pull away until the arc crackles then snaps out. Somewhere between the two is the ideal distance away from the workpiece.

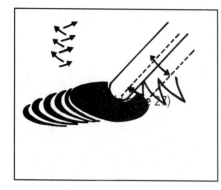

▲ Figure W4A. Once you have got the hang of moving the rod along, try swirling the end of it by just the smallest amount which helps to give better penetration. (Courtesy SIP (Industrial Products) Ltd)

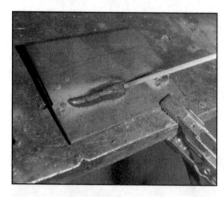

▲ W5. It is important that the correct arc length and correct rate of progress are consistently maintained. If progress is too rapid the weld will be stringy and obviously weak. If too slow, the slag formed will flow in front of the puddle and be trapped within the weld, severely weakening it. This shot shows the weld with the slag in place on top of the weld.

▲ W6. After the weld has been completed, use the chipping hammer to knock the slag off the top of the weld.

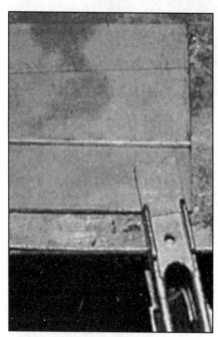

▲ W7. When you feel confident about running a bead along a flat piece of steel, try welding a lap joint. You will have to angle the rod towards the bottom piece rather than the edge of the piece on top because the weld will tend to burn furthest into the exposed edge. The exception would be steel which is a bit on the thin side when the top sheet would be favoured to reduce the risk of burning through the bottom sheet.

High Bead	Undercut	Overlap
CURRENT TOO LOW Arc is difficult to maintain. Very little penetration	CURRENT TOO HIGH Wide thick bead, undercut. Crater pointed and long. Rod burns away very quickly.	TRAVEL TOO SLOW Metal builds up producing a wide heavy bead which noticeably overlaps at sides.
Good Weld	**Splatter**	**Undercut**
NORMAL CONDITIONS Uniform ripples on surface of weld. Arc makes steady crackling sound.	ARC TOO LONG Surface of weld rough. Rod melts off in globules. Arc makes hissing sound.	TRAVEL TOO FAST Small bead undercut in some places. Rough surface and little penetration.

▲ Figure W5. Arc weld bead faults. (Courtesy SIP (Industrial Products) Ltd)

▲ W8. Start by placing a very short weld at the two outer edges. Known as 'sack' welds, these short welds hold the two pieces together and help to prevent distortion, as the heat of the weld would otherwise cause the two plates to part from one another at the end opposite to that being welded.

▲ W9. It is vital that all the slag is chipped off and, if necessary, wire brushed from the tack welds before the seam welds are run over the top, otherwise there will be slag inclusion in the weld.

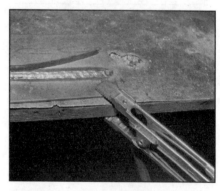

▲ W10. There is very little wrong with a weld where the slag peels off in one piece as the weld cools down leaving a beautifully even, rippled weld beneath it, like this one!

▲ W11. When welding a fillet weld, the hard bit can often be getting the vertical section to stay upright whilst you tack weld it!

▲ W13. Then with the rod angled at 45° to each of the two faces – or equidistant from each where they are not 90° apart – a seam weld can be run from one end to another.

▲ W16. External corner welds are always easier to carry out if the two pieces of metal are put together as shown, the two edges forming a narrow 'Vee' rather than one edge overlapping the other.

▲ W12. After tacking, there is always a certain amount of flexibility in the welds – the trick is in making the tack welds small enough to allow adjustments to be made but large enough for the workpiece to hold together while you tap it into place.

▲ W14. Always bear in mind that the more comfortable a welding position can be made, the more successful the weld is likely to be.

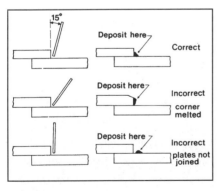

▲ Figure W6. Lap welding. (Courtesy SIP (Industrial Products) Ltd)

▲ W15. External corner welds are generally considerably easier than internal welds. Again the same procedure is followed – set-up; tack; clean-up; seam-weld.

▲ W17. Many welds have to be carried out in awkward places, so it is necessary to practise welds from different angles. This is a 'vertical-up' weld but 'vertical-down' welds (ie starting from the top and working down) are generally easier to carry out. They are best carried out with a smaller rod than normal, with a narrow gap between rod and workpiece (short arc) and by welding straight, without weaving. 'Vertical-up' welding is generally easiest with normal sized rods, a higher current setting than normal (so you have to take care not to burn through) and incorporating a weaving motion.

OVERHEAD WELDING

This can be a slow, tedious operation and should incorporate two or three runs over each joint. Slag and hanging drops of metal are prone to form and they must be chipped and ground away before continuing. The first weld pass should be straight, with no weaving, but subsequent welds can be carried out with a weaving action, covering the first weld. Try turning the power up by around 10 per cent but take care not to burn through. FOR SAFETY'S SAKE: wear a full head screen, leather apron and gauntlet gloves as a protection against red-hot spatter from the weld.

NB Always disconnect the vehicle's alternator before arc-welding because the current will damage it.

CARBON-ARC BRAZING

The carbon-arc torch is fitted with two cables: one to each carbon electrode. On welders with screw output terminals, the normal arc welding leads are removed and the leads from the carbon-arc torch are attached to the terminals in their place; one to the electrode terminal and the other to the 'work' or 'earth' terminal. (It is important that the welding cables are removed, because if the earth clamp is left connected to the work, it can have funny 'shorting' effects on the carbon arc in use.)

On welders with internally connected output cables, the leads from the carbon-arc torch have to be clipped into the electrode holder and earth clamp respectively. The electrode holder and clamp should be placed on a piece of wood or other insulating material.

The carbons are copper-coated, with a chemical core to give a smooth, even arc. (Earlier carbon-arc torches were supplied with ordinary copper coated carbons which were quite difficult to use; people who make the mistake of using non-chemical cored carbons designed for other purposes soon find the difference!) When the carbons are brought together and an arc struck, the resulting 'electric flame' then provides a heat source just as a gas flame does. It is then used with brazing rods, fluxes etc, much like a gas flame.

Of course, the carbon-arc torch is not as versatile as a gas flame but is a very good and economic substitute and it allows the owner of an arc welding set to carry out a far wider range of jobs with the set than would otherwise be possible. As well as steel, it is possible to join brass, copper and even aluminium by using the correct filler rods, although the latter material would be somewhat tricky to work with. The set could also be used for heating and bending smallish strips of steel and for freeing rusted nuts and bolts.

NB Always disconnect the vehicle's alternator before carbon-arc brazing because the current will damage it.

▲ W18. The first step is to remove any rust, scale or paint from the surface to be brazed, the mini-angle grinder being the ideal tool for the job.

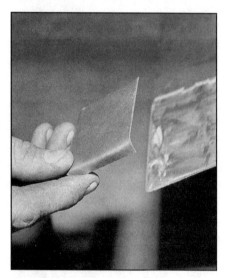

▲ W19. Then a repair patch can be made up to suit. The patch **must** take the form of a lap joint because there is not enough contact area in a butt joint to allow a sufficiently strong joint to be formed with braze.

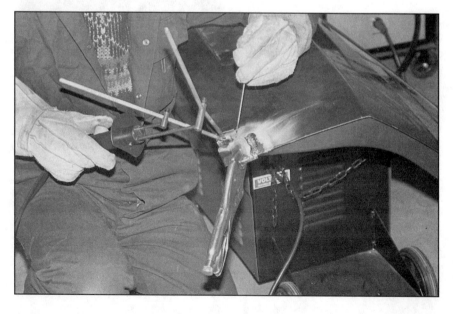

◀ W20. After clamping the repair patch in place, it should be tack brazed at regular intervals if it is a large patch. Either a pre-fluxed brazing rod should be used, which contains its own flux, or the end of the rod should be heated and dipped in the flux so that a quantity of the powder sticks to it. Then the carbon-arc rods are operated: the thumb slide on the handgrip is moved until the two rods touch, then moved just a little way apart so that an arc flares between the two of them.

▲ *W21. The arc is extremely bright as this picture shows, so **never** attempt to use the equipment without the headshield. (Obviously, unless you have three arms, the usual hand-held shield is useless.) But **never** use just dark goggles as these are designed only to shield the light of a gas flame. The intense light of an arc can cause permanent eye damage even through dark goggles and, in any case, a full face shield must be used to protect the skin from harmful UV rays. As the rods burn away, they have to be moved progressively together using the thumb slide. The heat from the arc is played onto the workpiece like a flame, the rod is fed in to the joint where first the flux then the rod itself melts and 'flushes' into the joint. Extra braze should be built up over the joint as you go along. The sound produced will be a 'buzz' rather than the crackle of arc welding when the gap between the carbon electrodes is just right.*

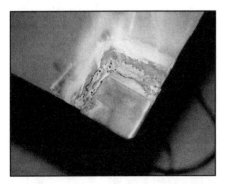

▲ *W22. Brazing is very easy to carry out and as long as the simple steps shown here are followed, the result will be a very strong joint, although unfortunately not strong enough for major structural or chassis-frame components on cars.*

OXY-ACETYLENE WELDING

Oxy-acetylene is the most versatile form of welding equipment to own although, as mentioned earlier, it does have its drawbacks. The most commonly used gases are, naturally enough, oxygen and acetylene although it is possible to gas weld with other gases. Some welding kits offer butane as a heat source, but this is too cool for anything but brazing although another alternative, Mapp gas, is hot enough for welding steels of the thickness of car bodywork.

Full-size welding cylinders can be difficult to get hold of for the home user (the companies involved will generally only hire out to business users) and in any case, the average DIY enthusiast would take ages to get through the gas contained in them. Also, the full size cylinders can be difficult to store and move because of their shape and weight.

Oxygen cylinders contain just oxygen under high pressure (and for that reason the cylinders are heavily reinforced – and expensive to produce). Oxygen is a stable gas and not particularly dangerous to handle, although oil and grease should be kept away from the regulator and other controls because when brought into contact with oxygen spontaneous combustion can occur. On the other hand, if acetylene were to be compressed into a cylinder in the same way as oxygen, it would explode, the critical pressure being as low as 15lb/sq in. To overcome this, the cylinder is filled with a porous material, such as asbestos, charcoal or balsa wood or some other absorbent material and the material thoroughly saturated with liquid acetone. Acetone absorbs acetylene like a blotter absorbs ink and then the acetylene can reach, say, 250lb/sq in although it has to be introduced into the cylinder very, very slowly indeed by the filling company.

Acetylene should be handled with care and respect because anything between 2.5 per cent and 80 per cent of acetylene in the air can be ignited with a naked flame. Also, it is possible for an acetylene bottle to explode as a result of a high level impact. Acetylene cylinders should always be kept in an upright position to prevent acetone being blown from the cylinder when the valve is opened.

SAFETY
Take careful note of all the safety comments contained within this chapter and refer to the additional safety notes earlier.

▲ *W23. The Portapack by Murex and BOC is an ideal if somewhat expensive way of equipping the keen amateur or portable professional workshop. Each item is built to top professional standards, but bear in mind that the better the equipment you buy, the easier the welding will be and the better the end product.*

▲ *W24. Here are the alternative, smaller sized bottles which, although rented for a full seven-year stretch, payable in advance, are cheaper to start off with than the larger bottles.*

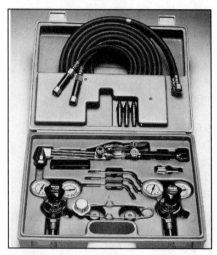

▲ W25. Gas welding equipment is available from a number of sources. This is the Clarke welding cutting kit in a carrying case. Make sure that the kit you buy is as good quality as those shown here and that it includes flashback arresters to prevent any risk of flame getting back into a cylinder.

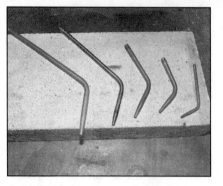

▲ W27. There are several different nozzle sizes appropriate for different applications. Portapack contains three nozzles, nozzles Nos 1 and 2 being the most commonly used for car bodywork. There is some overlap between the capacities of each nozzle size, but in general, too small a nozzle means that the welder is too close to the heat source while too large a nozzle means that the pressures have to be turned too low for the needs of the nozzle with risk of blowback – see earlier 'Safety' notes.

Nozzle sizes – applications

Mild steel thickness			Nozzle size
mm	inch	swg	
0.9	–	20	1
1.2	–	18	2
2.0	–	14	3
2.6	–	12	5
3.2	⅛	10	7

Note: in all cases shown acetylene and oxygen pressure should be 0.14 bar (2lb sq in)

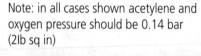

▼ W26. The Murex Saffire FN50 torch is the one supplied with the Portapack. The nozzle and mixer can be changed for a cutting attachment.

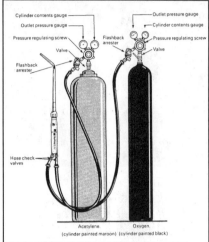

▲ Figure W7. High pressure gas welding outfit. (Courtesy BOC/Murex)

In the UK oxygen hoses are blue while acetylene hoses are red. In the USA, oxygen hoses are green and acetylene hoses are red. Before connecting the regulator to a new cylinder, the cylinder should be 'cracked'. This is the 'in' term for blowing out any water or dust that may have accumulated in the valves. All you do is to stand with your face turned away so that no 'UFOs' land in your eyes and briefly open each valve so that the pressure inside blows any unwanted stuff out of the valve.

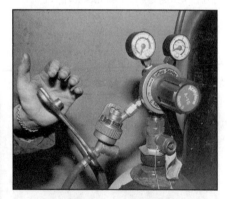

▲ W28. When connecting up, remember that all fuel gas fittings have left-hand threads, while all non-fuel gas fittings (oxygen, carbon dioxide, argon etc) have normal right-hand threads.

Also remember to leave the key on the acetylene valve during use (if that is the type of cylinder you are using; some have a wheeled valve) so that it can be shut down in a hurry if necessary.

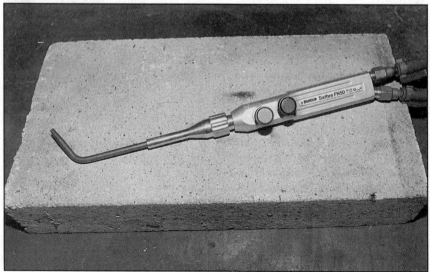

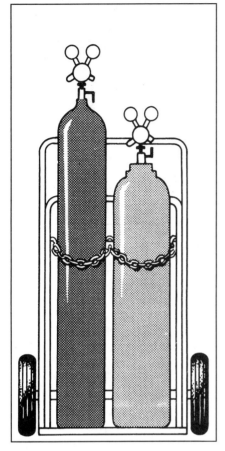

▲ *Figure W8. If you are using full-size cylinders, make sure before use they are contained in a trolley or safety-chained back to a wall. (Courtesy Murex Ltd)*

RODS AND WIRES

Mild steel applications

	Process	Rod/Wire	Melt-range	Diameters	Remarks
Plain	1. Welding (Oxy-Acetylene)	Sifsteel No. 11 (CCMS)	1450°C	1.2mm, 1.6mm 2.0mm, 2.4mm 3.2mm	No flux is needed. It is copper coated for long shelf-life.
	2. Oxy-Acetylene Brazing	Sifbronze No. 1	875°C-895°C	1.6mm, 2.4mm 3.2mm	Flux needed to suit application. This rod has a wide range of uses including joining galvanised steel without damaging the zinc coating.
	3. Oxy-Acetylene Brazing	Sifbronze No. 2	920°-980°C	1.6mm, 2.4mm 3.2mm	Contains 9% nickel, providing high strength joints. Excellent for building up worn parts.
	4. Oxy-Acetylene Brazing	Sifbronze No. 10	870°C-900°C	1.6mm, 2.4mm 3.2mm	Manganese-bronze free flowing rod. Suitable for use with gas fluxer.
Flux coated	5. Oxy-Acetylene Brazing	Sifredicote No. 1	875°C-895°C	1.6mm, 2.4mm 3.2mm	Pre-coated with flux. Ideal for use in high speed continuous welding or for DIY. Suitable for carbon arc brazing.
	6. Oxy-Acetylene Brazing	Sifredicote No. 2	920°C-980°C	2.4mm, 3.2mm	Pre-coated with flux. Contains 9% nickel for additional strength.
	7. Oxy-Acetylene Brazing	Sifredicote No. 4	875°C-895°C	2.4mm, 3.2mm	Special aggressive flux for cleaning action. Ideal for brazing where a difficult surface exists, such as rusty metal.
	8. Oxy-Acetylene Brazing	Sifserrate	875°C-895°C	2.0mm, 3.0mm	Pre-fluxed in pockets to ensure a measured flux-flow with minimum of joint cleaning. Ideal on clean metal.
	9. Gas shielded arc welding TIG & MIG	Phosphor-Bronze No. 8, MIG 8	–	0.8mm, 1.0mm 1.2mm, 1.6mm 2.4mm, 3.2mm	TIG & MIG brazing on mild steel. Also joining dissimilar metals and building up worn surfaces.
	10. Gas shielded arc welding MIG	MIG A18	–	0.6mm, 0.8mm 1.0mm, 1.2mm	Often referred to as CO_2 wire

(Reproduced with permission of Sibronze)

MATERIAL THICKNESS – CONVERSION TABLES

Inches (decimal) to nearest 0.0001in – Millimetres to nearest 0.001mm

▲ *W29. All the valves, however, open and close on the normal anticlockwise-to-open and clockwise-to-close principles. These cylinders are fitted with re-settable flashback arresters, designed to stop an instantaneous burn-back through the torch and pipe from getting into the cylinder with disastrous results.*

Inches (Decimal)	Millimetres	British Standard Wire Gauge	American Wire Gauge	Inches (Fractions)
0.0201	0.511		24	
0.0220	0.559	24		
0.0253	0.643		22	
0.0280	0.711	22		
0.0313	0.794			1/32
0.0320	0.813	21	20	
0.0360	0.914	20		
0.0394	1.000			
0.0403	1.024		18	
0.0469	1.191			3/64
0.0480	1.219	18		
0.0508	1.290		16	
0.0591	1.500			
0.0625	1.588			1/16
0.0640	1.626	16		
0.0641	1.628		14	
0.0781	1.984			5/64
0.0787	2.000			
0.0800	2.032	14		
0.0808	2.052		12	

Inches (Decimal)	Millimetres	British Standard Wire Gauge	American Wire Gauge	Inches (Fractions)
0.0938	2.381			3/32
0.0984	2.500			
0.1019	2.588		10	
0.1040	2.643	12		
0.1094	2.778			7/64
0.1181	3.000			
0.1250	3.175			1/8
0.1280	3.250	10		
0.1285	3.264		8	
0.1378	3.500			
0.1406	3.572			9/64
0.1563	3.969			5/32
0.1575	4.000			
0.1600	4.064	8		
0.1620	4.115		6	
0.1719	4.366			11/64
0.1772	4.500			
0.1876	4.763			3/16
0.1920	4.877	6		
0.1969	5.000			

THE FIRST WELD

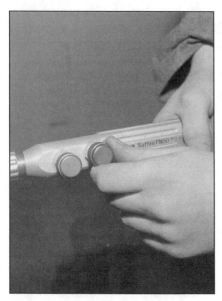

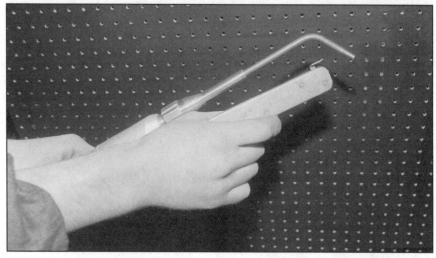

▲ W32. Use an igniter, held behind the end of the pipe, to light the acetylene at the end of the nozzle. (Oxygen turned off, of course).

▲ W30. Open the valve on the acetylene bottle and the valve on the oxygen bottle. Now open the oxygen valve (blue) on the torch for a few seconds to purge the system before closing down again. Repeat the process with the acetylene (red) valve on the torch, but leave it open whilst you carry out the step described in the following paragraph.

▲ W33. In practice, many professional users prefer to overrule the gauge reading (they can be inaccurate, especially on older, neglected, gauges) and turn the regulator until a bright bushy flame occurs.

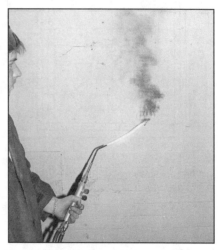

▲ W35. Now turn the valve on the torch down until the flame **just** starts to end in a smoky tip. (If you leave it in this state for long, the thick, lazy rolls of smoke will flutter back down as black soot marks all over the workshop!)

▲ W31. Next, open the valve on the acetylene cylinder and adjust the regulator to give the correct working pressure.

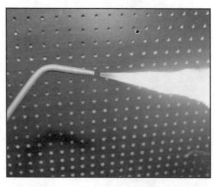

▲ W34. If there is an air gap between nozzle and flame, 'throttle back' until it disappears, then turn the acetylene up again until the bright flame is regained.

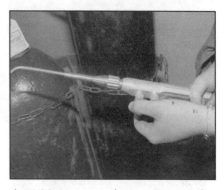

▲ W36. Now turn the oxygen on at the torch ...

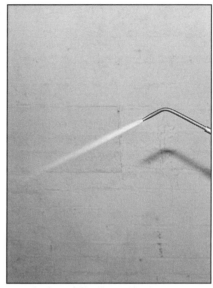

▲ W37. ... and again, if you wish, adjust the flame at the bottle regulator. Alternatively, and this is the usual approach for both gases, set the recommended pressure at the regulator and tune the flame at the torch.

▲ W39. Special nozzle cleaning reamers should be used to clean out a dirty nozzle (anything else will only be partly successful and could damage the shape or size of the nozzle).

▲ W41. Although the full brightness of the flame obscures the cone in this shot, this is how the flame should appear.

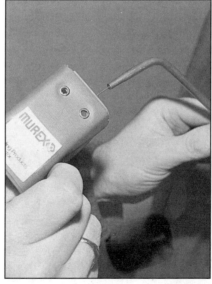

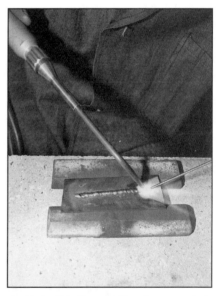

▲ W38. At this early stage, it could be seen that the flame was coming out of the nozzle at a slight angle, which indicated that there was a small obstruction in the end of the nozzle.

▲ W40. Simply select the wire reamer of the correct size for the nozzle and slide it in and out, rather like a stiff pipe cleaner. If the nozzle end becomes damaged, it can be restored to 'square' (ie 90° to the bore by rubbing it on a piece of emery paper held flat on a board.

▲ W42. The first weld has been carried out from (the operator's) right to left, which is normal for steel up to 5.0mm (³/₁₆in) thick. Note that the plate being welded here does not rest on a surface which could take the heat away from it. Do not, of course, weld on a flammable surface.

▲ Figure W9. Start off by holding nozzle and rod at the angles shown. Play the flame on the point where welding is to start, until a small pool of molten material develops – it will be easily visible through the goggles. Then begin to swirl or zig-zag the nozzle slightly, at the same time dipping the rod in and out of the weld pool at around ½-second intervals, or as often as necessary. If the weld pool forms too quickly, you are likely to blow through when you start welding, so turn the gas down a little. If it takes too long to form, turn it up a little. If more than a little adjustment is needed at the nozzle, go up or down one size of nozzle, as required. (Courtesy BOC Ltd)

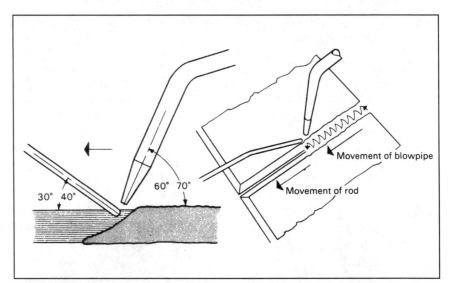

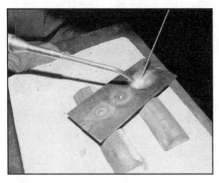

▲ W43. When joining two pieces of steel together with a lap joint, start by tacking them together at regular intervals. You may find that the pieces of steel move around between placing tack welds so that they have to be tapped back into place with a hammer, held with a clamp or pushed together by an assistant with a piece of steel bar.

▲ W45. Note also that if you try to start welding on the end of a piece of steel, you are likely to burn through before the weld pool forms.

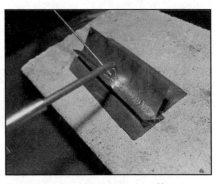

▲ W47. The trick is to get sufficient weld penetration: form the weld pool then push the nozzle a little way into the weld pool. If there is sufficient depth to the weld pool, you will see it separate.

▲ W44. Note that the edge of the overlapping panel heats and burns through quicker than the piece beneath. Swirl the flame but concentrate most of the heat on the flat steel at the bottom of the overlap.

▲ W46. When welding a fillet (or inside corner joint), support the pieces or clamp them together, then tack weld them.

▲ W48. You can weld outside corner joints without using any rod at all, although welding rod should be used to tack the pieces together. This type of joint is not uncommon when working on car bodywork.

▲ *W49. Butt joints in thin steel are rather prone to blowing through. Although you should have a gap between the pieces when welding thicker steel, try to close-up thin steel as far as possible. Don't play heat on the joint for too long – after all you are working with* **two** *edges of the type described in W44.*

▶ *Figure W10. Unfortunately, much welding on a car's bodywork is carried out in the sort of positions you never find when practising at the bench. These diagrams give an idea of how to approach upright, overhead and horizontal welding. (Courtesy BOC Ltd).*

SHUTTING-DOWN PROCEDURE

Shut off the acetylene first by closing the blowpipe control valve then follow with closure of the oxygen valve. Close the oxygen and fuel-gas valves on the cylinders, then open and close the blowpipe valves one at a time to relieve pressure in the system – ensuring the gauges register zero – oxygen first then acetylene. Wind back the pressure adjusting screws on both oxygen and acetylene regulators. If the equipment is to be used in the immediate future (ie within the next hour or two) it is not necessary to close the cylinder valves or the pipeline valves.

The only exception to the above procedure is when a sustained backfire occurs in the mixing chamber of the blowpipe. In this case the oxygen supply should be shut off first to stop burning internally, followed in rapid succession by closing off the acetylene valve. If this is not done melting of the blowpipe may occur. After quenching the backfire the blowpipe should be allowed to cool down and should be checked over before it is relit.

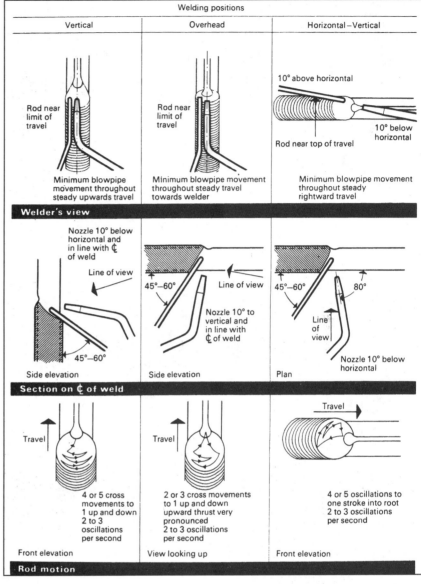

Welding positions

Vertical	Overhead	Horizontal – Vertical

Welder's view

Section on ₵ of weld

Rod motion

CUTTING

As an illustration of the versatility of oxy-acetylene welding, this section shows how to screw a cutting attachment on to the welder's torch and transform it into something that will cut cleanly through steel, which is very useful especially for thicker materials.

▶ *W50. First, unscrew the torch head by turning the screw in a clockwise direction.*

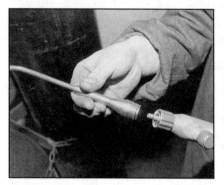

▲ W51. Then the torch head pulls from the torch body.

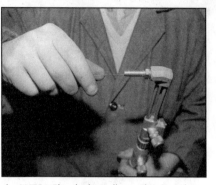

▲ W53. Check that all nozzles are clear using the reamers already mentioned. Set the oxygen to about 15lb sq in.

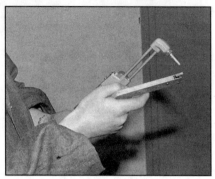

▲ W54. Turn on the acetylene and light the torch.

▲ W52. The cutting head pushes on to the torch body before the screw is retightened. The screw will **not** pull the cutter down tightly; it has to be pushed down hard and seated properly by hand first.

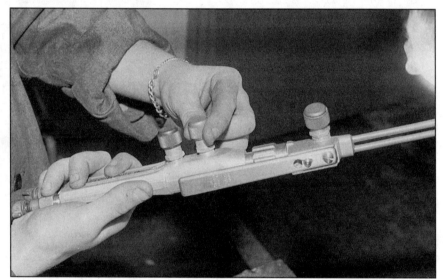

▲ W55. Turn the acetylene up to give a bushy flame just ceasing to smoke ...

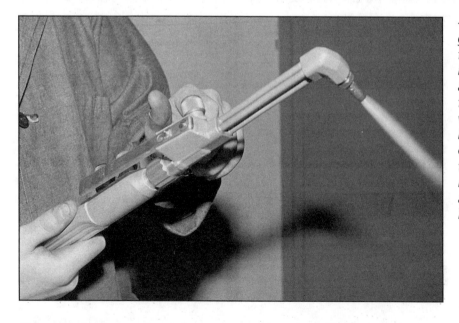

◀ W56. ... then turn up the oxygen to give a small cone in the middle of the flame, with the cone clearly defined. Next, depress the lever on the cutting attachment and readjust to a neutral flame with the blue oxygen heating valve. If it is found that some of the pre-heat cones are longer than others this can be rectified after shutting down the torch and bottles, then loosen the head nut and turn the nozzle through approximately 30°. Make sure that the head nut is re-tightened with a spanner.

SHUTTING DOWN

Close the red valve on the torch, when the flame will go out. Close the blue oxygen heating valve on the shank. Close the blue valve on the cutter. Turn off both cylinder valves. Open the red valve on the shank and close after releasing the gas in the hoses. Open the blue valve on the shank and the blue valve on the cutting attachment. Close the blue valve on the shank and the cutting attachment once the gas in the hoses has been released.

Note that propane is a perfectly acceptable substitute for acetylene when used with cutting equipment and is certainly a lot safer to carry around than acetylene; a point worth remembering if any work has to be carried out away from home, such as when a scrap car is being cut up for spares.

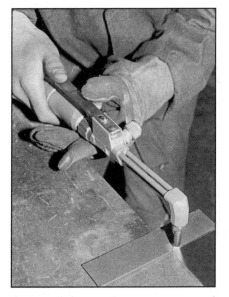

▲ *W57. When cutting, remove rust and scale, if possible, to give a cleaner cut. Heat the edge of the metal with the cutter until it glows bright red. Then press the cutting lever ...*

▲ *W58. ... and draw the cutter along through the material. Always wear at least one industrial glove (and preferably two) when using cutting gear.*

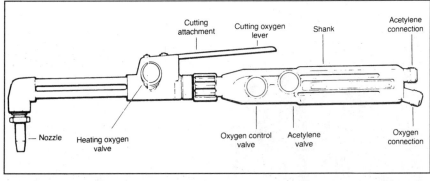

▲ *Figure W11. Cutting blowpipe and controls. (Courtesy BOC Ltd)*

HINTS ON WELDING STAINLESS STEEL

Use a welding rod of similar composition to the parent metal (a cut-off strip is ideal). Coat the underside of the joint with flux and use a neutral flame. Keep the rod in the flame the whole time and at the end of the weld, withdraw the flame slowly to prevent cracking. Do not stop in mid-weld and work as quickly as possible. Carefully remove all oxide and scale when the job is finished.

HINTS ON BRAZING ALUMINIUM ALLOYS

The recommended rod for use here is a 10 per cent silicon, 4 per cent copper aluminium alloy which has a lower melting point than most aluminium alloys. Make sure that the surfaces to be brazed are thoroughly scoured with steel wool, wire brush or file, back to bright non-oxidised metal immediately before use.

Use the correct aluminium brazing flux. The end of the rod is heated and dipped into the flux and the 'tuft' of flux adhering to the end of the rod is then touched down upon the surface of the joint to check the temperature. At the correct temperature the flux will begin to flow smoothly and rapidly forwards along the joint. The aluminium alloy **WILL NOT** change colour before it reaches the correct temperature or even exceeds it and melts and sags. It is most important that the filler rod is not melted into the joint until the flux flows freely. The force of the flame plus capillary action will pull the filler into the joint. Remove all traces of flux deposit as quickly as possible after brazing, or it will attack the aluminium alloy. If possible, buy a weak acid solution from your factor or chemist (drug store) and after using it to wash the joint, wash the joint again with warm water. (Check with your supplier regarding hazards associated with acid usage.)

OXY-ACETYLENE BRAZING

In welding, the workpiece melts as well as the filler rod, but in brazing only the filler melts, forming a strong bond with the workpiece.

Set up the equipment as if you were going to weld, but turn the oxygen on the torch up a little higher than normal to give an oxidising flame.

To minimise distortion, lightly preheat the panel, noting the points at which any initial distortion takes place, then tack it down at this point. On long welds, keep the heat as low as possible by making a series of short braze runs at intervals, going back to fill in the spaces later.

Heat the end of the brazing rod in the flame, then dip into the flux. Heat the workpiece and right away feed the end of the rod into the flame. The flux will melt and then, after a little more heating, the braze will run into the weld. If you use a pre-fluxed brazing rod, it will not require any additional flux added to it. You just push the rod into the flame and the flux inside the rod coats the workpiece before the rod melts.

Brazing is actually a lot easier to carry out than oxy-acetylene welding and there is less distortion because less heat has to be used. Do remember, however, that cleaning the steel to be welded can make all the difference between

successful and unsuccessful brazing. Remember also that a brazed joint is not as strong as a welded joint, and so should not be used where the car's structural safety could be put at risk.

HEAT-SHRINKING A PANEL

Every sort of welding depends upon heat to melt the metals being joined together. Unfortunately, it is physically impossible to keep the heat only where you want it (although MIG and TIG come nearest because the gases they blow onto the work help to cool it rapidly) and in the case of gas welding, more heat is transmitted away from the weld area than is used in the weld itself! The result of all this surplus heat is to expand and buckle the metal being worked on, and the flatter it is and the larger the area, the more prospect there is of bad buckling taking place.

Another way of causing metal to buckle is to panel beat it for too long or using the wrong technique. This causes the metal to go thinner, to expand and thus, to buckle – and it can be really difficult for the beginner not to let this happen.

A third and, perhaps the most common, form of buckling occurs when a car is involved in an accident and the metal becomes stretched as it is distorted.

In each of these cases, the metal will form a bulge which can often be 'popped' through from one side to the other without pausing in its correct position, halfway between. The following technique is used to shrink a panel so that the area becomes restressed and reverts back to something much closer to its correct shape. Note, however, that shrinking does have its drawbacks. The metal will not be perfectly flat when it is finished and it will be necessary to use filler or body solder to true it up. The other problem is that metal which has been shrunk can be very prone to rusting. It should be

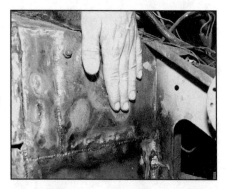

▲ HS1. There are three ways of judging whether a panel is buckled. The first is simply to look at the panel; all too often any buckling present will be just that obvious! A second way, shown here, is to feel the panel by rubbing the flat of the fingers over it, when any lumps and bumps will be clearly felt. The third way, and the most suitable way for large panels, is to hold the edge of a really true straightedge against the panel and to look for any gaps between panel and straightedge.

◀ HS2. In shrinking a dent, the centre or highest point of the stretched area must be found because that is where the first shrinking operation should take place. Select a welding nozzle of the size correct for welding the thickness of steel you are working on. Heat a small spot around ¾ inch (18mm) to a cherry red heat, holding the flame far enough away so that you don't burn right through the metal. As the metal comes up to cherry red heat, you will see it blister upwards.

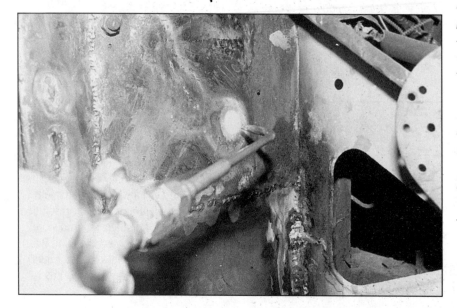

▲ *HS3. Take away the torch, hold a flat dolly at the back of the panel (or a curved one if dealing with a curved panel) and give several quick, sharp, squarely placed blows with a panel beater's hammer. This pushes the raised metal down but, because the black metal around it is harder than the considerably softened red-heat metal, tends to shift metal into the heated spot, which produces a tightening effect. For this reason, the hammering operation should be carried out before the metal returns to black heat. In practice, it will be found that the metal is far softer than cold metal and hammers down easily. Don't hammer too much, or you will just repeat the stretching process.*

▲ *HS4. When the metal has cooled to black heat again, quench it with a substantial rag soaked in water. This will pull the metal tauter again in the area close to where you have been heating. Don't quench the metal whilst it is still red hot, or you will cause the metal's grain structure to crystallise which will make the metal brittle and difficult to work. Replace the rag in a bucket of water right away after use and don't touch that part of the rag that has been against the red hot metal – it could scald!*

emery-clothed back to shiny metal and painted as soon as the work is finished.

If one shrink is not sufficient to remove the buckling, it is quite in order to use a number of shrinks but it is best to leave a wide space between them. The heating tends to 'deaden' the areas that have been shrunk, so leave plenty of taut, springy metal around and between each shrink. Make sure that you thoroughly cool the whole panel and those surrounding it after each shrink (you don't want another buckle taking you unawares somewhere else) and remember that a number of small shrinks are better than one large one – as Groucho might have said!

SAFETY

It is strongly recommended that anyone interested in carrying out oxy-acetylene welding applies to his local institute of education where night classes may be run in the use of oxy-acetylene equipment. In the following paragraphs, a few of the hazards associated with this type of equipment are listed.

• Leaking oxygen can gather in clothing and cause a flash fire or even lead to an explosion. Never drape clothing over bottles and never leave leaks unchecked.

• Acetylene cylinders should always be kept upright.
• Cylinders should always be kept away from sources of heat and should preferably be stored out of doors.
• Cylinders must not be dropped or bumped sharply.
• Chain cylinders to a wall or trolley and keep upright when in use.

• No oil or grease should be used with oxygen equipment, as under pressure it can cause an explosion.

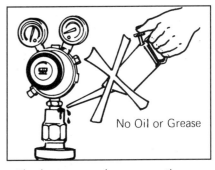

No Oil or Grease

• Check compressed gas connections with a weak solution of washing-up liquid.

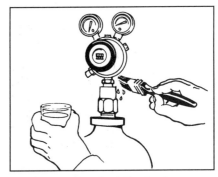

• Make sure that the following hose colours are obeyed: In UK: blue for oxygen; red for acetylene; orange for propane; black for argon or argon mix. In the USA: green for oxygen; red for acetylene.
• Never use oxygen as a substitute for compressed air. This is a *highly dangerous* practice!
• Always ensure that hoses are not cracked, split or chafed and that all connections are adequate.
• Never use oversize welding or cutting blow-pipes for the job in hand.
• Don't risk working with damaged regulators.
• NEVER weld without the correct type of goggles. The risk of eye damage is too great.
• Always purge both hoses before connecting them up to a welding torch or after changing cylinders.
• Always make sure that the nozzle is clean because a dirty nozzle can lead to a flashback. It is strongly recommended that a flashback arrester be fitted to each cylinder.

• Always 'purge' (ie allow gas to flow from each outlet for a short while) before lighting the torch. This helps to prevent a 'flashback' down the pipe and into the cylinder.

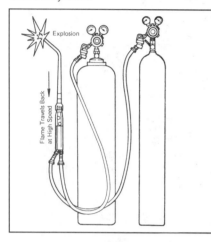

• Use adequate body, hand and foot protection, especially when working beneath a weld.

▲ HS5. Chubb are the leading manufacturer of fire extinguishers and the only one, at the time of writing, to have taken a decision to stop using halon. This is because halon, in spite of its relatively low cost, damages the earth's ozone layer.

Take advice from your supplier before selecting a fire extinguisher because not all types are suitable for workshop use.

The list of safety points can make it seem that the process is highly dangerous. If used correctly it is certainly not. BOC Ltd point out that, 'Estimates of one major incident in every 50,000 hours of oxy-fuel gas working (in industry) are an indication of its safety level'.

Just make sure that *your* hours of working don't include that one in 50,000!

Thanks are due to Les Ness of Murex Welding Products Ltd Training School for his assistance with this section.

TIG WELDING

This is a specialised process but one which is particularly suitable where a lot of aluminium welding has to be carried out. For that reason, it is briefly mentioned here. (TIG stands for 'Tungsten-Inert Gas'.)

▲ W59. Here a TIG tack-weld has been made. The 'torch' has a tungsten electrode which makes an arc, but unlike any other form of arc welding, the electrode is not consumed in the process. The shield around it blows argon onto the weld, similar to the MIG welding process shown here.

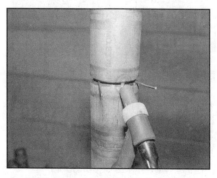

▲ W60. The pieces of aluminium to be joined are fused together by the addition of a hand-held rod, as in oxy-acetylene welding.

▲ W61. Good penetration and excellent results such as these can be obtained with aluminium. The process is exceedingly bright and full protective gear must be worn. The argon has to be blown onto the aluminium for a little while after the welding itself is completed.

MIG WELDING

Although the name sounds somewhat similar to that of the preceding section, there is all the difference in the world between them from the user's point of view. MIG welding (the acronym stands for Metal, Inert Gas) is easy to use, gives splendid results with little distortion, and reduced risk of heat damage to surrounding areas. It's just about the quickest way of welding thin steel and in terms of material consumption it must be the cheapest too.

▲ W62. A MIG welder of 100 to 120 amps will be enough for all car bodywork repairs and a 150 amp model will also let you repair larger steel items, such as a garden gate. (Illustration, courtesy Clarke International)

▲ W63. Small cylinders like these are convenient, but expensive if there's a lot to do. Full cylinders are far more economical. 'No gas' MIG welders allow you to keep welding when you run out, although weld quality drops away considerably with a large amount of spatter. (Illustration courtesy Clarke International)

▲ W65. Inside the machine is the spindle (on left) on to which the reel of wire has to be fitted, and the feed mechanism which pushes the wire out and along the supply pipe.

▲ W64. MIG is a form of arc welding, except that instead of using an electrode in the form of a stick which has to be changed once it is worn out, the machine contains an almost endless reel of wire which passes down the supply pipe shown here and out of the end of the handset. So, there is no stopping to change rods and no continuous re-adjustment of the distance between torch and workpiece.

▲ W66. The supply pipe also has to provide an electric current and this is simply passed into the welding wire at the handset end of the supply pipe. It is this current which melts the weld pool and the wire at the business end.

▶ W67. Now this is the interesting bit! Inside the machine, argon or an argon/carbon dioxide mix is fed through an on/off tap into the supply pipe. Then, when the trigger is pressed, the wire is pushed out and the electricity turned on, and the gas (known as shielding gas for reasons that will become clear) is pumped down the supply pipe and out of the end of the handset, to surround the weld.

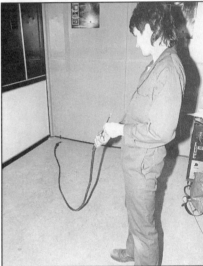

▲ W68. Aluminium alloy can also be welded with MIG. It just takes argon gas in preference to argon/CO_2, aluminium-compatible welding wire, and a new supply pipe liner, coated with teflon. This prevents the 'sticky' aluminium wire from binding in the supply pipe.

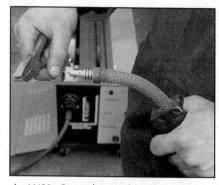

▲ W69. Once the machine has been set up, the wire is fed through the pipe by holding the trigger 'on' until it emerges, then cutting it off to length ...

▲ W72. It is possible to fit and use a CO_2 bottle of the sort that your local publican uses for making all those things fizzy in the cellar. You have to use a special adaptor and in cool weather the whole thing is liable to freeze up as the high-pressure CO_2 is released. (Industrial users of CO_2 use special and expensive heaters to prevent this from happening.) Argon-mix also gives a better result with a smoother weld, better penetration over a wider spread and less spatter, so it is certainly preferable to CO_2.

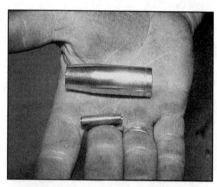

▲ W70. ... before screwing and clipping into place the correct tip for the wire to pass through and the shroud which goes around it and directs the gas.

THE FIRST WELD

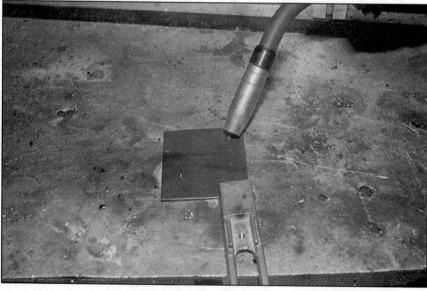

▲ W71. BOC Ltd have become aware of the great demand for these small MIG welders and have brought out a range of small Argon-mix and argon bottles, which are absolutely ideal for the DIY user and small garage. They are changeable at any of the many BOC centres.

▲ W73. Simply set the machine to the settings indicated in the handbook for the thickness of plate being welded and clamp the earth lead into place. Then hold the nozzle at 70° or so, with the nozzle opening pointing in the direction that the weld is to take. The end of the nozzle should be held just a little way from the surface of the workpiece.

▶ W74. When you're ready, pull the mask in front of your face, press the trigger and move the handset at about the speed of drawing a very slow line with a felt-tipped pen. Note how clean the weld is when the machine is set up correctly and there is no paint or rust to inhibit the weld. The gas, blown around the weld, is an inert gas which does not react in any way with the weld, but keeps it clear of the (oxidising) gases in the air until after the weld has 'frozen'. It also helps to cool the weld and so helps to cut down on distortion.

▶ W75. **Important**: MIG welding is really very bright, so follow the safety instructions for arc welding. The UV light given off can be very damaging to anyone (even any pet) watching with unshielded eyes. You can tell whether a MIG weld is going well just by the sound. It should give a crisp crackling sound. If the wire speed setting on the machine is too high, the weld will start off burning deep into the metal and then quickly burn through, or the wire may 'bounce' on the workpiece. On the other hand, if the wire speed is too low, the weld will progress with a spluttering sound and may burn back into the wire feed tip.

▶ W76. Next try a butt-weld, which is of course much closer to 'real' welding. Select a couple of pieces of scrap of the thickness you intend using, place them close together and hold the handset so that the wire is touching the gap. There is no risk of causing a weld to flash across accidentally because, unlike standard arc welding, no circuit takes place until the trigger is pressed. Hold the mask in front of the face and 'tack' the two pieces together. Run a seam down the joint, zig-zagging very slightly, so that the weld pool feeds equally into both pieces. There is far less risk of burning through with MIG than with any of the other main methods.

▲ W77. Before carrying out a fillet weld of this type, place sufficient tack welds to hold the material in place while any necessary adjustment is carried out.

▲ W80. Note how the first seam weld was stopped and then restarted with no risk of inclusions as with other weld types. This time, it is important to gain sufficient penetration into the lower piece, so it may be necessary to favour it just slightly at the expense of the edge of the top piece.

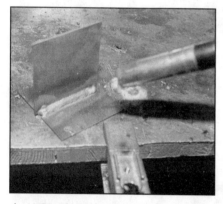

▲ W78. Bisect the angle between both pieces with the welding nozzle and be prepared to work the nozzle very slightly from side to side, to ensure that there is sufficient penetration into both pieces.

▲ W79. Here, the more common lap-joint is being tried. Again tack welds have been positioned first.

▲ W81. When welding an external angle, try tacking the two pieces together to form a 'vee'. This is much easier to weld and gives a stronger joint than having one piece overlap the other.

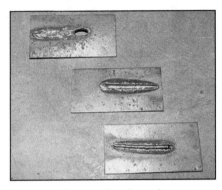

▲ W82. The top plate here shows a weld where the amperage and/or wire speed settings have been too high; the lower plate shows a thin, stringy weld where either the settings were too low or the handset passed too quickly over the plate; while the centre plate shows a weld that is just about right!

Experienced oxy-acetylene welders should beware that the torch should not be 'swirled' as would be an oxy-acetylene torch. You can weld in either direction but right-to-left for a right-handed person gives better visibility whilst the weld is taking place and improves gas flow over the weld.

MIG WELDING IN AWKWARD PLACES

Whenever possible, welds should be carried out flat but sometimes, of course, this is just not possible. Tipping the car over just to run a weld up a split wing is not exactly practical! Vertical welds are best carried out 'downhill', starting from the top, with the smaller sized machines being considered here; butt welds require a straight-on approach while fillets are best tackled with slight zig-zagging. Forehand welding (ie in the direction in which the nozzle opening is pointing) is recommended for all vertical or horizontal welds, so that the best gas shielding is obtained.

MIG welding out of doors is not recommended unless unavoidable because the wind tends to blow the shielding gas off the weld leaving a poor, untidy weld. Try building a localised wind break around the job and turn the gas flow-rate up higher.

▲ W83. Holes, like these superfluous dashboard holes, can be filled up by welding one side of the hole (say, at the 3 o'clock position) then the other (9 o'clock) then the remaining (12 o'clock and 6 o'clock) positions can be welded, and so on until the hole is filled. The tendency will be for the welder to burn through. Get over this by just pulsing the welder for a couple of seconds at a time.

▲ W84. These short-sharp welds can then be cleaned up to a perfect finish with the finisher, proving that no weakening inclusions are found in a MIG weld.

MIG SPOT-WELDING

▲ W85. Here, a repair patch is being MIG welded to the corner of a car tailgate. It is held in place first with a self-tapping screw to ensure a good fit with minimal distortion.

▲ W86. Small holes are drilled through the top plate only.

▲ W87. Then, the MIG nozzle is changed for a spot-welding nozzle, which simply holds the wire guide a set distance away from the workpiece. The nozzle is pressed down on to the job rather than held away as in seam welding.

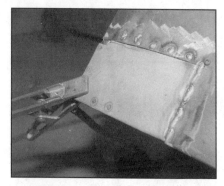

▲ W88. The right-hand edge was seam welded, but the neat button-spot welds can be seen along the top. There is no point in allowing too much build up. Always practise on scrap metal first and try to lever the finished weld apart with a screwdriver. This proves that settings and timing are correct. All SIP machines larger than the 120N have a timer built in so that pulsed welds and spot welds can be programmed automatically.

▲ W89. After welding, clean the 'spots' off flush with a minigrinder.

NB Always disconnect the vehicle alternator before MIG welding because the current will damage it.

SAFETY
In general, follow the safety rules for arc welding (see relevant section and 'Safety' section at the beginning of the book) and remember that newly MIG-welded panels are still hot enough to burn when touched. Care should be taken when flammable materials are near the weld and when a fuel tank is nearby, even though heat spread is less from MIG than any other form of welding except spot welding proper.

SPOT-WELDING

▲ W90. With a spot-welder, two pieces of steel are fuse-welded at the point where the two electrodes on the machine are squeezed together using the handle shown. At the point where they come together, an electric current is passed between them, melting the steel at that point and making the weld.

▲ W91. All modern cars are put together with thousands of spot-welds; factories are dominated by the awe-inspiring efficiency of spot-welding robots dancing and twirling rapidly from one set of welds to another. A spot-welder enables you to carry out quick, clean, original-type welds.

▲ W92. A spot-welder gives the cleanest welds of any system and is probably the easiest to use, but it still has to be set up and used correctly. First, these out-of-alignment electrodes have to be correctly lined up and the electrode tips cut back to the correct profile with the spot-welder.

▲ W93. The arms can be adjusted by slackening them off with an allen key or they can be changed for various shapes and sizes of arm, designed to reach round many of the obstructions found in car bodywork.

▶ W94. The amount of pressure has to be adjusted according to the maker's instructions and on models equipped with a timer, the correct length of weld can be pre-set for the material being used.

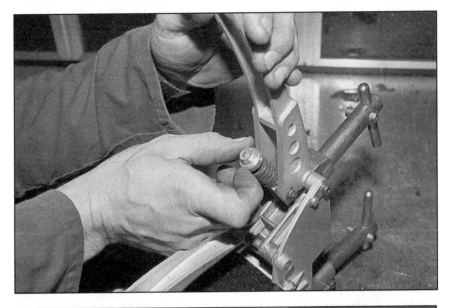

▶ W95. Try out the settings on scrap metal before starting to work. Metal **must** be clean and free of rust, paint or any other impurities and it must also be clamped close, without relying on the spot-welder arms to pull the pieces together. The weld on the left looks perfect, but the one on the right looks as though the timer was given too high a setting or, with a 'manual' spot-welder, the lever was held down for too long. Always check weld strength on the practice piece by trying to prise it open with a screwdriver. Weak welds are, quite obviously, a great danger.

◀ W96. The spot-welder in use. In an ideal situation there will be little or no sparking. If there is too much going on, suspect the weld strength. No special protective clothing or eye shields are needed when spot-welding but take all the usual precautions when working with electrical equipment.

SPOT-WELDING – NOTES

• If you are spot-welding thick metal, line the electrodes up with the metal held between the tips.
• If too much pressure is set, the spot weld will be a deep dimple; if too little, the weld will arc and burn.
• If the tips glow red hot, the welder has been left on for too long, or the tips may need cutting back to the correct profile.
• If you burn right through, the reason will be: metal rusty or contaminated; or, too little pressure set on the arms; or, welder left on too long coupled with too much pressure.

BRAZE WELDING ALUMINIUM

Welding aluminium is extremely tricky using oxy-acetylene, and TIG welding equipment is beyond the pocket of most mortals. However, there's a braze-welding system that allows even beginners to successfully weld pieces of aluminium together.

Durafix aluminium welding rods can be used to repair aluminium and alloys, zinc, 'pot' metals and die-cast. In fact, almost any non-ferrous metal (but including galvanised steel), including dissimilar metals, such as copper to aluminium can be braze welded.

This invaluable product uses no flux, making it easy to use and environmentally safe, and it has a low working temperature of 392°C (732°F).

Welds made with the rod are clean and free from slag, and produce a sound joint which is stronger than the parent metal. Aluminium of almost any thickness can be welded successfully, easily and cheaply. Durafix can be applied with any handheld torch – oxyacetylene, map gas, propane or butane.

It's worth remembering that Durafix will not work on ferrous metals, including stainless steel, or on 2000-grade aluminium, nor will it work on lead, mazac, zamac, tin or pewter.

Braze welding, by the way, is not simply a matter of two pieces of metal being 'glued' together as some people think. Brazing means that the brazing rod material is physically combined with that of the metals being brazed together. In other words, it really is a form of welding, and is capable of making an extremely strong joint.

▲ BWA1. For best results, the two pieces of aluminium being braze welded together have to be marked out...

▲ BWA2. ... and cut accurately, so that the joint between the pieces of metal is precisely formed.

▲ BWA3. If you use an angle grinder, be sure to use the correct cutting disc for the type of metal you are cutting.

▲ BWA4. If a disc intended for steel is used for cutting aluminium, it risks clogging, overheating and shattering, with extremely dangerous consequences. The correct discs can be bought easily from suppliers such as Screwfix Direct.

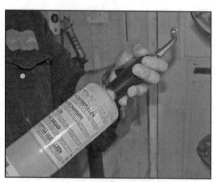

▲ BWA5. In addition to selling the welding rod, Durafix can also supply a suitable torch and either butane or the slightly hotter map gas in disposable containers.

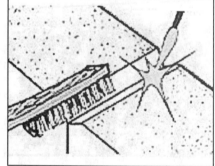

▲ BWA6. The surface of aluminium oxidises in minutes, and this layer needs to be removed before applying the Durafix welding rod. Sometimes, heating and vigorously brushing the surface with the stainless steel wire brush supplied with the Durafix kit is the best way of removing the oxides...

▲ BWA7. ... though we had no difficulty doing so on this thin aluminium sheet by simple brushing. If the aluminium has been anodised, the surface will need to be ground or filed back to bare aluminium.

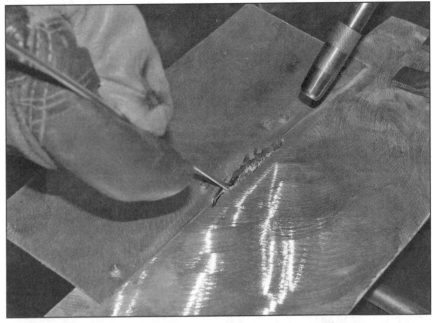

▲ BWA9. The Durafix rod now has to be pushed vigorously and rubbed onto the heated metal. You can keep heating the aluminium with the blowtorch, but it's important that the rod is not melted onto the workpiece, but is melted by the heat of the workpiece itself.

▲ BWA8. The area to be welded must now be heated evenly along the length being welded. The length of the weld to be carried out at any one time will be determined by the thickness of the aluminium.

▲ BWA10. Incidentally, note that thin material needs to be fixed so that it can't distort and bend away from its partner. We used a line of self-tapping screws that were removed later.

▶ BWA11. The finished weld should be nicely flushed into the joint, as shown here. You'll obtain a neater finish the more practice you get. After removing the screws, we tried breaking the weld and found that the aluminium broke away from the edge of the weld, though the weld itself stayed intact.

▲ BWA12. We also tried braze welding the thicker aluminium shown being cut earlier. Note that we used supports to ensure that the joint remained square while the welding was carried out.

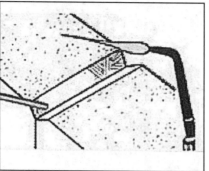

▲ BWA15. As before, the joint is heated and the rod pushed and rubbed into the joint...

▲ BWA18. But this is what happened when we tested the joint; it broke away! The weld had obviously not taken on one half of the joint, which could have been because oxides were not removed, or because the workpiece was not heated evenly.

▲ BWA13. You can see that here, the joint has been chamfered to allow a greater depth of weld and a greater surface area. The joint was heated...

▲ BWA16. ... until the point comes where the joint is hot enough to melt the rod.

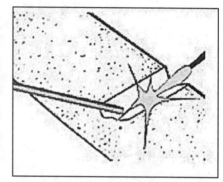

▲ BWA19. We tried again, and this time followed alternative instructions on the Durafix leaflet. After heating the joint, the surfaces of both pieces of metal were tinned with a thin layer of welding rod. While it was still molten, the stainless steel wire brush was used vigorously, some of the welding rod inevitably splashing off each side.

▲ BWA14. ... and vigorously wire brushed. Note that Durafix say you should not use any type of wire brush other than stainless steel, because it can contaminate the surface of the aluminium and prevent the weld from forming.

▲ BWA17. Here, the torch is being maintained at a small distance away from the joint to keep the workpiece hot without melting the rod directly.

▲ BWA20. This time, the weld appeared much smoother and, after the rod had gone in, a little more rod was applied to level out the surface.

▲ BWA21. When the top face had cooled and hardened, the workpiece was turned on its side and each edge welded in turn. As you can see, an old pair of pliers enables you to use almost all of the welding rod.

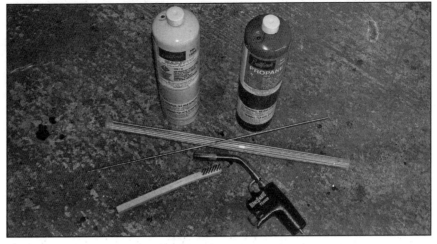

▲ BWA24. For information on where to purchase Durafix, see either: www,durafix.com or www.durafix.co.uk.

▲ BWA22. The finished weld was built up slightly higher than the surface of the workpiece...

▲ BBWA23. ...so an aluminium grinding disc was used to make a level surface.

PLASMA CUTTING

As with most developing technologies, early versions of plasma cutters were too expensive for everyday users to even consider, but subsequently cheaper versions have come on the market.

A narrow opening in the torch tip constricts the plasma and accelerates it towards the workpiece at very high temperatures of up to17,000°C and speeds of 20,000kph, while the plasma arc torch spins the gas around an electrode. (Incidentally, most manufacturers recommend using ordinary compressed air as the cutting gas.)

The force of the plasma arc thrusts through the metal, blasting away molten material. Metal that is not cleanly blasted away remains stuck around the cut as dross.

▲ PLC1. It's said that, once you've experienced the benefits of a hand-held plasma-cutting machine, you won't want to use any other cutting process. That's partly true, though there are downsides, especially where cheaper machines are concerned. (See 'Dross', on p.53.)

◄ PLC2. The arc on a plasma cutter results from electrically heating a gas (usually air) to a very high temperature. This creates a plasma arc in the chamber between the electrode and torch tip, which ionises the gas atoms and enables the gas (the 'plasma gas') to conduct electricity.

51

START CUTTING!

BEFORE STARTING:

▲ PLC3. Connect earth/ground/workpiece cable, the control cable and the torch cable to the machine.

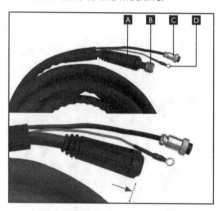

▲ PLC 4. Follow the recommended safety procedures in the owner's manual. These are the connections to be made to the BOC Smoothcut. (Courtesy BOC)

- Wear the correct safety equipment.
- Grind off rust and paint from the area you intend to cut and the point where you will be securing the earth (ground) clamp.
- Check that you have sufficient air pressure at the compressor.
- Set the amperage control, normally to maximum.

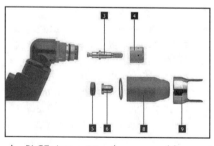

▲ PLC5. Inspect torch consumables (these are those of the BOC Smoothcut (Courtesy BOC)...

▲ PLC6. ...and replace worn parts if necessary.

STEP 1

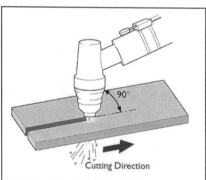

▲ PLC7. Note that the arc starts immediately when the trigger is pressed. Place the stand-off guide (or 'drag shield'), if fitted, on the edge of the base metal, or hold the cutting tip the correct distance (typically 2 or 3mm) above the workpiece, directing the arc straight down. (Courtesy BOC)

TIPS:

- As a general rule, for cutting amperages below 40A, the cutting tip can be dragged on the cutting surface, though dragging the tip will reduce its life.
- Higher amperages require a stand-off distance. Manufacturers normally supply a stand-off guide.
- You can use an extended electrode to improve visibility when cutting.

STEP 2

▲ PLC8. Once the cutting arc starts, slowly move the torch across the metal, adjusting your speed so that sparks are seen going through the workpiece and out the other side. (This is not the ideal cutting direction, but may sometimes be necessary.) The cutting speed will depend on the material type, thickness and amperage.

- Try not to hold the torch too firmly – it will make your hand shake more.
- Travel at the correct speed to produce a clean cut with little dross on the bottom of the cut and little or no distortion.
- If travelling at too slow a speed, the metal will become very hot and form more dross.

▲ PLC 9. It's very difficult to cut evenly 'freehand'. The cut will reflect all hand movements, and you may consider using roller or circle cutting guides. These make it easier to cut a straight line or circle while holding the torch at a consistent height and preventing the tip from touching the workpiece. Some guides also provide independently adjustable wheel height to allow you to easily cut a bevel angle.

▲ *PLC10. For a one-off, you could use a pre-cut piece of ply as a guide, though note that there is a risk it can catch fire! Work away from anything flammable and have a fire extinguisher to hand.*

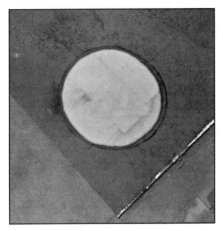

▲ *PLC11. This enabled us to easily cut a good hole in stainless steel sheet.*

DROSS

Dross accumulates when you force a machine towards its maximum cutting ability. To minimise dross, increase travel speed or reduce amperage. See the machine's recommended cutting speed.

STEP 3

At the end of a cut, turn the angle of the torch slightly towards the edge you're cutting towards, to go right through the metal. Air continues to flow to cool the torch, for 20 or 30 seconds after releasing the trigger.

TIPS:

If you can't see sparks beneath the workpiece, the arc is not penetrating the metal. This can be caused by:
- Moving the torch too quickly
- Too low an amperage
- Directing the plasma stream at a sharp angle
- Poor earthing (grounding)

PIERCING

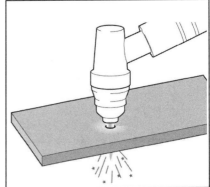

▲ *PLC12. To pierce material (ie, create a hole) the cutting torch should be held at an angle of 40 to 45° to the workpiece. Once piercing is established, bring the torch tip up to 90°, and the arc will pierce the base metal in the normal manner.*

- *Always protect the surrounds, and direct the arc away from the operator when initiating the cutting arc, as sparks and molten metal will be ejected from the cutting point.*
- *Piercing thickness is dependent on the power of the machine, and is generally 50% of its maximum cutting thickness.*

GOUGING

Gouging can remove old welds or imperfections from the metal's surface. When gouging with plasma, it's best to use a gouging tip supplied by the torch manufacturer, if available. The torch should be held at an angle of 30 to 45° to the surface. An arc length of 20mm should be used, and the torch moved in the direction of the material to be removed, adjusting torch speed, arc length and angle as required. Do not cut too deeply on one pass; several small cuts should be made to remove unwanted material.

Chapter 2

Panel beating

The operation of beating metal is the highest skill in the whole business of vehicle body repair. The ability to control the intensity of the blows delivered, together with the knowledge of how and where to direct the blows, anticipating the result to be expected, is the mark of the expert. Expertise can only be achieved by continued practice, once the basic requirements are understood, so it would be foolish for the complete beginner to start with an ambitious project. If you're interested in panel beating, practise on scrap metal first and take things a stage at a time.

This whole section has been produced with the close assistance of Sykes-Pickavant Ltd, manufacturers of the finest panel beating tools, in a range to suit the beginner and most accomplished expert alike. Fine tools, such as these, cost a little more to buy, but, because they last, cost less in the long run and because they are well balanced and well made, are easier to use than cheap products.

INTRODUCTION

So, to the first principles. When a sheet metal panel is bent by accidental force or impact, the force passes through the panel to give an area of direct damage at the point of contact and a wider area of indirect damage. This leaves a series of valleys, 'V' channels, or buckles across the surface, the ridges that appear being hard, rigid areas. In accident repair work it is important to know, or determine, the direction of the force causing the damage, so that exactly the opposite sequence can be applied to correct it. This means that in general, the indirect

damage is corrected first and the direct damage last.

Before any repair procedure can be carried out on a panel, the inner and outer surfaces must be thoroughly cleaned, and deadeners and underseal and other foreign matter that might interfere with the application of corrective forces removed. Most of the anti-drumming and other undercoatings used today can be removed by a scraper, or putty knife after softening by the application of heat to the outside of the panel. (Use a large tipped welding torch with a mild reducing flame.) The outside of the panel should be washed down with clean water and any traces of oil, road tar, or asphalt removed with a solvent-soaked rag. The panel preparation will make hand tool straightening more effective, coupled with a reduction in wear and tear on the dollies, etc. The first step in the restoration sequence is to unfold the valleys, 'V' channels and buckles in the indirectly damaged areas as gently as possible, without further stretching or reforming as they are brought up to something like their original position and contour.

The reshaping should continue with alternative working on the ridges and the low areas as the metal is slowly raised up into line with the surrounding sheet.

Figure PB1 shows a double end hand dolly and suitable beater in such a sequence. The actual force delivered to the metal surface will also depend on the weight of the beater used.

The weight and size of the dolly or spoon and indeed the area of actual

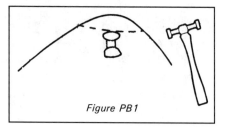

Figure PB1

contact with the panel will be factors to take into account. Too great a force between beater and dolly can stretch the metal locally, moving it outwards or inwards, as the metal cannot move sidewards to be absorbed within the panel. This action will involve further correction by shrinking (see later paragraphs).

The beater is held loosely, the shaft resting against the base of the thumb and the same distance from the heel of the palm, the fingers hooked over the shaft as shown. Now, by closing the fingers to grasp the shaft, the head of the beater is thrown forward by the strength of the fingers, to a position at 2, passing through an angle of about 80°. This method of beating is most useful when working beneath surfaces, when the beater, or the working area may be out of sight.

When trying this method of beating for the first time, only feeble blows may be possible. Strength in the fingers can only be developed with practice. Throw the head of the beater at the palm of the other hand, without movement of wrist or elbow. Alternatively use a block of soft wood to show if the blows are being received squarely.

Striking with the combined action of the fingers and wrist can be developed by following through from the above

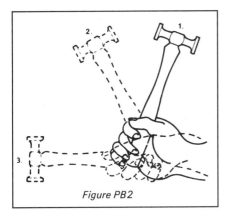

Figure PB2

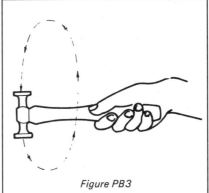

Figure PB3

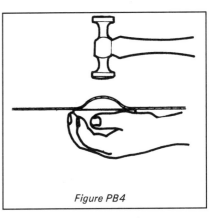

Figure PB4

description with added wrist action. The movement from 1 to 2 in Figure PB2 is achieved in exactly the same manner as described above. A follow through action of the wrist will cause the beater to make contact with the panel at position 3.

Some difficulty may be experienced at the initial attempt to strike with this co-ordination of movement so that practice is again essential. Heavier blows, for roughing-out purposes, become more in line with the natural movement of the elbow and shoulder, as in the use of ordinary hammers so that no description is deemed to be necessary here.

In the early attempts at panel beating, some difficulty may be experienced in aiming the beater at the panel so that it strikes squarely on the dolly below. Place a small dolly below the panel and tap the top surface lightly with the beater. Find the high surface of the dolly by checking for maximum rebound. Once this can be achieved, move the dolly about, following the movement with the beater to develop co-ordination until fairly rapid action is possible.

METALWORKING TECHNIQUES

Beaters should be well balanced ie the length of the shaft should give a feel of balance, when the tool is held in the hand, at a point about three quarters of the shaft length from the head. The handle should not be gripped tightly as this can cause fatigue in the arm muscles when beating over extended periods. When beating on metal the blows should land squarely on the surface. In all dinging

operations the beater should travel in a circular path (Figure PB3) with rhythmic action of some 100 to 120 blows per minute. In this manner the metal receives a sort of sliding or glancing blow resulting in but a small area of contact with the surface. To level out a panel the beater should be moved about in regular rows, striking the metal at intervals of about 10 mm, with light blows until levelling is completed. Beaters of sufficient size and weight such as those used for roughing-out and bumping are often used alone, or in conjunction with a piece of hardwood to raise the elastic areas of the metal. The non-elastic outer ridges are then re-shaped by 'Spring-beating' or 'On and Off the dolly' techniques. 'On-the-dolly' or 'direct' beating is shown in Figure PB4. The dolly is selected so that its contour, to be held under the ridge, is near to the original shape of the panel at this spot. Beating is then directed at the peak of the ridge, commencing with light blows, increasing in intensity to a level sufficient to push the ridge back. Work along the ridge from end-to-end in a progressive manner, ie do not flatten the ridge completely in a localised area, but take it all down gradually.

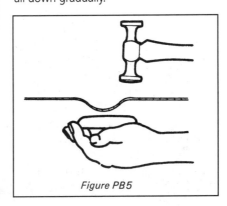

Figure PB5

In the case of a ridge with an associated depression on one side, 'off-the-dolly' or 'indirect' beating is applied. Again, the dolly is selected to be close to the original panel shape, and held under the depression (Figure PB5). Beating on the ridge away from the dolly, will cause a reaction to produce an alternating impact on the panel. First impact with the beater and then the impact from the dolly alternatively until the depression is removed. 'On-the-dolly' beating can then be resorted to, bringing the panel up to the final stages of levelling. In panel finishing (Figure PB6) small low areas should be raised by using the side of the round face of the beater, initially. The surface is now checked with the body file to highlight any remaining low spots. Each spot should be raised individually with a blow, or a series of tiny blows, with the pick. Care must be taken not to strike the low spots too hard, otherwise they will become rough and 'pimply' and the metal stretched.

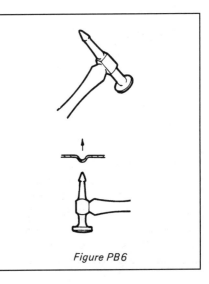

Figure PB6

MALLETS

Mallet heads are usually made of hardwood fitted to ash handles, to form a complete mallet. Standard round mallets have cylindrical heads. The bossing mallet is sometimes referred to as the 'pear-shaped' mallet. Both patterns are now available in other materials, such as rubber, rawhide and the softer metals, as in copper-faced mallets.

Rubber mallets, with interchangeable screw-on heads, are ideal for use on aluminium and may be used in the repair of panels in sheet steel. Hollowing (Figure PB7) is a process of thinning metal from the centre of a given blank, to produce a double-curvature panel. This can be accomplished by the use of a bossing mallet and a sand-bag. Beating of the metal commences in the centre of the plate, working outwards in increasing circles, until the required curvature is obtained. Uniformity in the intensity of the blows is important to produce a regular shape.

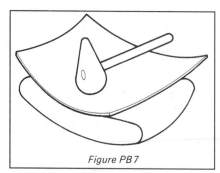

Figure PB7

APPLICATION OF BEATER AND DOLLY

RESHAPING A FLANGE

The utility dolly is placed in the damaged flange (Figure PB8) using the edge most suitable to the shape and size of the original flange. An upward and outward pressure is applied to the dolly. The flange is now reformed by 'on-the-dolly' beating; starting at the inner edge of the flange, gradually working to the outer edge as indicated, until it is back to its original form.

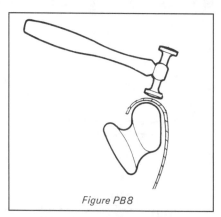

Figure PB8

SPOONS AND THEIR APPLICATIONS

Spoons are used for bumping and prying (prising), they are also used in place of dollies when direct access to the rear of the panel is obstructed by the internal frame structure. The choice of the spoon for a particular job will depend on the original contour of the metal, the amount of access, the proposed action (roughing or levelling) and the general shape and the length of the spoon.

GENERAL PURPOSE SPOON

The reshaping of the roof panel (Figure PB9) may be possible by the use of a general purpose spoon instead of the curved dolly. Figure PB10 shows the application. The use of a backing piece to prevent local damage to the cant rail and reduce the pressure in this area by distributing the force at the fulcrum will depend on clearances at this point. Prying upwards from a-to-b with a steady force, accompanied with external beating on any ridges that may be present, will restore the shape.

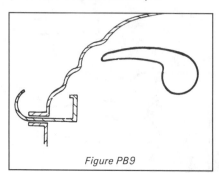

Figure PB9

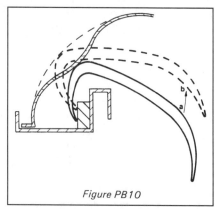

Figure PB10

Provided that a backing piece is employed a certain amount of prying fore and aft may assist the work.

INSIDE PRY AND SURFACING SPOON

Assuming that the outer panel only is damaged, making the repair an economical proposition, the car door provides an example of a double skin structure to illustrate the application of body spoons.

When the door is stripped of interior trim and window glass it should be placed panel down towards the floor or bench, resting on two pieces of wood as Figure PB11. This prevents the panel scraping the floor and gives space for the panel to move, or spring, as force is exerted on the spoon. After roughing out, the spoon can be reversed so that 'on' or 'off' the spoon beating can be used to complete the straightening procedure. Access for this spoon will depend on the pattern of the piercing through the inner structure. If direct access is not possible a Long-Reach Dolly should be employed. Alternatively circular holes may be cut in the inner panel for access and covered by the trim on assembly.

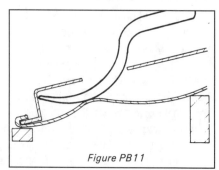

Figure PB11

HEAVY DUTY PRY SPOON

This spoon can be used for separating outer panels from the inner frame structure, when they have been damaged and squeezed together (Figure PB12). It can be driven between the plates, prying sidewards, or up and down until the desired amount of separation is achieved. The blade can then be used as a dolly, to dress out the outer panel and the inner structure if required. The blade is reduced to a very thin section that can be used for opening door panel flanges or breaking spot-welded joints that have been previously drilled through the panel or section to be discarded.

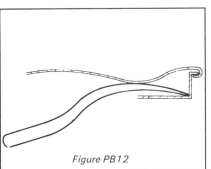

Figure PB12

HIGH CROWN SPOON

The high crown, with its broad working surface and high crown is an ideal tool as a dolly, or a spoon for work in confined areas, such as headlamp housings and high crown sections of the body above the waist line (Figure PB13).

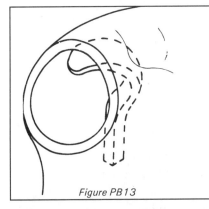

Figure PB13

SPRING BEATING SPOON

A light pressed-steel spoon is designed specially for spring beating on ridges. The spoon is placed directly on the ridge (Figure PB14) and sharp blows with a beater are delivered to the back of the

spoon, spreading the force over a large area. In this manner marking of the panel is prevented and the damage corrected in many cases without injury to the paint work. The intensity of the blow should be closely controlled so that the area is not forced down below its normal position. This spoon is not made for prying or levering, and its surface, as with other panel tools, should be kept clean and highly polished. Any irregularities on the surface will be reproduced on the panel, in reverse.

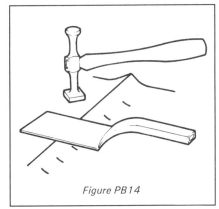

Figure PB14

BUMPING BLADES

Bumping blades are used for slapping out dents, with or without the backing support of a dolly. For slight dents or a wavy surface, a dolly is not required. The bumping blade should be applied so that glancing blows are received by the panel

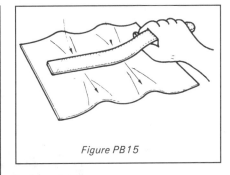

Figure PB15

(Figure PB15). The blade serrations hold the metal within the area of contact to avoid stretching. Limit the use of blades to slight or moderate damage, as they are not intended to take the role of the body spoon or beater and dolly. Experience will indicate when to use them; try out as a semi-finishing tool.

PANEL FINISHING

SHRINKING

In the final stages of panel finishing, some slightly stretched areas of metal may be encountered. The repairer determines the exact location, size and shape of the area by 'hand-feeling' (running the palm of the hand over the surface), by 'eye' or, in the case of a large flat area, such as a door panel, by the use of a straight edge. To increase sensitivity when 'hand-feeling', a lightweight cotton glove could be used to 'feel' the panel. On a paint-finished car body a spray of light oil and a strong light source can be used to show slight irregularities in the surface. Once the stretched area is located the treatment will depend on the amount of stretch involved. (See also 'Heat-shrinking a panel' in the Welding chapter.)

SHRINKING BEATERS

For slightly stretched areas shrinking beaters may be used (Figure PB16). The square faced end of the beater is cross-milled. In using this type of beater small amounts of metal are forced into the spaces created by the cross-milling. They can be used on aluminium in a cold condition, but working on sheet steel will be speeded if heat is applied to the

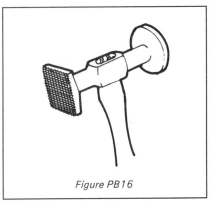

Figure PB16

area. Be careful, however, because excess heat can itself cause more stretching. Whenever possible such beating should be carried out on the inside of the panel to minimise resurfacing work prior to painting.

GRID DOLLY

A special dolly is available to facilitate shrinking work. This is the grid dolly which has a large crowned grid face on the upper surface. The base is a shallow face for normal finishing work.

▶ *SP1. Here, metal is beaten into the groove in the grid dolly, forcing the surplus metal downwards and 'out of the way'! In cases of severe stretching, a second groove can be made, at right-angles to the first, forming a cross.*

For information on heat shrinking, see relevant section in this book. In general, Sykes-Pickavant recommend leaving the panel-beating surface marginally lower and under no circumstances should high-spots remain because these are impossible to disguise. The beginner is strongly recommended to leave any small indentations below the surface out of harm's way, rather than to attempt to beat them out, when the result would probably be to stretch and 'belly' the metal. Finish off with a plastic filler: the quantity of filler you have to use will be a good guide to how well your expertise has developed! But once again, go for a successful finish rather than a macho attempt at beating out every last imperfection, because it's the finish that counts, assuming that the job is sound.

ANNEALING

When beating metal, the action of the beater tends to work-harden it. This happens quickly with aluminium; less so with steel. The result is that the metal becomes hard and springy and almost impossible to work. With steel, the solution is to heat it up to red heat then swirl the torch over the heated metal, withdrawing it slowly so that the steel cools slowly. Use this technique only when fabricating a repair panel which needs a lot of working: the risk of distortion is too great with a full body panel. Aluminium should also be heated to anneal it, but remember that it will melt at less than red heat. It will anneal whether allowed to cool in the air or if quenched in water. Quenched steel will not anneal properly.

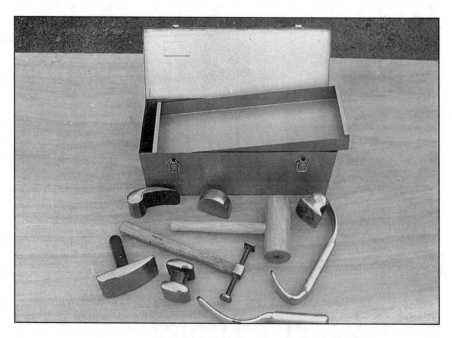

▶ *SP2. Sykes-Pickavant make kits ranging from the 'Service Station Kit' for the occasional user and the beginner, through to the 'Master Set' whose name speaks for itself. All are highly commended by the author as fine examples of craftsmanship in themselves!*

Chapter 3
Getting rid of rust

Rust is your classic car's greatest enemy. While its engine, gearbox and running gear can be made to go on for hundreds of thousands of miles given remedial treatment when needed, the corrosion of steel is more or less inevitable. You *can* slow it down, and in so doing considerably extend the life of your car, but you can't entirely stop it. Corrosion is part of the nature of things, the process of creation and decay that affects everything around us. Iron ore, a brown rock, is mined from the earth, melted down and alloyed with a small amount of carbon and other elements. This turns it into strong, usable steel. As corrosion sets in, however, the iron content rapidly starts to turn itself back into a brown, crumbly substance, useful only for resmelting and making back into steel again.

To protect steel against corrosion, it is necessary to create a barrier between the surface of the steel and its environment. Car manufacturers have always applied paint to their steel panels, of course, and traditionally, it was considered enough to keep rust at bay for the car's life with the first couple of owners. Today, pressure from the customer has meant that the manufacturer has had to do much more about keeping rust at bay, and competition has meant that he has had to back up his protection claims with a long-term guarantee. Such procedures make it all the more important to reintroduce corrosion control when repairs to minor bumps and panel replacements are carried out.

HOW CORROSION OCCURS
The process of corrosion actually happens as the result of an electric current passing from one section of metal to another. As in the case of a battery, there must be an electrolyte between the two sections (salty water? That'll do nicely!) and oxygen must also be present. As ions flow from the positive 'terminal' (the anode) to the negative 'terminal' (the cathode), the anode breaks down; in the case of steel it rusts. Rusting stops if water, oxygen or the electrolyte are completely excluded, but if any of them get through and the temperature is above freezing point it starts off with a vengeance. Poultices of salt-soaked mud and dust, industrial pollution and soil rich in agricultural chemicals provide corrosion with the perfect opportunity to take a hold on the steel sheets that make up the body of your car.

FIGHTING BACK
The most effective steps in excluding corrosion are taken during the manufacturing process when a car's internals are most accessible. Obviously, there's not much the owner of a classic car can do about this except when carrying out restoration work.

Once the car is in use, there are two steps that can usefully be taken by the owner to hold back the rust that takes a hold in the enclosed structural sections and those beneath the car. The first is to wash mud and dirt from underneath the vehicle at least twice a year. This can be done in an effective way by many garages at moderate cost using a pressure blast of steam. Steam cleaning removes all the mud from the traps and

crevices at which the steam is directed and it also removes any loose paint or underseal which, if left in place, can only accelerate corrosion.

Clearly, it is important to examine those areas that have been cleaned and to touch-up any bare patches. For the keen DIY enthusiast, a fairly effective way of dislodging mud from beneath the car is to make up a lance from ½in or 15mm copper tubing and hold it in the end of a piece of hosepipe with a jubilee clip. The business end of the tube can be hammered into a flat slit giving a water jet of increased pressure. But be prepared for a drenching!

The second is to apply rust preventer every couple of years, but beware! It is a fact that where any rust preventative is applied, any small areas which are missed by the treatment will be much more prone to electrolytic action than if no treatment had taken place at all. So make sure you do it thoroughly!

PART I – RUSTPROOFING

Most car handbooks give joke information on how to maintain your car's bodywork. They tell you to wash the car regularly, to oil the hinges and how to touch up stone chips. Dirt and dropped hinges have never sent a car to the great scrapyard in the sky yet! Rust can take a hold from the outside, through untreated paint chips, but I've never yet seen it send a car to the crusher! Ninety-nine point nine per cent of rusty cars are scrapped because of rust that starts on the inside and works its way out. If you understand the basic principles of rusting, it's easy to see what should be done about it.

As already mentioned, minute electric currents pass between areas of unprotected steel panels. This is known as electrolytic action – or rusting to you and me. Electrolytic action works best between dissimilar pieces of steel held close together. Separate sections held together with spot welds fit the bill admirably. Electrolytic action needs close physical contact, the presence of both air and moisture, and it loves a temperature which is just over freezing. Salt helps the process along wonderfully well.

Therefore, a perfect rust bath consists of mud from the road thrown up against joints in steel work, such as under wheel arches and in chassis sections. Then, in winter and the months that follow, salt water can soak in to form a damp poultice to work away when the temperature rises above freezing.

Also, a real boost to rust formation is a film of moisture trapped against the surface of the steel. Underseal (of the old-fashioned, paint-on variety) creates the perfect spot as it dries out and becomes brittle, trapping water beneath where it lifts from the steel it is meant to protect. Electrolytic action hates having water and air excluded, and it also thoroughly dislikes having salt water closed off. So, the basic principles of rustproofing are extremely simple: shut out air and water and you shut out rust!

On the outside of the bodywork, paint does the job of keping air and water away from the surface of the metal. Paint underneath is fine – but only for a short while. Beneath the car there is a constant shot-blasting factory at work. In addition, the salt and mud poultices work their way beneath the paint in a very short while. That's why underbody protection is needed. But as I said before, when it goes wrong by drying out and going brittle, it adds to the problem that it was put there to solve.

When it comes to older cars, where rust will invariably have made a start, the process of rust prevention is simple, but it requires you to be thorough. It also

needs you to repeat the treatment on a regular basis. Although it never appears in any workshop or service manuals, if you really want to keep your classic car

▲ RP2. A skirmish with an unknown enemy in a car park has left this patch without paint. Application of primer will stop the rust spreading, though it is in your own interest to get some finish paint on the damaged area as soon as possible because primer is more porous than finish paint.

▲ RP1. Paintwork will chip just about anywhere it can – not just on the leading edge of the bonnet, though that is obviously a major area. If you can't stop the paint coming off, at least you can stop the rust spreading outwards from the paint chips by using a suitable touch-up primer. In the top of the can is a handy brush made specifically for dealing with small areas. It unscrews and with this you can treat the affected areas in seconds.

alive, you must regard body maintenance as an essential part of servicing.

First of all, here's how to keep the car's outer panels in shape.

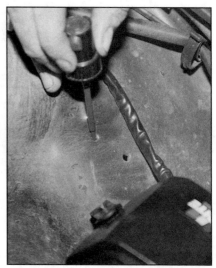

▲ RP3. Another use is when you drill holes in the bodywork. You should always make a point of tidying up any burrs or rough edges from new holes you drill, and rustproof them – otherwise rust will get a hold and make the hole considerably larger! Once again, always cover primer paint with touch-up paint.

▲ RP4. Here, some finish paint in an aerosol can is being sprayed into the cap from where it will be brushed on with a fine paint brush. Paint for spraying is too thin for brushing straight from the aerosol, so leave it to stand in the cap for a while to let the paint thicken. Alternatively, you can buy touch-up paint in a small tube with an applicator, similar to that shown previously.

Beneath the car, the process is a lot more 'earthy' and it becomes even more essential that you carry out rustproofing properly. None of the work is what you might call pleasant but the first time you do it will be the worst. The majority of cars never receive this treatment; and the majority of cars rot away before they should. The choice is yours! A word of warning, however. Some manufacturers of rustproofing products make it sound as though, by using their process, you can effectively rustproof your car with very little effort. I'm sure it helps them to sell their product but I'm equally sure that it doesn't work that way.

Don't waste your time by rustproofing your car in the winter time. The underside will be wet, it will be unpleasant to work on and, worse still, the rustproofer might not work properly. This essential part of body maintenance should be carried out twice a year, however – once before the onset of winter and once at the end.

Rust prevention should be regarded as a regular maintenance job, by which means you can extend the life of your car by many years. You will have to inject rustproofing fluid into all the enclosed box sections and 'chassis' sections on your car. In many cases you will find access holes already in place; in others, you'll be able to take off a cover, a piece of trim or a door lock in order to gain access. But in quite a few cases, you will need to drill holes to gain an entry point. Decide on your drill size with reference to the size of the injector nozzle and the size of grommets that you can obtain for blanking the holes off again afterwards. (This only needs to be done if the hole faces forwards or up, in which case you will want to keep water out, or if it is visible, such as inside door openings.)

The hand pump injectors that can be bought from DIY shops are often worse than useless. They don't usually make a proper spray, but simply squirt a jet of fluid that does nothing to give the all-over cover required. Make a dummy 'box section' out of a cardboard box – cut it and fold to make it about 4–6in (100–150mm) square – and try a dummy run. Open it up and see if it has worked. If you haven't obtained full misting of the fluid, you could be making the problem worse. Remember: if you only partly cover the internal areas to be protected, rust strikes even harder in those areas that aren't covered than it would have done previously, gathering all its force on the unprotected areas, as it were. So, consider investing in a full professional rustproofing gun. They are expensive but the cost is minute compared with the cost of rebuilding your classic car. Consider buying jointly with friends; persuade your car club to buy one and hire out or attempt to hire from a local body shop. And hiring a compressor from a tool hire shop keeps the cost down. Alternatively, consider taking your car to a garage with suitable equipment and having them do the work for you. It may not be quite as thoroughly carried out as it would be if you did the work yourself – unless you are allowed to 'lend a hand' and point out the areas where you would like fluid to be injected – but full, professional injection equipment as shown in the following picture sequences will make the fluid reach much further and deeper than amateur equipment.

If you carry out the work at home, place newspaper beneath the car to catch the inevitable drips that will flow out of bodywork drain holes – if you use enough rustproofer, that is! Make absolutely certain that you don't clog drain holes by injecting far too much fluid – especially in door bottoms where water could gather and form a veritable indoor pond.

Safety Note: Before using rustproofing fluid, read the manufacturer's safety notes. Keep it off the exhaust or any other components where it could ignite. Keep it away from brake components – cover them up with plastic bags before starting work. Wear an efficient face mask so that you don't inhale vapour, and goggles to keep material out of your eyes. Follow the advice under Safety Sense with regard to safe working beneath a car raised off the ground.

▲ RP5. Remove the mud that traps the salt water from beneath your car and you eliminate a potent source of corrosion. You can scrape it off by hand, use a pressure washer such as the one shown here or even make your own by hammering the end of a length of copper tubing to create a thin, flat nozzle; then fitting a hose pipe to the other end, holding it in place with a jubilee clip.

▲ RP6. Gather together all the materials and equipment you will need to carry out the work. All the better rustproofing materials manufacturers, such as Würth, make two types: one which is 'thinner' for applying to the insides of box sections and another which is tougher and is for application to the undersides of wheel arches and anywhere that is susceptible to blasting from debris thrown up by the wheels. The Würth applicator needs a compressor to power it.

AROUND THE CAR

▲ RP7. Some rustproofing fluids in aerosol cans are thin enough for injecting behind chromium trim strips and badges but some people find that they are inclined to leave a stain on the paintwork around the trim. As an alternative to a rustproofing fluid, you can use a water dispersant or a thin oil.

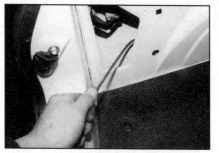

▲ RP9. Remove the pull-away side trims and work the nozzle into the space between the outer wing and the boot/luggage bay 'floor', paying particular attention to the lower joint which forms the wheel arch. It is a good idea to remove the rear lights also, in order to reach the box section beneath them and to treat the upper corners of the wing adequately. Insert the flexible nozzle into the box section that crosses the boot at the rear – holes provided for the wiring harness will give access to this section. Spray the spare wheel compartment (after removing the wheel!) but remember to wipe away any excess fluid before replacing it.

▲ RP11. Remember to treat the joints between wings and body, and the wing fixing bolts/washers. Apply fluid behind and beneath the front 'slam' panel, down the seams between the inner wing and bulkhead, and around the headlight/sidelight apertures. At each end of the bulkhead, work the nozzle up into the windscreen pillars, spraying as it is withdrawn.

▲ RP8. Drain holes provide good access to the tailgate interior, although it is best if the trim can be removed. Direct the flexible nozzle into all the strengthening ribs and seams, spraying as the nozzle is drawn out. 'Wiggle' the nozzle up into the sides of the tailgate around the rear screen aperture if possible, otherwise apply copious rustproofer and allow it to run down the channels. When spraying is complete, close the tailgate so that fluid drains down into the bottom seam. Make sure the drain holes remain clear on the bottom edge.

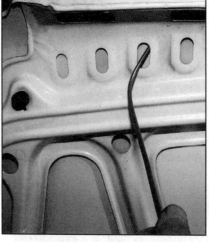

▲ RP10. Inject fluid into all strengthening ribs and channels on the underside of the bonnet. Some models have a fibre-board insulation cover clipped to the underside – remove this first. Pay attention to the front, rear, and side-seams of the bonnet, making sure sufficient fluid is applied to penetrate the layers of metal. As with the tailgate, close the bonnet after application so that fluid runs down to the front seam.

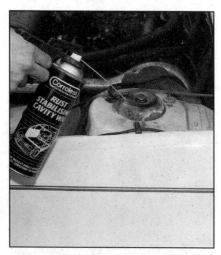

▲ RP12. Apply fluid to the suspension tops, around the projecting studs and nuts, and also to the edges of the overlapping panels on the suspension turrets.

UNDER THE CAR

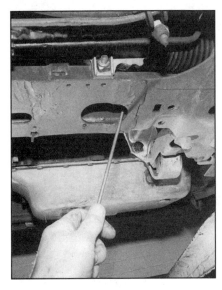

Get yourself prepared for this job! Disposable overalls or old clothes are a necessity and none more so than some form of headgear to protect your hair. Gloves and a face-mask are also essential.

First of all, the thinner, 'creeping' type of fluid is sprayed into and on to every seam. (This goes quite a long way into every joint but would wash away if not covered over.) Then, it is time to cover the entire surface with the tougher type of protectant. For this process the thicker, black underbody fluid is used – note that this needs to be warmed by standing it in a bucket of very hot water for 20 minutes or so before use. Make doubly sure that the car is safely raised and stable.

Spray the fluid while it is still warm and 'thin' taking care to ensure an even coverage with no gaps. When spraying over fuel and brake pipes make at least two passes with the spray gun, at different angles, so that the fluid isn't masked by the pipes which would leave an unprotected 'shadow' behind them. Start at the front of the car and work backwards.

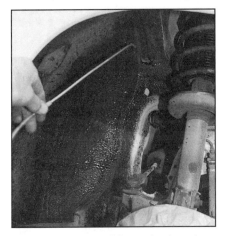

▲ *RP13. Work the flexible nozzle along the cross-members and spray as it is withdrawn, paying particular attention to the end-seams where they join the inner wing out-riggers that travel forwards through the engine bay. Use the flexible nozzle to treat these sections too, gaining access through the many drain holes already provided. Also, treat all other underbody box sections.*

▲ *RP15. Remove all four wheels and wrap plastic bags around the brake discs or drums. If your car is fitted with plastic inner splash guards it is a good idea to remove them so that the fluid can be applied to the 'hidden' seams and surfaces, because they can still get damp, if not wet, and consequently will corrode. Pay particular attention to the outer wheel arch seams – spray 'outwards' from inside the wheel arch to ensure good penetration and sealing. Spray also up into the coil spring recesses (suspension tops), varying the angle of the spray gun as the fluid is applied.*

Finally, clean any fluid overspray from the bodywork, including the door sills where fluid will have dripped from the door drain holes. Use a good glass cleaner if fluid has found its way on to the windows (it usually does!). Also, clean the wiper blades, as traces of fluid will be smeared across the screen when the wipers are next used and you're unlikely to see much through it! The last job is to fit any grommets into holes you may have drilled – dip them in rustproofing fluid before fitting, which will provide a very effective seal when the fluid turns to wax.

▲ *RP14. Work the flexible nozzle into a hole in each sill, drilling new ones if necessary, every time spraying as it is withdrawn. Make sure drain holes are clear by poking with a short length of stiff wire. Fluid should issue from all such holes, if you've applied it sufficiently!*

PART II – NEUTRALISING RUST

This section has been produced in association with Fertan. This unusual arrangement is because I had become rather cynical about the efficiency of rustproofing products. But I tested Fertan, treating rusty steel and leaving it unprotected over a period of six months, and the results were surprisingly good. I've now used the treatment on each of my classic cars.

Every year, more and more classic cars end up rusting in peace. This is partly because they've been around for so long, and have often been repaired before, and partly because, rust proofing on classic vehicles when they were new was vastly inferior to that on modern cars.

When planning rust control, it is important to remember that more than 75% of car body rust takes place from the inside outwards. Really effective protection must therefore strike at the root of the problem: inside cavities, double skinning and welds.

It's worth remembering that mechanical rust removal, such as sand blasting, can fail because only loose rust is removed. There are three grades of 'cleanliness' of mechanically blasted steel: SA3 (white metal), SA2.5 near white metal and SA2 (commercial blast). Just by painting with Fertan Rust Converter you can achieve a standard of rust removal exceeding SA2.5, and enjoy considerable cost savings and environmental benefits.

▲ NR 1. Fertan is a water-based product that penetrates the rust, converts it chemically and leaves 'bronzed' metal on the surface. It is important to note that Fertan doesn't cover the rust, like some other products, but dissolves it. The resulting black powder can simply be washed off, and the layer which lies underneath is extremely well-protected by a new bond to the metal. It is also very effective in cavities, joints, etc. because of its viscosity.

Fertan can be used as a protective coating on lightly rusted metal, stubborn rust and rust-free steel, but it also forces its way into overlaps and seams, double skinning, welds and joints, and even blistered paint, and then reacts. It can be used on both dry and damp metal. It is not damaging to rubber, chrome, plastic, glass and undamaged paintwork, though it can mark paler surfaces, so you should cover the surrounding areas.

Fertan only becomes active when it encounters metal or rust. It can be removed from all other surfaces simply by washing it off with water. It is not damaging to health, either by inhalation or by contact. In addition it is non-flammable and minimises the environmental damage of rust removal. As long as the surface treated is also treated with a protective coating, Fertan is effective for years. Fertan should not be applied at temperatures of less than 5°C.

SURFACE PREPARATION

▲ NR2. Because it is water-based, Fertan can't effectively react with rust in the presence of dirt, oil, grease or silicone, so first, clean the surface to be treated, removing loose rust at the same time.

TREATMENT

SAFETY:

● On contact with skin, a simple rinse under running water is sufficient.
● Do not swallow the product.

▲ NR3. Next, apply Fertan with a brush, roller, sponge or appropriate spray-gun attachment. After about an hour, dampen the treated surface (not necessary in damp conditions, especially inside cavities). Now allow Fertan to work for at least 24 hours (or 48 hours in temperatures of less than 12°C). Before further treatment, always clean the surface with water.

In areas such as box sections, a compressor and an injector with a 360° spray head are essential. You must periodically wash out the spray attachment with water.

A litre of Fertan is sufficient for an area of about 15m². In a closed container, Fertan will keep practically indefinitely. Store Fertan in a frost-free place.

PROTECTION

Further treatment is particularly important to protect sound areas on the vehicle and, also, the Fertan layer.

Prepared metal surfaces can be left from a few days to a maximum of six months before applying further treatments. Before doing so, the black dust created by the rust conversion process should be rinsed from the surface with water, or wiped off with a soft cloth.

FOLDS AND SEAMS

▲ NR5. Before treating folded door seams, removal of trim is usually recommended, partly to improve access and partly to avoid soiling trim parts.

▲ NR4. IMPORTANT NOTES: In cavities, you should only use cavity wax, and nothing else, after treatment. Remember never to use any product that hardens, such as colour coat, primer, etc. In the case of underbody protection, a summer-use or concours car for instance won't need three layers of underbody protection, and a cosmetically attractive paint layer in body colour might be best, protected by transparent, fully-hardening wax. You must decide for yourself, but don't forget that wax as a final coating gives noticeably better durability than bitumen- or tar-based products.

▲ NR6. Sometimes it's best to remove a whole bolt-on panel.

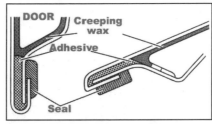

▲ NR7. First, the outer areas of folded seam are sanded smooth. Any rust pits and pinholes should not be treated until after the work on the folded seams has been completed, so as to avoid problems when applying filler, etc. (Illustration, courtesy Fertan)

▲ NR8. Rust proofer should be applied directly to the inside of the folded seam with a spray gun, using a pressure of about 4 bar (60psi), and because of its viscosity, it will then partly penetrate into the fold and partly emerge from its lower parts. To avoid marking, excess material should be washed off with water as quickly as possible; however, this isn't important if the area is being painted afterwards.

Allow Fertan to act for 24 hours, and then liberally treat the fold with clean water. Water, as well as dirt and dust, will flow out through the water drain holes, and it is therefore vital that these remain open. Once the folds are absolutely rust-free, they are finally protected with wax. The outer areas of folds are finally treated with paint in the normal way. On door seams and folds, Ferpox can be used as the first stage, for extra protection, on top of the Fertan-treated surface. However, as this material involves an extra layer of coating, it should be omitted on bonnet and boot edges where the final cosmetic appearance is more crucial.

▲ NR10. Access can often be gained by removing mirrors or trim…

▲ NR12. Insert the injector nozzle…

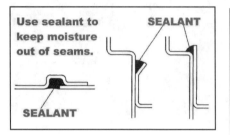

▲ NR9. External seams should also be cleaned, treated and sealed with PU sealer such as Würth Bond & Seal. (Illustration, courtesy Fertan)

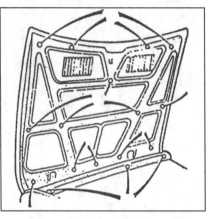

▲ NR11. …or by looking for existing access holes. (Illustration, courtesy Fertan)

▲ NR13. …and wipe off excess with white spirit on a rag.

CAVITIES

It is always better to paint panels before treating cavities. When treating cavities in bonnets and doors, a cavity spray attachment must be used, preferably in conjunction with a high-pressure spray gun, in the same way as with other cavities. The difference is that in these applications the openings are often much smaller than usual, and can't be reached with a normal (8–10mm) attachment.

Wax, the final protection medium, should not be applied so thickly that it creates problems later during painting. If bonnet, boot or door panel cavities show signs of excess wax leakage, this should be cleaned off with white spirit or panel wipe.

In very thin cavities and correspondingly smaller openings, Fertan can be applied with a hand spray and a 4mm diameter probe. Cavity wax can be applied with a spray can with a very thin probe attached.

BOX SECTIONS

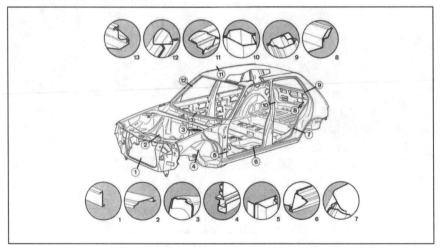

▲ NR14. The rusting process in box sections begins largely as a consequence of condensation forming on inner surfaces. There, this dampness is enriched by salts, which combine to form an acid which aggressively attacks the metal, and any protective coatings which are present, and in the course of time causes massive damage. On some vehicles, because of the design of the chassis, particles of dirt are thrown up, get lodged and baked hard, and then cause heavy corrosion when they get wet again. Research has shown that large quantities of water and very high humidity levels are generally found in box sections and cavities. (Illustration, courtesy Fertan)

Daytime temperatures inside box sections can reach nearly 90°C in summer, but when the temperature drops in the night, there will be a noticeable increase in atmospheric humidity. This means that box sections and cavities are usually damp, or even wet, all of the time, day and night.

This often affects classic cars, because in these vehicles active corrosion protection was either wholly or partially absent. Welds and seam overlaps are often in the critical weak spots.

Protecting an already-rusted box section only with a sealing layer of protection, such as paint, wax or underseal, means that any rust, and the damaging chemicals present in the rust, are merely sealed in and can start to cause new, even more serious corrosion. Therefore, it is vital that the rust is removed at the beginning, and damaging chemicals are removed.

On vehicles with loose flakes of rust which peel off and lie on the base of the box sections, two applications of Fertan are recommended, because these flakes must firstly be sufficiently loosened so that they can later be removed by rinsing with water. For this first application, you can mix Fertan with up to 50% water for the first treatment, spray it in and allow it to react for at least 48 hours at 20°C. During this time the vehicle can be used normally. If the temperatures are lower than 20°C, for instance at night, the reaction time allowed should be at least doubled. Fertan should not be applied at temperatures of less than 5°C.

RINSING

After the reaction time has elapsed, rinse the box sections and cavities thoroughly with water. Use approx. 15 litres of water for every litre of Fertan used, and operate the pressure gun at a pressure of 6 bar and the cavity gun at 4 bar. For this important rinsing, do not park the vehicle on a light-coloured surface, such as concrete, tiles, paving stones, etc, because the run-off water will stain it.

Now spray unthinned Fertan into the still-damp box sections, as described previously, and allow to react again at 20°C for at least 24 hours. Again, the vehicle can be used normally, and the reaction time can be stretched to 6 months without any problem.

Before the final treatment of the box section with protective wax, it is vital that the box section is rinsed out once more with clean water.

This treatment may seem involved, but it's the only way that all rust and damaging chemicals can be successfully removed from the box section.

Incidentally, rinsing water used in this process won't cause any new corrosion, because the layer which has been created on the surfaces of the box section is completely insoluble in water. Also, running water washes away rust-causing electrolytes, which noticeably slows the rate of corrosion. Be sure to dispose of rinsing water in an environmentally responsible way.

To ensure that no rinsing water remains in the seams and low points, raise one side of the vehicle and then the other with a jack and allow all water to run out. When the box section or cavity has been rinsed out completely, it is free of rust and damaging chemicals, and after the surface has been dried it can be coated with wax.

TIPS:

- DON'T drill holes before obtaining grommets – chances are you won't find grommets to fit.
- Coat the drill bit with grease to gather swarf before it can enter the box section, as it could cause corrosion later.

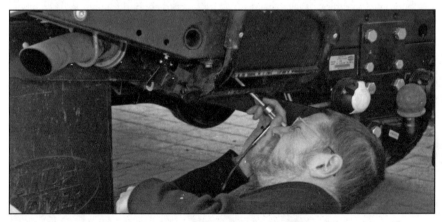

▲ NR15. Preliminary checking should, if possible, be carried out by means of an endoscope, as demonstrated here by Alan Thomas from Fertan, after which, the product should be injected into all the box sections by means of a cavity injection gun and a 360° probe.

- Take care to ensure that with a pressure gun, the pressure is kept at 7–9 bar and that with a cavity gun it is 3–4 bar.
- Use of a hand spray gun is only recommended for doors, bonnets, etc, because such a gun can only be used with a maximum pressure of approx. 1.2–1.5 bar, and that is not sufficient for complete atomisation of the Fertan product in normal box sections.
- Note that the product must penetrate into all cavities, seams and double-skinned areas in order to work effectively.

▲ NR16. In order to be able to treat box sections and cavities to the best effect with a cavity gun, water drain holes must be opened up. If they are blocked, covered with underbody protection, or are not present, new holes should be made in areas which do not affect the appearance or integrity of the bodywork. Before doing so, obtain suitable sealing grommets and then drill holes of the correct diameter.

FINAL PROTECTION

Final protection of box sections and cavities should only be carried out at temperatures of over 20°C.

When applying a protective wax, always observe the instructions on 'Wax Treatment'. When using NANO-Layer NT 10 you should additionally ensure that the cavity or box section is completely dry. The application process for wax is described below, followed by details of the NT 10 process.

WAX TREATMENT

Fertan protective wax contains resin which prevents run-out from the cavities, or at least reduces it. So, rather than a thick layer collecting at the base of the box section, the whole of the cavity wall is effectively protected for many years by a thick and homogeneous layer.

The recommended pressure for applying cavity wax protection is 7.5–9.5 bar for a pressure gun, and 3.5–4.5 bar for a cavity gun.

▲ NR17. Protective wax should always be applied in several thin coats. Allow each layer to dry before application of the next coat. If possible, assist the process by blowing air through the cavity at low pressure. Work should be carried out at a temperature of at least 20°C, because at low temperatures the fluid has less 'creepability'. If the wax is being applied in an unheated hall or garage, the application should, if possible, take place only at a warm time of the year. This should be easy to achieve because of the long reaction time of the Fertan.

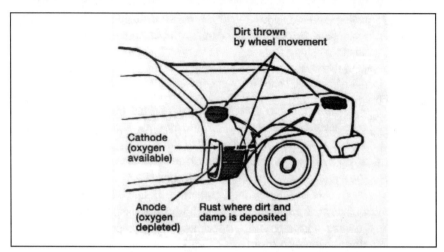

▲ NR18. However, during the course of use, the protective layer is repeatedly attacked by many temperature changes, heavy dampness, water ingress, salt, dirt and other environmental hazards, and gradually loses its elasticity. To pre-empt this, it is advisable to supplement the wax layer every 5–7 years or so with a new, thin layer of wax, in order to slightly dissolve the surface of the old, pre-existing layer and stabilise it. (Illustration, courtesy Fertan)

REMOVAL OF RUST AND CORROSION IN THE UNDERBODY

When restoring a classic car, complete removal of the old underbody protection is always recommended.

Within six months of applying the Fertan, the chassis should again be thoroughly washed with water. There are several protection options available, depending on expected vehicle use. The undersides of vehicles used only in summer, or primarily for shows, are often painted in body colour. This paint coat can be very effectively protected by a transparent underbody wax, or a glass-clear wax, such as Protewax BP 527. This is also suitable for painted suspension mountings, steering parts, etc, though it isn't recommended for vehicles used all year round and exposed to road salt in the winter months. In those conditions, a more durable coating must be used.

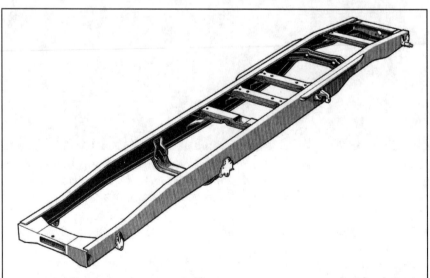

▲ NR19. First, the chassis should be cleaned of loose dust, dirt, oil, grease and silicon contamination. A pressure washer is recommended for this. (Illustration, courtesy Fertan)

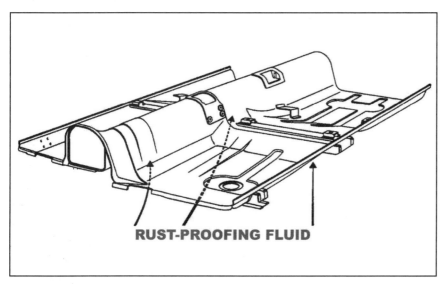

RUST-PROOFING FLUID

▲ *NR20. Fertan is then applied to the chassis or underbody while it is still wet, by means of a spray gun or possibly a Schutz gun, at a pressure of approx. 1–3 bar. The remains of the old underbody protection should be removed as far as possible. This also applies to the remains of PVC treatments, which are often used in the area of engine mountings. Treatments and layers which are securely attached to the underbody may be allowed to remain, because in general no corrosion is present here. However, a careful check should be made that there are no areas where the rust has lifted areas of the paint and penetrated under it. (Illustration, courtesy Fertan)*

DERUSTING WINDSCREEN/ WINDOW FRAMES

By the time this happens, the protective layers situated behind the window frames are already destroyed, and must urgently be replaced if greater rust-through is to be avoided.

Treat these areas as follows:
1. Remove glass.
2. Remove all traces of any remaining sealant.
3. Mechanically remove superficial rust as far as possible.
4. Thoroughly clean the surface with a silicon remover (but be sure not to use any other product, and in particular, no mineral products).
5. Apply Fertan with a small brush to the affected areas and allow to react.
6. After the Fertan has been allowed to react, clean the surface with water but, to avoid marking paintwork, do not allow run-off of Fertan or water to dry on the bodywork.
7. After drying, treat the area with appropriate coatings, primer and paint, and then refit the glass.

▲ *NR21. Where the treated panel will see year-round usage, Ferpox (a 1-part epoxy primer) or Over-4 may be used as a base coat. These coatings can both be overpainted.*

If a paint coat is omitted, Over-4 provides a long-lasting stone-chip layer.

On vehicles which are subjected to flexing, or heavy stresses as part of their construction (eg, convertibles), or normal service (eg, 4x4s), it is recommended always to use a non-hardening coating, such as UBS 220. This flexible coating will almost never crack.

▼ *NR22. (On many older vehicles, rust builds up under the windscreen and window frames. Affected by dampness which finds its way in, in conjunction with aggressive chemicals from the atmosphere, first of all the paint layer and then the protective coatings underneath, are damaged and finally the phosphate coating may be removed. Then the destructive process inevitably begins and will lead to further corrosion if it is not halted. This problem is visible when damp, and possibly rainwater, leaves brown stains trailing from the window frames onto the bodywork. Unfortunately, these visible signs are not always present in the case of more modern (bonded) screens, and the damp remains, causing corrosion in the seams. (Illustration, courtesy Fertan)*

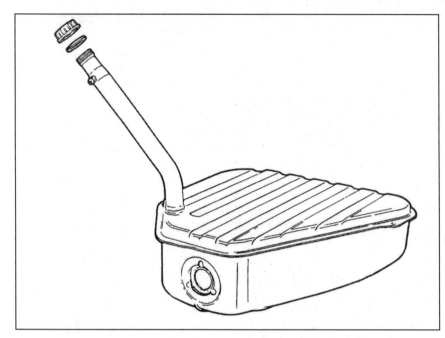

TANK DERUSTING

FeDOX Derusting concentrate is a product developed specially for derusting the inner surfaces of tanks, and for derusting steel parts, and it makes possible a complete removal of the oxide layer, so that the inner surfaces of the tank and the steel parts are completely shiny.

Immediately after the completion of the treatment, the (ideally still damp) metal surfaces should be treated with Fertan, in order to prevent atmospheric corrosion.

The product is added to water in a 10% solution.

TANK COATING

Follow the manufacturer's instructions to the letter, and in particular all health and safety information, when carrying out this work on a fuel tank. TAPOX is a specially-developed 2K hard epoxy coating for tanks. After hardening (72 hours at approx. 20°C and relative humidity under 70%), the product is resistant to all fuels, lye, and many acids. It builds an extremely resistant layer, which is highly resistant to abrasion. TAPOX may be used for the inner coating of tanks, but NOT for drinking-water tanks.

▲ *NR23. Follow the manufacturer's instructions to the letter, and in particular all health and safety information, when carrying out this work on a fuel tank. (Illustration, courtesy Fertan)*

PART III – PAINT AND RUST STRIPPING

Before metal can be painted or treated in order to prevent future corrosion, all traces of old paint, underseal and rust have to be totally removed. This can often be a major, messy job, so let's see what the alternative methods are.

▲ *PAR1. This is part of the seat support of my plastic-bodied Citroën Mehari – a kind of French buggy. Rust had started to pit the surface and there was very little paint left.*

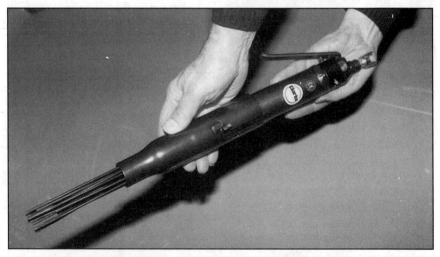

▲ *PAR2. First, I tried to shift the rust with this Clarke needle gun. It is connected to an air line and the steel needles sticking out from the end of the gun chatter powerfully against the steel, getting rid of corrosion – at least that's the theory!*

▲ PAR3. The needle gun might be useful for larger areas and for removing heavily scaled rust but for this job it was painfully slow and kept slipping off the edges of the narrow sections. You need to wear ear defenders when using a needle gun.

▲ PAR5. The first stage in the dipping process is when the components are boiled in caustic solution which strips off all of the paint.

▲ PAR4. The next step was to make a radically different approach. The seat sub-frame and part of the body's tubular framework was taken to a company in Birmingham which specialises in stripping components back to bare metal. Stan, wearing all the necessary protective gear, examines the steelwork prior to dipping it.

▲ PAR6. The parts are then lowered into a huge, unfriendly looking vat of hydrochloric acid which removes rust – although it would remove the steel too if it was left in there for too long.

The cost of having the work carried out is dependent on the amount of hand work involved, in addition to the cost of the dipping process itself. Components with a lot of nooks and crannies in them which can involve hand work to clean out, or tubular items without adequate drain holes can be among the most time-consuming. Specialist companies say that it is not only a matter of importance that all the acid is washed out, but it is also a legal requirement that nothing passes out of their factory still containing any discernible traces of acid. If a tubular structure has closed-off ends and takes a long time to drain out, it will have to be suspended first at one angle and then another while someone watches to make sure that the draining process is complete, this being something that has to be done a number of times until all the acid has been washed away.

One of the main disadvantages of dipping a panel containing spot welds is that it is not possible to remove every trace of the caustic paint-stripping material from the spot-welded seam. This material will be drawn into the seam by capillary action and then leach out slowly over a long period of time, causing a paint reaction in future which is virtually unstoppable.

▲ *PAR8. This Citroën Méhari seat frame still showed evidence of pitted corrosion and this became even more evident when the protective film of oil was cleaned off. This steel was most certainly not suitable for painting because corrosion would simply have continued underneath the paintwork. A fair amount of the hard work had been saved, however.*

▲ *PAR10. This time, after stripping, there were one or two places where the steel had obviously rusted right through, because the hydrochloric acid left small holes. However, it was now a far simpler job to strip off the redundant surrounding panels, cut out and repair rusty areas and reuse the headlight backs.*

▲ *PAR9. These Split-Screen VW Camper headlight backs were stripped at the same time. The headlight shells were to be fitted to later panels, the only ones available at that time.*

▼ *PAR11. Some specialists offer a paint-stripping service for complete bodyshells which involves putting them in an oven and baking them at a high temperature.*

▲ *PAR7. The tubular structure was stripped more successfully than the channel-section framework. This was probably because the rust was not so deeply etched into it. I later learned of someone who had had a VW Kharmann Ghia body dipped in its entirety, by a different company. It had then stood for about 12 months and severe corrosion was then found to have taken place in all of the welded seams. To avoid this, after the dipping I spent some time flushing the tubular sections through with water from a hose pipe.*

▲ *PAR15. The grit is poured into the container and, when the compressor is up to pressure ...*

▲ *PAR12. This is an extremely effective way of removing every scrap of paint, although all the surfaces have to be cleaned down thoroughly, of course. There are two possible objections to the process: one of them involving time but the other is potentially more serious. The first is that every single item has to be removed from the shell before it can be paint-stripped and this can be a time-consuming business. The other is the question mark over whether the high temperatures involved can soften the steel used in the body panels. It has certainly been found that springs (accidentally) left on a car have lost their elasticity and so it would seem to follow that the temper of the steel in the bodywork may be changed. In the case of a car with high tensile steel panels, it is difficult to see how the tensile strength of the steel could survive in its original form. Similarly, the steel used in any vehicle would be based around a required tensile strength which may be altered by the heating process. If you wish to have a specialist carry out this work, you would be strongly advised to check out these issues with them first.*

▲ *PAR16. ... and the gun connected back up again, rust is blasted away magically.*

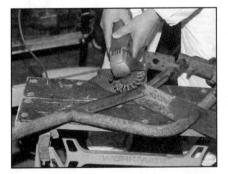

▲ *PAR17. Note that the grit gets absolutely everywhere! I'm wearing disposable overalls with elasticated cuffs and ankles and a hood to keep grit out of the hair; goggles and a face mask (the grit seemed to get through one but not both); a breathing mask and rubber gloves. The work is best carried out either over a completely hard area where the grit can be brushed up and disposed of, or over grass where it can be brushed in and left.*

▲ *PAR13. Back at the home-workshop level, one of the very best tools I have come across for stripping off both paint and even moderately pitted rust, is this special type of wire-wheel which is fitted to an angle grinder. The wire bristles are arranged in twisted tufts around the wheel which makes them strong and very long lasting. It is essential to wear goggles when using a tool of this kind. You'll find them at most suppliers of panels or paint.*

▲ *PAR14. Back to that Citroën seat frame again! The wire-wheel would not have penetrated the rusty corners and so Clarke supplied us with a compressor and sandblasting gun to try – so that I could report on it for this book. The Clarke Rebel Air 60 is supposed to be powerful enough both for this grit-blasting gun and for the Clarke Shot Blast Cabinet, shown later. I found that plenty of breaks were needed to allow the compressor to catch up with itself, which becomes frustrating when there is a lot of blasting to do.*

For very heavy duty sandblasting, suitable for cleaning down vehicle chassis, see Chassis and sub-frame repair.

▲ PAR18. The steel surface was immediately coated with Würth Rust Converter which turns any residual traces of rust into a black substance which is less likely to start rusting again. It is MOST IMPORTANT that any surface which has been stripped of paint or rust is immediately protected against further rusting because bare metal will corrode extremely quickly.

◀ PAR20. For smaller components, the Clarke Shot Blast Cabinet, when connected up to the compressor mentioned earlier, is an effective way of cleaning off rust in a controlled environment. The cabinet prevents any but the smallest amount of grit and dust from flying around the place although I found it necessary to wear the face mask otherwise a fair amount of dust does get into your respiratory system, which could be dangerous. Clarke also recommend the wearing of goggles.

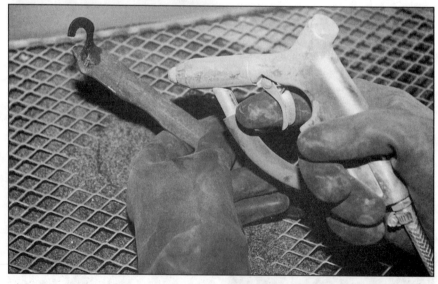

▲ PAR19. An alternative method of rust removal is Hammerite Rust Remover which is said to work by simply immersing the rusty component in the acidic fluid for a given period of time.

▲ PAR21. Inside the cabinet, the grit is constantly recycled from the sump in the base of the cabinet and blasted through the gun on to the work piece.

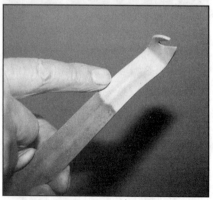

▲ PAR22. This engine bracket, which was quite heavily rusted, has come up absolutely rust-free – you can see clearly where I stopped blasting.

▲ PAR25. This pair of aluminium tailgate hinges, one before and one after, shows how useful the bead-blasting facility is. Do remember that you have to protect aluminium immediately after blasting it otherwise invisible oxides form on the surface and prevent any paint or varnish from adhering to it. Alternatively, for items such as engine components, you may prefer to use regular polishing to keep future corrosion at bay.

▲ PAR23. This is a pair of brackets, the one on the right has been cleaned up while the one on the left is in its original state. The sandblaster gets into every crevice and is the best system I have come across for cleaning small components in the course of repairing or restoring a car.

There's an air outlet on the back of the cabinet. If you buy a cheap, second-hand vacuum cleaner and connect it up to the cabinet, the air extraction system cuts down dramatically the amount of dust that gets into the air and also keeps the inside of the cabinet clearer while you are working so that you can see what you are doing.

▲ PAR24. If regular grit is used on aluminium components, you will blast the item away! Therefore you need to use glass beads in the cabinet for aluminium parts but you must make sure that every last trace of the regular grit is removed before using them. I used that second-hand vacuum cleaner again to make sure that every piece of grit was sucked up.

▲ PAR26. Most professional workshops remove paint and surface rust with a sanding disc on a rubber-backed pad fitted to the angle grinder. It's quick but can be fierce and is not good for removing deeply pitted rust.

PART IV – RUSTPROOFING SURFACES

Whether you're dealing with areas of bodywork or underbody that have been stripped of paint and corrosion, or new metal, you will want to keep corrosion at bay for as long as possible, and indefinitely if you can.

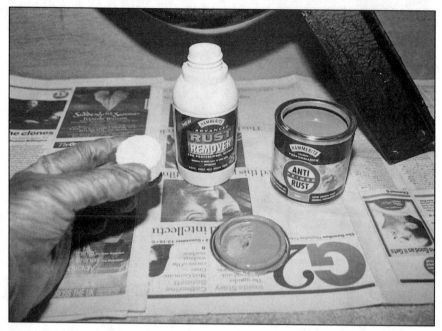

▲ RPS3. If you have been successful in removing all traces of rust – see previous section – or if you are using new material, you may wish to consider starting off with a primer such as Hammerite's Anti-Rust Primer.

▲ RPS1. As was said in the previous section, you need to get a protective coating on to stripped steel and aluminium as soon as you possibly can. The best coating for steel is something like Würth Zinc Spray because aerosols are so quick and easy to apply and also because zinc is an active disincentive for rust to make a start – which is why galvanised buckets are so successful.

▲ RPS2. For smaller areas, aerosol primers and finish coats will be ideal because of their speed of use and the fact that you don't have to waste time and money in cleaning brushes afterwards.

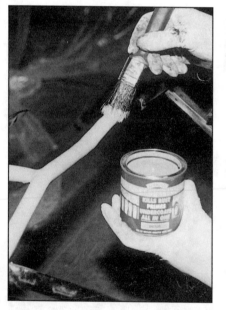

▲ RPS4. If you fear that some residual traces of rust still remain, as on this buggy's space-frame, you should use something such as Hammerite's No. 1 Rust Beater which helps to kill off any traces of rust.

▲ RPS5. I have been using Hammerite Hammer Finish Paint ever since my college days and I can tell you that, with the right preparation and primer, it really does work! For under-body surfaces this is one of the most durable paint finishes around. Do note that you have to apply a second coat immediately the first one is touch-dry or you will have to wait weeks before applying the second coat. It really is quite unusual paint!

▲ RPS6. You can use ordinary 'gunwash' cellulose thinners for cleaning brushes but it can't be used for thinning any of the Hammerite paints successfully – special Hammerite brush cleaner and thinners are needed to do the job so as not to lose the special properties of the paint. (Been there; tried that!)

▲ RPS7. Würth products are designed for the professional but there's no reason on earth why anyone else shouldn't use them and they really are among the best available. Underbody Protection and Stone Guard require a gun to apply them but give a tough, good-looking finish. Stone Guard can be used beneath finish paint on sills and other vulnerable bodywork.

◀ RPS8. Waxoyl Underbody Seal is designed for the DIY market and is easy to apply, although it does take a little time to harden before you can use the car on the road.

Würth Brush-On Body Sealant is a rubberised product that adheres exceptionally well and is superb for sealing joints and seams.

Chapter 4

Painting

The spray gun has a history that predates the motorcar itself. Right at the start of the story, a familiar name pops up. A Dr DeVilbiss, practising in the United States in the latter half of the last century, was irritated by the problems of getting droplets of nasal medicine into his patients' throat and nose passages. He invented his own solution to the problem and the DeVilbiss atomiser, or nasal spray, soon saw production and began to overshadow the good doctor's medical ministrations. Of course, as we now know, the idea of atomising and spraying went far beyond the world of medicine, and the DeVilbiss company is now a world-wide organisation and acknowledged as one of the foremost manufacturers of spray equipment.

Spray guns are precision tools. Any spray gun will blast paint onto a car, but in general, the more you pay for the gun, the better the quality of finish. To the professional, that matters a very great deal because the better the finish 'straight from the gun', the less work has to be done afterwards, but to the home sprayer, especially to the beginner, the

difference may not matter quite so much, until he or she carries out more spraying and becomes more critical.

The way in which the paint is supplied to the nozzle of the spray gun determines whether it is a suction-feed or pressure-feed gun.

SUCTION FEED

These guns have a flow of air through the top of the gun which pulls the paint up out of the paint pot by a vacuum effect, somewhat similar to the operation of a car engine's carburettor. All suction feed guns have an opening in the lid of the paint pot (to allow air at atmospheric pressure to push down on the paint) and the fluid tip, the centre part of the nozzle, protrudes a little way

beyond the front of the air cap. This system is sometimes known as 'syphon feed'. These guns often consume a larger amount of air but are generally used by the 'trade'.

PRESSURE FEED

This type of gun pushes air down into the pot itself and so pressurises the contents. It is better at lifting heavy materials, such as spray putty, out of a gun with a lower air consumption than the Suction Feed type of gun. Identification: there is no hole in the lid and the fluid tip does not protrude out of the front of the air cap (these are generally internal mix air caps).

There is yet another distinction between types of gun!

▶ Figure GL1. A simple spray-painting set-up. Nowadays, there are many different types of spray gun in industrial use, some of them involving the use of no air whatsoever. But for the home resprayer the choice is much more simple. (Courtesy of DeVilbiss)

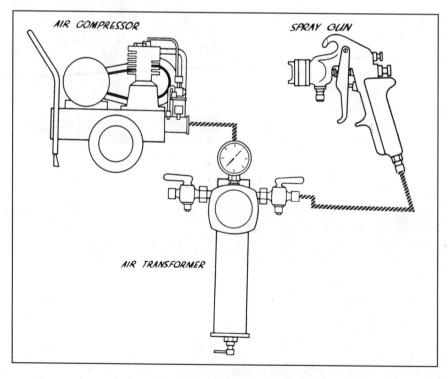

AIR COMPRESSOR

SPRAY GUN

AIR TRANSFORMER

BLEEDER TYPE

These guns discharge air through the air cap of the gun the whole time the compressor is on, although paint only comes out when the trigger is pressed. They are for simple spray set-ups where there is a small compressor with no air receiver (tank) and so no auto-mechanism for shutting the compressor off when the tank is filled. With this type of compressor, the air created has to go somewhere, so a bleeder type of gun is used.

NON-BLEEDER TYPE

Here the air and the paint are both shut off at the gun when the trigger is released.

There are also two different types of air cap available, which are:

INTERNAL MIX

Here the air and paint are mixed inside the air cap, but if quick-drying materials are used, such as most car finish paints, this type of air cap clogs up much too quickly. Internal mix air caps are always used with pressure feed guns.

EXTERNAL MIX

These air caps are the ones fitted to most guns and, here, the air and the fluid are actually mixed in the space outside the air cap.

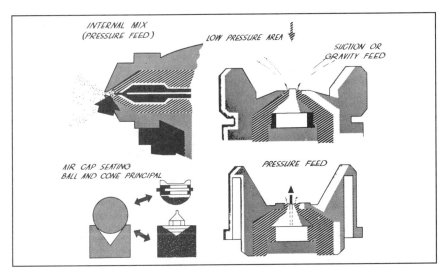

▲ *Figure GL2. Simple air cap types. (Courtesy DeVilbiss)*

CHOOSE YOUR WEAPON

If you buy a complete compressor/spray gun set-up, the choice has already been made for you. But if you're buying your own set piecemeal, or if you want to uprate the quality of your gun, this is for you.

The primary disadvantage of the suction feed type of gun for the DIY sprayer is that it requires quite a lot of air

▼ *Figure GL3. The DeVilbiss JGA; the full professional gun. (Courtesy of DeVilbiss)*

and therefore rather a large compressor to deliver it. The home sprayer is likely to have a smaller compressor with an inadequate capacity for the operation of a suction fed spray gun. If the compressor is fitted with an air receiver (and all but the smallest are), the reservoir of air would allow the compressor to cope for a short while but it would soon be spluttering breathlessly.

The major advantage of the pressure-feed system, however, is that it can work perfectly well for the DIY-er on a reduced pressure or volume of air. Its disadvantage is that the spread of the spray will be reduced, giving slower operation than the suction-feed type of gun but that is not generally too important to the home sprayer. Also, the pressure-feed system actually wastes less material in the form of potentially harmful overspray. The external-mix type of cap is a 'must' for the car sprayer, while the owner of a compressor without air receiver must use a bleeder type of gun. If your compressor has got an air receiver, the bleeder type will probably work but a) it will waste air unnecessarily and, b) it will not necessarily be a high performance gun, being built for lower priced spray set-ups. The 'Apollo' sprayer, DeVilbiss 'Tuffy' and 'Beaver' and the SIP 'Jet 30' are all examples of spray set-ups based around the bleeder type of gun and receiverless compressor.

In conclusion, whatever level of attainment you have reached, go for an

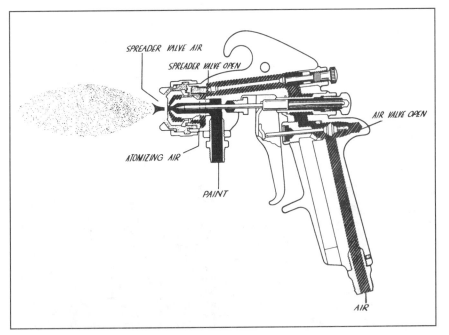

external-mix nozzle on your gun. Buy a suction feed gun if your compressor will cope with it (ask your supplier for advice) and if you want fast, professional standards of finish; buy pressure feed if you have a medium-small compressor and go for a bleeder type only if your compressor has no air receiver, or tank.

▲ GL1. The SIP 'Jade' spraygun has such versatility that it can be adapted for suction or pressure feed, bleeder or non-bleeder use or with a special setting for low-pressure use. The Anglo-Italian instructions are a trial, however!

CLEANLINESS COMES LAST!

So much for selecting the appropriate gun! There is also a wide range of fluid tips, needles, and air caps available. Their choice and selection is a complex matter, however, and as far as the DIY user is concerned, it's best to stick to standard offerings and to take advice from the factor or manufacturer's Customer Relations Department if specific problems are encountered. What the individual *can* do to improve standards of workmanship is to learn how to spray properly (see appropriate section for guidance) and to make special efforts to maintain the gun because standards of gun cleanliness and efficiency are absolutely critical in terms of spray quality. It may sound a little bit Lewis Carroll, but in spraying the end comes first. In other words, the quality of respray depends to a considerable degree on the cleaning carried out after the

previous job was complete. It's important to leave time to clean the gun out well after spraying. The following sequence shows how DeVilbiss, at their Bournemouth, England headquarters, recommend that it be done.

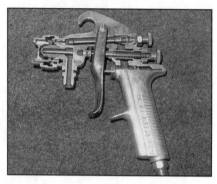

▲ DeV1. This special cut-away spray gun shows just how many passageways and chambers there are in a modern spray gun – and, therefore, just how much there is to keep clean.

▲ DeV2. After spraying, pour away the unused paint (store it for future use unless it is 2-pack paint in which case it must be thrown away, because it will go 'off' into a solid mass). Then, pour thinners into the spray gun pot. **Only** use thinners of the same type as that used for spraying, otherwise there could be a reaction which could create a blockage in the spray gun.

▶ DeV5. Blast the thinners through the gun so that it cleans all the passageways through which the paint has passed. Carry out this operation two or three times to ensure a thorough clean-out. Be careful where you spray the old thinners; remember that it still contains paint pigment and that it can carry over any nearby vehicles or household fittings.

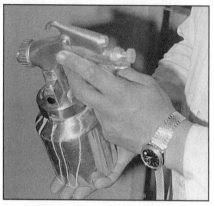

▲ DeV3. Screw the paint pot back onto the gun and shake thoroughly. Empty out the pot, to remove the worst of the paint residue and put more thinners into the pot. Don't leave paint to go hard on and in the gun and NEVER immerse the whole gun in thinners; this will destroy the effectiveness of the gun's sealing glands and allow dirt to get into the airways.

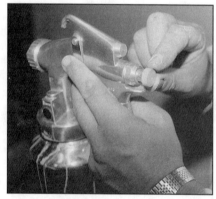

▲ DeV4. Now unscrew the air valve in an anticlockwise direction, so increasing the rate at which the gun will deliver fluid when it is triggered.

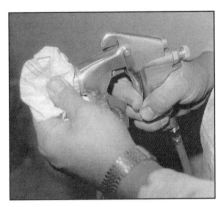

▲ DeV6. Take the paint pot off, cover the air cap with a rag and trigger the gun. This will push the thinners back into the container and dry out the suction tube.

▲ DeV7. Next, unscrew the air cap locking ring, remove the air cap and clean the fluid tip that sits beneath it.

▲ DeV8. Don't just wipe this area with a rag; you need to use a brush to stand a chance of getting inside all the nooks and crannies and the depths of the thread.

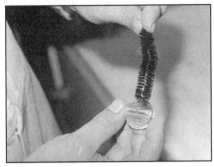

▲ DeV9. Pay particular attention to cleaning the air cap (a build-up of paint can easily form inside it) but resist the temptation to poke through the jet with anything metallic. The jet sizes are finely determined and they can easily be mis-shapen which would ruin the shape of the spray pattern.

▲ DeV10. Clean the fluid tip remembering that it, too, is a critical component in determining the quality of the spray pattern.

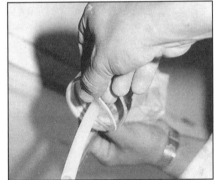

▲ DeV11. Inside the neck of the spray gun cup you will find a sealing washer of some sort. (It is best to have a spare standing by; a split or broken sealing washer, or one that has bedded down and which fails to seal, will allow drips through the top of the pot.) Remove the seal, clean it...

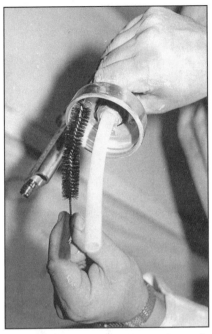

▲ DeV12. ... and also clean underneath it and inside the threads and the air chambers found there. Remember to push the 'flue brush' up the feed pipe, too. Then (for this area at least) put more thinners into the pot and give it a last blasting through ...

▲ DeV13. ... before taking off the pot and wiping it down externally.

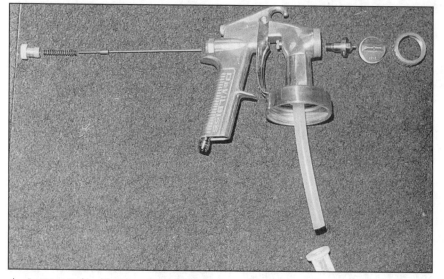

▲ DeV14. It shouldn't be necessary to strip out the fluid needle every time you use the gun, but it is a good idea to do so every few spray sessions. When you need to do so, take out the air valve all the way but be careful that the fluid needle spring doesn't jump out and launch itself into oblivion. The needle itself simply draws out backwards. Be careful not to bend the needle end or to abrade or damage the pointed 'business' end in any way.

▲ DeV15. To adjust the fluid needle gland nut, tighten it until the trigger starts to feel stiff, then slacken it off slowly and gradually until the trigger becomes completely free again. Keep the gland lightly oiled.

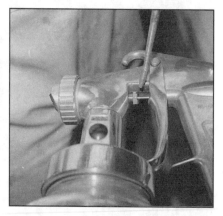

▲ DeV16. It is important that the trigger should be as free as possible. Although it might seem easy to pull at first, after a lot of spraying has been carried out, the spraying hand can become very tired – and fatigue leads to mistakes.

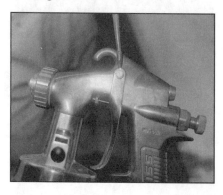

▶ DeV17. Also, oil the trigger pivot, where it hinges on the gun body.

PRINCIPAL PARTS OF THE SPRAY GUN

The most important features of a spray gun are the following three parts. **The Fluid Tip**, which meters out the paint. **The Fluid Needle**, which starts and stops the flow of paint. **The Air Cap**, which atomises the paint and forms the spray pattern.

It is important to remember that just any combination of these parts will not do; they must be teamed together correctly for the type of paint to be sprayed, the surface to be covered, the amount of compressed air available and the speed permissible on the job, although, for general purpose work, the right combination will automatically be supplied with the gun.

The rest of the spray gun consists of the body and handle, the trigger which actuates the fluid needle and the air valve, the spreader adjustment valve and the fluid adjustment screw.

The air valve, controlled by the trigger, starts and stops the flow of compressed air through the gun. The spreader adjustment valve (where fitted) controls the width of the spray pattern, and the fluid adjustment screw sets a predetermined maximum flow of paint by restricting the travel of the fluid needle.

PUTTING ON THE PAINT

In the motor trade, body repair shops depend for their existence largely upon their ability to turn out cars with a high shine. Naturally, the owner demands a perfect finish, whether the car has been totally resprayed or just spot repaired and so the trade has developed a wide range of techniques for ensuring that the depth of shine achieved is far greater than with paints used years ago. At the same time modern paint is both more durable and cheaper to apply. However, some modern paint systems demand a high level of investment on the part of the bodyshop owner and there are some health and safety snags that need to be considered.

The home car sprayer can most certainly achieve the best standards attainable in the best of the professional bodyshops. The methods for achieving this, however, are likely to be different, particularly in the following areas.

EQUIPMENT

For the home sprayer to attempt to achieve a set-up like that of the best equipped professionals would be foolish. A full professional spray booth and ancillaries could easily cost as much as, say, a top line Jaguar – hardly a cost effective exercise for someone who just wants to spray an old VW 'Beetle'!

There is, however, a great deal of small-scale spray equipment around which will give a first-class spray job, if used in conjunction with the guidelines which follow.

TIME

This is where the amateur scores over the professional every time. Whereas the body shop *has* to carry out work in a certain amount of time to ensure that profit does not slip into loss, the home sprayer has no such problem. Say, for instance, that through inexperience, you spray a really heavy coat of paint which then fails to smooth itself out and stays with an 'orange peel' finish. All you have to do is buckle down to several hours of hard polishing to leave a paint finish that is not only smooth but is fantastically shiny! Meanwhile, the pro who did the same thing would have cursed himself for losing a couple of hours and would have finished his machine polishing well before you, the amateur. But then, you wouldn't have been paying his wages. The third main difference comes down to ...

EXPERIENCE

The professional who has received years of training or practice will have a very wide range of skills that the amateur can't hope to gain. The answer is for the home sprayer to concentrate just on the skills needed for the job in hand, to read up every scrap of information in this book and in manufacturers' own data

sheets (such as those available from the factors who sell you the paint) and to spend some time trying out the new skills on a scrap panel or board before attempting the car itself. Again, you can be one up on the pro here: he often becomes stuck in his ways and fails to keep up with the latest developments whereas your information will be topical right from the word 'go'.

PAINT – THE CONSTITUENTS

To use something without understanding it is asking for trouble. It's a bit like driving a car without knowing what the water in the radiator is for. It's fine as long as everything is OK but when there's trouble you don't know what to do and so the problem worsens. So here is just a little bit of theory ...

Paints have come a very long way from the days when cavemen exorcised their fears of sabre-toothed tigers by drawing likenesses on the walls of their caves, and indeed, modern paints can be extremely complex chemical brews. All automotive paints, however, are made up of three basic parts which determine their use – pigment, binder (or 'vehicle', as it is sometimes called) and solvent (or thinner or reducer).

PIGMENT

The pigment in paint is a finely ground powder which gives it its colour and also can carry out other functions. For instance, the pigment in 'red-lead' primer helps to protect against corrosion while the pigment in spray putty gives a good depth of a material that, when dry, can be flatted. The function of pigments in metallic paints are especially important and these will be dealt with later.

BINDER

This carries the pigment (hence 'vehicle'), binds the pigment together and makes it adhere to the surface beneath. It also forms a protective, glossy film over the pigment when the paint has dried.

SOLVENT

This makes the paint runny so that it can be applied. Although it is obviously an essential ingredient, it has no other use and so it is made of a highly volatile substance (ie one that evaporates quickly). The solvent evaporates both during application and after application leaving the pigment and its binder to form the coat of paint found on the car. Different types of solvents are matched to different types of paint and, when paint is being 'thinned' to the correct degree of 'runniness' for its use, it is essential that the correct solvent is used.

VEHICLE MANUFACTURERS' PAINT TYPES

Just a few years ago it would have been hard to get confused over common paint types: there were just two. One has the grand sounding name of nitrocellulose lacquer (generally known as cellulose paint, for short) while the other, synthetic enamel, is a cousin of old-style coach paint and of ordinary household gloss paint. However, these paints are now used by a minority of professional finishers while the car manufacturers use paints better suited to mass production systems.

ENAMELS

Two types of enamel paint are used by manufacturers, both of which form a solid coat of colour by hardening rather than by simply drying. A close analogy is in the difference between 2-pack glue and ordinary wallpaper paste. The paste works by the process of the water (the 'solvent') in the paste evaporating. The 2-pack glue, however, sets by chemical reaction. It is not at all affected by the amount of moisture surrounding it, but like all chemical reactions its setting is affected by heat; the warmer it is, the faster it sets.

The two types of enamel paint used by car producers act in the same way. However, they also contain some 'reducer' to thin the paint down to the correct thickness for spraying. This is allowed to 'flash off' before the hardening process takes place.

If you own one of the many cars made by a small-volume producer such as Jensen, Morgan or TVR note that virtually any type of paint may have been used, though it is more likely to be one of the 'refinisher' paints than one of those used by the large scale manufacturers. Glass-fibre-bodied cars may well have their colouring impregnated in the outer coat of the glass-fibre. See section on 'Glass-fibre bodywork' for more information on spraying GRP.

ACRYLIC LACQUER

This is the type of paint usually found in aerosol cans but it can also be used through a standard spray gun. Acrylic Lacquers have excellent gloss colour retention qualities and they dry very rapidly indeed. However, after surface drying full hardness drying can take up to sixteen hours. It is usual to have to compound the paint after spraying in order to bring it up to the highest gloss. It is best if ordinary 'cellulose' undercoats are not used under acrylic lacquers but instead that thinners and undercoats specifically recommended for this type of paint are used. Furthermore, because different manufacturers use different formulations in the production of this type of paint, it is important not to mix different makers' versions of acrylic lacquer otherwise the paint may craze or crack. Because acrylic lacquers form a thin paint film it is necessary to use a number of coats to build up sufficient depth of paint.

Lacquer paints dry and harden when the solvent evaporates. However, 'Thermoplastic Acrylics' (TPA) as used by the manufacturers, also contain an element of plastic content which can be softened by heat. Consequently, TPA-sprayed cars are baked on the production line to a high temperature. This dries the paint, then softens and smooths the plastic content. TPA can be repaired at home with other lacquer paints where it is allowed simply to air dry.

REFINISH PAINT TYPES

Manufacturers' paints are not often suitable for refinishing. For instance, if a whole car was baked at a sufficiently high temperature to soften TPA paint, it would also melt the car's plastic trim, seats and wiring! So special paints have been formulated by the paint companies, designed especially to be used for refinishing.

They are available from paint factors under manufacturers' brand names, but their *type* names are: lacquer paints; oil and synthetic resin based paints; low bake enamels; and two-pack paints.

LACQUER PAINTS ('CELLULOSE')

This dries very quickly which makes it most suitable for use as a DIY refinishing paint, for the problem for most home sprayers is the settling of dust into the paint as it dries. Obviously, the quicker the paint dries, the less chance there is for dust to settle into it. In order to obtain a high gloss finish, 'cellulose' or lacquer paints usually have to be compounded (polished) after the painting has been completed. This type of paint is less expensive than the more exotic, newer, concoctions, carries fewer health hazards (although some still remain) and is fairly durable. The main disadvantage, however, is that it may not be compatible with the paint already on the car, although it is possible to spray a coat of isolator to form a barrier between the two quarrelling paint types. Overall, 'cellulose' or lacquer paints must be considered as the most highly favoured paint type for the amateur. 'Cellulose' paint films are thin, therefore a number of coats have to be sprayed in order to build up the necessary depth of paint.

ENAMEL (OIL-BASED PAINTS)

Enamel paint is the close cousin of old-style coach paint and today is generally favoured by refinishers of commercial vehicles. It is, like lacquer, a fairly durable paint and it is probably the least expensive type of paint available. It has the advantage that it causes no

reaction with any other type of paint that lies beneath it but it also has a number of huge disadvantages. The first is that it takes rather a long time to dry and can pick up every scrap of neighbourhood dust (and twice as many flies as you would have believed possible), while it does so. Secondly, and this can be a real headache for the beginner, it can take days (if not weeks) to harden off sufficiently to be flatted again – so what do you do if you get runs? (Incidentally, enamels *dry* first in the conventional way, then *harden* by oxidation ie, the effects of oxygen upon the chemical structure of the paint.) The third problem is that almost every other type of paint reacts by crazing and wrinkling if sprayed on top of enamel, especially if the enamel has fairly recently been applied. And the fourth problem is that it can't be compounded (polished) if you fail to get a shine straight from the gun, although, to be fair, enamel is one of the best paints for instant shine. If a car is to receive a last respray before being run into the ground, or if the car or small commercial has previously been sprayed in enamel then use it. Otherwise, forget it!

TWO-PACK PAINTS

These are the 'magic mixture' paints, the witches' brews of chemicals and compounds that give a fantastic (if rather 'plasticky') gloss from the gun and an extremely hard durable finish together with pigments that seem to fade less than any others, especially in the fade-prone red and yellow ranges.

The big disadvantage with these paints has nothing to do with the paints themselves (although, in being designed for use with low-bake ovens they can be slow to dry and harden unless used with specially activated reducers to give speedier hardening), having more to do with the user's prospects for a long and peaceful life. In short, they can kill if misused. If breathed in whilst in the form of airborne spray, 2-pack isocyanate paints can be lethal. On rare occasions, they have caused fatal spasms after first contact; on other occasions, long-term users of the paint who have not used prescribed breathing apparatus, have been suddenly struck down in the same way. If the correct breathing apparatus is used religiously, there should, according to the manufacturers, be no inherent risk and DeVilbiss, for example, make an excellent filtration/breathing set for around the price of four ordinary tyres. Most ordinary users will conclude, however, that the risks are simply not worth the improved finish, even though, in the motor trade, well over half of all refinishing work carried out is undertaken with this type of paint. Non-isocyanate air-drying 2-pack paint systems are currently under development, but it is understood that there is a problem in getting paint to go hard in a sensible sort of time. Do watch out for this paint, though. When, and if, a safe non-isocyanate 2-pack paint becomes available, it will be the DIY-ers dream!

LOW BAKE PAINTS

Low bake enamels are baked at a minimum temperature of 80°C (175°F) and give super results for those bodyshops in the refinishing trade who can afford the large investment of low bake spray booth/ovens.

METALLIC PAINTS

It is important to understand how the increasingly popular metallic paints 'work' in order to understand how to use them. They achieve their metallic effect by the inclusion of tiny flakes of aluminium in the paint. These aluminium chips act as reflectors giving the familiar metallic effect and also the characteristic changes of light and shade in the apparent colour of the paint. The reason for this is quite simple: if the surface of the paint is viewed from above, reflections from the chips of aluminium will be direct, making the surface of the paint seem lighter. If the paint is viewed from one side, the aluminium chips won't be reflecting much light back at you so the surface will seem darker.

Unfortunately, the same car can have areas which vary by how much this is true. In places where the paint has been

put on thinly, the flakes of aluminium will have arranged themselves flat against the panel, so the differences between the appearance of the paint from above and from the side will be great. In other places, however, the paint may have been put on too heavily. Where this has occurred, the aluminium flakes will have floated around in the relatively deep paint and will have come to rest at all sorts of angles as the paint dried. In this case, the differences in shading will be small. Next time you see a car painted in metallic paint, try to judge which areas are which. Then, when it comes to spot painting a panel which has been painted in this type of paint, try to ape the style of the person who originally sprayed it so the metallic shadings blend in with the surrounding paint. Metallic paints can be made up of any of the types already shown, the metallic content simply forming a part of the pigment.

CLEAR-OVER-BASE

This is a painting technique that is becoming popular with some manufacturers. Using this system the colour coat is not applied as a topcoat, but as a matt 'undercoat' which is then covered by one or more coats of clear lacquer. An example of dealing with this type of finish as a refinish task is given in Chapter 5 in the 'Front wing damage repair' section.

UNDERCOATS

It is often said that a successful paint job depends upon successful preparation. That is perfectly true, and it is in the selection of undercoats that the difference between amateurs and professionals is most marked; picking the right undercoat for the job can cut preparation time dramatically and make it so much easier to avoid blemishes which show through the paint and which might even cause outright failure.

Primers are designed to make sure that the paint adheres well to the surface of the panel and to resist corrosion when

used over bare metal. Many are required to perform at least one other function. Like everything else a primer should be chosen with a specific purpose in mind. The various types are as follows.

ETCH PRIMERS

These contain an acid which eats microscopically into the surface of the bare metal being primed and increases the hold of the paint onto the metal. An etch primer will also help to prevent the spread of corrosion beneath the paint should the paint film become scratched right through, because it holds on tight and makes it more difficult for corrosion to get at the metal.

PRIMER FILLER AND PRIMER SURFACER

These are probably the most versatile primers and can be used directly onto bare metal provided two coats are applied to ensure full coverage even after flatting. Primer surfacers and fillers achieve a compromise between giving good adhesion and also a reasonable level of 'build' – in other words, they leave quite a deep film which hides very minor scratches and blemishes and can then be flatted down.

SURFACERS AND FILLERS

Surfacers and fillers do not attempt to do the job of primer alone and as such are not suitable for use on bare metal but they are superb at filling scratches and blemishes. They give a considerably higher 'build' but they flat out easily to give a fine finish. It is most important that you don't try to overcook the goose when using spray fillers. If too many coats are sprayed on in one session, the coats beneath will not have had time to dry out and the paint coats could take a long time to dry.

Polyester spray fillers, on the other hand, go hard after the addition of a hardener to the paint before spraying. Since they don't need to dry out, polyester spray fillers can be built up as deeply as you like. Unfortunately the same dangerous health considerations apply to this paint as to the 2-pack paint already mentioned.

SPRAY PUTTIES

These have a very similar effect to that of the spray fillers already mentioned, although they give an even deeper build. They are 'cellulose' based and so much safer than the 2-packs. They should be left to dry thoroughly *before* flatting, or they may shrink back further after flatting and expose the scratches and chips they were meant to conceal. Spray putties have to be sprayed on without the addition of extra thinners and so they need the services of quite a powerful compressor to pull the thick paint out of the pot.

If your compressor is powerful enough, using a spray filler or spray putty, will help cut down enormously on preparation time. After all, it's the way the pros do it!

ISOLATOR

This relatively expensive but very useful primer is used as a barrier between two incompatible paint types. It can be water-based, wood alcohol-based, or based on anything else that will act as a non-reactive solvent with the common paint types. Just to be sure that it has done the job, try out the first non-compatible coat on a small panel first. *Always* spray a primer-filler over the top within the time specified by the makers and *never* flat the isolator itself.

SEALERS

These are rarely used nowadays and were used as a groundcoat to help the final colour match. Modern paint colour pigments don't need such help but note that a 'sealer' was meant to 'seal' in the colour of the primer and that it won't do the job of an isolator.

CHIP RESISTANT PRIMER

Chip resistant primers are made to cut down the risk of paint chipping in vulnerable areas such as on sills and aprons and they are worth using when spraying the underside of large flat panels such as bonnets because they also help to cut down drumming noise as well as giving improved resistance to corrosion.

The paints market is an especially competitive one and international manufacturers are coming up with new ideas all the time. It is well worth going into paint factors with an open mind; if you ask to buy something specific you'll get it without comment but if you ask the factors' advice they will be able to advise on the best product to suit your particular purpose.

PRE-SPRAY GARAGE PREPARATIONS

▲ *PSG1. The biggest problem in DIY spraying is usually the presence of dust. You don't really notice it under normal circumstances but the blast of air from your spray gun and the movement of your feet around the car will stir up enough dust to make the surface of your newly shiny paintwork look almost like sandpaper if you don't take the right precautions. Start by vacuuming the roof, especially around any beams and also do the walls and any other nooks and crannies where dust can lurk.*

▲ *PSG2. It almost goes without saying that you should sweep the floor out and you should also be prepared to move any dust-gathering lawn mowers, push bikes and any other garage paraphernalia because not only will they have trapped dust but they could also be damaged by overspray and paint dust from the air settling on them when you spray.*

◄ *PSG3. While you're cleaning out the garage, you may be tempted to do something a bit more permanent about the state of your floor. Hammerite Floor Paint can be applied by brush or roller to give a shiny but non-slip, easy to clean floor surface. Before spreading on the floor paint, you must scrub the floor with a broom using lots of detergent, to shift any soaked-in grease, then paint the whole floor with old emulsion paint to seal it.*

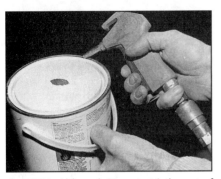

▲ *PSG4. Although it's not strictly part of the garage itself, the paint tins you will be using could well have been stored in there during the great 'spring clean' so be sure to blow any dust from around the tin lid before opening up. An air line does the job best of course, but make sure you don't blast any specks into your eyes.*

PREPARING TO SPRAY

The first 'must' is to find out what type of paint you are spraying onto. As you will have noticed, some paints cannot be sprayed on top of other paints, otherwise a reaction will take place in the new paint leading to cracks and crazing. So it is really important to make sure you are not working with incompatible paint types.

If you are sure that your car has never been resprayed, find the colour code tag (sometimes on the maker's identity plate, sometimes by itself but sadly – sometimes not there at all, especially on older cars).

If the car has been resprayed, try using the paint-type identification chart shown here or take the car along to the paint factors and ask them to take a look at it. An experienced eye can sometimes tell you which paint type has been used with a high level of probability of being right. If, as most home sprayers do, you opt to spray in 'cellulose' paint, try wiping some thinners on to an area that is not important such as the inside of a wheel arch or the bottom of a door. 'Cellulose' thinners is strong and so, if any reaction is going to take place, it will probably happen fairly quickly. If in doubt, you can always use an isolating primer, but if the

surface of the paint shows signs of reaction to earlier applications of refinishing paint, you would be wisest to strip the paint down to bare metal, at the very least in those areas where reaction is apparent. Stripping the paint is also highly desirable if too many coats of paint have been applied. One more can be just too much and cause bad crazing all over the car and especially on the horizontal surfaces.

CHECK BACK

If you are not sure of the quality of the paintwork that has gone before, *now* is the time to sort it out. Follow the plan of work shown here:
a) Clean the paintwork really thoroughly.
b) Catch the light on the paintwork and look really carefully for signs of paint film problems. The biggest problems usually occur on horizontal surfaces, so check for: cracking (checking); crazing; micro blistering (hundreds of tiny eruptions in the paint caused by dampness getting into the air lines or primer); cratering.
c) Look out for variations in the paint gloss. Where the paint is dull check for b) again but this time with a magnifying glass.

d) Make sure that the paint adheres well to that beneath it. Cheap resprays often don't include sufficient flatting of the old paint. See if the paint film has broken away from any edges leaving glossy paint beneath. Any such loose paint will have to be flatted through to the paint beneath.
e) All of the problems mentioned in b) are best dealt with by stripping to bare metal all those areas affected. Cratering is caused by silicones (from polish) forming no-go inverted islands into which paint cannot run but instead stands off around the silicone spot making a crater. Clean the panel with silicone polish remover *before* and after working on the panel and be sure that you don't transfer the silicone onto any of your tools or equipment. Indeed, it is highly recommended that the whole of the paintwork be cleaned down with a spirit wipe made specially for the job before work commences. It will also remove all traces of dirt, wax oil and petrol on and embedded in the paint.

If you're not sure what type of paint has been used on your car, try the following tests:

Test	Outcome	Paint type
1. Rub the paint with a rag soaked in 'cellulose' thinner.	A) The colour of the paint comes off on the rag, or the paint dissolves or softens, then –	'Cellulose' paint, or Acrylic lacquer
	B) The paint reacts quite badly, then –	Old oil based enamel paint. Air dry synthetic (not fully cured)
	C) The paintwork is unaffected by solvent, then –	High bake synthetic or acrylic enamel. Air dry synthetic enamel (fully cured)
If the outcome is as B), then perform Test 2.		
2. Flat with medium grit abrasive paper.	The paint clogs flatting paper, goes into balls, feels rubbery, then –	'Young' enamel paint

To determine the finish type:

Test	Outcome	Finish
3. Rub paint with cloth dipped in polishing compound.	A) The paint colour shows on cloth, then –	Orthodox paint finish
	B) The polishing cloth doesn't mark, then –	Basecoat and clear topcoat

FLATTING (OR SANDING)

Many home sprayers relegate the job of flatting with abrasive paper to the level of washing the dishes; it's a necessary chore but one to be got out of the way as rapidly as possible. In fact, flatting is crucially important to the finished appearance of the job and should be carried out in the right sequence

The first stage is the shaping of the filler to produce exactly the right contour and shape, especially over repaired areas. The second stage is to make all surfaces true and to remove the deep marks left in stage one. The third and fourth stages involve working through medium grade to fine grade abrasive paper ensuring that each grade takes out all the scratch marks of the one that went before.

Professional body shops use a lot of machine flatting equipment which is very time saving, but if you do have access to these tools make sure that you don't press too hard and cause deep scratching or undulations in the surface.

Flatting can be carried out using either wet-or-dry paper which, in spite of its name is always used with plenty of water, or by using dry flatting paper.

A useful tip when using wet-or-dry is to put a spot of washing up liquid into the bucket of water used for the supply of lubricant. This helps the water to stay on the panel rather than run straight off and it helps to slow down the clogging of the flatting paper. Plenty of water should be used when flatting but the water should be clean to start off with. Be careful not to pick up any grit out of the bucket and if you drop the paper on the floor, wash it thoroughly under the tap to avoid scratching the surface with grit. Each time you change to a finer grade of paper, you should also change the water to avoid picking up particles of the heavier grit used before.

Dry flatting is carried out with 'open coat' abrasive papers, some of them incorporating a dry powder lubricant within them. Grade for grade, open coat papers produce a finer surface than wet-or-dry paper.

On the face of it, open coat flatting is greatly preferable to wet-or-dry. After all, why introduce unnecessary water onto the job when it can cause humidity blisters if not thoroughly dried, it can lodge behind masked off areas only to slither out under the force of compressed air when spraying, it takes time to dry out and it can cause light rusting on bare metal.

Whichever system is used, be sure to clean all traces off after use. Wet-or-dry leaves a paint residue which, if allowed to dry on the panel forms a hard-to-move alkaline residue (so sponge each panel off with clean water as it is finished) and the stearate lubricating powder used in some open coat papers can lead to poor adhesion of the colour coats.

HOW TO FLAT

Start with a coarse grade of paper over areas of new filler where there may still be some marks from the use of the coarser abrasive used in shaping the filler. When all the deeper marks have been removed transfer to a medium grade paper. It is important now that all the marks from the grade you have used previously are removed with the grade you are working with. Don't imagine that the finest grade of paper will

remove the coarsest paper scratches – it won't. If you are simply flatting sound but dull paintwork it should be enough to start with a medium grit paper and then, in all cases, finish off with a fine grit. And again, if you are flatting between coats use the finest grade of paper.

When flatting small areas or concave curves, flatting should be carried out with the flats of the fingers rather than with the finger tips, so that the load is spread evenly over a greater area. At the same time, the fingers should be at right angles to the direction of rubbing. This can seem an unnatural way to move at first but it is important because it prevents 'grooving' caused by the pressure of the individual fingers. When flatting always rub in straight lines. If you flat in circles, the scratches will always show through the paint but if you rub in straight lines, the scratches will not be visible.

Use a rubbing block for more level results on flat or slightly convex surfaces. Remember that the object of flatting is to produce a level surface which is keyed with fine scratches to assist in the adhesion of paint, but is also to eliminate deeper scratches which will show through the paint. It is *not* to remove road tar, polish or other contamination and indeed, flatting will simply push the

▶ *Figure P1. Abrasive paper grades. As a rough rule of thumb, Coarse, Medium and Fine grades of abrasive paper involve the following grade numbers:*

	Open coat papers	Wet-or-dry papers
Very coarse	up to P80	
Coarse	P100-P180	P100-P220
Medium	P180-P400	P220-P400
Fine	P400-P500	P500-P1200

The grit sizes shown above with the prefix 'P' conform to the European standard. The grit numbers are compressed compared with the older grading and the two types can be compared as shown opposite.

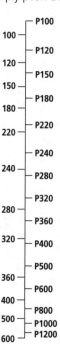

100	P100
120	P120
150	P150
180	P180
220	P220
240	P240
	P280
280	P320
320	P360
	P400
360	P500
400	P600
500	P800
600	P1000
	P1200

contamination deeper into the surface. So make sure that you spirit-wipe the surface to be flatted very thoroughly before commencing work.

FEATHER EDGES

Where rust bubbles have formed, where new paint has been applied after a repair or even just where paint is thin, the edges of the paint have to be flatted in such a way that there is no ridge of paint marking where it begins. Flat the paint edges gently to prevent the edge crumbling and flat over a wide area to blend in the edge gently so that it will not be visible under the paint. This process is known as feather edging. As a general rule, attempt to feather edge, to taper the paint back, by two inches for each coat of paint.

GUIDE COATS

Filler, primer and flatted paint are all matt surfaces and are notorious for hiding faults. These faults will show through, however, once the glossy paint is applied, so find out where they are first. Either use an aerosol can or spray a very heavily thinned coat of cellulose lacquer onto the panel with the spray gun. This gives an almost transparent gloss coat of paint which shows up such faults as are there; they can then be cured with the use of thin stopper. If there are large high and low spots, the guide coat will help to pick them out too, because as the panel is reflatted, the guide coat will go from the high spots first, leaving the low spots crying out to be filled or stoppered flat.

Try to avoid the use of reds or yellows when applying the guide coat because these colours are more likely than most to 'bleed' through subsequent layers of paint. Do choose a colour that contrasts with the panel, however.

MASKING OFF

The one major disadvantage with spraying compared with painting is that the spray goes everywhere! This makes it essential to mask off areas not to be sprayed.

The well-trained pro would often dismiss the use of newspaper as a material for masking off but for amateur use, newspaper is fine; it's plentiful and free. If you are masking off a newly painted surface, however, it would be best to use some other plain paper to avoid the risk of the ink bleeding into and staining the paint.

Choose your masking tape carefully. Some tapes are almost flat and these are frustratingly hard to 'bend' round corners. Others have lots of corrugations built into them and these are the ones to use since they will 'bend' nicely. If your tape won't stick to rubber, don't necessarily blame the tape – old rubber simply won't always take masking tape. If the worst comes to the worst, try painting clear lacquer onto the rubber and letting it dry before attaching the tape. When masking off along a duo-tone line where there is no body moulding bead, be sure to press the tape down carefully all along its sealing edge otherwise paint will seep beneath it.

The worse thing you can do when masking off (next to letting paint through) is to leave crinkles and ridges in the paper. Flatten all folds right down and seal them right off with masking tape.

Avoid wrapping masking tape round and round like the bandages round *The Invisible Man*. This makes the tape really hard to get off afterwards. Apply tape alone to the edges of all surfaces to be masked off, then add tape and paper to the tape already down – it's the most accurate way of doing the job.

PREPARING TO PAINT – SUMMARY

1) Wash the car.
2) Spirit-wipe the area to be painted to remove contaminants.
3) Wash off again with detergent and dry thoroughly.
4) Flat the entire area to be painted, using the following as a guide:
   Where primer is to be applied, use P280 to P400 grade.

Where colour is to be applied, use P500 to P1000 grade.
5) Feather edge all bare metal areas.
6) Spirit wipe panels once again.
7) Mask off.

SPRAYING THE PRIMER

Earlier in this section, mention was made of the wide number of types of primer available. Greatest mention was made of primer fillers, but perhaps it is worth pointing out that where the highest standards are sought such as when preparing a Classic car for concours respray, or when spraying a panel on a new car, it is worth applying a primer pure and simple. Bare steel should be treated with phosphoric acid cleaner which is washed over the bare steel, following the manufacturer's instructions (including those on safety) most carefully. The phosphoric acid must then be washed off thoroughly before it has a chance to dry.

An etching primer can be sprayed onto bare steel but aluminium panels could, and galvanised metal should, be given a coat of zinc chromate primer as a first coat. **NB** Primer designed for steel will cause paint flaking if used direct on aluminium or zinc plating.

If the work to be carried out is simply a repair to an older car, the quality of the finish may matter less than simple uniformity of colour! In this case the use of a straightforward primer/filler would be fine.

If an older car is to be given a complete respray with a 'glossy from the gun' finish with the minimum of preparation, go for a 'non-sand' undercoat and just use it on the repaired or 'dodgy' areas; where the paint is sound, flat that and use it as your undercoat.

Primer should be sprayed using an approximate pressure of 45lb sq in and with the gun held about 6 inches away from the workpiece. Spraying primer is excellent experience for someone who has never sprayed before but remember that colour coat flows (and therefore runs) much more easily.

After you have sprayed with undercoat, don't make the mistake of leaving the car out in the rain because primer absorbs moisture and trapped moisture can destroy the finish months after you have painted the car. Isolator is actually hygroscopic – in other words, it seeks out moisture from the air, so never leave it for more than a few hours without a coat of undercoat on top.

SPRAYING THE COLOUR COAT

Once again, base a decision on what type of paint to use upon the type of car being worked upon but also bear in mind the facilities you have. If you are lucky enough to have the correct, safe and necessary breathing apparatus and a fairly dust-free environment in which to spray, the use of two-pack ought really to be the first choice. If you can get hold of a non-isocyanate two-pack (ie non-poisonous), then use it by all means, but the problems regarding dust settling into the paint must be taken into account. Do bear in mind that there are special thinners available for speedier air drying.

Otherwise stick to 'cellulose' lacquer for most jobs (and especially for older 'classic' cars where the too-good-to-be-true shine of two-pack paints may look out of place) and benefit from the speedier drying times. Some special customising colours are only available in acrylic paint so be prepared for some hard polishing if you want to go for metal flake shocking pink coachwork!

If your car is an oldster with paint of dubious parentage and you don't want to go to the trouble of stripping off the paint, spray safe and use a synthetic, oil based paint whose thinners are highly unlikely to react with the paintwork already on the car.

When using two-pack or synthetic paint, there is a lot to be said for introducing some heat into the spray area (but beware of fire hazards, use only non-flame heaters such as the electric convector type) unless you are working in high summer. This will encourage the paint to surface dry or go off much more quickly and reduce the risk of dusting. On the other hand, the extra heat could cause dust to circulate ...

START SPRAYING!

The following picture sequence shows how the DeVilbiss company, makers of what is widely recognised as being the best spray equipment in the world, set about preparing and spraying a door panel at their British HQ in Bournemouth, England. For the purposes of the demonstation, the DeVilbiss personnel used a special extraction booth, so that explains the peculiar looking waterfall present in the background of some of the later shots!

▼ SS1. DeVilbiss chose this perfectly standard door panel to demonstrate the correct techniques. First of all, they ran all the tests to determine paint type and fetched a half litre of colour coat from the stores.

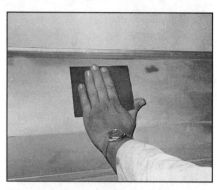

▲ SS2. Before commencing work, the door was washed, dried, then wiped down with a spirit wipe. Then the panel was flatted all over using a fine grit wet-or-dry. Here the panel is being flatted in straight lines, left to right. Note how the fingers are held flat, the wrist close to the panel and – especially important – the fingers are at right angles to the direction of flatting.

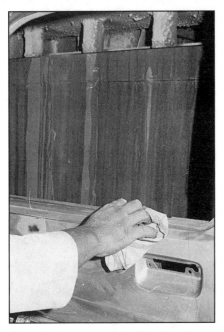

▲ SS7. Use your air line to blow dust out of the top of the tin **before** opening it. There is nothing more infuriating than to open the lid and see evil little flakes of dirt snuggling down into the shine on the top of the paint.

▲ SS3. Out comes that old spirit wipe again! If you haven't been able to get hold of the correct stuff, it may be OK to use thinners although there is a small risk that thinners will cause problems with cellulose stopper or fairly new paint.

▲ SS5. The quality of the air coming into the gun is all too often neglected. Compressors large and small are all prone to introducing water vapour into the air line and thus into the paint. If you haven't got a water trap in your air line or fitted to the compressor, a gun mounted moisture separator is an essential for successful work. This DeVilbiss separator is fitted with a small cock for regular draining. It simply fits on the handle of the gun and the air line fits to it.

▲ SS8. Pour as much paint as you need into a thoroughly cleaned disposable tin. If you have a graduated measuring stick, place it in the tin first (a steel rule would do, provided that you remember to clean it afterwards) or use the following tip for a 50/50 mix. Hold a clean stick upright in the paint, lift the stick until the bottom of the stick just touches the top of the paint you have just poured in and top-up with thinners until the level reaches the high paint mark on your dipstick. Good idea?

▲ SS4. On the Continent of Europe, gravity feed spray guns similar to this one are the norm rather than the exception but they are mainly used in the UK for spot work only. There are no real advantages or problems either way – it's simply a matter of what your hand gets used to spraying with!

▲ SS6. If water is the enemy in the air line, dirt in the paint is another major foe. A last line of defence in every gun should be a simple, cheap little filter fitted to the end of the tube.

▶ *SS9. Now you need to know whether the paint is at the right viscosity, ie whether it is runny enough or too much so. This is a cheap, plastic viscosity cup – invest in one because it's a 'must: Stir the paint and thinners very thoroughly together. Now dip the viscosity cup right into the thinned paint so that the cup is brim full. Watch the paint until it reaches the shoulder set in the cup. Start watching the seconds counter on your watch just at that point.*

▲ *SS13. Shoulders are much in evidence! Here is the point above which you have overfilled the pot!*

▲ *SS11. When buying the paint, buy a few disposable filters, too. Filter the paint into a pouring jug or into the spray pot itself. If the pot opening is too small for the filter make it a tighter cone shape by folding one side of it.*

▲ *SS14. Next job is to regulate the spray fan size and the flow rate. Use the regulator screw(s) (depending upon the type of gun) at the rear of the gun head.*

▲ *SS10. Here the camera has caught the very split second when you must* **stop** *counting; it's at the instant that the steady flow of paint stops and first begins to break into globules.* **Don't** *wait until all the drips stop too! You may need to try this out a few times to get the hang of it. The paint manufacturer's literature will give you the correct viscosity timing (pick the literature up when you collect the paint – it's free). Make sure that the paint is at the same temperature as the place where you are going to spray. If the paint is too cold it will be 'thick' and if warm it will be 'thin'. Then, when you take it into the spray area, it will take on the wrong viscosity altogether.*

▲ *SS12. Really, it's best to have all your clean, filtered paint in a pouring jug. Then, when you run out of paint during the respray you can top-up without all the hassle, spills and so on of having to filter the paint just when you want to be getting on.*

▲ *SS15. The gun should be held 6–8 inches away from the surface being sprayed. Conventionally, this is around a hand span with the middle fingers opened. Even the experts try out the gun, the pattern, etc before commencing work. Don't tilt the gun. Holding the gun close causes runs while holding it too far away causes orange peeling.*

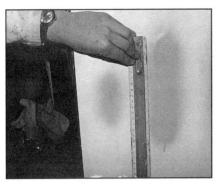

▲ SS16. A strip of paper was sprayed with the gun held the right distance away. Various fan settings were tried and the one that gave the correct, vertical pattern 8 to 9 inches in length was chosen.

▲ SS17. Before spraying anything, whether it be a whole car or just a panel, decide upon a plan of action. Our DeVilbiss expert sprayed the rear upright first, starting at the bottom and working up. Note how he has rocked the gun – but **slightly** – so as not to have the full, concentrated vertical spray pattern causing runs.

▲ SS18. Then he worked forwards and down the front of the window frame, maintaining the right distance away from the work the whole time.

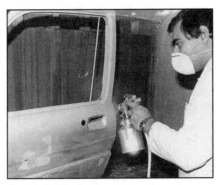

▲ SS19. His first pass was along the top of the door skin, front to back. After every 'strip' was painted, he shut off the gun momentarily, then restarted it again just before he hit the panel with the paint. In other words, the end and the start of every stroke are aimed at thin air.

▲ SS20. He worked down the panel, the top of every new 'pass' aimed at the middle of every previous one, so that in effect the whole panel gets covered twice. Note how he has bent his whole body and his arm so that the gun remains at right angles to the workpiece the whole time. The finished door looked terrific!

BITS IN THE GLOSS COAT? – DON'T PANIC!

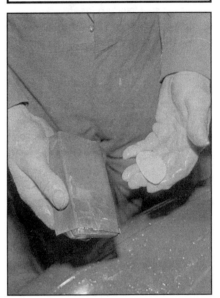

▲ BGC1. If you find lots of bits in the surface of the paint, either as a result of poor filtering, or airborne contamination, don't despair; at least, not if the paint is thoroughly cured 2-pack or cellulose. Get hold of some P1200 grade wet-or-dry paper and rub soap onto it to soften the effect of the abrasive still further. Rub the paintwork down in the normal way

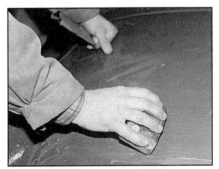

▲ BGC2. Use a rubber squeegee to scrape the paint residue from the surface of the panel and examine it minutely for the presence of blemishes. Obviously, you can only do this where you have a good thickness of paint, and in any case, you don't want to take off more paint than is necessary. (The edge of the rubbing block – if you use the rubber sort – makes an excellent squeegee with the flatting paper removed.)

▶ BGC3. When you have removed all the blemishes, set about putting back the shine. Cover an area of about a couple of feet or so square with polishing compound. (Note that 2-pack paints demand a special ammonia-free compound otherwise the surface of the paint will retain a slight haze.)

▲ BGC4. This is the Black & Decker polisher which is ideal for the professional and conscientious amateur alike. The depth of shine brought up by this machine had to be seen to be believed, and being electrically powered, it neatly sidesteps the problems of capacity created by air operated polishing mops and the need for a large compressor. The mop operates best, as Black & Decker recommend, used under its own weight, with no downward pressure to burn the paint, and it is especially important not to use the polisher excessively near to edges or on sharp convex curves or it can polish right through the paint. The highest shine is obtained by completing the polishing process with compound and then washing the mop and giving the panel a final polish all over with a fine abrasive such as T-Cut.

PAINTING POINTERS

• Try wetting the workshop floor with a watering can before spraying commences. This stills the dust, especially on a concrete floor, but don't put so much down that the water lies in puddles; you might splash the car and ruin the wet paint finish.
• If the workshop ceiling is very dusty, try vacuuming it clean. You could even pin up a sheet of clear plastic onto the roof's rafters.
• If you're spot spraying just part of a panel with 'cellulose' lacquer and the paint colour match is not perfect, try fading the edges of the panel. Mask off a much wider area than would normally apply and at the end of each stroke, turn the gun at an angle. The colour of the new paint will then fade into the old and the unavoidable dry spray at the end of each stroke can be polished to a high gloss.
• When spraying an outside corner such as the edge of a door frame, or an inside corner, such as the bottom of a boot or footwell, use Figures GL4 and GL5 as guidelines.

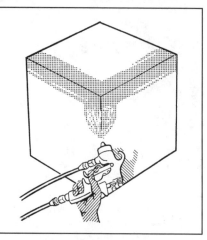

▲ Figure GL4. Method of spraying an outside corner. (Courtesy DeVilbiss)

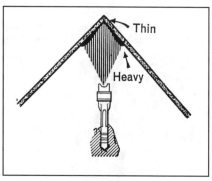

▲ Figure GL5. Method of spraying an inside corner. (Courtesy DeVilbiss)

• Always mask off the engine bay. The blast of air around the area can blow dirt onto the panel surfaces and spray can easily creep on to the components inside.
• Never immerse the gun in cleaning fluid; it destroys the lubricant in the fluid needle and air valve packings. Get into the habit of cleaning the gun whilst the paint is soft, right after using it.
• If the paint runs out and there are just a few square inches left, try holding the gun upside down. It may just drain it of the last few drops and save the day!

SPRAY GUN TROUBLE-SHOOTING

No matter how excellent spraying equipment is, sooner or later some small trouble shows itself which, if it were allowed to develop, would mar the work done. But this trouble can usually be very quickly rectified if the operator knows where to look for the source of it.

The following list contains the causes and remedies of all the trouble most commonly encountered in spraying.

1. Sometimes the gun will give a fluttering or jerky spray, and this is caused by: (see Figure GL6).
a) Insufficient paint in the cup or pressure feed tank so that the end of the fluid tube is uncovered.
b) When a suction feed gun is used, the cup is tilted at an excessive angle so that the fluid tube does not dip below the surface of the paint.
c) Some obstruction in the fluid passageway which must be removed.
d) Fluid tube loose or cracked or resting on the bottom of the paint container.
e) A loose fluid tip on the spray gun.
f) Too heavy a material for suction feed.
g) A clogged air vent in the cup lid.
h) Loose nut coupling the suction feed cup or fluid hose to the spray gun or pressure feed tank.
i) Loose fluid needle packing nut or dry packing.

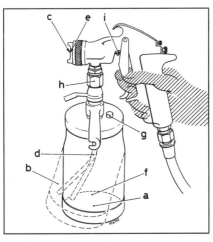

▲ *Figure GL6. Spray gun components.*

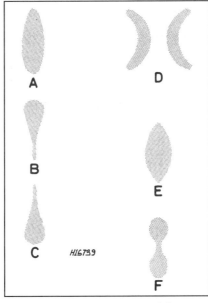

▲ *Figure GL7. Spray pattern defects.*

A Normal   D Heavy right/left
B Top heavy   E Heavy centre
C Bottom heavy   F Split spray

2. The normal spray pattern produced by a correctly adjusted spray gun is shown in Figure GL7, as are defective spray patterns which can develop from the following causes:

a) Top or bottom heavy pattern caused by:
(i) Horn holes in air cap partially blocked.
(ii) Obstruction on top or bottom of fluid tip.
(iii) Dirt on air cap seat or fluid tip seat.

(b) Heavy right or left side pattern caused by:
(i) Right or left side horn hole in air cap partially clogged.
(ii) Dirt on right or left side of fluid tip.

c) Heavy centre pattern caused by:
(i) Too low a setting of the spreader adjustment valve on the gun.
(ii) Atomising air pressure is too low or the paint is too thick.
(iii) With pressure feed, the fluid pressure is too high, or the flow of paint exceeds the normal capacity of the air cap.
(iv) The wrong size fluid tip for the paint being sprayed.

d) Split spray pattern is caused by the atomising air and fluid flow not being properly balanced.

Remedies for defective spray patterns

For defects (a) and (b) (top or bottom heavy pattern, or heavy right or left pattern) determine whether the obstruction is in the air cap by spraying a test pattern; then rotate the air cap half a turn and spray another test. If the defect is inverted the obstruction is obviously in the air cap which should be cleaned as previously instructed.

If the defect has not changed its position the obstruction is on the fluid tip. When cleaning the fluid tip, check for fine burr on the tip, which can be removed with 600 wet or dry sandpaper.

To rectify defects (c) and (d) (heavy centre pattern, or split spray pattern), if the adjustments are unbalanced readjust the atomising air pressure, fluid pressure, and spray width control setting until the correct pattern is obtained.

3. If there is an excessive mist or spray fog it is caused by:
a) Too thin a paint.
b) Over-atomisation, due to using too high an atomising air pressure for the volume of paint flowing.
c) Improper use of the gun, such as making incorrect strokes or holding the gun too far from the surface.

4. Runs or sags on a sprayed surface.
a) Sags are the result of applying too much paint to the surface, possibly by moving the gun too slowly. Runs are caused by using too thin a paint.
b) If the gun is tilted at an angle to the surface, excessive paint is applied where the pattern is closest to the surface, causing the paint to pile up and sag.

5. An 'orange-peel' defect such as that sometimes obtained with cellulose and synthetic materials is caused by:
a) Using unsuitable thinners.
b) Either too high or too low an atomising air pressure.

c) Holding the gun either too far off or too close to the surface.

d) The paint is not thoroughly mixed or agitated.

e) Draught blowing on to the surface.

f) Improperly prepared surface.

6. Paint leakage from the front of the spray gun is caused by the fluid needle not seating properly, due to:

a) Worn or damaged fluid tip or needle.

b) Lumps of dried paint or dirt lodged in the fluid tip.

c) Fluid needle packing nut screwed up too tightly.

d) Broken fluid needle spring.

7. Paint leakage from the fluid needle packing nut is caused by a loose packing nut or a worn dry fluid needle packing. The packing can be lubricated with a drop or two of light oil, but fitting new packing is strongly advised.

Tighten the packing nut with the fingers only to prevent leakage, but not so tight as to bind the needle.

8. Compressed air leakage from the front of a non-bleeder type of gun is caused by:

a) Dirt on air valve or air valve seating.

b) Worn or damaged air valve or air valve seating.

c) Broken air valve spring.

d) Sticking valve stem due to lack of lubrication.

e) Bent valve stem.

f) Lack of lubrication on air valve packing.

g) Air valve gasket damaged.

9. If the air compressor pumps oil into the air line, it is for the following reasons:

a) Strainer on air intake clogged with dirt.

b) Clogged intake valve.

c) Too much oil in crankcase.

d) Worn piston rings.

10. An overheated air compressor is caused by:

a) No oil in crankcase.

b) Oil too heavy.

c) Valves sticking, or dirty and covered with carbon.

d) Insufficient air circulating round an air-cooled compressor due to its being placed too close to a wall or in a confined space.

e) Cylinder block and head being coated with a thick deposit of paint or dirt.

f) Air inlet strainer clogged.

PAINT FAULTS

See Colour section for examples of typical paint faults.

If you have carried out your first respray and you find a few minor faults, you'll probably be so pleased with the general improvement in the appearance of the car that you will hardly notice. However, those who go on from there generally become more critical of what they are doing. The following chart of paint faults and what to do about them has been compiled by the experts at International Paint, so even the most pernickety of operators should be able to see why any fault, large or small, may have occurred and what to do about curing it.

1) ADHESION LOSS

Description

In severe cases, the topcoat is easily detached from the primer surface/filler or the old finish, or the complete system detaches from the metal. Generally, this loss of adhesion is limited to areas which are susceptible to abrasion or impact, eg stone chippings, etc. Loss of adhesion will usually be noticed in the paint shop when the masking tape is removed.

Cause

Poor adhesion is the result of improper bonding or wetting of the paint film to the surface being finished. This can occur initially because of poor surface cleaning and preparation, or adhesion can be destroyed later by moisture or other film deterioration.

a) Inadequate surface cleaning and preparation – failure to remove surface contaminants in or on the surface before painting, eg wax, oil, water, rust, flatting dust etc. Thus preventing the subsequent paint films from obtaining a good key to the surface.

b) Insufficient flatting of the primer surfacer/filler coat before overcoating will also increase the risk of poor adhesion.

c) Improperly mixed materials. The make-

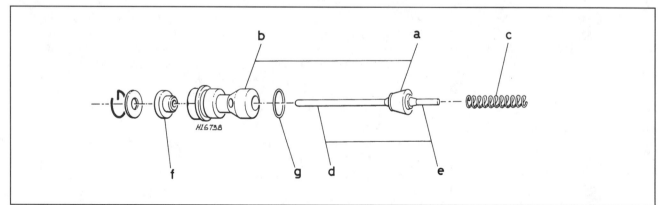

▲ *Figure GL8. Air valve components.*

Continued after Colour Section

TOTAL RESPRAY

The best way of carrying out a total respray, especially after the restoration of a vehicle, is to strip the bodyshell. This is my Volkswagen Golf MkI Clipper Cabriolet, which has been totally restored and is off to receive bodywork fettling and respraying at the spray shop.

▶ TRS1. The stripped-out bodyshell is mounted on a rolling frame – something you will have to think about if you intend moving your stripped-down bodyshell around.

▶ TRS2. The best way of removing stuck-on decals is to apply a heat gun – a hairdryer would do the job – to soften the glue holding the decal on and then peel it off carefully.

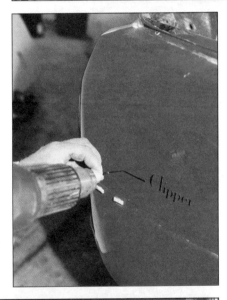

▼ TRS3. Volksmagic's Brad uses panel wipe to get rid of all traces of decal adhesive. Before starting work, you will need to clean the whole of the bodywork with the same type of wipe to remove all traces of grease or silicones.

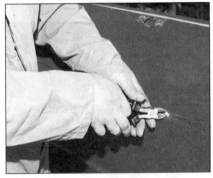

▲ TRS4. Plastic trim clips need to be removed in order to prepare the surface. Sometimes they are reusable; on other occasions, such as here, they are not, and can simply be cut away.

▲ TRS5. Over the years, even a bodyshell as fundamentally sound as this one receives lots of dings and dents. Brad uses a sanding disc on a rubber backing pad on an angle grinder to take off paint, back to bare metal . . .

▲ TRS6. . . . and then the random orbit sander to feather the edges of the paint and take off the rough grinding marks from the sanding disc.

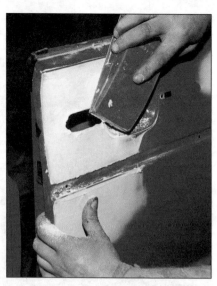

▲ TRS8. You may have to apply filler several times before you get it just right, rubbing down with coarse paper on a rubbing block after it has completely hardened off.

Two-pack paint: This gives the best possible paint finish but is emphatically not suitable for home use since the paint spray contains potentially extreme health hazards. It is the paint used here by Volksmagic.

Water-based paint: This has fewer environmental problems than any other paint and is the only type which the larger bodyshops are allowed to use, by law. It is anticipated that this regulation may apply to smaller bodyshops too, in certain countries, by the time you read this.

Cellulose paint: Provided that there is appropriate ventilation, that there are no possible hazards present from flame or ignition; and the user wears appropriate breathing equipment – cellulose paint is suitable for use in the home workshop. Autopaint International can supply the full range of cellulose enamel paint and its application is almost identical to that shown here for two-pack paint. The main differences are that cellulose paint dries rather than hardens and usually requires more coats than two-pack.

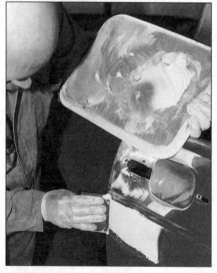

▲ TRS7. Filler is mixed on a plastic, non-fibrous board (otherwise fibres pick up in the filler) and is then spread carefully over the low areas.

▲ TRS9. The random orbit sander is used once again to feather the edges of the filler and prepare the now flat surfaces for primer.

▼ TRS10. It's not always as easy as it used to be to obtain all the materials you will need for a home respray. U-POL has a wide range available for trade and DIY use.

▲ TRS15. After the guide coat has dried, you can flat the surface down, removing almost all the black paint so that what is left will be . . .

▲ TRS11. Brad starts with an etch primer and this is applied to all the bare metal areas on the car. It provides better adhesion than any other paint and resists the formation of rust beneath the paint surface, something that can otherwise happen if the surface is damaged by a scratch or stonechip.

▲ TRS13. Brad sprays on two coats of high-build two-pack primer. If you are using cellulose primer, you must be aware that it is less capable of covering small imperfections than the two-pack variety. This is because the cellulose primer shrinks as it dries – and it takes a considerable time to dry off completely. It will then reveal imperfections beneath the paint surface even after you have put the top coat on. If using cellulose primer, spend more time preparing the surface prior to using the primer. Two-pack primer doesn't shrink anything like as much and can be used almost like a very light skim of filler over the whole surface, allowing you to flat it smooth before applying the top coat.

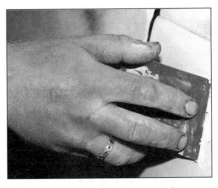

▲ TRS16. . . . the low areas or air bubbles highlighted by the black paint which you didn't remove when sanding. Brad applies stopper – a fine version of filler – to get rid of a small blemish before a final careful sanding down.

▲ TRS12. Next, the primer is mixed with thinners and hardener (you don't need the latter in the case of cellulose paint) and pours the mixture into the paint pot ready for application.

▶ TRS14. This might look bizarre, but Brad is applying a guide coat, using black paint from an aerosol can. The paint is sprayed on to give an extremely light coverage, holding the can further away than he would normally for spray painting.

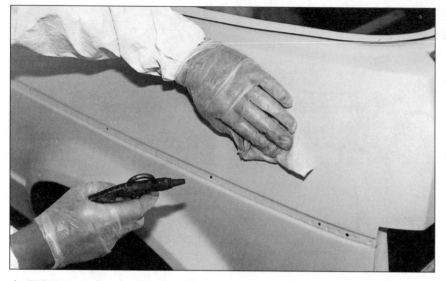

▲ TRS17. Now that the flatting and sanding is complete you can see there are no traces of the black aerosol spray paint – the guide coat – because it has all been flatted away with fine grade paper. Brad is preparing to paint by wiping down the whole surface with something called a Tak Rag – a sticky cloth which picks up bits from the surface – and an air gun on the airline to make sure dust is blown out of the nooks and crannies.

▲ TRS21. After thorough stirring, the paint is poured into the paint pot through a disposable filter.

▲ TRS18. Now it's time to paint! Brad pours in the finish paint, taking enormous care to ensure that exactly the correct amount is measured out.

▲ TRS20. . . . followed by the prescribed quantity of hardener (not needed for cellulose paint).

▲ TRS22. Suitably clad in gloves, all-over overalls and an air-fed mask, Lee starts painting at one corner of the vehicle . . .

◄ TRS19. The correct amount of thinners is added and stirred in . . .

▶ *TRS23. . . . completing each panel in vertical strips, and then working all around the vehicle until it is complete.*

The following tips will help you to get it right:

i) Start and finish each vertical paint strip at a logical stopping-off point, such as the edge of a panel.

ii) Most painters like to paint the small, fiddly areas first before going back to put on the main bulk of the paint. In other words, wheel arches, light apertures and the like are given a coat of paint before doing the whole vehicle, otherwise there will invariably be paint runs if you have to stop to do those fiddly areas when putting on the main body of the paint.

iii) Each coat of paint must be allowed 15 minutes or so 'flash off' time before putting on the next. This allows the build up of the solvent to evaporate before the next coat of paint goes on.

iv) The very first coat of paint should be a very thin one. It doesn't matter if you can see the primer through it – in fact you should expect to. If the first coat of paint isn't thin, you will be far more likely to have runs in the paint.

▶ *TRS24. The finished car is now out of the booth and the masking up has been taken off. And here's the tip we referred to earlier: Brad is fitting suspension parts to enable the shell to be wheeled about. If you were to do this before painting the car, you could fit scrap components from your local breakers yard, and that's what Brad is doing here.*

▶ *TRS25. The beautifully painted vehicle is carefully fitted up again and now looks quite superb!*

TYPICAL PAINT FAULTS

Refer to the main text for confirmation on what to do about them! *(Illustrations courtesy Rover Group)*

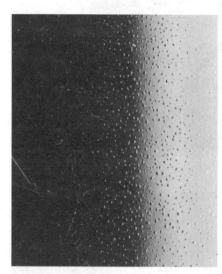

▲ *PF1. Blistering.*

▲ *PF3. Solvent pop.*

▲ *PF5. Cracking. This instance of cracking could have been caused by the application of paint which is incompatible with the paint already on the surface of the panel.*
Solutions: strip back to bare metal or sand right through the cracks to a smooth surface and apply an isolator.

▼ *PF2. Sand scratches. This is an example of scratch marks left by a disc sander.*

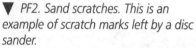

▼ *PF4. Cracking. This is a case of cracking, probably caused by a far too heavy application of paint.*

▼ *PF6. Crazing. Sometimes, the paint takes on a crazed rather than cracked appearance when the problems mentioned under 'Cracking' are encountered.*

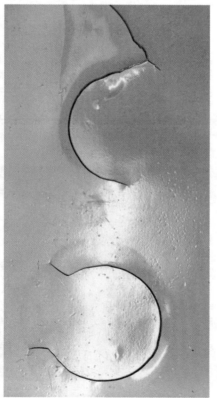

▲ PF7. Cratering.

▲ PF9. Orange peel.

▼ PF10. Intercoat adhesion failure. Paint flaking can occur over large or small areas and can go right through to the metal, although it is usually confined to flaking down to a poorly flatted gloss coat from a previous paint job.

▲ PF11. Pin-holing.

▼ PF8. Low gloss.

▼ PF12. Dirt. This is the result of a severe case of dirt inclusion.

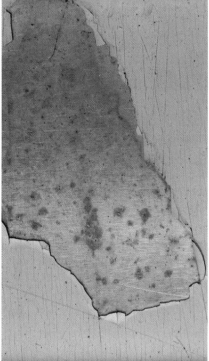

FLAME CONDITIONS FOR OXY-ACETYLENE WELDING

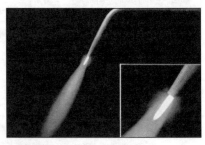

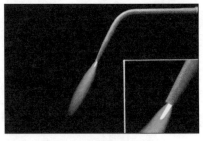

NEUTRAL

Use: Mild steel, stainless steels.
Setting: After lighting the torch as described in the text, adjust the valves until you see a white cone clearly defined with the merest trace of acetylene haze.

OXIDISING (EXCESS OF OXYGEN)

Use: Brass and bronze.
Setting: Adjust the valves to give a tighter cone and a pale flame colour. It may cause the nozzle to 'pop'.
(Illustrations courtesy of Murex Ltd)

CARBONISING (EXCESS OF ACETYLENE)

Use: Cast iron, hard surfacing and stellite.
Setting: Adjust the valves to give a lengthened inner cone. If made too long, insufficient heat may be produced.

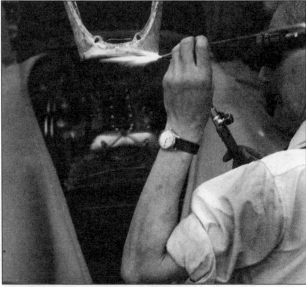

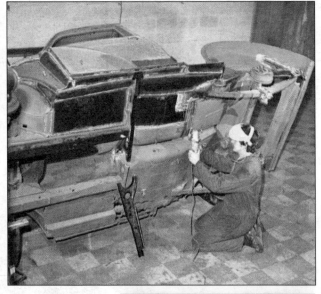

▲ *W1. (Above left) Gas welding is ideal for repairing thin sheet components and ...*

▲ *W2. (Above right) ... for welding in replacement panels, and patch panels of the type shown being cleaned up here.*

◄ *W3. Although more troublesome for use on thin panels the electrical welder is a good DIY alternative for much general work including ...*

► *W4. . . . that of brazing when used with an attachment.*

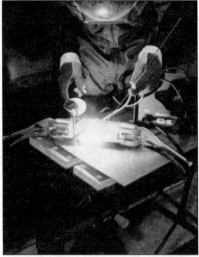

up of paint is such that maximum surface wetting and contact with all components is most important.

d) Use of the incorrect undercoat for either the metal or the topcoat, and poor application, eg dry spraying.

e) Failure to use the proper surfacers; use of a surfacer minimises the risk of poor adhesion.

f) Use of incorrect or cheap thinner, or underthinning.

g) Masking too soon on a new colour in a two-tone system. Careless masking may cause bridging which is removal of the paint from the surface when the tape is peeled off.

h) Excessive oven bake time or temperature.

Cure

a) Remove the finish by sanding over an area considerably larger than the affected area, so as to obtain a good sound base (to metal if necessary).

b) If loss of adhesion is due to faulty masking technique, flat and feather edge the affected area, and then respray.

2) MOTTLING

Description
Spotty, non-uniform, blotchy appearance of metallic paint. Small, irregular areas darker in colour, or spots in solid colour paint.

Cause
a) Spray viscosity is too high, causing too wet a film.

b) Solvent is too slow to evaporate. This is a fairly rare occurrence.

c) Atomising pressure too low.

d) Fan on gun too narrow.

e) Fluid delivery too high.

f) Applying too much of total film on final coat.

g) Gun too close to panel.

Cure
In all these cases the paint surface must be reflatted and a new topcoat applied.

3) BLEEDING

Description
Bleeding occurs when pigment from the original finish dissolves in the solvents of the refinishing material and discolours it. This usually only occurs with red or maroon coloured finishes.

Cause
a) Failure to test the original finish before proceeding, by applying a full coat of the colour to be used to a small flatted area.

b) Failure to use a bleeding inhibitor sealer or isolator as directed.

c) Failure to remove overspray of a bleeding finish from the surface before painting.

Cure
a) Bleeding sometimes does not occur until several coats of undercoat and finish have been applied. In this case, the complete removal of the affected paint, and refinishing from bare metal is necessary.

b) When bleeding occurs after an initial coat of undercoat or finish, the faults can be sealed off with a bleeding inhibitor sealer or isolator.

4) BLISTERING

Description
Blistering appears as pimples or bubbles, which can vary considerably both in size and density, in the paint film. It can affect newly applied and aged films, commonly occurring during periods of high humidity followed by sharp frost spells.

Cause
Trapped moisture or air under a paint film causes blistering. Even the best paint films are permeable to water vapour, and when the paint film is subjected to abrupt changes in temperature, the entrapped moisture expands and builds

up pressure. This weakens the adhesion between the various coats, and so leads to the formation of blisters.

a) Inadequate surface cleaning and preparation – the most common cause of blistering is the presence of contaminants, either between the primer filler and metal, or between the topcoat and primer filler. Typical contaminants are oil from air lines, grease from finger marks, flatting dust, dirt and salt. Therefore, ensure that the surface is clean and dry before spraying.

b) Wrong thinning – use of non-recommended thinner.

c) Excessive film thickness and insufficient drying time between coats may trap solvents which, when they later escape, cause blistering of the paint film. Therefore, allow each coat to flash off naturally, do not fan as this merely dries the surface.

d) Insufficient undercoat/topcoat – adequate film thickness or primer undercoat and topcoat is essential.

e) Exposure to wet weather or high humidity before the finish is really hard, and also continuous exposure to such conditions will often promote blistering.

Cure
a) In cases of severe blistering, the finish must be stripped off down to the bare metal. Then reapply the complete refinish system.

b) In less severe cases, sand out the blisters, and resurface or re-topcoat as necessary.

5) SAND SCRATCHES

Description
A film that appears low in gloss and shows primer and metal imperfections in

the topcoat. Normally the film has flowed smoothly with no evidence of orange peel or mottling.

Cause

a) Film thickness too low.
b) Poor surface preparation or use of too coarse a grade of paper when flatting.
c) Poor curing of undercoat or primer.
d) Poor primer hold-out.

Cure

a) Where the film thickness is too low the solvent content of the finish coat should be reduced so that a heavier weight of solids is applied.
b) In most other cases, reflatting should take place followed by careful repreparation of the surface using further foundation coats (where necessary) and a topcoat of the correct viscosity.

6) SOLVENT POP

Description

Small bumps in the paint film which, under close examination, can be seen to have small holes in the top. The condition is most likely to occur on edges or areas where film build is the heaviest.

Cause

Solvent pop is caused by too great a film depth being applied in one coat as a result of:
a) Too high a fluid delivery.
b) Too high an air pressure.
c) Too high a paint viscosity
d) Moving the gun too slowly, or treating a narrow area to the full spray pattern will over-paint the surface.
e) Too much overlapping in the spray sequence will over-paint the surface.

Cure

Allow the surface to harden well (bearing in mind the paint depth will affect drying times of oil-based paints) before reflatting and applying a further finish coat.

7) BLOOMING/BLUSHING

Description

Blooming or Blushing appears as a milky white haze or mist on enamel films. When blooming is seen on a colour coat, the undercoats may also have suffered from this condition. Note that this may not be visible as undercoat surfaces are usually matt – but blistering or loss of intercoat adhesion may occur later.

Cause

Blooming can occur when paint films are applied during cold, humid conditions and is caused by moisture being trapped in the wet film. During the spraying operation air currents are generated which, combined with the rapid evaporation of the solvents, result in the sprayed surface being at a lower temperature than the paint shop. This causes moisture in the surrounding air to condense on to the wet paint film, resulting in a milky white haze.
a) Use of cheap thinner.
b) Use of fast thinner in cold or humid conditions. Under such conditions, a non-bloom thinner should be used to prevent blooming. However, use the minimum amount required, otherwise the drying rate will be slowed down considerably.
c) Wrong gun set-up and technique or excessive air pressure.
d) Lack of adequate air movement and heating in the paint shop.
e) Fanning the sprayed surface with the spray gun to speed up solvent release.
f) Draughty paint shop.

Cure

a) Slight blooming/blushing – allow the paint film to harden and remove the defect by polishing with polishing compound.
b) Respray the affected areas using paint thinned with non-bloom thinners.

c) Respray the whole of the affected area with neat non-bloom thinners. Under some conditions this will remove the milky haze.
d) If none of the above remedies work, then the temperature of the paint shop must be raised by at least five degrees and all direct draughts avoided.

8) CRACKING AND CHECKING

Description

Checking appears as a large number of unattached very small cracks, which normally require a magnifying glass to be seen clearly. The paint film appears dull and lacking in gloss when checking occurs. Cracking appears as a number of random cracks, often in the form of three-legged stars, which resemble mud cracks present in a dry pond or river bed. The cracks are generally quite deep, penetrating through the top coat and sometimes through the primer/filler coat as well. Cracking is usually the result of a weakness in the paint film such as checking or blistering being exaggerated by normal exterior conditions.

Cause

Cracking occurs mainly as a result of paint film weaknesses that are exaggerated by extended periods of outdoor exposure and so occurs rarely with good quality modern paint finishes that have been properly applied.
a) Excessive film thickness. Application of excessive topcoat or primer/filler coats will magnify the stresses and strains normally present in paint films and can result in early cracking, even under normal conditions.
b) Insufficient flash time. The risk of cracking increases when heavy coats are applied without adequate flash off time between successive coats.
c) Inefficient stirring of the paint before use – this can lead to paint components being improperly mixed. This is particularly important where surfacers are concerned, as failure to stir thoroughly may affect film strength, flexibility and adhesion. The resulting paint films may therefore be weakened and more susceptible to cracking.

d) Inefficient cleaning and preparation of the surface before cleaning.

Cure
The affected areas must be sanded down to a smooth, sound finish, although in the majority of cases it will be necessary to strip down to bare metal and reapply the complete refinish system.

9) CRATERING (FISH EYES OR CISSING)

Description
Cratering is the appearance of small, crater-like openings (small rounded indentations) in the paint film, and can occur either during the spraying operation or immediately after completion.

Cause
The main cause of cratering is silicone particles. These particles (and also other contaminants) repel the paint film so that it fails to form a smooth continuous film, ie containing craters or holes in the film. Many modern waxes and car polishes contain silicones which are the most common cause of cratering in freshly painted surfaces. Silicones adhere strongly to the paint film and require extra effort to remove them using a proprietary brand of silicone-removing spirit wipe.
a) Inadequate surface cleaning and preparation. Failure to remove contaminants will invariably cause problems, such contaminants being dried soap, detergent or metal pre-treatment residues. Precautions should be taken to remove all traces of silicone and other likely contaminants, by thoroughly cleaning the surface with wax and grease remover.
b) Airborne contamination of the surface prepared for painting. Minute quantities of silicone in sanding dust, contaminated rags or even from car polish being applied at some distance from the prepared surface can cause contamination and result in cratering.
c) Oil in the air line to the spray gun.
Note. The use of silicone containing

additives to prevent cratering is not recommended. These additives can contaminate the paint shop and other work around and also lead to future adhesion failure.

Cure
Reflat the affected areas and apply a further finishing coat.

10) DRY SPRAY

Description
A rough, irregular paint surface.

Cause
a) Too fast an evaporation of the solvent either because of incorrect solvent type or low humidity and high ambient temperature.
b) Paint viscosity too low.
c) Air pressure too high.
d) Film build is too low.
e) The gun is being held too far from the surface.
f) Poorly prepared primer coat.

11) FEATHER EDGE CRACKING OR SPLITTING

Description
This appears as fine cracks or splits at the feather edge of a spot repair. It occurs during or shortly after the topcoat is applied over the primer surfacer.

Cause
a) Excessive film thicknesses – heavy applications of primer surfacer/filler without adequate flash off times between successive coats will encourage solvent entrapment and so cause feather edge cracking.
b) Inadequate stirring and the application of improperly mixed, thinned primer-surfacer, will result in a film containing loosely held pigment particles, with voids and crevices throughout – similar to a sponge. When the topcoat is applied, this structure may be broken, causing shrinkage and splitting resulting in feather edge cracking.
c) Too fast a thinner for the primer-

surfacer, thus preventing the primer particles from flowing together.
d) Improper surface cleaning and preparation. When feather edges of spot repairs are not properly cleaned, primer-surfacer coats may crawl or draw away from this edge due to poor wetting and adhesion.
e) Fanning the primer-surfacer after application with the spray gun will dry the surface before the air or solvent from within the film can escape so resulting in shrinking and splitting on later drying.

Cure
Remove finish from the affected areas and refinish.

12) LOW GLOSS

Description
Poor light reflection in relation to expected standard of the paint finish being applied. Note that some paints, such as 2-pack paints, have a much greater from-the-gun gloss than others.

Cause
a) Film thickness is too low.
b) Sand scratches. See item 5.
c) Mottling. See item 2.
d) Poor paint batch.

Cure
Reflat the surface and apply a further finishing coat.

13) ORANGE PEEL

Description
Orange peel appears as an uneven formation on the film surface, similar to that of an orange skin.

Cause
Orange peel is caused by the failure of atomised paint droplets to flow into each other when they reach the surface and is known technically as poor coalescence. When this occurs the droplets remain as they are formed by the gun nozzle, thus causing a rough surface. Ideally, the droplets should be wet enough when they reach the surface to blend completely or flow into each other, and so form a smooth film.
a) Wrong gun adjustment or technique. Too high or too low an air pressure, excessive gun distance, too little paint flow or too wide spray fan width.
b) Too high shop temperature, in which case use a slower thinner to overcome this.
c) Non-uniformly mixed materials. Many finishes contain components which aid coalescence or flow. If these are improperly mixed, then orange peel can occur.
d) Excessively thick or thin film application.
e) Wrong viscosity or thinning.
f) Incorrect flash time between successive coats, and gun fanning to increase drying rate, will promote the risk of orange peel.

Cure
a) After the colour coat has thoroughly hardened, rub out the orange peel with rubbing compound or Grade P1200 paper, depending on the severity of the condition. Restore the gloss with polish.
b) In severe cases, flat with Grade P1000/P1200 paper and respray.

14) INTERCOAT ADHESION FAILURE

Description
One coat of finish peels off or can easily be stripped off with masking tape from another layer of finish underneath. This problem can occur with refinish or original paint applications.

Cause
a) Contamination between coats by oil, sanding dust, water etc.
b) Excessive bake time or temperature of base coat or topcoat.
c) Very low film basecoat or topcoat.
d) Poor inter-coat flatting, thus providing poor paint keying.
e) Incompatibility of primer coats and finish coat.

Cure
Flatting of the surface down to the problem base coat and thorough decontamination or keying as a result will normally solve the situation. In rare cases, where successive earlier refinishing has taken place it may be necessary to go back to bare metal.

15) SAGS OR RUNS

Description
Tears or curtains of paint on vertical or inclined areas of bodywork.

Cause
a) Too much slow speed solvent in paint.
b) Too heavy a film build.
c) Film applied too rapidly with no flash-time between coats.
d) Gun too close to surface being sprayed.
e) Air pressure too low.
f) Fluid delivery too high.

Cure
The affected area should be allowed to harden off before reflatting takes place. Bear in mind that oil-based paints 'dry' rather slowly and the depth in a run may be significant. In many cases addition of a further finishing coat will not be necessary.

16) OVERSPRAY

Description
Overspray appears as dry or semi-dry atomised paint from the spray gun and so causes unabsorbed paint particles on the painted surface.

Cause
a) Failure to ensure continuity of painting sequence resulting in dry overlaps, eg due to the use of a paint with too fast a drying rate.
b) Use of cheap or incorrect thinner, eg too fast a thinner in hot, dry conditions.
c) Poor spray gun technique, eg careless overspray of adjacent (painted or unpainted) areas.
d) Excessive rebound, due to incorrect air pressure, viscosity or spray gun set-up.

Cure
a) Lacquer overspray is normally dry and non-adhesive and can, therefore, be rectified by polishing the partly dried film.
b) Synthetic enamel overspray is normally wet and strongly adhering to the surface beneath when sprayed. Many of these materials are not easily polished when young and so to remove overspray requires wet flatting and recoating.

17) PINHOLING

Description
Pinholing appears as tiny holes – often grouped – in the finish.

Cause
Pinholing can occur for a variety of reasons and is caused by trapped solvents, moisture or air being released from the film while drying. This is often

due to poor preparation or application techniques and can occur in the primer-surfacer, putty and body filler or topcoat.

a) Wrong gun adjustment or technique. Gun held too close to the surface, too wet an application or insufficient atomisation of the primer filler or topcoat. Pinholes will occur when the air or excessive solvent is released during drying.

b) Fanning a freshly applied finish can drive air into its surface, or cause a skin dry.

c) Application of colour coats over an undercoat or colour coat that has been dry sprayed.

d) Contamination. Moisture or oil in the air line will enter the paint while being applied.

e) Application of heavy coats with an insufficient flash off period between successive coats.

f) Poor knifing technique when applying stopper or body filler. Using the knife at an acute angle causes the material to roll under the blade, forcing air bubbles in.

g) *Failure to spot-in areas of body filler or stopper with primer-surfacer before painting.*

Cure

a) Where the pinholing is only slight and confined to the colour coat, remove the defect by compounding, or by flatting with Grade P1200 paper and then compounding.

b) In other cases, wet flat the affected paint to a depth ensuring complete elimination of the holes and then refinish, or remove the affected paint and refinish from bare metal.

On no account attempt to bridge pinholes with successive dry applications of primer-surfacer.

c) Pinholes exposed after flatting body filler or stopper should be sealed off with a thin spread stopper, applied with the knife held at 90° to the surface. This technique ensures that the stopper is forced well into the holes and also that it is not dragged out again as the knife moves on. **Note**: When pinholing is a problem in the paint shop, check and adjust all the conditions that cause rapid surface drying, ie paint viscosity, thinner, shop temperature etc.

18) DIRT

Description
Almost always, except in a case of seed condition (see below), dirt will show up as a rough finish characterised by an irregular pattern with an irregular particle size.

Cause
Dirt can find its way into the finish surface either through the paint in application or after the paint has been applied. In either case, the root cause is likely to be sloppy housekeeping or the use of paints which are unsuited to poor working conditions.

a) Contaminated paint or solvent. It is unlikely that a new batch of paint or solvent will be contaminated prior to opening the container, though subsequent contamination can occur easily if dusty lids are removed, or if the paint is stored carelessly after part-use.

b) Dust from primer sanding not removed.

c) Airborne contamination either from the area immediately surrounding the work, or from more remote sources. Slow drying paints such as enamels demand a clean, closed application area on two counts. First, the extended drying time allows ample opportunity for dust to settle and embed itself in the finish. Secondly, unlike 'cellulose'-based paints the surface cannot be compounded back and repolished to restore the gloss.

d) Poor cleaning of equipment and filters will lead to a dirty finish. Quite often a recent colour change, requiring a higher solvent content, will dislodge residue from inside the gun, upstream of the final (pick-up tube) filter.

Cure
To ensure that there is no subsequent breakthrough of the dirt particles, which themselves may be contaminated by oil, solvent etc, the dirty layer must be removed. This can be done by careful sanding down to an unaffected level. Such action is not required when the problem is localised and has been caused by hardened paint deposits being flushed from the gun. In this case merely reflat and then refinish.

19) SEED CONDITION

Description
This appears as a uniform distribution in the film or particles of a regular size and pattern.

Cause
a) Very low paint film.
b) Contamination of the paint and poor filtration.

Cure
Reflat the affected areas and apply a new finish coat.

20) POOR OPACITY

Description
Poor opacity will be found when the original finish or undercoat, etc can be seen through the topcoat.

Cause
a) Inefficient mixing, ie failure to stir the paint sufficiently to incorporate all the pigment throughout.
b) Overthinning.
c) Use of excessively slow thinner, causing the paint to sag before a sufficiently thick coat is obtained.
d) Use of cheap or incorrect thinner.
e) Failure to apply an adequate number of coats.

Cure
Allow the paint to flash off and then recoat, or allow the paint to harden completely, wet flat and then recoat.

21) SINKAGE

Description
As drying proceeds, the finish loses gloss and eventually shows all the underlying imperfections, such as the contours of stopper patches and metal scratches, etc.

Cause
a) Excessively heavy application of any one, or all the materials used in the painting or preparation stages.
b) Insufficient drying time between coats.
c) Dry spraying of undercoats, resulting in porosity.
d) Failure to spot-prime body filler, stopper and sealer patches, etc.
e) Failure to stir highly pigmented undercoats before use, or poor curing of undercoats.
f) Use of too coarse a grade of sandpaper.
g) Poor drying conditions: confined, cold, humid, unventilated.
h) Underthinned paint.
i) Use of incorrect thinner, particularly in primer-fillers. **Note**: Insufficient weight of colour coat will give the appearance of sinkage.

Cure
a) Allow the paint to harden thoroughly. Depending on the degree of linkage, use either rubbing compound, or Grade 1200 paper to level the surface, and then polish.
b) In severe cases, wet flat with Grade P500-P1000 paper and respray.

22) SLOW DRYING

Description
The paint film takes an excessively long time to dry and harden.

Causes
a) Excessively heavy coat application, leading to surface skin drying and trapping of solvents in the paint film.
b) Poor surface cleaning and preparation – painting over wax, oil paint stripper or grease contaminants.
c) Poor drying conditions: confined, cold, humid and unventilated.
d) Poor application conditions – lack of air movement or warmth.
e) Insufficient drying time between coats.
f) Excessive use of retarder.
g) Use of cheap or incorrect thinner, eg too slow.

Cure
a) Generally, slow drying can be overcome by moving the vehicle to an area of improved ventilation and temperature, or by the application of low heat. If slow drying is due to extra heavy coats, wrinkling may develop, unless great caution is observed so as not to apply the heat too rapidly or directly to the panels of the vehicle.
b) If the slow drying is due to contamination (from paint stripper not properly washed off, for example), neither improved drying conditions nor heat will dry the paint film. In this case, strip to bare metal, thoroughly clean and refinish.

23) OFF COLOUR

Description
The paint does not match the colour standard.

Cause
a) Poor mixing of paint either in main tanks prior to distribution or in small-scale storage.
b) Low film causing transparency and 'see-through' to primer coats. This may be caused by poor application, or as a result of imperfections in the paint.
c) Poor application techniques when applying metallic paint.
d) Variations in the application processes between the original finish and repair finish.

Cure
Flat the existing topcoat and refinish.

24) WATER MARKING AND SPOTTING

Description
Water marking cannot be removed by rubbing with a cloth, and occurs when a drop of water evaporates from a painted surface, leaving an outline of the drop behind. If a white spot is left behind, this is known as water spotting.

Cause
a) Exposure of the paint film to rain, before it is fully hardened.
b) Abnormal weather conditions, when showers are followed by very strong sun.
c) Excessive wax application.

Cure
a) If repeated heavy applications of wax polish are suspected of being the cause, thoroughly clean off the old wax using plenty of rag, and wax and grease remover. Polish with a liquid polish initially, followed with a coarser polishing or rubbing compound afterwards, depending on the depth of the mark or spot.
b) If repeated polishings are not effective, wet flat the affected area and

respray. **Note**: In severe cases, the water marks or spots may reappear a few days after the polishing. This may be rectified by repeating the polishing operation once or twice more.

25) WRINKLING

Description
Wrinkling is confined to synthetic enamels ie those which dry by a process of oxidation or a thermosetting process in an oven. It appears as a surface distortion or shrivelling, generally during the drying process, although it can occur while the topcoat is being applied.

Cause
Wrinkling is caused by non-uniform drying within the paint film. Synthetic enamels generally dry from the surface downwards ie the surface tends to set to a skin due to its contact with the oxygen in the air. When these coats have been applied, the lower coats are not able to release the solvents and set at the same rate as the surface layer, thus resulting in a distortion and wrinkling of the paint film.
a) Non-uniform drying.
b) Excessive film thickness.
c) Use of incorrect or cheap thinner ie too slow a thinner.
d) Non-uniform shop temperature; this will cause localised skinning in uneven patterns.
e) Improper drying. When a freshly applied topcoat is baked or force dried too soon, softening of the undercoats may occur, which will cause swelling and wrinkling.
f) Insufficient flash-off time between successive coats.

Cure
a) When wrinkling is slight, allow the film to harden thoroughly. Then flat to remove all traces of the defect and respray.
b) When the condition is severe, strip to bare metal, clean thoroughly and then refinish.

26) SOFT PAINT

Description
The paint surface can be marked easily even after full drying has been allowed.

Cause
a) Too great a film thickness.
b) Incorrect quantity of catalyst in 2-pack paint.

Cure
The paint surface must be removed by sanding, although almost all paints, but particularly enamels, will respond to some extent to increased drying time. (The information contained in this Section was provided by courtesy of International Paint, Birmingham, England. Cartoons and captions courtesy of International Paint and Paint & Vinyl Operations Ford Motor Co. USA.)

PAINT STRIPPING

Paint stripper is highly caustic and should be handled with great care. Always wear rubber gloves, cover up bare arms and wear goggles when using it. Also, read the manufacturer's instructions on what to do if you spill some onto your skin or into your eyes.

▲ PS1. Begin by brushing a heavy coat of stripper on the area to be stripped. Try to restrict your activities to no more than, say, a couple of feet square (around half a metre). Be sure to protect any surrounding paintwork with **several** layers of masking paper.

▲ PS2. Let the stripper attack the paint for a little while before starting work with the scraper. The outer layer of paint, being the newest, will still contain a relatively great amount of solvent and so it should bubble and wrinkle quite considerably.

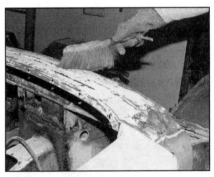

▲ PS3. Brush all of the old loosened paint off the surface so that you can see what you are doing. Don't forget that the paint is still coated in caustic paint stripper. Bundle the waste up and dispose of it before it has a chance to do any harm. It could burn your pets (and your children!) quite badly.

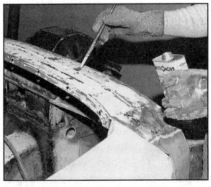

▲ PS4. Coat the next layer with more stripper. It is important to note that each successive layer will become progressively slower to wrinkle and that the lower coats may only soften.

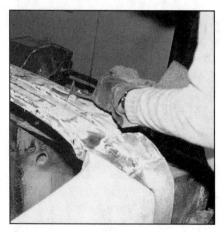

▲ *PS5. Extra weight can be put behind a glazier's three-sided scraper, the sort you pull towards yourself. Remember that scrapers will benefit from being sharpened as much as any cutting tool (although it's necessary only to restore a crisp edge, not to make the scraper razor sharp), but be careful not to dig deeply into the metal.*

▲ *PS6. Corrosion of this sort is best tackled after stripping the surrounding area. If only a small area is to be tackled, try stripping it by softening the paint with a blowtorch, but be careful not to cause heat-distortion in the panel. Be prepared for the stripped paint to reveal even more damage, especially since paint stripper works well on polyester resin (the plastic in glass-fibre). For that reason, a special type of stripper has to be used on a glass-fibre car (if you have difficulty obtaining it, try someone who specialises in Corvettes in the 'States, Lotus or Reliant in the UK or try a boat chandler. Stripper for glass-fibre panels is much slower acting than that used on steel panels).*

COMPRESSORS – CHOICES AND USE

There is more bull in advertisements for compressors than anything since the hi-fi was invented! No wonder most people buy these extremely useful tools on price and looks above all. A compressor is an indispensable tool for anyone who takes spraying half-seriously and it is also useful for jobs such as blowing up tyres, blasting grease remover onto engines and other mechanical parts, powering a small sand-blaster and also for powering any air tools you may wish to use such as an air chisel, for rapidly cutting away rusty or damaged metal, or a grinder, polisher or random-orbit sander. In fact, when you start taking body repairs seriously, a compressor is the first major item to buy.

A compressor consists of an electric motor (or occasionally petrol or diesel engine) driving a piston in a cylinder, rather like that in a car engine. In this case, however, the piston provides energy in the form of compressed air which is fed to the equipment it powers via air lines.

Whether you are buying new or second-hand, perhaps from a garage which is closing down, there are certain points to watch out for. After deciding how much you can afford to spend the first check to make is on the capacity of the machine and it's here that the makers' 'lack of clarity' – shall we call it – sets in.

Larger machines really must be equipped with an air receiver to take out the fluctuations caused by the pumping action of the piston. There are some very small models on the market with no air receiver but, with this type of compressor, progress is very slow in any case so that the pulses in the spray of paint coming from the gun hardly matter. SIP have brought out a tiny compressor which incorporates its own tiny air receiver, which manages to smooth out the flow of air. Compressors which have a larger air receiver have an added advantage in that they can power for short bursts equipment which requires a high flow rate and which the motor itself is not capable of keeping up with. One example would be an air chisel, which uses a great deal of air to keep going flat out. In practice, an air chisel is rarely used for more than a few seconds at a time, the pauses in between giving the compressor time to catch up on the capacity of the air receiver. In general, though, it is false economy to buy a compressor that is going to have to work its heart out to keep up with equipment which you are likely to put to a lot of use. You have to decide how often you will want to use the machine and how much it will bother or inconvenience you if you have to wait for the machine to pick up pressure. At the very least, the compressor must keep up with the type of spray equipment you intend to use and if you use a top-line gun like the DeVilbiss JGA, you will need a machine which delivers, say, 9 cubic feet per minute (CPU) minimum (250 litres per minute) although there are many less 'greedy' spray guns.

Watch manufacturer's delivery figures like a hawk! Often the figure quoted is the machine's theoretical output which bears little relation to the practical output and is related to the *displacement* figure, which is the volume of the cylinder stroked by the piston. Because of losses and inefficiencies, however, the usable amount of air given out is generally a little over half of this figure. The truly usable capacity of the machine is its *Free Air Delivery* (FAD) and it is the FAD figure which must be related to the tool or tools you intend to use. Air-driven polishing mops, for instance, can consume a hearty 18cfm (500lpm) and need that level of output for minutes on end, so you would have to buy a very expensive compressor just to keep up. But most equipment is used only intermittently, so you can make allowances for the time when you are not using the tool and the compressor is rebuilding its tank pressure.

The other figure to look at is the speed at which the machine is running. Smaller DeVilbiss compressors run, typically, at around 650rpm, SIP run at around 900rpm, both of which are sensible speeds which ensure reasonable compressor life, but some units which claim a fantastically high output from low purchase cost, run at anything up to a staggering 3,000rpm, with around 1,400rpm being the average. Obviously the faster a machine runs, the faster it will wear out.

Other 'quality' pointers to look out for are: safety guards to British Standards Institute, or equivalent, levels of safety; a good quality motor built by a firm with a known reputation; a large air receiver which, as well as the benefits already mentioned, cuts down on condensation because, as the air expands and cools, any moisture in it will condense into droplets and the tank will act as a trap to collect the water, rather than letting it get out onto the job; a tank pressure gauge which gives a visual indication of unusual tank pressure if the cut-off valve goes wrong, room for top-mounting an air regulator, because there is not always sufficient depth for the regulator body with side mountings; the presence of an inlet filter. Remember also that pressure is far less important than air delivery (FAD *not* displacement). Also, belt-driven compressors are generally quieter running than direct drive.

IN USE

Leakage in the air line or connections can cause quite a dramatic drop in the potential of the machine. For instance, a hole measuring only 3mm across will lose 11 litres of air per second, which is just about the flat-out capacity of the very smallest compressors, so check all connections for tightness. Also, do not choose air lines of too narrow a diameter, especially for longer runs of pipe, because the frictional loss inside the pipe can reduce the air flow volume a great deal. In general, select a pipe size that matches the size of the outlet on the compressor.

You should try to keep the lubricating oil *in* the compressor and water *out*. Accomplish the former by keeping the oil topped up to its recommended level, but no higher, and by renewing the piston rings, when they become worn out. The latter is achieved by draining the tank and/or regulator after every use and by allowing the compressor to run

somewhere relatively cool and where it will not draw in particularly damp air. Compressors are best sited outside workshops, if they are to receive very regular use, or inside with a cover and an air inlet to the fresh air, so that abrasive and dirty particles are not drawn into the machine from the air in the workshop. In any case, change the inlet filter or filters at regular intervals. It is all too easy to forget them until they become choked and the machine really has to struggle to keep up.

RESPRAYING A REAR WING

No, there is no reason why a 'Beetle' wing spray should be any different from that of any other car! It's simply that when the author visited the headquarters of International Paints in Ladywood, Birmingham, it was a Beetle that was selected by their man-on-the-spot Ian MacAlister as a suitable car for the demonstration he was about to give. Actually, Ian is very used to being 'on the spot' because as International's Technical Sales Representative he is the man who visits dozens of commercial premises each year as a troubleshooter: finding the cause of difficult problems and demonstrating ways round them.

IDENTIFYING THE CORRECT REFINISHING PAINT

Ian pointed out that the first step, before carrying out any work whatsoever, is to

determine the type of paint that has already been used on the car. Knowing the original paint system used is no help at all unless the car's history from new is known. Newish cars may have been accident damaged and older cars are almost certain to have been given a 'blow-over' at some stage by a dealer operating in the knowledge that the seductiveness of a shiny car is a real forecourt asset. There are four principal paint types in use and certain combinations are so incompatible that putting the wrong combination together, such as applying a car with cellulose paint on top of an oil-based paint, will cause a reaction almost as extreme and unsightly as if paint stripper had been sprayed on to the car.

The paint type test in 'Preparing to spray', earlier in this chapter will allow you to deduce what the existing paint type is; the accompanying chart shows which combinations of paint can or cannot be used on top of one another.

Cellulose paint was once overwhelmingly the most popular paint for original equipment and refinishing use. It does not require sophisticated equipment in its use, it is very quick drying so minimising dust problems and it is relatively inexpensive. It has the ability to be polished back to a high shine (albeit after many hours of elbow grease in many cases) and so if the amateur's initial finish is not perfect, the problem can be remedied. Coupled with its low toxicity (you don't tend to drop dead upon coming into contact with it!)

Original paint	Cellulose	1-pack Acrylic	2-pack Acrylic	1-pack Synthetic
Refinish Paint				
Cellulose	O	X	O	X
1-pack Acrylic (eg aerosol cans)	O	O	O	X
2-pack Acrylic (Isocyanate cured hydroxy acrylics)	O	O	O	O (if aged)
1-pack Synthetic (oil-based paint)	O	O	O	O

Note: O denotes acceptable case.

cellulose must remain favourite with the home sprayer.

Where touching-in is concerned, however, 1-pack Acrylic, which is frequently used in aerosol spray cans, is an excellent product and, of course, use of paint in this way involves absolutely minimal outlay. See the section on 'Bodywork repair from a can' for further information.

2-pack Acrylic paint is relatively new to the UK although it has been used for some time in Continental Europe. Its qualities are stunning: it completely hides small scratches and so requires less flatting, it can be used over any other paint, it gives a very tough, hard finish and it retains its deep lustrous shine for years and years, requiring only a wash to bring it up like new. But, life being what

▼ BWS1. Ian MacAlister turned up at PPG Paint's Refinishing School in a fairly well-preserved 'Beetle' complete with a few bashes in its rear wing where the owner had argued briefly with a gate post – and lost. Ian knew that the car had previously been sprayed in 2-pack because it had been sprayed previously at the same place. Had he been unsure of the compatibility of the paints being used he would have tried wiping some paint or its solvent onto an unobtrusive area such as a wheel arch flange, or some other out of the way part of the car to be sprayed, then waited to see if any reaction took place.

it is, the enormous advantages are matched by a potentially bigger disadvantage – inhaling the spray can be lethal! The match between the words Isocyanate and cyanide is no idle coincidence – they are both killers! Isocyanate 2-packs must be used in a sealed booth where the operator is wearing an air-fed face visor so that he breathes only good air from outside the booth. At the time of writing, there are rumours of a non isocyanate, air-drying 2-pack being on the verge of being launched, and if that is as good as it promises to be, it could virtually kill off the use of cellulose paint. For the moment, however, 2-packs are simply too dangerous for anyone to even consider them for home use.

The fourth major paint system is 1-pack Synthetic, or oil-based paint, a very close cousin to the coach paint found on very old Vintage cars. Synthetics are used by the commercial respray trade simply because the areas to be sprayed are usually so vast and synthetic is the cheapest paint around. The same virtue makes it attractive to the lowest end of the car respray market but it is possessed of some serious disadvantages: it is very slow to dry and so the risk of its being affected by dust inclusion is commensurately higher; but worst of all is the fact that if there are problems such as runs in the paintwork, it can take weeks before the paint is hard enough to be

flatted down again. In addition, apart from another Synthetic, only 2-pack Acrylic can later be used over the top of Synthetic without provoking a reaction and then only if the paint beneath is years old and thus is 'well-cured'.

Actually, it is not quite true to say that nothing can be sprayed over Synthetic paint. It is possible to buy a special barrier paint called an isolator paint which can be sprayed onto an area suspected of being prone to reaction and which seals it off. Isolators are known to be hygroscopic if used incorrectly (they absorb water from the atmosphere) which means that if a car is left covered in isolator, its paint will act like a sponge. Later, when the finish coat is sprayed on,

▲ BWS2. The next job is to establish the exact colour of the paint. It is possible to identify the colour by its name such as 'Silver Fox', or 'Connaught Green' or whatever. However, it is not always obvious what the colour is called: a visit to the paint factor will bring the assistance of someone with a book of colours called paint chips but the best way is to find the manufacturer's paint code number. Check of course, that the car is in its original livery. Look inside the engine bay and under the carpets to find the original colour. If the paint is original, the code number will be invaluable because there are often production line variations even with one particular colour name and these 'variants' should be indicated in the code number. Code numbers are usually on a plate in one of a variety of possible hiding places. Look along the front panel, where there is usually a range of information to be found. Alternatively, the plate may be found underneath the spare wheel in the spare wheel well.

nothing untoward will occur, until the next good hard frosty spell. Then the tiny droplets of water beneath the surface will freeze and expand, and the surface will erupt with a covering of tiny pimples known as micro-blistering. The answer is to spray a coat of primer over the isolator within the hour and so effectively seal it off from the atmosphere. (It must be said, however, that even primer will absorb moisture if left for a length of time without any top coat – and for that reason, it should never be left outside in the rain.)

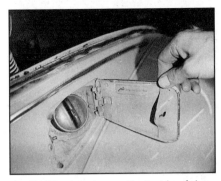

▲ BWS6. ... and even the inside of the fuel filler flap ...

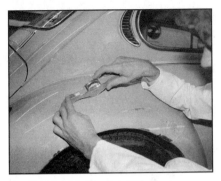

▲ BWS9. This fiendish little device measures the thickness of the paint already on the panel; the paint factor will probably have one and could do the job for you. Older cars often have layer upon layer of paint on their bodywork and this can eventually cause problems; you can reach the stage where one coat too many can cause a reaction with the paint beneath, necessitating the stripping of the entire panel.

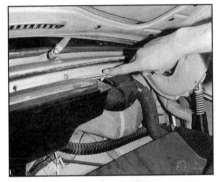

▲ BWS3. Another favourite spot is at the front edge of the bulkhead.

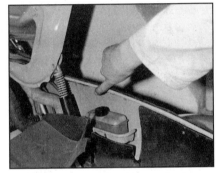

▲ BWS7. ... as well as the engine bay flitch plates (but, remember, this is a Beetle with its engine at the 'wrong' end).

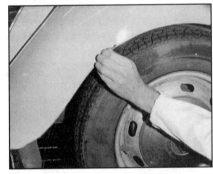

▲ BWS10. Ian next looked at the blemishes on the panel which, of course, had to be remedied before any painting took place. Here the paint was flaking around a light area of damage. Surface rust had formed and possibly spread a little way beneath the paint film.

▲ BSW4. Further 'hiding places' are the door hinge pillar ...

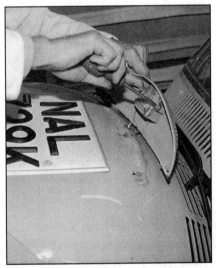

▲ BWS8. If you can't manage to take the whole of the car to the factor, you can usually find a small part of the bodywork to remove and take along. Here, Ian removes the number plate lamp for the purpose of taking it along to International's own range of paint chips, just to be sure.

▲ BWS11. Fortunately, the wing was basically quite sound, apart from a shallow dent towards the front of the wing.

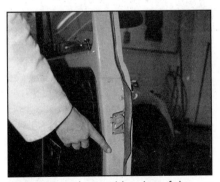

▲ BWS5. ... the outside edge of the door itself ...

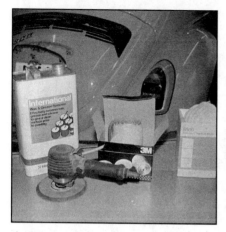

▲ BWS12. Ian began by reassembling the equipment he would need for the first stage in the process of repairing the wing: at the front is a random orbit sander (easily replaceable by a free commodity called 'hard work',) and from left to right is a tin of wax and grease remover, a box of sanding papers and a packet of face masks of the type designed to stop the wearer from inhaling dust.

▲ BWS14. Before trying to get rid of the dent, Ian sanded the whole area down to bare metal; it's the only way of being certain of what's under the paint.

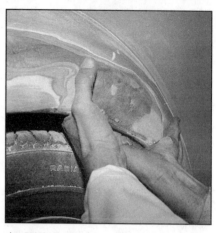

▲ BWS15. He then 'popped' the worst of the dent by pressing very hard on the back of the panel. Of course, the finish was not perfect but it was good enough for the job in hand. Some enthusiasts might prefer to aim for a perfect finish to the surface of the steel. See the section on Panel Beating.

▲ BWS13. The use of wax and grease remover is most important before any abrading work is carried out. Polish, especially silicone polish, can play havoc with paintwork, causing it to form 'fish eyes' where the paint surrounds spots of silicone but doesn't cover them. If silicone is sanded, it is simply pushed further into the remaining paint or steel where it is virtually impossible to remove.

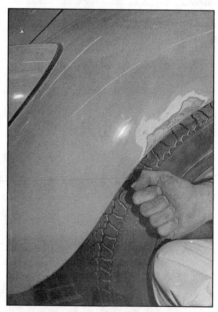

▲ BWS16. The dent at the rear of the wing couldn't be pushed out so Ian thumped it once with his clenched fist and out it came! An alternative is to use a soft-faced hammer, but it is generally a mistake for the less experienced repairers to use a steel hammer because it can cause more trouble than it prevents, by causing the steel to stand out from the panel.

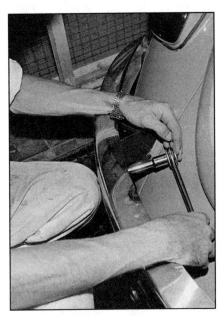

▲ BWS21. Notice how Ian held the spreader as flat as possible and also shaped it to the contour of the wing. Filler should be left slightly proud, but the closer to the correct shape, the less wastage will occur and the better the final profile is likely to be.

▲ BWS17. Optional: you could, at this stage, remove the bumper so that it does not get in the way of the flatting and painting processes. Be prepared for bumper retaining bolts to be difficult to undo. If they are tough going, try: pushing the spanner with your foot; applying releasing fluid to the nut well in advance; heating the part with a welding torch or even a small butane torch, provided that nothing flammable is in the area.

▲ BWS19. Ian judged the amount of filler to be used and scooped it out onto a clean board using the spreader supplied. The hardener was squeezed out next to it. The proportions of hardener to filler paste are not critical but should be 'about right'. Manufacturers usually supply enough hardener in the pack to satisfy the quantity of filler paste it accompanies, so try to use the proportion of the quantities used as a guide. Remember, though, that if you are working in hot weather, filler 'goes off' (sets) much more quickly while in winter it can take much longer. Mix only on a fibre-free surface. Onion boards have sheets you tear-off and throw away.

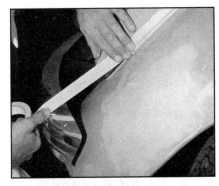

▲ BWS22. Masking off is best carried out using two layers of masking tape. The first is carefully and accurately placed over the edge to be masked off...

▲ BWS18. With all the offending areas thoroughly sanded down, Ian then provided himself with a tin of polyester filler and the tube of hardener required to make it set.

▲ BWS20. It is important to mix hardener with filler evenly and thoroughly. The contrasting colours help. Do avoid getting the filler paste on your hands; it is very advisable to wear gloves – follow the manufacturer's safety instructions supplied with the filler.

▲ BWS23. ... while the next is placed over the edge of the masking paper before the paper is stuck down to the tape already in place. Ian carefully folded the paper in on itself as neatly as a Christmas parcel.

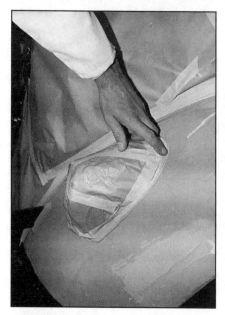

▲ BWS24. All the edges were then sealed down with more masking tape so that no dust could get trapped in there. Dust blown about by the pressure from the spraygun is the resprayer's Public Enemy No. 1 and great lengths have to be gone to in order to prevent it from causing blemishes on the paint finish.

▲ BWS26. The professional way of feeling a panel to check for ripples and bumps is to run the flat of the hand lightly over the panel. At this stage a panel can appear to be perfectly flat to the eye, but once it is painted every ripple will be cruelly exposed.

▲ BWS28. Belatedly, Ian remembered that he should really have masked off the wheel before sanding the filler down to avoid an accumulation of dust there. He used the air line for the task.

▲ BWS29. More brown paper was used to mask off the wheel. Paper is better than cloth because the latter harbours dust.

▲ BWS25. Ian used the powersander to flatten the filler. An ordinary disc held in a drill is not nearly as good; the random orbit device in this special sander prevents scratching in the surface of the filler. See the section on 'Bodywork repair from a can' and also 'Tools and Equipment' for more tips on hand sanding.

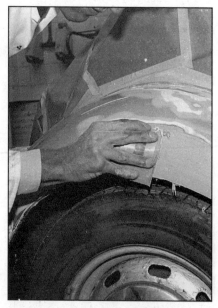

▲ BWS27. As usually happens, it was necessary to apply a second layer of filler. This time, a really thin skin was all that was necessary.

▲ BWS30. Ian demonstrated a rapid method of removing filler by using a Sykes-Pickavant body file. It has single cut teeth which resist clogging and can be adjusted to give a flat or a concave or convex blade shape.

▲ BWS31. After a further bout of flatting, the surface of the filler was found still to contain small pin holes and other very minor blemishes. It is thoroughly recommended to use a 2-pack stopper to deal with these imperfections. This is a very fine filler paste which is far less prone to shrinkage than the old-fashioned cellulose stopper. The usual guideleines for safety apply as with all 2-pack products and remember to wear gloves.

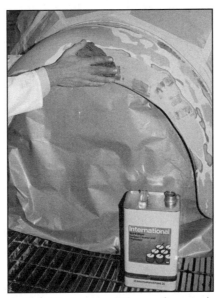

▲ BWS33. A clean cloth was then used with some PPG Spirit Wipe/Degreaser. It is most important to remove all traces of grease at this stage.

▲ BWS36. Ian next took a piece of card and sprayed it with just a little of the paint that he was about to use. He then compared it with the shade of the paint on the car's bodywork. If there is a difference between shades, it is better to take the paint back to the factors at this stage where they can often blend the colour to the required shade; after all, paint can fade over a period of time and when that happens, no amount of colour code identification will give you the right shade. Reds and yellows are generally thought of as the most fade-prone colours.

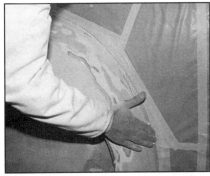

▲ BW32. Stopper sands very easily and the small areas treated were easily hand flatted using the flat of the hand, fingers facing across the direction of sanding to minimise the risk of creating grooving.

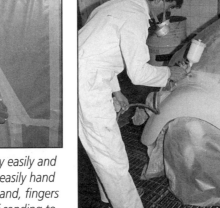

▲ BWS34. A couple of coats of primer/filler were next blown on ...

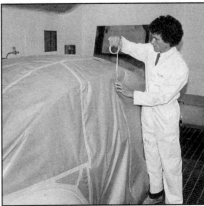

▲ BWS37. Ian had removed all of the masking paper, put there to prevent any damage to the surrounding panel as well as to stop overspray from the primer. His justifiable obsession with dust told him that the old paper was likely to have trapped pockets of the stuff. When masking off a second time, Ian really went to town with the masking paper to make absolutely certain that no overspray whatever could reach the surrounding panels.

▶ BWS35. ... and then sanded again with fine grade of paper on a sanding block. This had the effect of highlighting any blemishes that may have escaped attention earlier. A little more stopping was used on the small blemishes discovered. If necessary, more filler would have been used at this stage and, while the professional might rarely need to go back to filler after flatting the primer, the less experienced home resprayer may have to be prepared to do so in order to achieve a first class finish.

◄ BWS38. Before starting to spray, wipe the air lines and the surface of the gun itself to ensure that there are no particles there. This is an important and often overlooked step, important because the forward flow of air which jets out of the front of the gun tends to pull in air – and thus particles if they are present – from behind the nozzle of the gun.

◄ BWS39. The 'man from Mars' outfit that Ian is wearing while spraying the top coat is not just for effect. It's a necessary safety precaution when spraying with 2-pack paint. Fresh, filtered air is fed into the sealed face mask and this keeps out the toxic spray of paint. Needless to say, once the paint has landed and hardened, there is no danger whatsoever. DeVilbiss market an excellent air-fed visor kit complete with all the necessary plumbing at reasonable cost – an essential investment if spraying 2-pack!

◄ BWS40. Two-pack paints can be baked (ie the spray booth doubles as an oven to heat up the car) so that the paint goes off more quickly. If the paint is to be allowed to dry and go 'off' in the air, it is necessary to use a special airdrying 2-pack thinner to allow the process to take place within a reasonable time. An important difference between cellulose and 2-pack is that cellulose hardens mainly by a drying process and is thus liable to shrinkage while 2-pack hardens mainly by a chemical reaction, rather like that in filler and so suffers very little shrinkage. With the paint dry, the masking paper and tape can come off. Tape should not be left in place for more than a few days or it can be the devil of a job to remove.

▶ BWS41. The newly painted wing looked absolutely splendid! But it was interesting that the surrounding panels, painted a couple of years previously in the same PPG 2-pack paint, looked virtually as good.

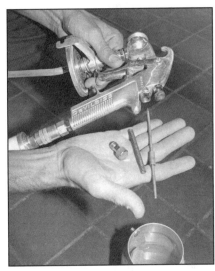

▲ BWS42. Ian went to great lengths to strip and clean the DeVilbiss gun he had been using, but see the section on 'Spray Gun Care, produced with the assistance of DeVilbiss themselves, for more detail.

SPRAYING WITH AEROSOLS

Safety Note: Aerosol paint has many of the health hazards associated with conventional paint spraying. Read carefully the safety instructions on the can. In particular: use only in a well-ventilated area; keep sparks and flames away from spray vapour; do not puncture the can or apply heat to it. Wear gloves and keep wet paint and mist away from skin and eyes.

▲ AP2. Before starting to spray, the primer can was taken outside, shaken vigorously, and the nozzle cleared.

▲ BWS43. At around the time that Ian MacAlister was respraying the Beetle wing, someone else was carrying out some experimental work on spraying plastics which are finding increasing use in today's cars. (This is a Ford Sierra wing mirror back, receiving attention.)

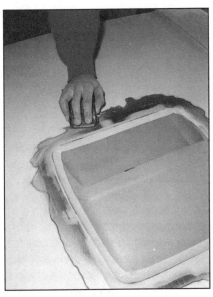

▲ AP1. Wet-or-dry paper was used with water to feather out the filler, leaving no trace of a hard edge.

▲ AP3. The can was held about six inches away and red oxide primer sprayed on to the bare metal.

▲ AP4. High-build spray putty was sprayed on to the whole area and then, extending a little wider than the area of the original red oxide primer, a second coat of spray putty was applied after the first had dried.

▲ AP7. Now here's a tip from the experts. Holding a tin of black spray paint about 12 inches (300mm) or more away from the job, dust a light coat on to the work surface. The idea is not to change the colour of the panel but just to put an even sprinkling of paint over it.

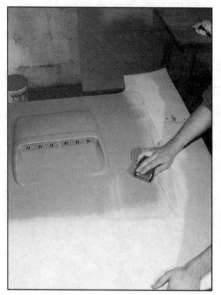

▲ AP5. Provided that the filler work was carried out properly, the use of high build spray putty will allow you to remove every last blemish when you sand it out with fine wet-or-dry paper supported on a flat rubbing block.

▲ AP6. We chose to spray on grey primer paint as a barrier colour between the yellow and the white top coat to follow. Red and yellow have a nasty habit of 'grinning through' white surface coats above them. When choosing your primer colour, use red for dark shades, grey for lighter coats, and grey or preferably white for white top coats and metallics. Plenty of water, a few spots of washing-up liquid and the finest grade of wet-or-dry and the final primer coat was prepared for finish painting.

▲ AP8. Sand the entire panel all over once more with the finest grade of paper and the guide coat, as it is called, will be sanded off in all but the low areas. After you wipe off with a dry cloth, any low spots and blemishes will stand out like a sore thumb!

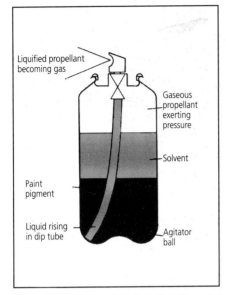

▲ *AP9. How an aerosol works. The paint and pigment separate in the can. You have to shake and shake so that little metal ball mixes them thoroughly! This diagram also explains why paint stops coming out when you invert the can.*

Paint Matching: Some companies, such as Hycote, can mix aerosol paint colours to match your car. Ask your retailer for details.

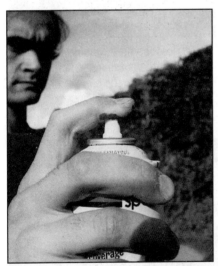

▲ *AP10. If you do what comes naturally, the part of your finger sticking forwards catches the edge of the spray which builds up into a drip which is then shot forward as a blob on to your lovely handiwork. Most annoying! Hold the nozzle down with the top of your finger or, better still, buy an accessory trigger sold with some brands of aerosol paint.*

▲ *AP12. The first coat should be applied in regular strips up and down the bonnet, concentrating on obtaining an even coat without trying to blanket out the colour underneath. That's the way to achieve runs! You must leave a few minutes for the solvent in the first coat to 'flash off'.*

▲ *AP13. The second coat, as already suggested, follows in a pattern which crisscrosses the first and this time the colour beneath will usually disappear from view. Ideally, you will apply another one or two coats. If any little bits of dust land in the paint surface, you may be able to polish them out with fine cutting compound, but be most careful not to go right through the paint and don't try it until the paint has had several days to dry really hard.*

◄ *AP11. It's best to practice your spraying on a spare scrap of sheet metal. Hold the can too close and the paint will run; too far away and you'll have a 'dry' look finish.*

▲ *AP14. This shield does an excellent job of keeping the tyres clean while you spray the wheels in situ. You would be better off taking the wheels off the car so that there is no risk of overspray getting on to the bodywork. The outsides of the wheel flanges, covered by the shield, have to be brushed in later, by hand. (Courtesy The Eastwood Company)*

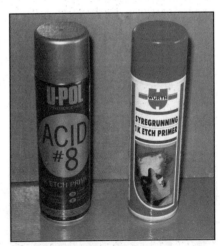

▲ *AP15. If you're painting aluminium or galvanised metal, new paint will peel after a while, unless you use an etch primer. It's available from U-POL and Würth in aerosols for small areas.*

'MOBILE' PAINT REPAIRS

Here, these happen to be repairs to front and rear plastic bumpers – see also Chapter 5, Part III: Repairing plastics or the relevant information on plastic repairs. The paint repair part of this job is common to all types of material however.

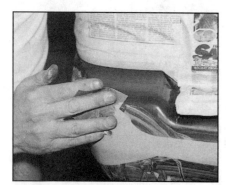

▲ MPR1. Tony Mousley from Paint Technik had already repaired the damaged plastic on the front and rear bumpers – the results of everyday parking knocks over a couple of years' period – and here he is flatting down the repaired area in readiness for applying the paint. If the damage had been to a steel panel, he would have carried out a similar repair to the one we described in Small Dent Repair, shown earlier.

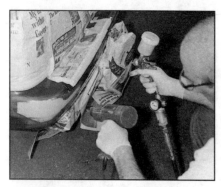

▲ MPR2. A useful tip from Tony Mousley is to use a hot air blower – a hairdryer would do the job just as well – to dry off the surface and heat it slightly, if there is any damp in the air. Don't, whatever you do, apply so much heat that you damage the paint!

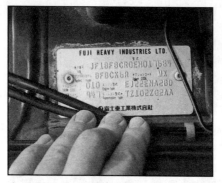

▲ MPR3. Tony's first job was to find the car's VIN plate and to look for the paint code number shown on there. On some vehicles, the paint code may be on a plate or sticker on some other part of the vehicle, such as inside the petrol filler cap cover or inside the luggage bay aperture. (Consult your vehicle handbook if necessary.)

▲ MPR4. In the back of his van, Tony has a complete paint mixing scheme. He consults the microfiche reader to find out what combination of paints he will require and mixes enough paint for the repair.

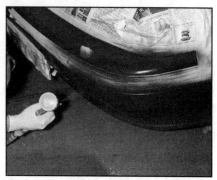

▲ MPR5. Both front and rear bumpers, having been carefully masked off, were painted by Tony with his small spray gun powered by the mobile workshop's on-board compressor.

▲ MPR6. When the paint is completely hardened off – but not before! – the masking paper can be removed.

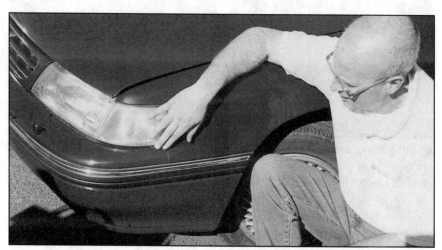

▲ MPR7. The next day, Tony gave the finished job a final polish and the results were as good as new.

Chapter 5

Bodywork repairs – Part I

The major part of any restoration invariably involves body repairs. This chapter sets out to describe the ways in which panels are stripped and removed, and the ways in which minor accident repairs can be carried out to your classic. We cover everything from the most minor repairs, to major chassis/frame replacement. But to start off with, you'll always need to remove body trim and fittings, so here goes!

Not unnaturally, car makers fit their trim and body fittings in such a way that often you can't readily see how they're fitted from the outside. But since it is really only possible to glue, clip, screw or bolt fittings in place, a little creative thinking usually shows how it's done. The following section shows some of the usual ways of holding body fittings in place.

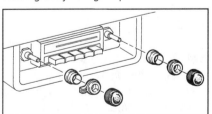

▲ BF1. Inside the car, most radios and radio/cassettes are removed after first easing off the knobs, bezels and other controls, then undoing the nut behind each control. (Courtesy Austin-Rover)

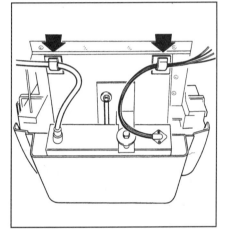

▲ BF2. Behind the dash there is almost always another mounting bracket. The aerial/antenna wire plugs into the set but the feed and speaker wires will have to be disconnected either at source or at their first junction. (Courtesy Austin-Rover)

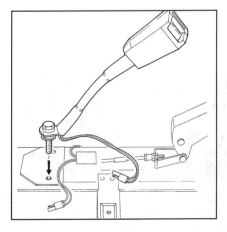

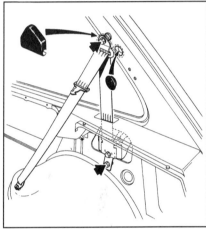

▲ BF3. Where inertia reel seat belts are fitted, they are bolted to a sturdy mounting, often behind a trim panel. High-up brackets are usually covered in a clip-on cover. When unbolting, be certain to keep track of the sequence of all spacer washers otherwise any swivelling movement in the bracket will be lost. (Courtesy Austin-Rover)

◄ BF4. Floor mountings are straightforward but, this time, the wiring for the seat belt warning light also has to be uncoupled. (Courtesy Austin-Rover)

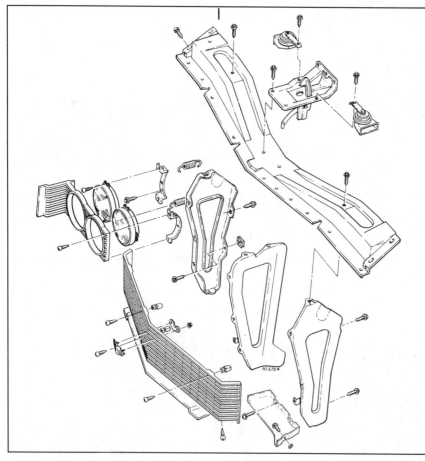

▲ BF8. This VW Golf/Rabbit wheel arch shield is held on in this way. The nuts are simply spannered off in the normal way.

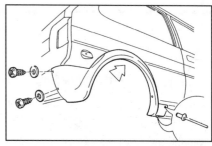

▲ BF9. Here self-tapping screws hold the rear of this wheel arch flare while the front is pop-riveted into place. To remove them, it is necessary to drill the head off (taking care not to allow the drill to bite into the plastic) and fit new pop-rivets when refitting. (Courtesy Rover Group)

▲ BF5. External fittings can be held on by a variety of means. The extensive grille components from this model of Chevrolet are held on with a mixture of hex-head and screwdriver head coarse-thread screws.

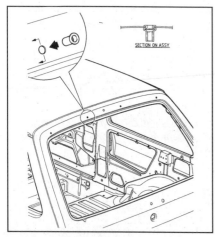

▲ BF6. A Metro tailgate spoiler is held on with screws which screw into plastic anchor nuts which are pushed into pre-stamped holes. (Courtesy Austin-Rover)

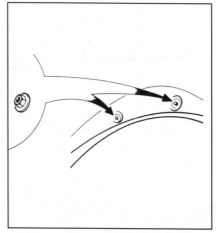

▲ BF7. Sometimes, threaded screws are built into parts which are then held into place with plastic nuts. They have built-in washers which cannot be separated from the nut. (Courtesy Rover Group)

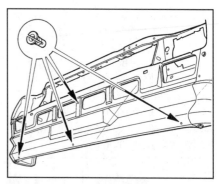

▲ BF10. Where self-tapping screws are used, Locut nuts are pressed into ready-cut holes, or, on some applications, special spring clips are fitted into which the screw is fed. (Courtesy Rover Group)

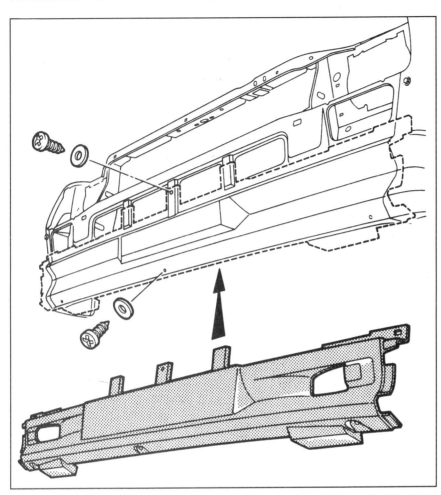

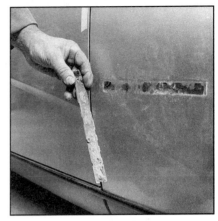

▲ BF14. The sticking medium is usually a double-sided tape. Obtain some from your local friendly body shop rather than having to buy a complete roll.

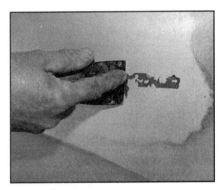

▲ BF11. In this case, the Locut nuts enable a front spoiler to be fitted without the risk of the self-tapping screws cutting into the body and causing corrosion.

▲ BF12. Almost all trim strips clip down onto special clips. Remove them by carefully prising up from beneath. The clips themselves usually fix in place with special pop-rivets, built into the clips. Buy them from the relevant main dealer.

▲ BF13. Usually badges are stuck on. Remove by pushing a thin-bladed scraper under and along the badge; don't try to prise the badge off.

▲ BF15. The old tape can then be scraped off the body ...

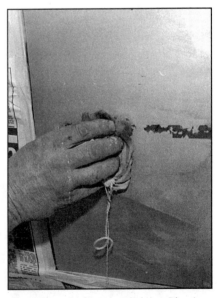

▲ BF16. ... before the sticky residue is removed with a spirit wipe or white spirit.

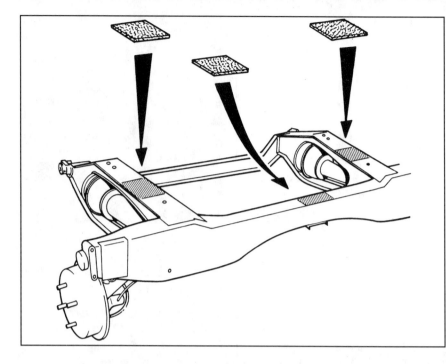

▲ BF17. Where major components are bolted together, such as where this Metro rear sub-frame fits against the body, or where some fuel tanks bolt tight against bodywork, be sure to use self-adhesive rubbing pads to prevent squeaks and groans from rubbing bodywork. (Courtesy Rover Group)

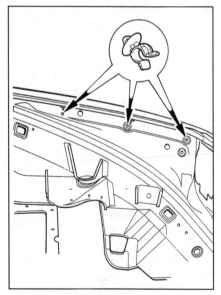

▲ BF18. Using the correct clips for wiring, fuel and brake pipes is essential for both neatness and safety. These plastic clips push straight into pre-drilled holes ...

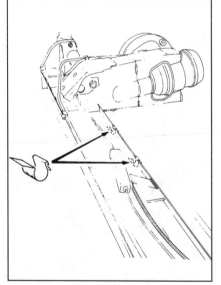

▲ BF19. ... while these clip tight over the edge of a panel. (Courtesy Rover Group)

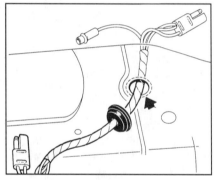

▲ BF20. Other clips are self-adhesive and these can be really useful when wiring in new components or where old clips are missing. Be sure to thoroughly degrease the mounting area with some kind of spirit wipe to ensure good adhesion. (Courtesy Rover Group)

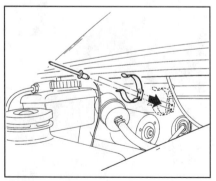

▲ BF21. Whilst on the subject of wiring, always use and re-fit the correct grommets, especially to the bulkhead/ firewall area. It is surprising how much in the way of fumes and noise they can keep out. (Courtesy Rover Group)

▲ BF22. This fuel filter clip is held on with a couple of pop-rivets, direct to the bodywork. (Courtesy Rover Group)

REMOVING STUBBORN FIXINGS

One of the most basic rules in carrying out any sort of dismantling work is to make a plan of action before the work actually commences. The reason for this is two-fold. First, it enables you to ensure that no unnecessary work is carried out – and just about every mechanic can tell of the time spent in dismantling a stubborn part only to find that it didn't need to come off at all! Secondly, it enables you to get plenty of releasing fluid on all the parts that are likely to be seized-up with rust, and heaven knows, on older cars there are certainly enough of those! The most heavily rusted parts will come off a lot more willingly if they are soaked in releasing fluid on each of three days before the work is carried out.

One of the most versatile methods for the freeing of rust-seized nuts and bolts is to get some heat on the seized parts. This is one of those occasions where every enthusiast wishes he had an oxy-acetylene outfit but in fact the heat from the increasingly popular carbon-arc torch fitted to an arc-welder or even that available from a simple butane torch can make quite an amazing amount of difference. What happens is quite simple. The two parts which have been sitting in cosy proximity for so long that they have virtually welded themselves together with rust are made to move against each other by the action of the expansion of metal, thus helping to break down the bond between them. Also a nut will tend to expand making it a looser fit on the bolt so it is obviously sensible to remove said nut while it is still hot.

Of course, where a lot of heat is being applied safety precautions are of the greatest importance. Under no circumstances should parts situated near to a fuel tank be heated; that much is common sense. What is sometimes not realised, however, is that on more modern cars the fuel line itself is made from plastic which will easily melt and cause a nasty fire if heat should be accidentally played on it. Rubber bushes

can also catch fire and if one of those should burn you could end up with the awful situation where you find yourself in more trouble than you started with. Remember also to clear everything flammable from inside the car in the area to be heated, such as plastic trim and carpeting. Also bear in mind that fumes given off by the car's battery are highly flammable. It is best to have a helper keeping an eye on things, armed with a washing-up liquid bottle full of cold water ready to use as a fire extinguisher, just in case something you hadn't thought of, such as rust proofer in the box sections, underseal or mastic, goes up in flames. Also have a proprietary brand of workshop fire extinguisher available in case of more serious problems. Don't assume that a proper fire extinguisher can be dispensed with; always have one to hand when using any heat source.

Sometimes a really unfriendly nut is encountered; one which refuses to budge no matter how much encouragement is applied. It is then best to cut your losses, admit defeat and remove the thing by less delicate means. Wherever possible the nut should be sawn off rather than chiselled off to avoid risk of damage caused by the action of chiselling. In picture RSF1 you can see the technique of sawing a nut by making a cut in its thinnest part which is parallel to the hole in the nut. By this means it is often possible to preserve the bolt intact and it can often mean less sawing than trying to go through the whole bolt. In any case, in trying to saw underneath the nut the saw usually encounters the spring washer which, being hardened steel, can't be sawn through with a hacksaw blade. However, where there is room to get under the nut, a hacksaw blade held in a pad-saw handle can often be used where there is insufficient room for an orthodox type of hacksaw. In practice, there is sometimes no room to wield a hacksaw of any sort and then a nut just has to be chiselled off. Where this is the case a hole should first be drilled down the nut (again parallel to its hole) before chiselling down (not across) the much weakened

▲ *RSF1. Removing a nut by hacksawing across the thinnest part.*

nut. Incidentally, chisels should always be ground sharp before use in this way, and it is better to use a relatively heavy hammer (say, a 2 pounder) and wield it lightly than to try using a light hammer heavily – the user loses a lot of control that way.

On occasions the nuts themselves cannot be reached or, as in the case of bumper bolts, it is virtually certain that the nut and bolt will be impossible to remove. (Bumper bolts are held in place by a squared portion of the shank of the bolt, just under the dome. This sits in a square hole punched into the bumper blade, which allows sufficient purchase for the bolt to be held firmly in place for the first couple of years of the car's life but thereafter there are nearly always problems in removing the nuts). After centre-punching the centre of the bolt head (do it well to break through the chrome plating) the head can be drilled off the bolt allowing simple removal of the bumper.

Coach bolts, which are used in bolting bodywork to woodwork, are virtually the same shape as bumper bolts. The process is older than cars themselves (hence the name) but was still being used in volume production as late as 1971 on the Morris 1000 Traveller. Unfortunately, coach bolts can be just as awkward as bumper bolts, usually simply

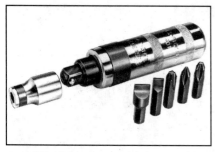

▲ *RSF2. The indispensable impact driver set. (Courtesy Sykes-Pickavant)*

turning in the wood when they are being untightened instead of being held in place by the square on the shank. If they stand proud of the surface of the wood it is sometimes possible to saw a screwdriver slot on to the dome but if, as usually happens, the dome has sunk below the surface of the wood it will be necessary to remove the nut or the bolt head in one of the ways already described.

A more modern but no less problematic method of fixing bolt-on bodywork is by bolting into captive or caged nuts. In their struggle for freedom these nuts often bend their cage outwards as an attempt is made to undo the bolt, particularly if the threads are tight. When this happens the best solution is to chisel off the cage completely using a slim but sharp cold chisel. Then a spanner can be placed across the flats of the square nut to be found underneath and when the bolt is replaced it can be held with an orthodox type of nut held tight by a spanner.

There are occasions when all the 'trad' methods have been tried and there seems to be no way out. It is then that one of the various gadgets on the market can come in useful. One device which most people wonder how they ever managed without once they have got one, is the impact screwdriver. The impact screwdriver consists of a fat screwdriver body, like that shown in picture RSF2 inside which is a ratchet. The ratchet is operated by striking the end of the screwdriver with a hammer and can be adjusted to work in either direction, enabling it to work with either left- or right-hand threads and for either screwing or unscrewing. Before using an

impact screwdriver it is essential to clean any rubbish out of the screw head, otherwise the point of the screwdriver will not seat properly and rounded screw heads could easily be the only result. With most models, it is also possible to substitute a ½in socket drive for the screwdriver tip, giving another weapon in the armoury against seized nuts.

A poor man's impact screwdriver can be made up for emergency use by selecting a screwdriver with an impact resistant handle, fixing a self-grip wrench to the upper end of the blade and while putting a slight rotational pressure on the wrench, tapping the end of the screwdriver firmly with a hammer.

Frequently nuts are rounded off by the application of the wrong size spanner or by the ravages of corrosion. A self-grip wrench can sometimes solve the problem. Obviously the nut is already ruined and so further damage is totally irrelevant. A pipe wrench (or Stillson wrench) will give even more grip since once it is properly adjusted it actually gets tighter and tighter as pressure is applied to it.

And don't forget that when a nut and bolt are scrap, you could always grind off the entire nut using a mini-grinder with grinding disc attached.

One gadget which should not be overlooked is that painful sounding old faithful, the nut splitter. This consists of a chisel point which is driven into the nut by tightening the bolt on the splitter. It is a very clean and effective way of removing a nut but it does have the disadvantage that it is not always possible to get the tool into a constricted space and in many cases, small nuts just won't reach far enough into the body of the splitter to enable it to do its job properly. Having said that, the nut splitter does such a good job when the circumstances are right for it that it is a tool well worth investing in.

What if all the above ideas have been to no avail and all that has happened is that the nut has gone 'free' as it has been turned. 'It's coming off at last!' you think, before the stud or bolt shears and drops on the floor. All too often the remains of a vital stud is left in place

which has just **got** to come out. It is here that a good stud extractor will prove its worth. The extractor takes the form of a tapered rod with spiral fluting with a left-hand 'thread'. To use a stud extractor a hole has first to be drilled in the end of the stud before the extractor is inserted and turned in an anticlockwise direction. When inserted into the pre-drilled hole and rotated until it can go no further it should – you hope – turn the stud itself. So much for the more obvious type of fixing. But what about trim such as door trim or chrome beading which snaps onto concealed fixings? Removal of this can all too often damage paintwork, bend the chrome plated strip or damage the door panel. Several tool makers make a tool especially for the job of removing such concealed fixings, which consists of a double pronged fork, rather like the claw on a claw hammer, which is extended into a handle.

Even when armed with the best gadgets that money can buy, there can be no universal way of freeing stubborn fixings. The best ammunition is the sort of advice that has been presented here coupled with the most important ingredients of all – the ingenuity and common sense of the person working on the car. In a vicious combination, Murphy's Law (If a Thing Can Go Wrong – It Will Go Wrong) and Sodt's Codicil (– And In The Most Difficult Circumstances Possible) will always place ingenuity at a premium. And who knows, your ingenuity could lead to the invention of the gadget that everyone has been waiting for and a fortune for the inventor. After all, even Mr Snap-On had to start somewhere.

BONNET/FRONT DAMAGE REPAIR

▼ MGB1. The front of any car's bonnet is vulnerable to accident damage. In a big crash, there's usually nothing to do but replace the bonnet, but in the flyweight class of High Street butting, damage is usually slight. In the case of the MGB shown here, damage to the front bumper overriders was rectified by slackening the overrider bolts and repositioning them, and the grille was very easily pulled back to shape and a new badge was purchased.

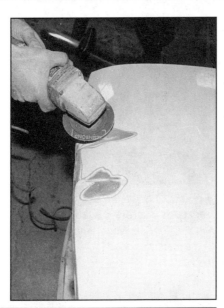

▲ MGB2. The bonnet had taken a punch right on the end of its hooter and looked just a little bit crumpled.

▲ MGB3. With the bonnet lifted and grille removed, the front panel could be seen to be just a little bit put back. Its leading edge was crinkled slightly, so this was straightened out using a flat dolly below and a hammer with a cross-pein above.

◄ MGB4. Sorting out a supporting structure first is always the best way of working. Once the front panel was finished, the bonnet itself could be sorted. It is important to establish that you are working with sound metal and so the paint around the damaged area was finished off back to bare metal. In this case, there was no filler clogging up the works.

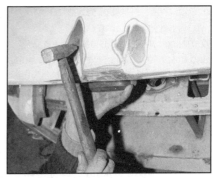

▲ MGB5. The shape of the bonnet at this point was slightly curved and so a dolly with slightly **less** curve was held beneath the panel. Again the cross-pein hammer was used and the 'edge' of the hammer used in a series of sharp, accurate blows along the crest of the upwards kink. This had the dual effect of pushing the kink back down and also pushing the leading edge of the bonnet back where it belonged. It was important not to heat the kinked area because, although it would have made it easier to get rid of the ridge, the soft metal would have compressed into itself without pushing the front edge of the bonnet further forwards.

▲ MGB6. Any very slight ripples remaining can be lightly filed or flushed over with body filler. It then only remains to flat and finish, as detailed elsewhere in this book.

FRONT WING DAMAGE REPAIR

Cars like this Triumph TR7 are typical of modern cars, with apparently simple lines, but with complex shapes and compound curves. As a result, they can be quite tricky to repair. In fact, when anything more than light damage is encountered, it makes sense to fit a whole new panel. The other complication with this particular car – and it applies to many vehicles nowadays – is that it was painted with a clear gloss coat of paint over a matt colour coat. Check by very lightly flatting with a fine grade wet-and-dry. If the colour you remove is the colour of the car, the finish is **not** clear-over-base; if it's a virtually colourless, perhaps milky colour, you know that you are flatting a clear coat.

▲ FWR2. It is virtually essential to have rear access in a case like this. Here, panelbeater Ken Wright finds a way in to the mainly enclosed area behind the wing.

▲ FWR5. Then he works steadily forwards, towards the point of impact. It is vitally important not to hammer too much or the metal will stretch and you could be worse off than when you started. If the metal is stretched a little, it is better to have it slightly low and bring the surface up with a thin skin of filler than to have it too high.

▲ FWR1. You can pick out the high spots of dents and distortion best by lightly running the flat of your hand over it, like this. Use long strokes of the hand, keep it flat on the job and sense the hollows and high spots through the palm rather than the tips of the fingers.

▲ FWR3. He chooses a panel beating hammer with a general purpose head and a heavy spoon that will act as a dolly in this instance. (See 'Panel beating' section for more information.)

▲ FWR6. In order to dress the flange, Ken chose one of the Sykes-Pickavant dollies with a shape to fit inside the wheel arch.

▲ FWR4. Starting furthest away from the point of impact, Ken lightly taps the raised area while holding the spoon behind it. In one or two places where the panel is hollowed, he holds the hammer on the job and slaps inside with the spoon.

▲ FWR7. Then, with the dolly in place, he carefully beat the flange true ...

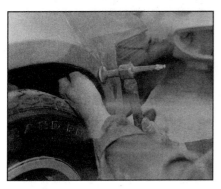

▲ FWR8. ... once again, working from the 'shock' damage which went through the panel, towards the point of impact.

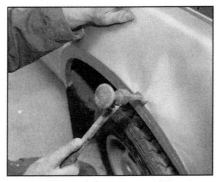

▲ FWR11. With the general shape looking good, Ken could now go back and get rid of one or two areas of very light damage. He uses a cross-pein hammer here to tap out the raised 'vee' ...

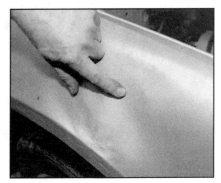

▲ FWR12. ... and then, feeling that much more hammering could stretch the metal, which could take a lot more time to remedy (and perhaps more skill than most DIY-ers could muster), he looks for the couple of slightly raised areas that remain and dings them down.

▲ FWR9. In reality, you can often be wholly unconventional and yet achieve a better job. A slight kink in the flange is bent out with nothing more sophisticated than a pair of pincers.

▲ FWR13. Next, he covers up the surrounding area, paying special attention to every scrap of exposed glass.

▲ FWR10. This can cause its own minor distortion and a couple of light taps are being used here to put matters to rights.

◀ FWR14. He also masks off the surrounding trim areas.

▲ FWR15. He uses the angle grinder with 40 grit sanding disc to finish the paint off, defining the full area of the repair first. Sparks from this tool can embed themselves immovably in the glass, which is why it must be covered. It makes sense to keep the whole engine bay clean, too.

▲ FWR17. ... when (and this is the reality, not the textbook theory!) it is possible to discover any remaining high spots that you may not be happy with.

▲ FWR16. The whole repair area is finished back to bare metal ...

◀ FWR18. Now body filler has a bad name because of its use over rusty panels, but in this case, to bring the surface back smooth without hours and hours of work, it is perfectly acceptable. Indeed, for the amateur who can cause more problems than are solved by trying to take panel beating too far, the use of filler as a surfacing agent is highly desirable!

▲ FWR19. Ken uses a half-round rasp to cut away most of the surplus filler, before going through the grades of sanding paper, as shown in several other places in this book.

▲ FWR20. When he has the surface as level and smooth as he wants it, down to about 120 grit dry (400 grit wet-or-dry), he chooses a high-build primer-filler. Good quality primer-fillers are very worthwhile; cheaper ones don't give the depth to get rid of small imperfections. Don't use a poor quality thinner because it will show through in the final paint.

▲ FWR22. When dry, a very light mist of finish paint is 'blown' over the primer and flatted, the contrast in colours showing up any minor imperfections.

▼ FWR23. The next job is to paint the panel with the base colour, starting with the inside of the wheel arch flange ...

▲ FWR21. The primer-filler is sprayed on more heavily than finish paint, although sags and runs do take a long time to dry. The repaired area and a couple of inches of the old paint (pre-flatted) are 'blown' over.

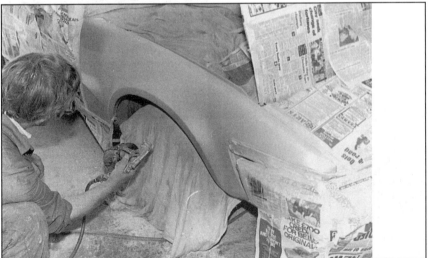

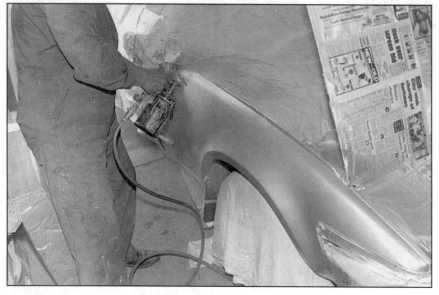

▲ FWR24. ... and going on to paint the whole panel in the normal way. Beware of any imperfections because they will show up right through the final coat.

◀ FWR25. The final coat is of clear paint and this brings the matt finish up to an incredible shine and also offers some protection. Be sure to use a cellulose base paint for both coats – there is a great deal of 2-pack clear over-base available, but it is unsafe to spray it without using the correct protective breathing apparatus.

▼ FWR26. The finished result shows the car looking 'as new' again and indeed it is, with even the rust-proofing on the insides of the panel undamaged. (For details of how the '2-litre' badge was removed and replaced, see 'Body fittings' section.)

ADJUSTMENTS – TIPS IN FITTING PANELS AND DOORS

BONNET

▲ A1. Correct adjustments start right back here, when you're carrying out major repairs to the car. When dealing with a unitary or monocoque construction, it is possible to weld major structural components, such as this MGB sill, in such a way that distortion is locked into the body, making it at best impossible to fit parts correctly and at worst, making the car unsafe.

▲ A2. The way to avoid this problem is to build replacement body structures around known datum points like doors, and to support the body structure in such a way that it cannot sag whilst old structural members are being replaced.

◀ A3. One of the most crucial gaps is that between the bonnet and wings. The catch at the front almost always has both up-and-down and (some) sideways adjustment, although the bonnet must be adjusted for side-to-side movement at the hinges.

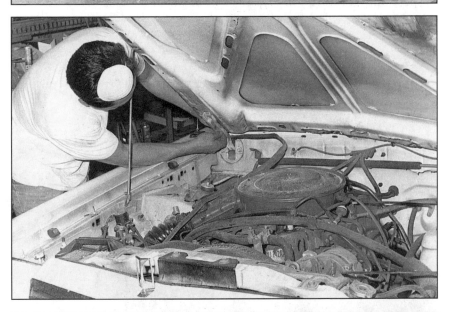

◀ A4. Adjusting a bonnet is best carried out by two people. Slacken the hinge nuts on both sides until the bonnet can **only just** be moved on its hinge adjustment. Bring the bonnet down and pull the panel one side or the other until the gap between it and the wings is the same on both sides and at the rear. Take care that the bonnet doesn't foul the firewall/bulkhead panel as it is lifted up.

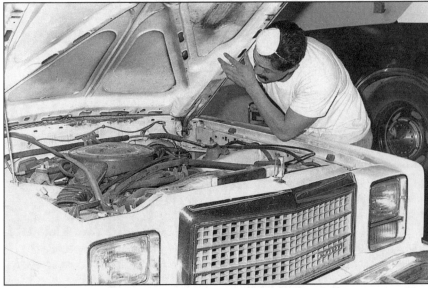

◀ A5. If the bonnet is low at the rear, lift both sides up on the adjustment so that when it is closed both rear corners are too high. Then gently press each side down until the correct level is attained, reopen the bonnet and retighten. If any of the bump rubbers are missing from the inside of the wing rain channel, they should be replaced because they also help determine the correct position of the bonnet.

WING

Many American cars have wings with adjustment brackets, which enables them to be moved around to give the best obtainable fit. However, many American and European cars' wings are welded on and there is, of course, nothing that can be done once they are in place, which makes it essential that they are fitted up around other panels, such as doors and bonnet in the first place. Bolt-on wings without special adjustments can be adjusted by filing out the holes through which the fixing bolts fit. It means that a great deal of time has to be spent putting on and taking off the panel until the fit is acceptable.

DOORS

Doors generally have some adjustment built into the points where the hinges join the hinge pillar and the door itself. It is not possible, of course, to adjust welded-on door hinges. The position of the door striker plate is critical to the fit of a door, both in the up-down plane and as far as door protrusion is concerned. Never try to fit a door accurately without the sealing rubbers in place as they can make a large difference to the fit. The same procedure applies to the boot lid, too.

If you come across a door which is twisted, so that when it is flush at, say, the top-rear, it is proud or low at the bottom-rear, you can usually twist it back quite easily, although the method sounds quite brutal! Place a block of wood between the door and the surface against which it closes, behind the rear corner where it is low. Shut the door against the wood and spring the high corner of the door inwards, taking the twist out of the door.

If a welded-on door or one without front-end in-and-out adjustment is fitted and the leading edge is below the level of the wing, you can level it up in a similar way. Place the block of wood between the front edge of the door and the door pillar and push the door as if to close it. (Don't push too hard!). The leverage on the door will spring the front of the door outwards but because you can easily overdo it, do it a little at a time.

TRIM

▲ A6. Bumpers, grilles and the like should always be polished before refitting because it is easier to be thorough that way. Be prepared to open out fixing holes in grilles or to adjust bumper brackets so that the trim looks even and square-on.

REPAIRING ALLOY WHEEL DAMAGE

If you have a damaged alloy wheel, or you are missing essential wheel bolt or nut components you *must* use the right ones! You may need to consult an alloy wheel specialist, such as A1 Wheel Renovation – see illustration AW7.

▲ AW1. It's all too easy to scuff an alloy wheel on the kerb but, provided there's no structural damage, repairs can be carried out reasonably economically. Tony Mousley of mobile paint and plastics specialists, Paint Technik, demonstrates how he carries out such a repair.

▲ AW2. This is the sort of job for which the Dremel is almost heaven sent! For very light damage, you may even be able to get away with using the polisher from the kit and polishing the damage out. No matter where the damage has occurred, the Dremel has enough different shapes and size of tool to enable you to reach it.

▲ AW3. Tony uses his to sand off the raised areas of aluminium.

▲ AW4. He then uses a special type of filler, available from most auto accessory stores, for filling aluminium.

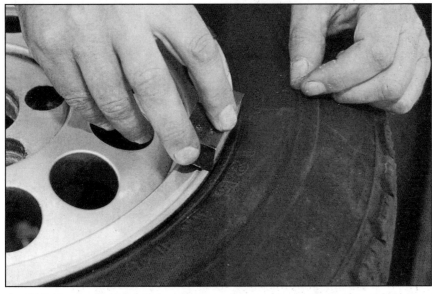

▲ AW5. Tony's experience helps him to sand the repair area down to match the original profile precisely.

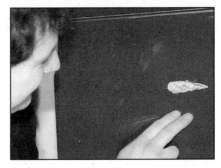

▲ SDR1. A small gouge or dent such as this one can ruin the overall appearance of your car – but be warned! If you carry out a poor quality repair you could make matters worse rather than better. Follow the advice given here and allow yourself plenty of time and you shouldn't go wrong.

▲ AW6. Part of the Paint Technik armoury is the ability to make exact paint matches and Tony uses one of the standard colours to complete the wheel's refurbishment. You should be able to buy a brand of paint which will give a pretty good match. Note that Tony has taken a lot of trouble to mask off the tyre and this is a key element in producing a professional-looking job.

▲ AW7. A1 Wheel Renovation can take a damaged wheel, weld damaged areas, refinish the surface and powder coat and lacquer the surface, so that they will last as long as new wheels. Leading wheel expert Roy demonstrates the difference!

▲ SDR2. It's not economical to consider carrying out extensive repairs from a can but for a small area, you may wish to consider using aerosols. These have the advantage that you don't have to lay out a lot of money on equipment but it won't be quite so easy to get a good result. However, if you buy the correct range of products, you'll stand a better chance of getting it right.

▶ AW8. Locking wheel nuts or bolts, new fixings and finishings can all be supplied by the impressive A1 Wheels!

▶ SDR3. The first job is to completely mask off the damaged area. This will keep dust away (it puts in a reappearance when you are applying the paint!), and prevents any risk of overspray.

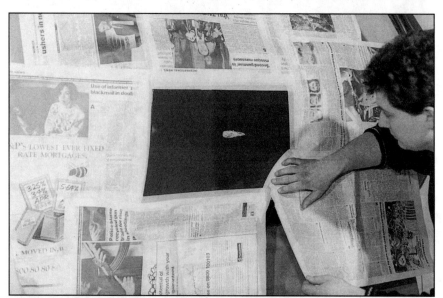

▲ SDR4. The next job is to use a sanding disc on a rubber backing pad and remove the paint from the area of the dent and the surrounding area.

▲ SDR5. Mix filler, trying to judge how much you will need (it comes with experience!) and only apply the correct amount of hardener. As a guide, the amount of hardener supplied is meant to match the quantity of filler in the can. Try to mix pro-rata. If, in hot weather, the filler goes off too quickly, cut back on the hardener next time round. It's important to mix filler on something like a flexible plastic board rather than anything fibrous, or the fibres of card, or whatever, will get into the filler mix.

▲ SDR6. Apply filler to the area of the repair and then sand it down.

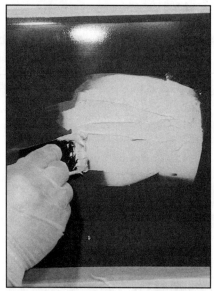

▲ SDR7. You never, ever have the right amount of filler first time, so be prepared to apply more filler, sand and continue to repeat the process . . .

▲ SDR8. . . . until the area can be sanded level. Note – not at this stage **smooth** but **level**. Smooth comes later!

▲ SDR9. After sanding the filler level, there will invariably be pin holes and other low areas. You could use filler but you would be strongly recommended to use something finer, such as stopper to spread over the pin holes before sanding off with a finer grade of paper.

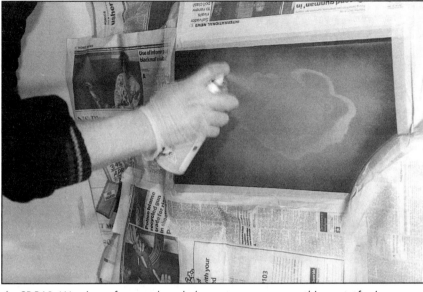

▲ SDR10. Wearing a face mask and gloves, spray on a very thin coat of primer. When it is dry, add another coat, and then another, until the colours of the panel and the filler beneath no longer show through.

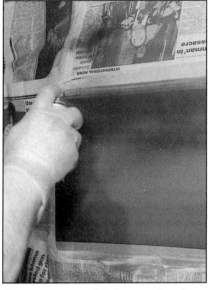

▲ SDR14. . . . and make sure that the first coat is a very thin one, otherwise the paint will run. Note the way that the can is being moved in straight, horizontal lines from left to right.

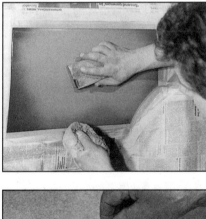

◀ SDR11. You can now sand the repair area down with a fine grade of wet-or-dry paper, as used here or, better still . . .

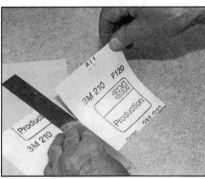

▲ SDR12. . . . use some of the white silicon carbide paper such as that produced by 3M. This has the advantage of not needing water to stop it from clogging and not adding water means that no moisture will be trapped in the primer, leading to micro-blisters forming under the paint the next time the car is left out in freezing weather. Tear it to the required size, using a steel rule.

▲ SDR13. Note that the correct way to press down an aerosol can is with the finger **not** sticking out over the front of the nozzle. Otherwise, paint will build up on the end of your finger and droplets will be blown on to the job, spoiling the finish. It pays to practise spraying first, holding the can about 10in (250mm) away from the surface and moving the can in a steady fashion. There's no point practising on paper or card because you won't find out how easy it is for paint to run. Practice on a piece of scrap steel . . .

▲ SDR15. Each coat must be allowed to dry off thoroughly before applying the next one. You will probably need to apply six, and possibly up to ten coats, to achieve decent coverage. Take care not to cause runs or sags. The first are avoided by not holding the can too close or moving too slowly; the second by allowing the paint to dry off thoroughly between coats. Be patient!

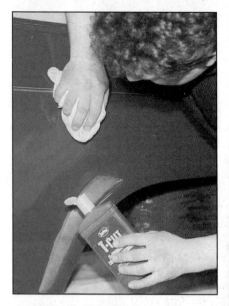

▲ SDR16. With very great care, an invisible repair can be achieved but note that you will have to use a very fine grit paper – about 1,000 grit – to flat the edges of the repair so that the new paint blends into the original paintwork. You can then polish the whole repair with an abrasive such as T-Cut. Note that you will need to leave the paint to harden off for at least a week, if not longer, before cutting it back and polishing it.

'MOBILE' DENT REPAIRERS

▲ DR1. When I caused this nasty looking dent to the rear door of my wife's car, I was less than popular! The paint was undamaged but there was a nasty vertical crease where I had cracked the door against a lamppost. Normally, a repair of this sort would involve stripping down the door and panel beating it or masking it off, filling it and rubbing it down as shown in the previous section, Small Dent Repair.

▲ DR2. When I heard that there are companies who will carry out 'magic' repairs to panels of this sort, with no dismantling, I was mightily relieved! I wasn't sure that it could be done, but the man from Dentmaster proved me wrong! He started by identifying high spots and skilfully tapping them down with a pointed nylon tool.

▼ DR3. He then inserted a specially shaped tool into the door panel, through the glass aperture and proceeded to lever, pry, twist and turn, pushing the dent out a little at a time.

▲ SDR17. A final note: if you are repairing aluminium or zinc-coated bodywork, you will not be able to use ordinary car body filler. If you try to do so, everything will seem fine at first but it will not adhere properly and it will crack and eventually drop out. You must use a proprietary type of filler for this kind of surface, such as the Würth product shown here.

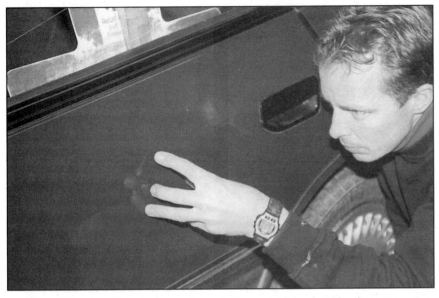

▲ DR4. He used touch rather more than sight to establish when the dent was perfectly removed . . .

▲ DR5. . . . and then polished the surface of the dent – or where it had been! – to get rid of any tiny blemishes on the surface of the paint.

◀ DR6. After a quick polish, there was absolutely no trace of my ghastly mistake. Although this is essentially a DIY manual, this is one instance where I think it would be best to consider using a professional service such as Dentmaster to carry out the work for you. There is no doubt that a good deal of skill comes into this and a poorly trained or disreputable specialist could no doubt fail to do the work as well as this – but boy, was I relieved!

AGREED VALUE INSURANCE

If you own a classic car and you take out the right kind of insurance, you might not need to carry out your own accident damage repairs!

Classic car insurance is usually cheaper than that for modern cars. This is because classic vehicles are generally used less than the main family vehicle and are used with extra care, making them a good risk. Naturally enough, there will be some restrictions to enable you to allow for classic car insurance. For instance, Hastings Direct specify that the car must be at least 15 years old (other companies have different age limits) and there are certain maximum mileage restrictions, but the lower the mileage the lower the premium, in general.

Steve Hudson, at Hastings Direct, advises that there is a cardinal rule that must be remembered when insuring your classic vehicle: 'Make sure you can agree the value of your vehicle with your insurers. It's the only way to protect your investment, should the worst come to the worst.'

If your vehicle is eligible, you really should consider taking out an agreed-value classic car insurance policy.

Bodywork repairs – Part II

USING BODY FILLER

Plastic body filler is one of the most useful materials around when it comes to repairing car bodywork. Unfortunately, it's gained itself a lousy reputation, mostly because the stuff is so good, so effective and so easy to use that a number of folk have been known to misuse it. Filler can be applied over any surface that will support it until it goes hard – and that *includes* rusty metal, or even a hole shored up with newspaper! Used properly, though, it's an absolute godsend.

First of all, it's worth mentioning that there are one or two places where it is best not to use plastic filler, because of the relatively brittle nature of the stuff. It is best kept away from the edges of door and door pillars, and any other part of the car with an exposed edge that might get chipped. Also it's no use expecting it to bridge a hole structurally unsupported. Finally, it *won't* hold back rust for more than a few winter weeks because it is porous.

On the other hand, it is stronger than most people realise and it clings very tenaciously to the surface, right up to the point where the surface may receive collision damage. There is no reason to believe that filler will ever lift or flake from a well-prepared surface, provided that the following rules are followed.

There are basically two kinds of filler in common use. One is a simple, smooth paste; the other contains chopped strands of glass-fibre which gives it a great deal of strength. You should always wear an efficient particle mask when sanding filler, especially when machine sanding, but a mask is ESSENTIAL when sanding filler with chopped glass strands in it.

PREPARATION

The first job is to wipe the damaged area with a spirit wipe, or a rag dampened with paint thinners. This removes all traces of contamination which is *not* completely removed by sanding, but which is often just stirred around by it, so that it pops up later and ruins the paint finish. Then, using a sanding disc in a drill or a mini-grinder, the paint should be sanded from the area being filled. (If you intend filling a rusted-out area, be aware of the fact that the repair will only be temporary, and take a look at *'Repair on a shoestring'* for project ideas.)

USE

Open the can of filler and if there are pools of liquid on the top mix it well. Use a clean plastic spreader with a dead-smooth edge and take a dollop of filler from the can. Place it on a smooth, clean surface and next to it, squeeze the right amount of hardener from the tube supplied. (Read the maker's instructions for advice on quantities.) The quality of the filler will be reduced if you use too much hardener and one maker's hardener may not work with another's filler which can leave you with a very sticky problem on your hands, and on your car, too!

Mix the filler and hardener very thoroughly and spread the paste over the repair. If you're not sure whether you are too high or too low, use a throw-away straightedge (eg the back of an old hacksaw blade) to gauge the correct amount. You will almost never get it right first time, so don't even try: make the first coat a foundation, with its high points as high as you want to go.

The important thing about filler is that it hardens by chemical action rather than drying by evaporation so there is little shrinkage and everything happens much more quickly. The filler should go off (hard) in around 20 minutes, to the point where you can't scratch it with your nail. When it's hard, take off the highest peaks and test the surface with a straightedge. Judge where the low-spots are and apply more filler.

BUT: Don't use the same scraper without thoroughly cleaning it; don't use the same mixing surface even if it looks clean because it will pick up hard bits which scour across the surface; and don't scoop out more filler with a dirty spreader.

Filler that hasn't gone off can get into the tin and set off all the material in a couple of days, or bits can get into the filler.

Sanding at this stage can be with a single-cut file or 40 grit paper. Go through the sanding/rubbing routine until you have the level where you want it, bearing in mind the advice on sanding flat in the two project chapters mentioned. Finally, use a cellulose or 2-pack stopper to get rid of the finest blemishes. Spread it on like ordinary filler but much thinner. Give cellulose stopper plenty of time to dry, because it dries by evaporation but 2-pack stopper is really a 'thinner' version of body filler. Both are about the consistency of face cream or margarine.

Two points that the first timer often gets wrong: don't use filler to try to get rid of high spots in metal by building up all around them. The result will look absolutely awful, so have the courage to tap the high spot down first. And when you're sanding filler, try to sand right across it. It's easy to make the outsides of the filler look level with the surrounding area but to leave a mound in the middle, which will stand out like a Dutch mountain when the car has been painted.

▲ *BF1. Filler must be mixed throroughly with its hardener before use. Only experience can tell you exactly how much hardener to use at a given temperature so, if you are a beginner, mix a relatively small amount at a time. Care taken when spreading the filler can save a lot of material, a lot of nuisance from dust, and a great deal of time and effort.* **Always follow the manufacturer's safety advice supplied** *– wear gloves.*

▲ *BF2. A single cut file is an excellent tool for removing filler quickly, and without the health hazards associated with the use of power tools. Also, it clogs a great deal less readily than the standard metal worker's bench file.*

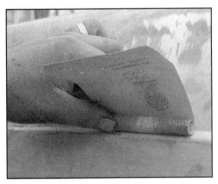

▲ *BF3. Where filler has been used in the area of a body moulding, a rolled-up piece of abrasive paper is often perfect for retaining the shape when rubbing down.*

USING BODY SOLDER

Have you ever wondered what the professional body repairer did before the days of plastic filler? In fact he did use a 'filler' of sorts for smoothing out ripples and shallow dents, and that filler was a far stronger substance than today's more common substitute. Old style filler, known as body solder, consists of an alloy of lead and tin and has the effect of strengthening repairs, unlike plastic filler which simply sits on top of them.

Most people have seen molten electrical solder and will know that it runs as freely as water. How then can body solder be persuaded to stay on vertical surfaces without simply running in an expensive stream onto the floor? The answer lies in the properties which tin and lead develop once they are alloyed together. Tin has a melting point of 450°F (232°C) and lead melts at 620°F (377°C). Whenever tin and lead are mixed together, however, the melting point of the resulting alloy is considerably lower than that of lead. Also, body solder, having a combination of 30% tin and 70% lead (and thus commonly known as 30/70 solder) has the remarkable property of going into a plastic almost putty-like, state at around 360°F (180°C) and staying like that right up to a temperature of around 500°F (260°C) at which temperature it turns to a liquid.

This means that body solder can be spread around like butter if it is kept within this temperature range, but of course, there is rather more to it than that ...

WHERE TO BODY SOLDER

There's no doubt that body solder is greatly superior to plastic filler in many respects though its advantages are often exaggerated. Plastic filler has earned some of its bad reputation for the paradoxical reason that it is so good! It can be used over any surface and so it's frequently used to patch rusty holes which, of course, break right through again. Body solder can't be used in this way. When plastic filler is used over totally sound metal however, it has excellent qualities. So, unless you are an out and out traditionalist, you will probably want to use body solder only in those places where it will do most good. The joint between two panels is one ideal place because the solder will run into the joint and both strengthen it and – more importantly – help to seal it against further corrosion. Another perfect place is where steel has become pitted on one side through corrosion, without having broken through. Here, the corrosion is sandblasted clear then the pitted area built up with body solder. A third area which is perfect for the use of the material is where a corner of a bonnet, or some other small projection, is completely missing. Again the area has to be completely cleared of any corrosion and this time a great deal of solder has to be used in one spot in order to build up sufficient material.

It has been emphasised several times already that the surface of the steel has to be thoroughly cleaned before soldering. This is because the solder will just not stick to steel that is not both chemically and physically clean. One of the strengths of solder is that it combines *chemically* with the surface of the steel, while plastic filler just sticks on top. If any contamination is left, it forms a barrier which prevents the process taking place.

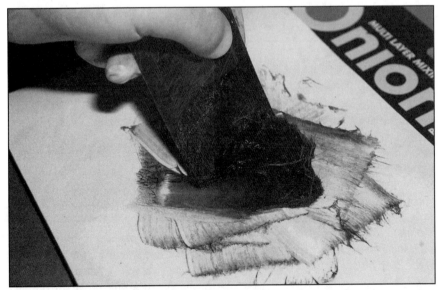

▲ *BF4. This is filler with chopped 'glass strands in it, to give additional strength. Any old, clean lids, can sides or pieces of stiff card can be used as a mixing board.* **Safety note** – *again, wear gloves.*

HOW TO BODY SOLDER

▶ BS1. On the right are shown a few sticks of 30/70 solder, next is a pot of solder paint and a brush. On the right is a stainless steel spatula used for spreading the solder while in between is the booklet supplied by the small UK firm, Radlen Body Products, which supplied all of the items shown here as a complete kit. Each of the materials shown can be purchased individually from paint factors and a spatula could be made from a piece of smooth wood. Since tin became one of the world's semi-precious metals, body solder has become expensive.

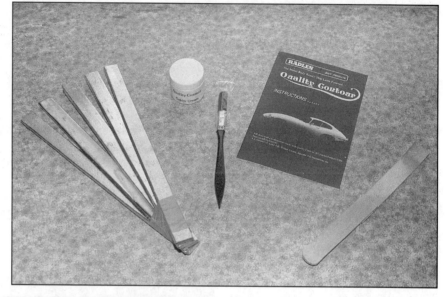

◀ BS2. This is an ideal place for the use of body solder. Here a classic car's wing has been repaired using three separate repair sections. One is a replacement wheel arch panel while the others complete the front and rear of the wing. Each panel was joined to the others via a 'step' in the adjoining panel so that there was a small overlap but the panels lay flush with one another. This left panels which lay beautifully flat and true but with joints that would be susceptible to corrosion in several years time, unless something was done about it.

◀ BS3. That something, at least as far as the outsides of the panel were concerned, was to lead load it. Before that could be done, the joint was thoroughly cleared of any of its protective paint with a spot sandblaster run from a standard compressor. This scoured out all of the paint right from inside the joint and also removed any traces of rust that might have developed. If no sandblaster is available, it is important to spend some time scraping and sanding every bit of corrosion out of the joint, otherwise the solder just won't take.

▲ BS4. The paint also was cleared off, about an inch or so back from the joint, using a medium grit sanding disc – until all traces of paint were removed. Paint can also be removed by heating it until it curls and then scraping off while it is still soft. Either the welding torch can be used with a soft flame to remove the paint or a butane torch, the sort that is mounted on top of a disposable cartridge, could be used.

Quite often, when metal has been dented or rippled it is extremely difficult to sand all of the paint or corrosion off the surface. A useful tip is to take a sanding disc and cut it into a square or an octagon shape. Then the 'points' of the shape will reach down into the concave parts of the panel.

▲ *BS6. The next step is to play a flame over the solder paint until the solder 'flushes'. In other words, the solder has to be melted at which point it flows across the surface of the steel. The point at which this takes place should be fairly obvious because the dull matt grey of the solder paint will be replaced by the silvery gleam of fresh solder. A common mistake when carrying out this job for the first time, especially for those who are used to welding, is to apply too much heat too rapidly. The biggest risk comes when a welding torch is being used, simply because there is so much heat 'on tap'. If the metal is overheated, the flame will burn the flux away and oxidise (blacken) the surface of the steel before the solder has had a chance to melt. If you intend using a welding torch, choose a medium nozzle, have a 'soft' flame (oxygen turned down a little) and play the heat lightly over the job from a respectful distance, not up close such as when you are welding.*

▲ *BS5. Old-timers would 'tin' the surfaces of the steel before starting to load the solder. This has the effect of putting a thin coat of solder all over the surface onto which the solder can be built up. Steel does not have the same ideal affinity for solder as copper, for example, so the tinning process must be carried out thoroughly. The old-style way of doing it was to coat the surface of the steel in flux first of all. Flux is necessary to stop the surface of the steel going black as it oxidises (reacts with the air); it melts at a lower temperature than solder, runs over the surface and keeps the air out long enough for the solder to flow over the steel and combine with it. Here, in the picture, you can see an alternative to flux and stick solder being used. Solder paint is being brushed onto the surface of the joint. This is simply flux in which powdered solder is held in suspension. Naturally it has to be stirred well before use because the solder grains tend to sink to the bottom, then it should be painted onto the surface fairly heavily.*

▲ *BS7. No matter how hard you try to clean the metal, there will almost certainly be some impurities left – so it's a good job that flux has a slight cleaning action to go with its ability to keep oxygen out. As a result, the flux throws up a small quantity of black waste on to the surface. This must be removed thoroughly before attempting to add any more body solder. The flux itself is water soluble and so it can be removed along with the waste by scrubbing it with a wet rag.*

▲ BS8. The next stage is just a little bit tricky to master and involves one of those sets of actions where you have to do and think about two different things at once. (After a while, of course, it becomes automatic – do you remember the first time you drove a car and how you seemed to have to do so much all at the same time?) The blowtorch has to be used to heat the panel over an area which covers no more than, say, the size of a playing card. At the same time, the solder has to be held on the edge of the flame so that it is being pre-heated, but not by enough to melt it. When, after a minute or two, you judge that the panel is hot enough, try pressing the end of the solder stick onto the joint. If everything is ready, the solder will become droopy and waxy and at the same time stick to the tinned surface of the steel. You should now try to deposit 'dollops' of solder at close, regular intervals along the joint or across the surface of the panel. Don't even begin to think about making a smooth surface; all you are doing at this stage is heating the solder to its plastic stage (between 360–500°F; 180–260°C) and depositing the material on to the panel.

▲ BS9. The next stage is the one where you smooth the solder out. Throughout this, and indeed throughout the previous stage, it is best to have a piece of steel on the floor beneath the area being soldered. You can waste an awful lot of the stuff, especially if you are inexperienced; as has been pointed out before, it's very expensive. When you have finished, collect together all the splash shaped scraps and store it. When you have enough, make up a mould from a piece of right-angled steel and blank the ends off with lumps of ordinary household glazing putty. Put the solder scraps into a discarded can and grip the edge with a self-grip wrench. Now heat the bottom of the can with the butane torch or with a **very** soft oxy-acetylene flame (keep it moving so as not to burn through the can) then, when the solder is melted pour into your mould. Hey presto, you've got a 'free' solderstick! And you'll be amazed at how much you can save!

The spreader (or paddle) used for spreading the solder can be stainless steel, although old-timers used hardwood paddles made of beech or boxwood which they kept smooth and burnished with oil. The beginner tends to get the paddle into the flame, so perhaps stainless is best – it doesn't burn. If you look at the range of temperatures between which solder is soft, it looks pretty wide, but in practice, the range seems narrow when you're actually holding the torch. Heat a blob of solder and hold the paddle close by. Periodically, remove the flame and press down on the solder with the paddle. At first the solder will start to move but in a rather crumbly way; heat it for a little longer and it will

spread like butter on a summer's day. Heat it too far, however, and it will slip in a silvery stream onto the floor – a demoralising sight! Again, don't worry too much about having a smooth finish at this stage. Try for a consistent even thickness which is slightly proud of the surface you want to finish up with.

▲ BS10. The solder can be filed down using a body file, which is a single-cut file and thus one which resists clogging. It is easy to take off too much of the solder, especially if the file is new, because of the softness of the solder relative to the hardness of the surrounding steel. Professional body repairers often keep a semi-blunt file solely for filing body solder, just to prevent digging-in. An important safety point here is that body solder should never be removed with a power sander. The lead would become air-borne dust which could then be inhaled with HIGHLY INJURIOUS CONSEQUENCES. Filing should be done from all angles, working from the outside edges of the soldered patch if it is a large one, and working inwards. Long, smooth strokes should be used wherever there is room and just enough pressure should be used to prevent the file from skidding over the surface without touching. Final sanding of the solder should be carried out with 80 or 100 grit paper.

Where the solder is found to be a little low, you have three options open. You can follow a risky, perfectionist's path and attempt to build up more solder; you can console yourself with the thought that the joint is sound and strong and finish off with a skin of plastic body filler or, if the depression is really shallow, you could follow the path of the old timers and use a skin of cellulose putty although really this is inferior to plastic filler with no real advantages.

Finally, a tip worth remembering in connection with the heat input involved. When applying body solder to a large, flattish panel such as a door skin for example, it is easy to cause heat buckling, especially if a wide area has to be covered. Buckling can easily be prevented by having a pail of water and a rag to hand and by soldering a small area at a time then quenching it with the rag afterwards. This restricts the flow of heat through the panel and shrinks the localised area back down to its original size, provided that it has not been expanded too far.

SAFETY NOTES

When using body solder particular attention *must* be paid to the health hazards encountered when working with lead and alloys. Whilst filing and sanding you *must* always wear a face mask and the wearing of gloves is also highly recommended.

SOLDERING ALUMINIUM

Aluminium can be soldered using ordinary 30/70 solder but it has to be prepared in a rather different way. It is possible to buy a special bar of solder which has to be used for tinning the aluminium first. The surface of the aluminium has to be thoroughly cleaned up first in the usual way and then the special tinning bar is melted onto the surface of the metal. Next, a slightly strange process has to be carried out. Whilst the tinned surface is kept molten, a sharp tool such as a scriber has to be scratched vigorously all over the area which has been tinned, reaching through the molten solder and scratching through the surface of the aluminium beneath. This has the effect of scratching away the outer layer of the aluminium while giving oxides no chance whatever to form and allowing the special tinning aluminium to combine with and key into the metal. From then on, the process is exactly the same as in using body solder on steel and exactly the same materials are used.

USING METAL LOADING BODY FILLER

If you particularly want to use a metal-based filler, Classic Metal Loading Body Filler is the modern alternative to using body solder. It is used in exactly the same way as ordinary polyester filler and as such it is far easier to apply than body solder. The powdered aluminium it contains makes it harder than polyester filler and therefore it provides a tougher repair. It is also non-porous. The usual safety advice relating to polyester filler applies – it is very important not to inhale any of the dust caused while sanding.

▲ *MKL1. Metal loading filler is mixed with a hardener in the same way as polyester filler. It does, however, feel rather different as it has a stiffer consistency.*
SAFETY NOTE: *ALWAYS wear gloves when handling any type of body filler.*

REPLACING A SILL/BODY ROCKER

The usual reason for replacing a sill/body rocker is because of corrosion but a part or the whole of the sill may need to be replaced because of damage.

On most cars, the sill assembly is a major structural component. Although details vary, the basic principles remain the same and are described here. Look out, on a few vehicles, for an extra inner

membrane and, on others, a jacking point built in to the bottom of the sill.

If corrosion is bad enough to have damaged the sill, be prepared to have to carry out work on surrounding areas and especially to the floor section where it is adjacent to the sill.

NOTE: Before cutting away the old sill, take a careful measurement of the door openings as shown in illustration RAS21.

▲ *RAS1. On this car, highly localised spots of rust rapidly became holes when Steve, of Kingfisher Kustoms, tapped them with his hammer. There was far less strength there than at first seemed to be the case.*

▲ *RAS2. Here, a replacement sill from SVG Ltd is offered up to the car by Steve so that he can get a feel for what needs to be cut away and what can stay. It pays to make a careful plan of action before you start!*

▶ *RAS3. With the sill temporarily clamped in place over the existing one, Steve draws around it with a scriber so that he can see where to cut.*

▲ *RAS4. This is the most tricky part and you must make sure that the bases of the 'A' and 'B' pillars are both sufficiently sound and have enough material left in them to weld strongly on to the new sill.*

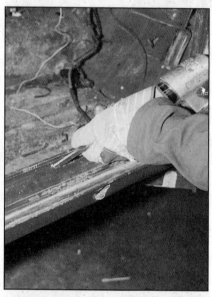

◀ *RAS6. Sills invariably join to the inner sill with a vertical flange around the door opening. Steve uses an air chisel a sharp broad-bladed bolster chisel and hammer will be just as effective if a little slower to cut all along the top of the sill . . .*

▲ *RAS5. Steve has marked a fresh cut line about 1in (25mm) in from the mark he scribed earlier. The idea is that there will be an overlap between the two panels. This is the conventional way of carrying out a repair of this sort and is best for both speed and strength. Unfortunately, the overlap in the steel may induce rust in future and some skilled and experienced welders prefer to make a butt joint, cutting the steel so that it matches edge-to-edge. But beware; it's not easy to avoid severe distortion and it is more difficult to make a strong weld.*

◀ *RAS7. . . . and when the cut is complete, the top of the sill can usually be folded down. This is because the seam at the bottom of the sill has usually corroded through to some degree. Note how vitally important it is to wear thick, industrial-strength gloves to prevent damage from all those sharp edges.*

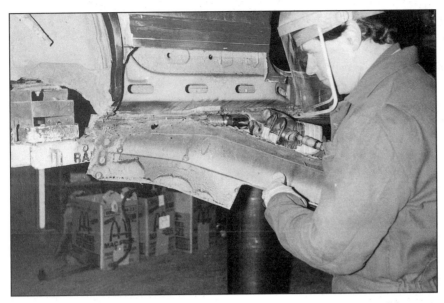

▲ RAS8. Where the bottom seam of the sill is still hanging in there, you will have to cut it away, just as you did for the top.

▲ RAS11. If this corrosion is not too severe, it is usually possible to cut away part of the inner sill, leaving the uncorroded portion in place. Do be sure to cut away every scrap of rusty steel because new rust will rapidly form where old rust is still present to provide a seed. Steve also cut away the outer edge of the floor which you can see here exposed behind the section of the inner sill which he has removed with the cutting disc on the angle grinder.

◀ RAS9. With the bulk of the sill removed, Steve found extra corrosion at the base of the inner sill and on the outer edge of the floor. This latter area is particularly important because the floor folds over to form a flange on to which both the inner sill and the bottom of the outer sill are welded.

▲ RAS10. Where an inner sill is very badly corroded, it will be necessary to fit a new one. Once again this is an SVG panel, and replacement sills are available for most models.

▲ RAS12. Steve made up a new section of floor, consisting of a strip of steel folded to a right-angle. This was welded to the underside of the floor, leaving the fold in place to form a flange to which could be fitted the new section of inner sill and the new outer sill.

▲ RAS13. The new piece of inner sill was then cut to shape, clamped in position . . .

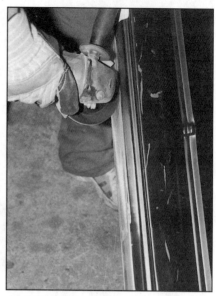

▲ RAS18. Steve takes a few moments off now to clean all the flanges on the new sill back to shiny, bright metal. Some are finished in weldable primer – check before you sand it all off! In any case, you are strongly advised to apply a coat of Würth weldable zinc primer to all the surfaces of the flanges to be welded. This will help to keep corrosion at bay and will not be burned away by the welding process.

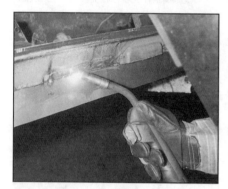

▲ RAS14. . . . and tack-welded into place. It can be seam-welded on to the inner sill but must not be welded at the ends at this stage until careful measurements have been taken across the door opening – see later.

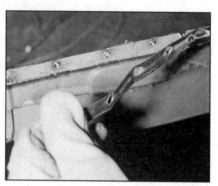

▲ RAS16. . . . which enables you to pull and chisel off the flange strip – the mortal remains of the outer sill – away from the inner sill.

▲ RAS15. All the flanges on the sill will have been spot-welded together at the factory. Use a proper spot-weld removing drill to cut through one layer.

▲ RAS17. It's best to use a sanding disc on a rubber pad to remove what is left of the spot welds, as well as any paint and rust, so that the new weld will take place between two level, clean surfaces.

▲ RAS19. Steve now pushes the new sill into place . . .

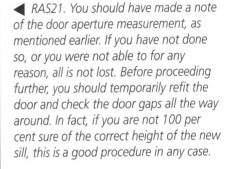 RAS20. . . . clamps it accurately into position – note that there are three thicknesses of steel to be lined up at the base of the sill – and checks that everything is true and level. It is easy to distort the sill at this stage but (and this is typical of a pattern part) you may find that there is some dressing, and even cutting and hammering to do, to make the sill fit perfectly at the 'A' and 'B' pillars.

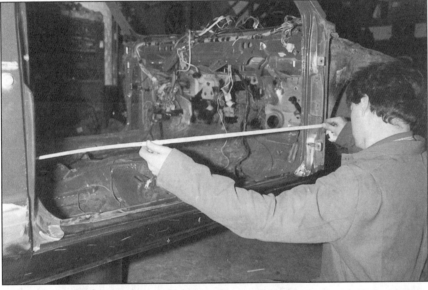

◀ RAS21. You should have made a note of the door aperture measurement, as mentioned earlier. If you have not done so, or you were not able to for any reason, all is not lost. Before proceeding further, you should temporarily refit the door and check the door gaps all the way around. In fact, if you are not 100 per cent sure of the correct height of the new sill, this is a good procedure in any case.

NOTE: This is the point in the proceedings where it pays to spend as much time as it takes to check that the sill alignment and door opening are absolutely correct. You can spend time now in clamping, unclamping and moving, tack-welding and re-checking until you are certain that everything is correct, but to have to change things later would be a very major operation!

◀ RAS22. Steve spot welds the two flanges at the top of the sill . . .

▲ RAS23. . . . and the three flanges at the bottom of the sill, using the manufacturer's original spacings between spot welds as a guide.

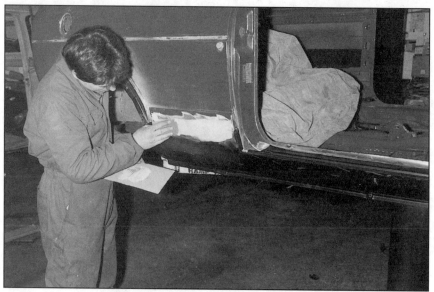

▲ RAS25. After cleaning up his MIG welds with a sanding disc on a rubber pad mounted on the mini grinder, filler is applied and rubbed down flat, as described elsewhere in this manual.

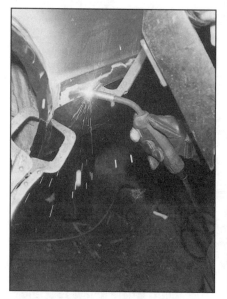

▲ RAS24. Steve had already added some extra curvature to the rear of the sill, where it fitted the rear wing so that the gap was correct, and one of the folds, around the vertical edge of the door aperture, had been remade. It is best by far to make the sill fit perfectly without forcing it into position. If forced into place, you will inevitably introduce distortion and some of the forcing will have the effect of pulling the original panel to fit the mis-shaped new one. Steve seam welds the rear of the panel in place.

▲ RAS26. This sill replacement was part of a major restoration and it was not going to be possible to paint the sill properly straight away. In such a case it is most important that primer is applied to all bare metal before fresh rust can take a hold. Otherwise, you'll be introducing the same problem that you started with!

REMOVING AND FITTING A CLASSIC CAR'S WELDED-ON WING

This 1960 Mk 1 Austin-Healey Sprite (known colloquially as the 'Frogeye' or 'Bugeye') was suffering from a severe state of corrosion in one of its rear wings. In many ways, the removal and principles involved are similar to those involved in fitting a replacement wing to a more modern car but there are significant differences worth pointing out here. The first problem is that classic cars very rarely have manufacturers' original panels available. (The exceptions to this rule are cars like the VW Beetle, the Mini and the MGB which had long production runs so that while the earlier examples are often fairly established as 'Classics', later panels can often be of use.) It is occasionally possible to pick up new panels for earlier cars from garages disposing of 'new-old' stock or from autojumbles, but you can't really bank on it. In the case of very rare and valuable cars, the only option open is to have wings specially built. This is a process beyond the scope of this book and is very skilled, labour-intensive and costly. Happily, however, more and more specialist suppliers are arranging to have panels produced in limited production runs while other manufacturers have gone into the business of making reproduction panels for a vast range of cars mainly to satisfy the demands of 'the trade'.

Wings produced by the former source are generally no-frills panels which may require some final detail work such as the cutting out and positioning of light apertures, while the latter group, the repair panels, are often crude in a different way. They are usually made to fit over existing panels (in the case of sills and chassis members) or over the remnants of wings, for instance, but not back to the manufacturer's joint line. Built to provide a cheap method of cobbling cars together where the cost of OE (Original Equipment) panels would be too high, they can be an acceptable medium-term solution to accident or corrosion problems, but they frequently do nothing to overcome inherent corrosion.

However, the main point about fitting non-OE panels of any type is that they will inevitably require some tailoring to make them fit, read on for more details!

▲ WW1. All steel wings are held on around the wheel arch by the in-turned flange which matches that on the inner wing. The drill for removal is to grind away the corner of the flange so that inner and outer panels become separated. The flange of the outer wing can be removed later as a separate strip of metal.

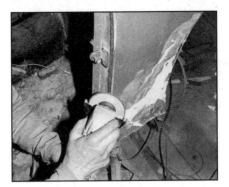

▲ WW2. Similarly, the edge of the door pillar has a flange which has to be ground away in the same way. If a rear wing is to be fitted to a saloon, a cut may well have to be made to separate the wing from the rear pillar. Carefully measure the replacement wing to determine where the cut is to be made and leave an overlap – it's easier to trim back later rather than to have to add on.

▲ WW3. There are a variety of ways of cutting sheet steel in these circumstances. Using a hare v. tortoise analogy, the Monodex cutter shown here is most definitely the tortoise; and it always gets there in the end! It's finger-achingly slow but it causes virtually no distortion whilst it carves a thin slot with its beak.

▲ WW4. Here a thin bladed bolster chisel is being used to cut 10mm or so away from the joint of the old wing. Make sure that the chisel is sharpened regularly: sharp tools are safe tools and, also, a chisel that requires less thumping with the hammer can be positioned more accurately and causes less percussion damage to the surrounding areas.

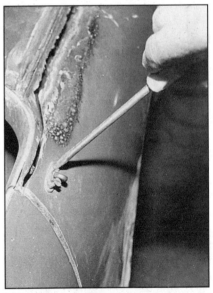

▲ WW5. It's too easy to overlook any fixtures and fittings, throw them away with the old wing and then find that they are irreplaceable. Take them off and store them safely in labelled plastic bags for easy reference, or leave them on the old wing which is retained until the job is finished.

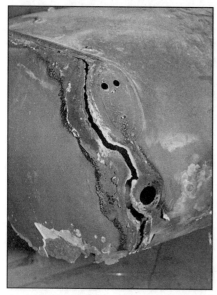

▲ WW6. At the rear of the wing things were looking a bit delicate and so, to prevent unnecessary damage, the oxy-acetylene cutting torch was used. Note that the base of the wing had corroded right out and so no cutting was needed there.

▲ WW7. The 'gas' cutting torch is used by holding it in place like an ordinary welding torch then, when the steel melts, the torch is turned at a steep angle as shown, the oxygen trigger pressed and a stream of almost pure oxygen directed through the metal. This cuts the metal rather than burning it and is capable of doing so quite neatly.

▲ WW8. As the old wing was lifted away the worst could be seen. Note that the edges of the old panel were razor sharp, especially where that had been ground away. It is always best to wear leather gloves when handling panels at this stage. Ray, one of The Classic Restoration Centre's panel beaters, whose hand is in the picture hates wearing gloves. But then they're his fingers.

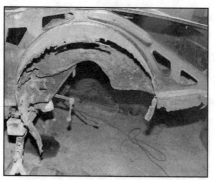

▲ WW9. The remains of the inner wing were an ugly sight. This is one of the biggest and most typical problems encountered when working on a classic. Because of the car's special interest status it will probably have had its outer panels cobbled together many times just to keep it looking good, but because of its age, the inner panels are likely to have deteriorated most severely. Before the inner panels were repaired, the rest of the old outer wing was still in place and needed to be taken off.

▲ WW10. The flange of the old wing, where it joined the two lamp mounting plates, had been spot-welded in place on the production line. The positions of the spot welds were found by finishing the surface of the steel, when they became apparent as small craters in the surface of the steel. The centre of each spot-weld was drilled out with a small drill. Sometimes the old flange comes straight off in this way but it usually needs to be helped off with a hammer and thin-bladed bolster chisel. If it seems to need a lot of bashing, you've probably missed some of the spot welds!

▲ WW11. We made a saw cut to separate the flange from the top of the top rear lamp plate. The point here is that every job is different and no prescribed pattern can be laid down for every job; you need common sense and sometimes a little ingenuity as part of your tool box. But then, that's what makes restoration so interesting!

▲ WW12. The top of the wing was joined to the inner panel by a concealed, downward turning flange which is virtually impossible to get at with a drill with the wing in place. Between the two flanges was a strip of beading and this, being part of an arc weld sandwich, had also to be drilled through.

▲ WW16. To digress at this juncture: a less severely corroded wing could have been repaired with a repair panel such as this one. Many classic cars (and non-classic) no longer have full panels available for them, but smaller repair sections are often to be had. Enquire at your local factor if the car is modern; at your specialist supplier or car club if the car is a classic.

◀ WW13. A further flange was wrapped around the outer edge of the door pillar and this too was removed after simply drilling out the spots.

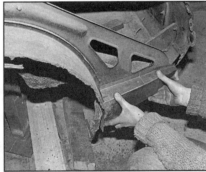

▲ WW15. The tapered box member, level with the boot floor at its top face, had totally disintegrated. It was a fairly complex shape and had to be tailored to fit the curve of the outer wing when it was fitted. The top and other surfaces were first made in card then transferred to steel. The base of the box was fitted up from the inside after the outer wing was fitted.

▲ WW17. Whether a repair panel or full panel is being used, the inner wing has to be repaired just the same. The easiest way to do so when no repair panel is available is to cut a piece of plywood around 10mm thick into the same curve as the wheel arch. Then use the plywood as a former around which a strip of steel can be folded – grip the steel to the ply with a series of self-grip wrenches. Make the sections in a number of short length pieces; it's easier to fold, easier to fit and more economical with the steel sheet that way.

▲ WW14. This trim strip was held on with a series of small nuts and bolts, most of which were easy to get at but one was virtually inaccessible with the wing in place. It was, of course, easy to remove with the wing taken off. It can often be easier to strip trim, mirrors and other fittings with the old wing taken off.

▲ WW18. With all the preparatory work out of the way, it's time to start fitting the wing. Offer it up and, unless it is a panel made by the original manufacturer, expect to have to carry out some tailoring.

▲ WW19. Blank plates were fitted to this wing at the positions of the rear lamps. The original plates were perfectly OK and so the spot welds holding the new plates in place were drilled out and the plates removed. The original plates were already drilled for the correct fitting of the lamps of course; the new ones would have had to have been correctly drilled and filed out.

◄ WW20. Holding the replacement wing in place can often require some ingenuity. Here a rack clamp and a pair of welding grips have been pressed into service. Self-tapping screws can be very useful for this purpose, especially if the wing is to go 'out' for its final welding into place.

◄ WW21. Underneath, the reverse flange was gripped with standard selfgrip wrenches. (The lamp is simply an owner's accessory.) This flange has to be welded up later, even though it is awkward to get at.

▲ WW22. In the final stages of fitting, the wing was tacked a few times with braze, to hold it solidly into place prior to welding. The advantage of braze tacking is that the braze can later be softened with the welding torch and the panel moved around a little if that should become necessary.

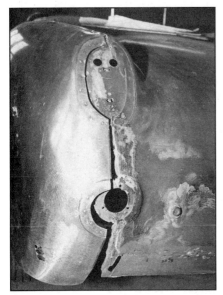

▲ WW23. Here is a typical problem with 'reproduction' panels: the bottom lamp aperture is set too low. The problem could only be overcome with a series of compromises. The braze at the top, rear was softened and the wing pushed up slightly. Then, with the wing held solidly at the top, it was carefufly raised further with the jack, so increasing the curve at the wing top. Any deficiencies that remained were made up by lead loading the area around the lamp mounting.

▲ WW25. The solution was to cut a narrow 'vee' out of the wing, to close it up until it fitted perfectly and then to MIG weld the joint back up again before finishing the weld flat.

SAFETY NOTES

When carrying out this operation it is essential to protect your hands, eyes and ears so wear good quality thick leather gloves (welding gauntlets are ideal), goggles and ear muffs – pieces of cotton wool are really not adequate. Remember the noise when grinding is tremendous and can severely damage your hearing.

Whenever possible, buy an original equipment door skin from the manufacturer rather than one from one of the many repair panel suppliers. The latter's panels are often poorly made and bear little more than a passing resemblance to the original! Skilled panel beaters can often make use of them (at the cost of considerable time) but the beginner should steer clear of them unless they are demonstrably of a good quality or unless there is no alternative.

▲ WW24. Another problem was encountered where the wing adjoined the sill. The front of the wing fitted perfectly but where it should have contacted the rearmost part of the sill it was simply too long.

RENEWING A DOOR SKIN

Replacing a door skin is a job which can be tackled by the sort of person who is serious about getting to grips with the simpler principles of panel beating but who may have done very little in the past. It involves the use of few special tools but the transformation in the appearance and structural condition of the door can be dramatic.

Professional body shops will often fit a new door skin in preference to carrying out quite minor rust or accident damage repairs to a door. The reasoning is simply that because doors consist of large, flat panels, they are difficult to make 'true' and flat again, and door skins are basically so straightforward to fit.

Basically, a door's structure is made up in two parts. The inner part (the door frame) consists of a large, pressed steel dish with a lip around three sides. The outer part (the door skin) is a more or less flat section which is placed onto the frame and the outer edges folded round.

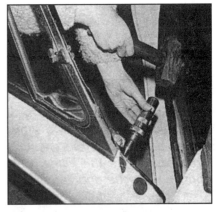

▲ DS1. Doors on older cars, such as this MGB, are often held to their hinges by three or four machine screws. They are often very tight and are best released with the aid of an impact screwdriver. Modern cars often have their hinges welded to the door or hinge post. In these cases, the hinge pins holding the two halves of the hinge together must be drifted out. It is possible to make up a drift to knock the pin part of the way out then grip it with a selfgrip wrench to complete the job. Hinge pin removal kits are available from good DIY motor factors.

◀ DS2. When you are ready to pull the door away, be prepared for its weight! This sports car door with all of its internals removed was not too bad, but a complete door from a medium sized 2-door car can be really quite heavy. It is not always necessary to strip out a door before reskinning it, but be sure to obtain new door weather seals and their clips because they attach to the skin itself.

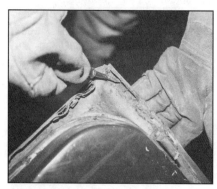

▲ DS3. Before deciding to fit a new door skin, go around the frame of the old door to make sure that it is sound enough to repair. There will always be more corrosion than you can at first see so if extensive repairs are needed to the frame, you will almost always be better off buying a new door.

▲ DS5. Steve, the body expert at Volkswagen specialist Kingfisher Kustoms, uses the new door skin as a template for marking out where the old one is going to be cut away.

▲ DS7. And, just to prove the point, Steve uses the air tool to complete the cutting away of this part of the old skin.

▲ DS4. Door skins from the original manufacturers (when available) give the best fit but can be horrendously expensive. This Golf door was fitted with a door skin from SVG Ltd in Birmingham. Good quality pattern parts are far less expensive to buy than manufacturers' parts but good quality ones, such as these, fit perfectly well.

▲ DS6. Kingfisher Kustoms normally use a power tool but here Steve demonstrates how it is possible to use hand tools for some of the work.

▲ DS8. This is how the outer edges of the skin are removed from the door frame. The Bosch angle grinder is fitted with a rubber backing pad and uses a P60 grit disc to sand through the outer edge of the skin at a 45-degree angle. Note that it isn't necessary to go all the way through all the way around and if you do, you will risk damaging part of the frame beneath.

▲ DS9. Steve goes all around the door, cutting through the skin . . .

▲ DS11. The same bolster chisel can be used to remove any sections of flange which remain in place. On the bottom of the Golf door, the skin is spot-welded to the frame rather than folded right around it. Steve has drilled through each of the spot welds and is now separating the two sections.

▲ DS10. . . . until it can be lifted away. Note that you can use a bolster chisel and hammer to cut through the skin where the sanding disc hasn't gone all the way through.

▲ DS12. The very bottom edge of the door frame was found to be rusty and in need of replacement – something that couldn't be seen when the door skin was in place. Steve completely cleaned up the flange with the sanding disc shown earlier and made up an angled repair section for the bottom of the frame.

▲ DS13. The replacement section was used to mark out the metal to be cut away and Steve can be seen here cutting away the redundant and rusty steel from the bottom of the door frame.

It is essential that you wear industrial work gloves because the steel from now on can have extremely sharp edges!

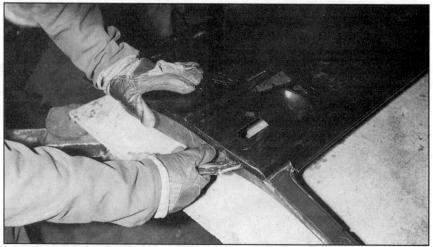

▲ DS14. Here, when welding the repair section in place, you can see a MIG welder being used to its best advantage it gives a clean weld and causes a minimal amount of distortion.

▲ DS17. You should take some time to correctly align the door skin on the door frame. Clamp it in place at strategic points around the frame.

▲ DS15. Steve recommends the use of Würth weldable zinc primer for all the bare metal areas and flanges of the door frame and skin. The extremely high zinc content gives excellent protection against corrosion.

▲ DS18. Some areas, such as at the top of the door skin, will need to be seam welded . . .

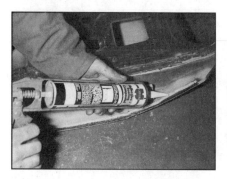

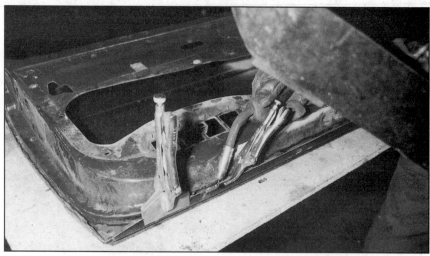

▲ DS16. Another favourite with body repairers is Würth Adhesive Sealing Compound, applied to the surfaces of any folded-over flanges. Here, the sealer is run along the flange after making the fold, and it is strongly advised that a bead of the compound is applied to the inside of the door skin before placing the door frame down on top of it.

▲ DS19. . . . while other areas will need to be spot or tack-welded, such as here at the bottom of the door.

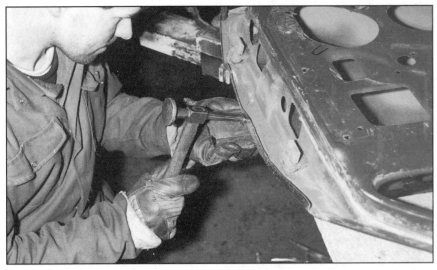

▲ DS20. Where the flange has to be folded over, the door must be placed with the skin down, with a soft surface, such as a piece of old carpet, beneath it. If you hammer the flange all the way over in one place and then work along the flange attempting to hammer the rest of it down as well, you will see ripples, folds and distortion starting to occur. Steve shows how it's done. You hammer the flange over a little say a quarter of the way over all the way along . . .

◄ DS21. . . . then take it a further quarter of the way, all the way along, followed by a 'run' of hammer blows to take it three quarters of the way over, all the time holding the metal dolly flat against the other side of the door skin, directly beneath the hammer blows. This keeps the fold tight as the metal goes over.

▲ DS22. Steve finally uses the flat of the hammer, still with the dolly held flat beneath the door skin, to produce a clean looking fold. (Sticking your tongue between the corner of your lips at this stage is optional!)

▲ DS23. All door skins have bridging pieces which need to be welded after making sure that the gap between the door skin and the door frame is parallel and correct all the way along. One of the bridging pieces can be seen here clamped up while the other is being pointed out.

▲ DS24. After using the sanding pad once again to clean up the seam weld...

▲ DS25. ...the finished door is ready for building up so that it can be fitted back on the car.

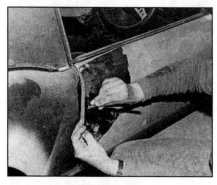

▲ DS26. Most doorskins come complete with lock and handle holes already formed. If there aren't any, a good way to ensure correct placement is to chop out a section from the old skin (avoiding distortion) and mark around the inside of the relevant holes.

▲ DS27. Suitable start holes can then be drilled and joined up to complete the desired cut out with a file.

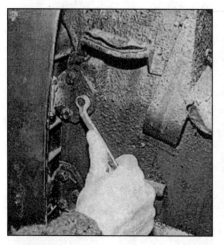

▲ DS28. Once back on the car, the door fit can be adjusted by slightly loosening the securing bolts ...

▲ DS29. ... and levering up and down ...

▲ DS30. ... and backwards and forwards with a suitable length of wood before finally retightening the bolts.

1930s BODY REPAIRS

In this section we have featured two 1930s built cars which were fairly typical of this period. The first is a 1936 Vauxhall Fourteen with Tickford convertible bodywork and the second an early 1930s Austin with Swallow bodywork. The fact that they both feature coachbuilt bodies almost certainly means there will be no new or repair panels available and so any replacement panels required will have to be specially fabricated. This is no easy task when it comes to complete new wings for instance, although with the use of modern equipment the job is made considerably less difficult. It is, however, always wise to try and retain as much original bodywork as is practically possible. In other words, try to replace just the rusted-out area of the wing rather than the entire panel. In a lot of cases, the car's simple design and the fact that there is a sturdy chassis to work from makes the job of replacing certain panels rather easier than you might at

▼ DS31. One solution, where there is insufficient hinge adjustment available, is to bend the door hinges out just enough to clear the obstruction. (It looks like a 'bodge' but is in fact standard bodyshop practice.) Place a block of wood in the gap between half opened door and hinge pillar and push the door towards the closed position. The leverage of the door acting upon the fulcrum of the wooden blocks, forces the front of the door slightly outwards.

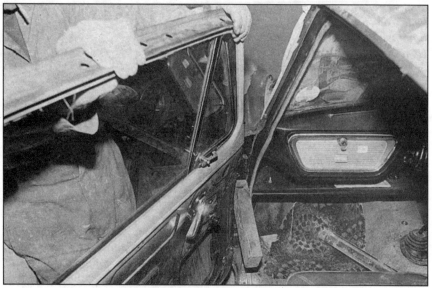

first think. The Golden Rule is not to rush into the job but to give some thought as to how the car was originally put together.

When welding in new sections of bodywork bear in mind that most cars of the 1930s, and older, will have been constructed around a wooden frame or 'tub' as it is called in the trade. There is therefore a great danger of the whole car going up in flames as soon as the welding torch is held near it! As with all welding tasks it is (especially so in this case) most important that you have an effective fire extinguisher close to hand. (See *Safety notes* in Chapter 1).

▲ *OT1. This was potentially one of the most difficult areas of the Vauxhall's bodywork to restore. The rear inner wheel arch is double-skinned in this area and corrosion has obviously started through the ingress of water between the panels.*

▲ *OT2. With the wing removed a heat gun is used to soften the old underseal and make it easier to scrape away ...*

▲ *OT3. ... whereupon we found this aluminium plate which was pop-riveted over more corrosion.*

▲ *OT4. We decided that, in this case, the easiest course of action was to remove the entire inner wheel arch, first of all drilling out the screws in the rail running alongside the chassis.*

▲ *OT5. An angle grinder is used to cut through the inner wheel arch, being very careful not to grind into the wood frame, whilst leaving a flange of at least an inch to enable the wheel arch to be screwed into the wood frame.*

▼ *OT6. The first skin of the inner wheel arch can then be removed. It must be stressed that, particularly when working with old rusty steel, the wearing of heavy-duty gloves is strongly recommended.*

▲ OT7. Having taken out the other fixing screws on the inside, the remainder of the wheel arch assembly could be removed. Notice how the panel has all but disintegrated along the 90° flange.

▲ OT11. The side of the new inner wheel arch panel is then clamped into its correct position and checked for fitting.

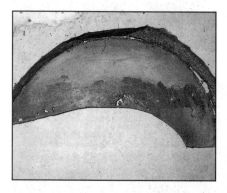

◄ OT8. The horrible remains! It would have been an impossible task to have made a satisfactory repair with the panel still in place on the car.

▲ OT12. With the panel removed, the next job is to spot-weld the horizontal sections to the flange. Again this process should be done gradually with a few spot-welds initially holding the horizontal sections to the flange and then working around the panel filling in the gaps, leaving a space of about one inch between spot-welds.

▲ OT10. With the side of the inner wheelarch carefully cut out using this chipboard template, the 90° flange has to be made along the outer edge. Having secured the panel with welding clamps to the chipboard template a panel beating hammer is used. Working along the edge several times, the 90 degree flange is gradually folded over. It is important to create the fold a little at a time to avoid the possibility of the folded-over edge stretching and wrinkling. The motto is: 'A little at a time!'

▲ OT9. Here is a plasma cutter being used to cut out the sections which make up the new inner wheel arch. There is so little heat build-up that even this plastic ruler could be used as a guide for a straight cut. The result leaves a very clean edge with no signs of distortion whatsoever.

◄ OT13. Offer up the complete new inner wheel arch to the car and ...

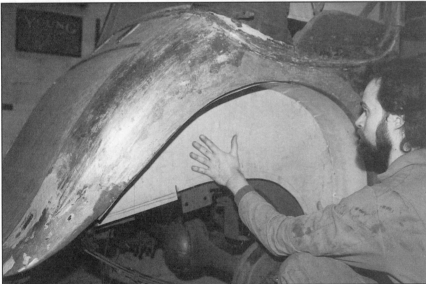

◄ OT14. ... push it firmly into place. We drilled the side of the inner wheel arch and screwed it to the side-rail, just as it was originally secured. We also decided to drill and screw the panel to the wood frame of the car which runs around the length of the wheel arch.

◄ OT15. Finally, a trial fitting of the rear wing was carried out to see how the wing fitted against the wheel arch.

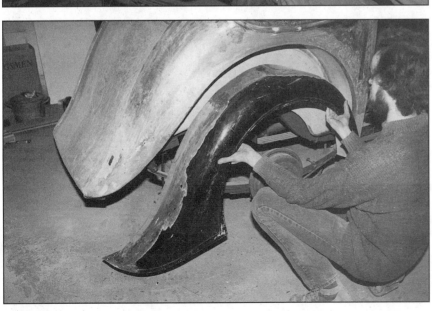

▲ OT16. The bottom corners of both windscreen pillars on the Vauxhall were found to be rather corroded. After the removal of several layers of polyester filler, the corroded steel was cut away and small repair sections ...

▲ OT17 ... gas welded into place. The windscreen was offered up to make sure the curvature of the repair was correct before finally welding. It is always advisable to wear heavy duty leather gloves when carrying out any welding operations

▲ OT18. The bottom of the bulkhead and footwell area on the Vauxhall, and this applies to nearly all 1930s built cars, is particularly vulnerable to rust as it is exposed to road dirt and stones thrown up by the front wheels. An angle grinder is used to cut the corroded section out, followed by ...

▲ OT19. ... using a bolster chisel to cut through the bottom edge.

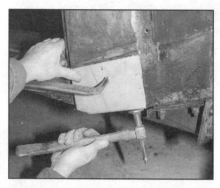

▲ OT20. A repair panel was fabricated and clamped into position. Using a panel beating hammer the repair panel was adjusted to give a close fit.

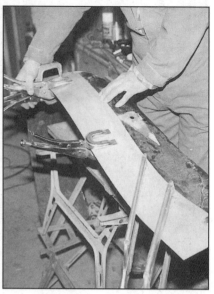

▲ OT22. The screwed-on rear wings on the Vauxhall are typical 1930s and therefore they are very easily removed for any repair work. Here the repair panel is securely clamped over the rusty area on the rear wing.

▲ OT21. Once the repair panel has been adjusted to exactly the shape required, it can be welded into position. It is important, particularly with MIG welding, that any surface-corroded bodywork you are welding to is thoroughly cleaned up using an angle grinder with a coarse sanding disc fitted.

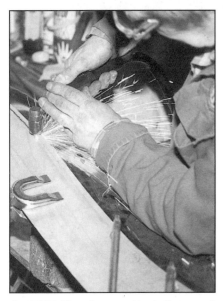

▲ OT23. The plasma cutter is then used to cut right through both the repair section and the wing itself. In this way the repair can be butt-welded in place which makes for a neater finished result.

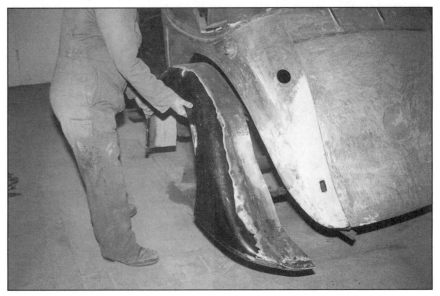

▲ OT25. With the repair section welded in position the wing is offered up to the car's bodywork and checked for fitting. Any minor adjustments can be made by panel beating the repair to achieve a close fit. Note that some brazing was also needed on the trailing edge of this wing to build it up to the correct shape.

▲ OT24. The repair section is first tack-welded to the wing along its entire length followed by in-filling between the tack-welds. The best policy is not to do a continuous run of weld but to leave a space between welds, going over to the other end of the repair whilst the first weld is cooling down. By using this method, distortion will be kept to an absolute minimum.

▲ OT26. Both front wings on the Vauxhall had corroded where they are joined together by means of this small bracket, directly below the radiator shell.

▲ OT27. The rusted metal was cut away and repair sections fabricated and welded into position. It was necessary to leave a flange on the lower edge of the repair to enable the bracket to be bolted to the wings and thus hold them securely together. This is typical of how many of your own 'bits and pieces' you have to fabricate when working on most older or rarer cars.

▲ OT31. ... but there's no reason why you should not be able to find a specialist capable of making the sections, leaving you to jigsaw-piece them back together. This repair section was made in two pieces, then spotwelded together: a case of modern equipment making an old-fashioned job so much easier!

▲ OT28. This early-1930s Austin with Swallow bodywork, belonging to Paul Skilleter, one-time Managing Editor of Practical Classics magazine, was beautifully built but ravaged by time. The rear wing, for instance, had rotted badly at its leading edge, near where it met the running board.

◀ OT29. Here, a repair patch has been made up, faithfully following the lines of the old wing, and the old rot has been cut away. Thicker steel can be used than on modern cars, to match the original, and that makes the job of welding so much easier.

▲ OT32. One of the front wings had gone right through where the tyre had rubbed against the wing on full lock. A piece was cut out with oxy-acetylene and a new one made up and welded straight in with butt-joints.

◀ OT30. Complex shapes such as these have to be produced on a piece of specialist equipment known as a wheeling machine. This work is really beyond the scope of the amateur ...

SECOND-HAND PARTS

SALVAGING A PANEL

Owners of rare or classic cars may not be strangers to the need to salvage what they can from spare parts. For this sequence the author can be seen using the small, handy but powerful welding set supplied by The Welding Centre.

▲ SP1. This is the remains of a scrapped Austin-Healey 'Frogeye' Mk 1 Sprite bodyshell. The only panel worth having from it was the rear centre panel, the place where the boot goes on most cars. This type of panel has no value if you don't need it, but for the person who wanted this particular one, it was invaluable; how else could you obtain one for such an old car other than from a scrapped car? Before removing a scrap panel, note carefully how it is fitted to its surround parts. Obviously it is better to cut too much metal away rather than risk ruining a hard-to-find part.

▲ SP2. Here the Welding Centre's kit really comes into its own. It's so light and easy to carry that it can be taken to the most inaccessible car. Make certain that there is no fuel tank nor any other combustibles around before starting work. Here the author is cutting using a welding torch; it is possible if it's all you've got but it is slow. Start by melting a hole in the metal then turn the oxygen up a long way, when you will be able to cut after a fashion.

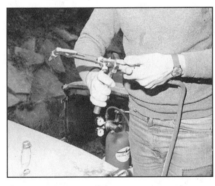

▲ SP3. You can fit a cutter onto the torch in place of the welding nozzle. See the appropriate section for more information on how to use a cutter.

▲ SP4. The only additional point to make regarding cutting technique is to tilt the flame in the direction you are travelling when cutting thin steel. This cut is being made about 1 inch (2cm) outside the flange holding the rear panel in place; in fact the wing is being cut through. The rear light housings were cut out complete; you can decide how much to trim off later.

▲ SP5. The whole rear panel is lifted away in one complete section. Although the rest of the car was a rotten hulk, this panel was sound at the base where they usually rot. Moral: just because your car has rotted in a certain place, don't assume that all the cars in the breaker's yard will have corroded in the same place. There can be remarkable differences between different cars, even those of the same model year.

FITTING A SALVAGED PANEL

Cars can corrode in some of the most ridiculous and unpredictable places! This Citroën Dyane was a very sound car in every area except its windscreen lower surround. There, corrosion had eaten right through the steel allowing torrents of water to come cascading into the car. One solution would have been to purchase a complete front panel from Citroën, but to let the whole panel in would have been an unnecessary extravagance and, in any case, the panel may not have included the dash top panel which was badly corroded. The answer chosen here was to visit a breaker's yard and find a Dyane with no corrosion in this area. The task proved simple as Dyanes rarely rot out in this area – and that's the whole point of this section. Cutting out a repair patch from a scrap car can save you a lot of money and you can also make sure that you get all the bits you need rather than the bits the manufacturer may have needed when the car was being produced.

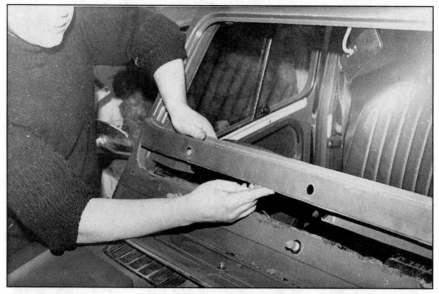

▲ SP7. This is the salvage panel removed from the scrap car. It had been cut out quite a lot bigger than it was required to be (see section on cutting out a salvage panel) and was then accurately cut back to a trim line (to disguise the welding) and to a width which suited the area of corrosion involved.

◀ SP8. The repair patch was seated well down onto the panel it was to replace, and the outer edges scribed around carefully. The panel did not go down quite far enough but that didn't matter at this stage because the panel that was in its way was going to have to be cut out anyway.

▲ SP6. The windscreen lower panel had rotted through to an alarming degree. The corrosion had not seemed to be anything like this bad until the windscreen had been taken out. It was well past patching with home made repair panels, or at least if it had been patched, the work involved would have been disproportionate to the value of the car.

▲ SP9. The Monodex cutter was used to cut the unwanted metal away. Although slow in operation the Monodex was chosen because it distorted the thin steel hardly at all. Vertical cuts were simply made with a hacksaw. The metal was cut away about ½ inch (10mm) above the marked line to allow an overlap.

▲ SP10. The panel was fitted first of all with a line of about 15 pop rivets and also by the windscreen wiper mechanism. This was to ensure that no movement and as little distortion as possible takes place. The panel was held in place by a series of short braze tacks; amply sufficient for this type of work where few structural loads are involved.

▲ SP11. Naturally, the paint in the surrounding area had burned off and this was thoroughly cleaned up with a wire brush. Special care had been taken not to ignite any of the wiring behind the dash; it had all been tucked away safely.

▲ SP12. In order to seal the gap off thoroughly and also to help prevent any filler from cracking, the joint was reinforced with glass-fibre. First, a coat of resin was painted on ...

▲ SP13. ... then two layers of very fine glass-fibre tissue was stippled into place. Ordinary glass-fibre mat would have been too coarse and could have been difficult to restore to an even surface. Finally, the area was filled, finished and sprayed, as detailed elsewhere in this book.

▲ SP14. Rollie's don't seem to throw anything away! Most yards seem to sell off the old engines, and other useless bits for scrap but when you find a yard that hangs onto its stuff, you can locate some real nuggets among the dross. Note the selection of grille panels hanging like trophies around the perimeter fence.

TYPES OF SALVAGE PANELS

The cost of new body panels can be frightening, especially if you own an imported car. Even small items like bezels, badges and clips can knock a hefty hole in your pocket, but fortunately there is often a way out.

Vehicle dismantlers do a roaring trade in good second-hand body panels and it's well worth visiting your local yard, or ringing round a few that are further afield to see what they have in stock.

The shots in this section were taken at Rollie's Auto Wrecking Yard, Sun Valley, California, but the principles involved are the same wherever you live, with the few exceptions pointed out in the captions.

▲ SP16. Complete front-ends in a unit are a US speciality. Check that the one you buy includes any hard-to-get trim and other details.

▲ SP17. Bumpers as far as the eye can see! They're often scuffed or slightly bent, so check carefully. Outside the sun belt, where corrosion isn't a problem, also check for corrosion at the rear and pitting through the chrome. Scrap-yard dirt can obscure such blemishes!

▲ SP15. Screens are shown stacked here with the model identification clearly chalked onto the glass.

◀ SP18. Wings and doors are commonly damaged in a light accident and can cost an arm and a leg to replace new. In addition, brand new doors come as bare as a new born babe and can take a good deal of fitting up while second-hand doors usually have their gear intact! In rust-smitten climates, check carefully for rust in used panels.

◀ SP19. Sometimes a panel will have escaped rust for no apparent reason, sometimes a car will have been fitted with a new panel just a couple of years previously, while there are some cases where a small amount of welding will make a panel which is a great deal better than the one you have got – but be prepared to haggle with the dealer.

◀ SP20. The days are generally gone when breaker's yards in the UK left old cars lying around like this, until all the useful stuff was salvaged from them. With present environmental legislation, cars have to be dismantled carefully so as not to pollute watercourses with fluids, for example. Still, if you can find a private cache or a specialist facility, you'll have found a goldmine – so mine it!

BLAST CLEANING

Anyone who has spent hours of backbreaking rust-scraping would be delighted to find a way of getting back to shiny metal without any effort at all. There is a way and it's the most efficient method there is because it gets right down into rust pits and other crevices: blast cleaning is the answer. Blast cleaning is the use of compressed air to blast an abrasive at a chassis or bodywork to scour all the old rust and paint away. It's so efficient that you would swear the operator was blowing clean shiny metal on, rather than blasting the rubbish off!

There are five main types of blast cleaning, not all of which are suitable for motor car use.

SHOT BLASTING

Blasting with round steel balls is suitable only for heavy industrial applications and is not suitable for any motor car work, being far too abrasive.

DRY GRIT BLASTING (PRESSURISED SUPPLY)

With this method a large container of grit is usually used which is pressurised from a heavy-duty compressor. All 'mobile' blast cleaners use this method. The material used is grit rather than steel balls and there are various grades available. This method is ideal for chassis but is often too robust for thinner panels. The pressure can create ripples in the panel even when it does not blast straight through, unless a fine grade of grit is used at low pressure. A lot depends on the user's expertise.

Clean off all underseal and grease because they absorb the force of the grit. They take ages to blast off – which costs you money and before they are blasted away, the surrounding area could have been blasted through. Remove all brake and mechanical components and wiring and have the work carried out well away from the house or workshop – the grit seems to go everywhere, and it's the very last thing you want near anything mechanical. If anything is to be left in place which must not be blasted, cover it with many layers of PVC insulation tape and point it out to the operator.

DRY GRIT BLASTING (SUCTION SUPPLY)

This is the sort of system which can be used by the DIY-er, but note all the earlier comments about dust and damage to certain components. Glass is easily etched by a blast cleaner.

DRY BEAD BLASTING

This uses glass beads which remove paint and contamination without affecting the critical tolerances of parts being blasted. It is much slower than dry-grit and so more costly and a dry bead blasted surface can be rather 'spikey' and difficult to clean.

VAPOUR BEAD BLASTING

Although more expensive than dry bead blasting, this is a superior system which gives the original 'polished' surface to aluminium items such as cylinder heads and gearbox casings. The glass beads are blasted on with pressurised water, which helps to close the grain of the surface of the aluminium and gives an even smoother finish.

Blast cleaning of any type will make it so much easier to work with elderly panels or components but, best of all, it chases corrosion out from every place it exists. But do entrust your work to a reputable firm. Once a part is blasted into extinction, it's gone for good!

▲ *BC1. A small gun costs about the average price of a tyre but takes a large compressor to run it continuously. If you are prepared to wait for pressure to build up every few minutes, you should be able to use one with a 9cu ft FAD compressor, (around 14cu ft displacement).*

(See the following sections for photographs of a dry grit blaster in operation.)

CHASSIS AND SUB-FRAME REPAIR

SEPARATE CHASSIS AND SUB-FRAMES

This is a brief story of an MGA chassis repair. Many older cars were built on a separate chassis to which the car's mechanics and body were hung. To repair them properly they have to be stripped down to the bare bones, which is, of course, a massive task. Detachable sub-frames, such as those on the BL Mini or 1100/1300 series, can be treated in a similar way to a full chassis, although the strip-out will require very much less work.

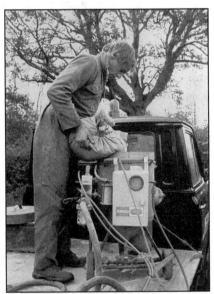

▲ *CRP1. Having gone as far as to strip the thing down, there's only one way to get rid of all the rust, and that is to sandblast it. A 'mobile' sand blaster was called in, carrying the blaster unit and sand on the back of a truck and towing a very heavy-duty compressor.*

▲ CRP2. Martin Griffiths, the fella doing the sandblasting could almost have passed for Neil Armstrong when dressed like this, which is some indication of the power of the blaster and the volumes of all-pervasive dust it gives off. Do it **well** away from a house or a workshop or any sort of machinery.

▲ CRP3. The blaster hosed rust off a treat, but didn't want to know about old undershield. To save a great deal of expensive sand-blasting time, always clean off all traces of undershield or other soft materials beforehand.

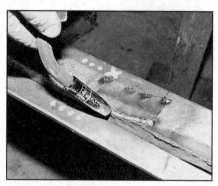

▲ CRP4. Back in the workshop, a system of sturdy axle stands and chains stretched down to hooks in the floor was used to hold the chassis rigidly. It was trued up in all directions with a spirit level.

▲ CRP5. Where a complete sidewall had rotted out, it was cut out and replaced whole, the jack pushing up lightly just to hold the member true.

▲ CRP6. A smaller area of rot was cut out with an oxy-acetylene cutting torch.

▲ CRP7. Then a plate was tacked down at one end, tapped down flat with a hammer...

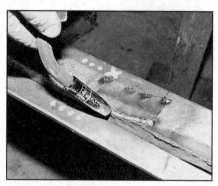

▲ CRP8. ... then after tack welding all the way round, seam welded with the MIG.

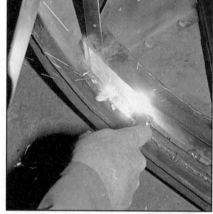

▲ CRP9. The floor bearers had corroded into insignificance along with one or two other small brackets. They were fabricated, generally from a thinner steel than that required for the chassis itself, and welded into place. Dimensional accuracy of every part is vital here because the chassis is literally the skeleton of the entire car. If you can't check measurements of one part from another symmetrically positioned part, (you should really measure any frail components before you have the sandblasting carried out), try to get hold of some original drawings from your specialist one make club, or perhaps just measure another enthusiast's car. Remember that accuracy and soundness are the keynotes to your chassis-based car's safety and appearance. In fact, you would be wise to have a specialist check your chassis on a jig before starting work and then again after the work is complete to ensure that the welding process has not caused any distortion to occur.

UNITARY CHASSIS

Manipulating the 'chassis' on a semi-monocoque framed car (ie one where the body itself provides a good deal of strength but where there are also 'chassis' rails welded in as an integral part) is a more skilled task. The following section shows how the job can be done but, if the damage is severe, there's no way that an amateur can do it or should attempt it. The following information holds true only for slight damage.

▲ CRP10. First, mount the car or body shell on stands, on a perfectly true surface. Check for level with a large spirit level used in several different directions.

▲ CRP11. Make sure that the shell is level by measuring from known datum points: don't just accept a couple of measurements but take several. You should then use a builders plumb-bob, which is a piece of cord with a pointed weight on the end. You hold the cord against two symmetrically-placed datum points at the rear, for example a particular pair of spring mounting bolts, and two at the front, such as points on the front suspension. Where the pointer on the bottom of the plumb bob touches the ground, an accurate pencil or chalk mark should be made. Measurements between the diagonally opposite points will give you an idea of whether the car's frame is twisted or not and the height measurements will give further clues. If the overall shape seems twisted, play safe and go to a specialist with a body jig.

◀ CRP12. Assuming that the damage is purely localised, it is sometimes possible to use a bottle jack to push out light damage. (Spread the load at both ends with timbers.) Incidentally, some bottle jack valves won't work in this position.

▲ CRP13. It may be possible to hire a professional hydraulic ram, which is capable of exerting great power. Go little by little and, again, spread the load.

▲ CRP14. You can sometimes help prevent all the pushing loads being taken in one area (particularly one you **don't** want to move!) by supporting it from behind with baulks of timber which go back to other structural members.

▲ CRP15. Once again, accurate measurement is the key to success, the distance between parallel members being an easy one to check.

▲ CRP16. Overall shape is best checked by measuring diagonals. Here a suspension strut to engine mounting is measured ...

▲ CRP17. ... while here the distance between the opposite pair is compared. Always measure from the edge of a hole or nut – otherwise you will be guessing the centre – and measure from the first digit on the tape rather than from the end, because it's more accurate.

REMOVING BODY FROM CHASSIS

In this section a Volkswagen Beetle is used to illustrate the body removal procedure with some additional photographs of the Triumph Spitfire/GT6 range. With the Beetle the underframe, which incorporates the floorpans, is not in itself particularly rigid as it relies upon the body to form a complete rigid structure. This method of construction is slightly different to cars utilising a separate chassis, which does inherently form the main structural strength of the vehicle, although the same principles regarding the separation of the body from the chassis or underframe remain basically very similar.

The combination of a welded body 'tub' and a separate, strong frame gives the Volkswagen an immensely strong structure. At the same time, the absence of nooks and crannies means that the body is less rust-prone than those of most cars, although many of the cars are by now rather old and in the end, rust will always have its way. It is also said that the Karmann-built cars, which includes the Cabriolets, were more rust-prone than the saloon/sedan models.

A complete restoration really requires that the body is taken from the frame and, needless to say, this is quite a major task! But first, a word of warning! Don't ever take off the body in order to repair it because, although it may make it easier to 'get at', there will be a very real risk, or even a likelihood that the body will become distorted and so not fit properly back onto the frame. Always carry out all the body repairs before lifting it off so that its inherent shape is not altered and so that the 'tub' is strong enough not to distort when lifted up. This advice is particularly important when dealing with a Cabriolet, of course. Note that there is no difference between the saloon/sedan models and the Cabriolet when it comes to body-to-frame mountings.

SAFETY NOTE:
It cannot be overemphasised that *any* chassis repairs should be checked over by a specialist with highly accurate equipment after they have been carried out, and if the repairs are more than of a very minor nature, they should be carried out by a specialist. A faulty door skin can ruin your car's looks but a faulty chassis can ruin a car's safe handling and cost lives.

In the photographs illustrating this section, you will see how House of Haselock lift off and replace the body using a power hoist. Naturally, home mechanics won't have access to this type of equipment and so the body will have to be lifted by hand. This is a job best treated as a social occasion and it could be that it will require the offer of liquid refreshment following the big event to get sufficient lifting power together! Four of us carried the Cabriolet body around after it had been removed at Haselock's and after it had been completely stripped out to the barest of bare shells, but two more pairs of hands would have made the job more comfortable, especially since when lowering and lifting, it is all too easy to cause an injury. Where a saloon/sedan body has to be lifted high enough to get it off a chassis I would recommend getting eight lifters together.

The body is held to the chassis by countless bolts, most of which pass upwards from beneath the car. Take out the bolts which are removed from beneath first of all, after raising the car up on axle stands or by driving it up ramps, not forgetting to chock the wheels on the ground. DON'T work underneath a car supported by a jack.

Provided that you lift and lower the car via the chassis, there will be no problem with having the underneath body bolts undone, then, with the car on the ground, the bolts reached from above can be removed, any other dismantling that is necessary can be carried out and the body lifted straight off. Have some trestles ready to lower the body onto, in order to save having to lift or lower to ground level and to make work underneath easier to carry out.

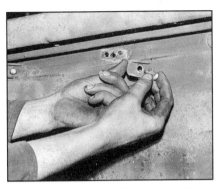

▲ BR1. Beneath the sills, all along the edges of the car there are M8 bolts (ie 8mm) and special washers tying the body down.

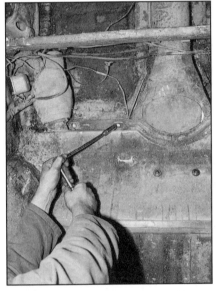

▲ BR2. Other M8 bolts are found beneath the rear seat area ...

▲ BR3. ... while M10 bolts hold the centre tunnel to this body bracket alongside the foot pedals.

◄ BR4. The frame and floorpan form a self-contained unit capable of being moved easily around. Later models, those with MacPherson strut front suspension have to be picked up at the front, with a trolley jack and 'wheelbarrowed' around because the front suspension is located on the bodywork and without the body in place the front wheels are free to slop drunkenly about. The bolts in the centre-side and rear-cross joints are, as stated in all previous captions, M8 whilst all the others are M10. The numbers superimposed here indicate the tightening order of the M10 bolts on early models.

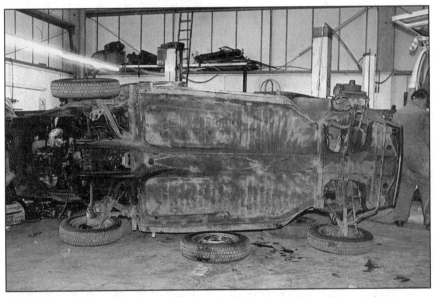

▲ BR5. One of the great advantages of having the body off the frame is that so many things become so much more accessible. You can tip the frame onto one side like this in order to clean it and paint it while mechanical components like brakes and steering become twenty times easier to work on.

◄ BR6. One job that you are strongly recommended to carry out is to clean out all the body mounting threads while the body is off. If you haven't got access to a tap, take a bolt, make a saw cut down its length and run it in and out of the thread a couple of times using releasing fluid as a lubricant

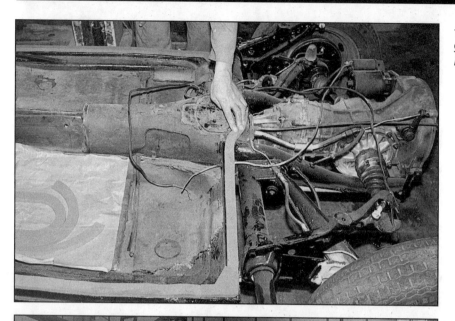

◄ BR7. It's important to use a new body gasket on the frame before lowering the body back into place.

◄ BR8. Here's a Cabriolet body on the hoist before being lowered back onto the frame. Note how the underbody and wing joint areas have all been painted in body colour and the frame painted in semi-gloss black, using ICI Autocolor 2K for longevity. Because of the MacPherson strut front suspension, the front end of the car has had to be supported on axle stands.

◄ BR9. The body must be lowered slowly and carefully into position, taking note of all the points raised in the notes at the end of these captions including the use of guide studs.

▲ BR10. Even more pairs of hands are needed when lowering on a MacPherson strut body because the strut has to be aligned with the tower on the body ...

▲ BR13. ... but don't tighten it down hard yet. See the section at the end of these captions for tightening details.

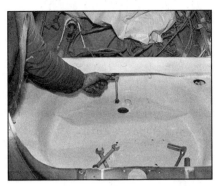

▲ BR16. ... two more bolts in the spare wheel well (later models – those on earlier models are further forwards than this on top of the front axle; see BR4) ...

▲ BR11. ... and the studs passed through the inner wing/fender. Nuts can be fitted and tightened later.

▲ BR14. Just as reminders, mounting bolts also go on the rear wing/fender mounting ...

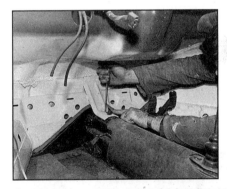

▲ BR12. You may find that the bracket down in the footwell doesn't align with the bolt holes straight away in which case insert a bar into one of the holes, lever the bracket into position and insert a bolt into the other hole ...

▲ BR15. ... at the ends of the front cross member there are two M10 bolts ...

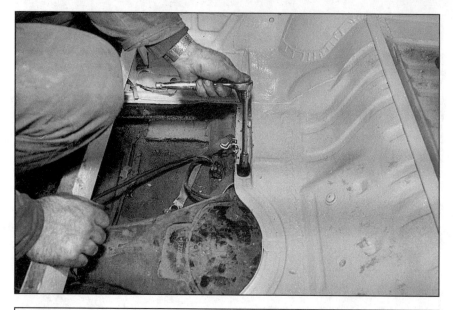

◄ BR17. There are also those that go down into the frame end plate beneath the rear seat area.

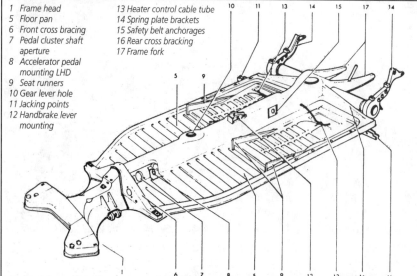

1 Frame head
5 Floor pan
6 Front cross bracing
7 Pedal cluster shaft aperture
8 Accelerator pedal mounting LHD
9 Seat runners
10 Gear lever hole
11 Jacking points
12 Handbrake lever mounting
13 Heater control cable tube
14 Spring plate brackets
15 Safety belt anchorages
16 Rear cross bracking
17 Frame fork

◄ BR18. The sturdy underframe is not in itself totally rigid, but relies upon combination with the so-very-strong body for its rigidity. Here you can see what's included – and it's virtually the same for every Bug/Beetle that has been built except that this is the 1600/1302/1303 front end. See BR4, for other type.

◄ BR19. This is a chassis from the Triumph Herald/Spitfire range shown being pulled out from underneath the body which was in this case suspended from a suitable framework inside the workshop. The same basic principles apply when removing the body of any car utilising this method of construction.

◀ *BR20. Of course when the body has been removed access to the entire chassis is superb and the opportunity should be taken to pressure wash and repaint the chassis even if no repairs are needed.*

◀ *BR21. It isn't a good idea to tighten any of the mounting bolts until they have all found their relevant homes in the chassis. Inevitably a fair amount of pushing and shoving will be needed for all the mounting holes to line up.*

◀ *BR22. In some instances shims are used between the body and chassis and some mechanical components. Due to tolerances during manufacture different cars will use a different number of shims making it essential to label them.*

BOLT-ON FRONT WING REPLACEMENT

▲ BW1. As with all rusty panels, there's more to be found beneath the surface than you can see at first. Behind this Subaru Justy front bumper, there was so much rust that the bumper mounting had become loose. Be prepared for more corrosion on inner panels.

▲ BW3. The first step is to remove surrounding panels and components, where necessary. In this instance, the front bumper had to be taken off. Some of the bumper fixings may be found behind the front grille panel, the front number/licence plate or beneath push-on cappings.

▲ BW5. Spray releasing fluid on to each of the fixing bolts and leave it to soak in.

▲ BW4. Don't forget to disconnect any lighting from the bumper and remember that almost all modern bumpers, once the fixing bolts have been disconnected, slide forwards off clips in the sides of the bumper. You may need to give them a good tug!

▲ BW2 Choose replacement panels with care. Subaru's own brand panels are extremely exensive but fortunately, we were able to purchase good quality replacements. Very cheap panels are usually more trouble than they are worth because they only fit where they touch – and they don't touch all that often!

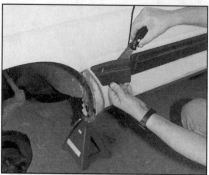

▲ BW6. In the meantime, disconnect lights, mud flaps and stuck-on trim, pushing a spatula through the double-sided tape behind the trim, when used.

▲ BW7. On some vehicles, especially older ones, the mounting bolts are cunningly hidden just where you can't get at them. Cut your losses (in every sense of the verb) and saw or chisel through the panel, exposing the hidden bolts.

Always wear protective gloves for this sort of job – unlike the stubborn mechanic shown here! – to protect your hands against the inevitable sharp edges.

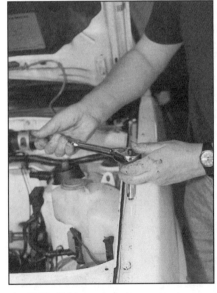

▲ BW8. With most bolt-on panels, there is a line of bolts down the side of the engine bay. These are easy to remove . . .

▲ BW9. . . . but you still have the problem of easing the flange away, because it is invariably stuck down with sealant. The rear edge of the wing may be similarly stuck down and on some vehicles, such as Volkswagens, the sealant is tough to shift!

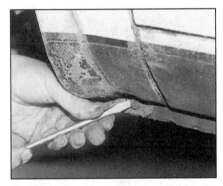

▲ BW10. Another problem will be bolts that are subject to corrosion. Here, you're usually best advised to use an angle grinder to remove the bolt head. Make **certain** that the sparks do not land on any glass because otherwise it will be permanently marked.

▲ BW11. This panel was easily removed but it was not to be scrapped, as will be made clear in the next section, Repairing Panels with Adhesive.

▲ BW12. In some cases, the mud shield will have had to be detached first. There will often be screws or bolts to undo in addition to push-on clips.

▼ BW13. This was a perfect opportunity to use a power washer to get rid of mud, loose underseal and flaking paint before continuing with the repair.

▲ BW14. We used Hammerite No. 1 Rust Beater to deter rust and to prime the existing panel. There was a small amount of corrosion which was cut out, going right back beyond the rusty metal. A repair section was cut out and is shown here being screwed into place with self-tapping screws. But don't be fooled! The repair was securely fixed using the technique shown in the next section. If more extensive corrosion is found, it may be necessary to weld in repair sections or even to completely replace the inner panel. See the relevant sections of this manual.

▲ BW15. The insides of the new panels were flatted down with a 3M Scotch-Brite pad to give a key to the new paint and then given a thorough coat of Hammerite Anti-Rust Primer. They were then given two coats of black Hammerite to provide what should be superb protection against future rusting.

▲ BW16. With the insides of the panels fully hardened off, the outsides were flatted off with 3M's Hookit dry paper on a good long sanding block. The advantages of this type of paper are that, unlike old fashioned wet-or-dry paper, no water is used and therefore no moisture is unnecessarily added to the panel; the paper is anti-clogging and stays useful for a long time. Hookit paper won't slip on the special 3M sanding block because of the tiny hooks which grip one to the other.

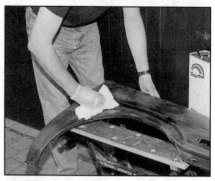

▲ BW17. Before and after sanding, use panel wipe fluid to remove all traces of grease and (especially!) silicones which will completely ruin the painted surface later on.

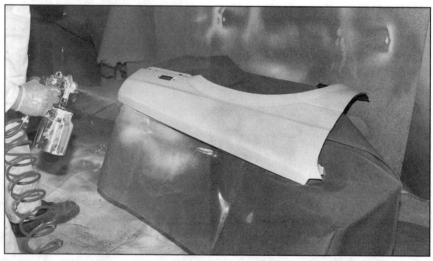

▲ BW18. After priming and painting the panel, as shown elsewhere in this manual . . .

◀ BW19. . . . the new panel proved to be an excellent fit when fitted to the vehicle.

▲ BW20. All that remains is to refit lights, bumper and trim. We used both double-sided tape and body adhesive to make certain that this trim didn't come adrift!

REPAIRING PANELS WITH ADHESIVE

In the previous section, we showed how to fit new, bolt-on front wings and in this one, we show how we repaired corrosion in the rear wheel arches without carrying out any welding.

Before going any further, let's be reassuring about the use of adhesives in car bodywork. As stated previously, the Jaguar XJ220, once the fastest production car in the world and still right up there with the best, is made entirely from panels and structures which are glued together. We were privileged to have access to the factory while these cars were being built, filming the process as it took place – that's what gave us the idea for the following sequence. After all, what's good enough for an XJ220 must be good enough for a humble Subaru Justy!

▶ RP3. . . . and another section was cut to fit the larger area of the wheel arch. If you need to buy repair panels, and you can't get the right ones for your vehicle, try drawing the shape of the wheel arch on a piece of card and taking this to your local panel supplier to see if there are any other rear wheel arch sections which will be close enough in shape to be adapted in the same way as these. You can see that the repair section has been put in place and drawn around with a felt pen.

▲ RP1. The first step is to obtain panels with which to replace the rusty ones. On this vehicle, the front wheel arches from the previously discarded front wings were, on the whole, in perfect condition. They were now to be cut out and used as repair sections for the rear replacements.

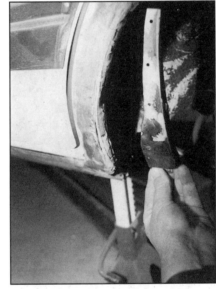

▲ RP2. A selected piece of the front arch was cut out to replace the lower part of the rear wheel arch . . .

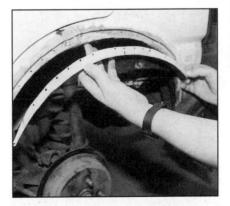

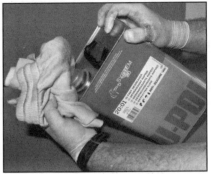

▲ RP4. I used an angle grinder to cut away all the rusty steel, right back to sound material. With all the paint sanded away, every trace of grease was removed with spirit wipe.

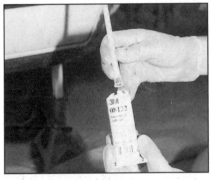

▲ RP5. The adhesive we chose was one made by 3M, which is purpose-made for the job. The mixing nozzle is fitted to the cartridge . . .

▲ RP6. . . . and as the adhesive and hardener is passed down the mixing nozzle the two components are thoroughly combined so that they begin to set strongly as soon as possible. The adhesive is then gunned on to the section to be repaired . . .

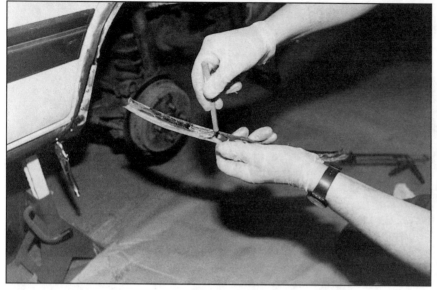

▲ RP7. . . . and its mating flange. Note that I'm wearing plastic gloves because of the potentially harmful nature of the material.

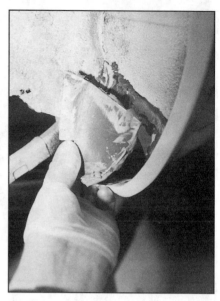

▲ RP10. As always, there is corrosion on the inner panels to match that on the outer. Repair panels were made up for these small areas, once the corrosion had been cut out completely.

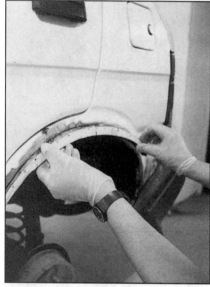

▲ RP8. The repair section is then offered up and fitted into place . . .

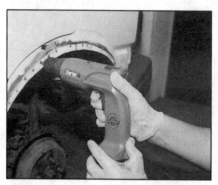

▲ RP9. . . . before being screwed down with self-tapping screws. It's worth making the following points:
The repair panel has previously been fitted 'dry', complete with pilot holes and self-tapping screws. This makes sure that it does fit and that it lines up correctly. Here, I am using a Clarke rechargeable drill which is especially useful in this context because speed is of the essence, and there's no worries with trailing cables to get in the way. 3M quote a fully set time of 24 hours for the adhesive. It will start to go hard well before that but **don't** be tempted to do what I did and take out the screws before the setting time is up. If you do, there will be some partial unsticking of the repair and you'll have to remove the panel and all the weary work will have to be done all over again.

▲ RP11. It wasn't so important to have a smooth-fitting repair and the surfaces to be fitted together were more undulating. Epoxy body adhesive requires that the two panels being fixed together are a very close fit, so I used Würth Epoxy Repair Stick. You take it out of the protective tube, cut off the amount you want . . .

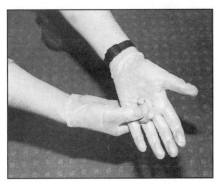

▲ RP12. . . . and roll it around in the middle of your (gloved) hand until the two elements are completely mixed together. It can then be used as a hard-setting filler/adhesive.

▶ RP13. The rear wheel arch was filled using body filler, in the normal way.

▼ RP14. Larger areas of body filler are best sanded down with a random orbit sander. This is an air-operated sander, produced by Clarke, but there is also a Bosch PEX 12 AE random orbit sander which will also be found invaluable for use around the house. See Tools and equipment at the beginning of this manual for why a random orbit sander is vastly superior to any other power-operated type when carrying out car bodywork repairs.

▲ RP15. Once again, we used a selection of 3M dry sanding paper, working through from coarse to fine, as described elsewhere in this manual.

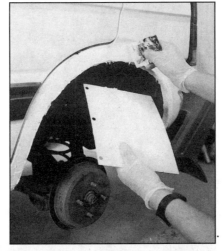

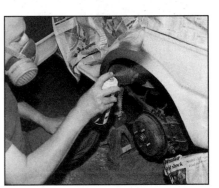

▲ RP16. After masking off the surrounding area, the wheel arch was sprayed with aerosol primer followed by finish coat. Note that you should always wear a face mask, even with aerosol, otherwise you will take in a surprisingly large amount of potentially harmful paint vapour and solids. This Würth mask has a double filter attached to it which makes breathing somewhat easier!

▲ RP17. With the surrounding components fitted back in place, the wheel arch looked as good as new.

Bodywork repairs – Part III
repairing plastics

REPAIRING A CRACKED BUMPER

▲ RCB1. Many professional bodyshops replace broken bumpers rather than repairing them because of the time involved. But the technology is available, and is widely used, for the repair of plastic bumpers as can be seen by the UPOL Plast 'X' repair system shown here.

▲ RCB2. You can purchase a complete kit to enable you to carry out bumper repairs using the Plast 'X' system.

◀ RCB3. There are different types of plastic but many can be softened by heat. If the plastic around the area has become distorted, apply heat and restore it to its correct shape. It is not possible to reshape some types of plastic, including glass-fibre, in this way. Use spirit wipe to get rid of all traces of grease or silicones from both the front and the rear of the bumper.

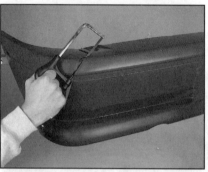

◀ RCB4. Any split will need to be enlarged so that the gap at the edge of the plastic is at least 3mm wide, tapering inwards to the point of the split. You could use a small saw or knife but it would be far easier to do so with the Dremel tool illustrated in 'Tools and equipment' at the start of this book.

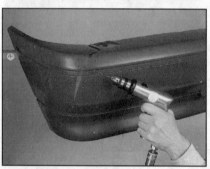

◀ RCB5. Make a small hole, 3mm from the end of the split and drill more holes 5mm apart along each side of the split, about 3mm from the sides.

▼ RCB6. Make a 'Vee' shape around the split to a distance of about 30mm from the edge.

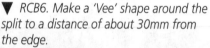
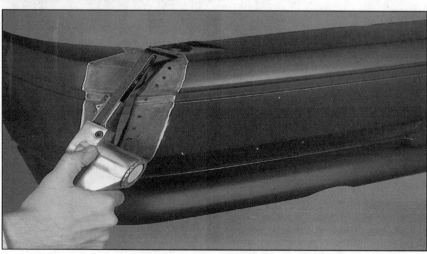

▲ RCB7. Take the can of Plast 'X' 1 Plastic Cleaner, spray some on to a cloth and wipe the damaged area both front and back. **Do not** spray directly on to the plastic part.

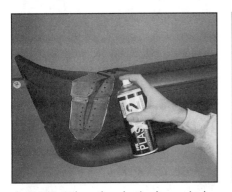

▲ RCB8. When the plastic cleaner is dry, spray an even coat of Plast 'X' 2 Adhesion Promoter, front and rear once again. Allow at least 30 minutes for the adhesion promoter to dry.

▲ RCB10. From the Plast 'X' repair kit, cut a strip of reinforcing film and another strip of contouring film, both of them 1¼in (30mm) longer than the split.

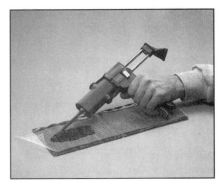

▲ RCB12. Operate the gun and pump out some of the adhesive on to a piece of scrap paper which can then be thrown away. This ensures that the mixing is taking place correctly. Now gun the adhesive on to the mesh side of the reinforcing film strip. There should be enough to slightly overfill the split. Take the mixing nozzle from the adhesive cartridge and replace the end cap on the cartridge. You'll have to throw the mixing nozzle away and use a fresh one next time.

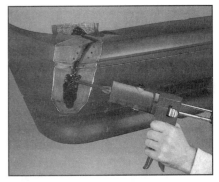

▲ RCB13. The reinforcing strip is pushed on to the rear of the bumper, wearing impervious gloves when doing so. You can now fill the front of the split into each drill hole. Begin gunning in from the narrow end of the split keeping the end of the tip in the adhesive during application. Slightly overfill the split and the holes, working quickly. The adhesive cures rapidly!

▲ RCB9. While you are waiting, take a sliver of plastic – perhaps some that has been cut out of the split – and place it into a glass of water. Use the results to tell you which type of Plast 'X' adhesive to use: a) If it **floats**, use Plast 'X' A Adhesive. b) If it **sinks**, use Plast 'X' B Adhesive.

▲ RCB11. Place the appropriate cartridge of adhesive into the gun and attach the mixing nozzle.

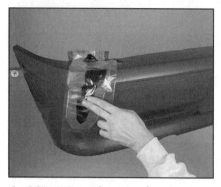

▲ RCB14. Press the strip of contouring film on to the adhesive but do not press it into the split itself. As far as possible, attempt to recreate the original contours of the plastic part.

▲ BSR2. Tony uses a Bosch Delta sander to take off the raised areas . . .

▲ BSR5. On the rear bumper, the damage had not gone too deep and it was only necessary to use the special Paint Technik high-build primer. Tony masked off a smaller area around the repair and used his heat gun carefully to dry off any residual moisture.

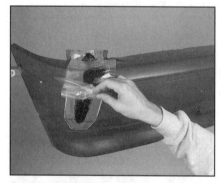

▲ RCB15. When the adhesive has completely set, you can remove the contouring film and the plastic backing of the reinforcing film before sanding down and finishing as shown elsewhere in this manual.

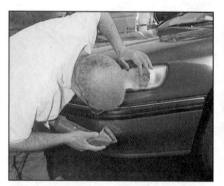

▲ BSR3. . . . on both front and rear bumpers. This particular shape of sander is ideal for reaching into the various nooks and crannies. As usual, the Paint Technik van comes fully equipped with everything needed to carry out the repair.

▲ BSR6. Tony sprayed on the primer filler, wafting the heat gun over the area to help each coat to harden off – it was a cool spring day and he was working outside . . .

'MOBILE' PLASTIC BUMPER SCUFF REPAIRS

▲ BSR1. We called on Paint Technik's Tony Mousley once again to show how to deal with the inevitable bumper scuffs that deface the appearance of our cars.

▲ BSR4. IMPORTANT: Before applying filler, refer to the sections Repairing a cracked bumper and Painting plastic for information on preparing the surface of plastics before applying the correct type of filler. Ordinary body filler is not suitable because it won't adhere properly.

▲ BSR7. . . . and then removed the smaller area of masking-off ready to repaint both bumpers. See Chapter 4, 'Mobile' paint repairs.

PAINTING PLASTIC

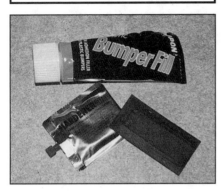

▲ PPL1. While the previous section showed how to carry out major repairs to a damaged bumper, there are often cases when minor repairs are needed such as to bashed or dented areas. Isopon's Bumper Fill is one of the products that enables you to carry out minor surface repairs to plastic products.

Before starting work on the bumper, wash it off using washing-up liquid and water, rinse and dry. You should then use Plast 'X' 1 Plastic Cleaner, as shown in the previous section, to clean the whole of the area to be painted. Do not spray directly on to the plastic.

▼ PPL2. You will now use a selection from the range of Plast 'X' products in order to complete the job. Note that there is a plastic filler in the same range (Plast 'X' 6) which is also suitable for repairing surface defects.

▲ PPL3. You must now apply a coat of Plast 'X' 2 Adhesion Promoter, as described in the previous section. Note that at least 30 minutes drying time must be allowed. You can then follow this up with light mist coats of Plast 'X' 3 Primer Filler, sprayed at a distance of 1ft (300mm) from the bumper. Allow three minutes between coats and a drying time of at least 20 minutes.

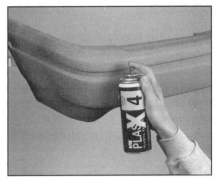

▲ PPL4. After sanding the primer filler in the usual way (see other sections of this manual) spray on the Plast 'X' 4 Texture Coat, using the fine or coarse grade as appropriate. Do not apply the high-build of texture coat – use two light mist coats sprayed at a distance of 12in (300mm) (fine) or 32in (800mm) (coarse). Allow three minutes between coats and at least 15 minutes drying time. Obviously, if your bumper does not have a textured finish, this stage will not be necessary!

◄ PPL5. Colour Coat is available in a range of three shades of grey plus black. Apply light, even coats at a distance of 1ft, allowing three minutes between coats and a final drying time of at least one hour.

▲ PPL6. I also experimented with another brand of bumper paint sprayed on to a VW Golf rear bumper. At first, the results looked excellent but after a while, the paint began to peel off again. This suggests that the one-can bumper paint may not be suitable for every type of plastic, in spite of the instructions on the can being carefully followed. Test the type of spray you are choosing to use, on the inside of the bumper, before causing unnecessary work.

WELDING PLASTICS

IMPORTANT SAFETY NOTE
When using power tools on plastic, note that plastic particles are as dangerous to the eyes as metal particles and safety goggles should be worn at all times.

▲ WP1. This process enables structural repairs – and if necessary, invisible ones – to be carried out to most types of plastic component. Welwyn Tool Co. have developed a range of products and techniques suitable for welding plastics – the cost is broadly comparable to that of low-end MIG welding equipment and I spent a couple of days with Clive Day of Welwyn Tool Co. learning how to plastic weld.

▲ WP2. The first step is to identify the type of plastic you intend to weld. Most plastic components have a code indicated on the reverse side. This is, among other things, to comply with recycling legislation and you can use it to identify the type of plastic you have. (Some older components may not have a code or one that is in common use, but Welwyn Tool Co. can advise on what some of the more obscure codes mean if they are contacted.) The following chart identifies most common plastic types.

This process enables structural repairs – and if necessary, invisible ones – to be carried out to most types of plastic component. Welwyn Tool Co. have developed a range of products and techniques suitable for welding plastics – the cost is broadly comparable to that of low-end MIG welding equipment and I spent a couple of days with Clive Day of Welwyn Tool Co. learning how to weld plastic.

For anyone who has gas welded, the process is not difficult, although there are techniques that you have to un-learn! In fact, I would say that plastic welding is easier to carry out than most forms of metal welding.

PLASTIC IDENTIFICATION CODES

Code	Plastic
ABS	Acrylonitrile Butadiene Styrene
ABS/PC	Polymer alloy of above
PA	Polyamide (Nylon)
PBT	Polybutylene Terephtalate (POCAN)
PC	Polycarbonate
PE	Polyethylene
PP	Polypropylene
PP/EPDM	Polypropylene/Ethylenediene Rubber
PUR	Polyurethane (Not all PUR is weldable)
PVC	Polyvinyl Chloride
GRP/SMC	Glass-fibre Reinforced Plastics (Not weldable)

It is important to note that plastics fall into two broad groups: Thermo-setting plastics and Thermo-plastic plastics. The first group included glass-fibre (although there are others) and is non-weldable. This is because thermo-setting plastics cannot be softened by heat and can therefore not be welded. Fortunately, the majority of plastics used on vehicles are thermo-plastic plastics. If you have to repair a glass-fibre (GRP) component, refer to the section on glass-fibre repairs in this chapter.

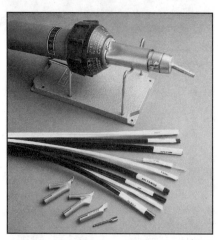

▲ WP3. The plastic welding kit supplied by Welwyn Tool Co. includes all the parts you will need and extra packs of welding rods are available.

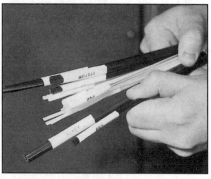

▲ WP4. Each pack of welding rod is marked with the plastic code shown in the above chart so, if you know which type of plastic to use, select the appropriate rods.

▲ WP5. If there is no way of identifying the type of plastic, use a rod that has a similar look and feel to it and try welding with that, on a part of the component that will not be seen and after first cleaning the surface. You may or may not be successful; there's no way of knowing in advance!

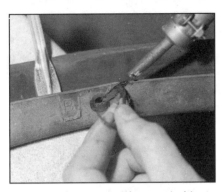

▲ WP6. Clive managed to repair this split in a 1980s Volkswagen wheel arch trim by cutting off a sliver of plastic from another part of the trim, where it wouldn't be seen, and used that as the welding rod. It worked, although the weld was not quite as neat as those we will be seeing later because of the high rubber content in the plastic.

If it proves impossible to weld the plastic component you are trying to repair, the only alternative will be a chemical repair as shown elsewhere in this chapter.

CRACKED BUMPER REPAIR

▲ WP7. The first part of the job is to sand the paint from around the area to be repaired and then using the rotary cutting tool supplied with the kit, form a 90° v-shaped groove along the length of the crack.

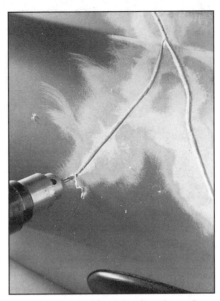

▲ WP8. Next, the ends of each crack should be drilled to prevent them spreading.

▲ WP9. The burring tool supplied with the kit is ideal for preparing the crack for welding. If you set the Dremel to a high speed setting, the tool is much less likely to jump out of the crack. Begin the groove about 10mm beyond the end of the crack and increase the depth progressively. When the groove is at the right depth, the welding rod should rest neatly in it with the upper curved face of the rod protruding 1mm to 2mm above the surface of the repair. This allows for weld dressing and cuts down the need for fillers while allowing enough depth of penetration for the rod.

TACK WELDING

▲ WP10. With the welding kit comes a chart showing types of plastic and types of weld and this enables you to set the heat gun to the required temperature. Before starting the tack weld, look up the required setting and apply it to your heat gun.

▲ WP11. The tack welding nozzle is fitted to the heat gun and drawn along the base of each 'Vee' groove. The nozzle should be held with its toe in contact with the base of the groove and the heel slightly raised. As the nozzle is drawn along, hot air softens the plastic below the heel of the nozzle and the toe draws the softened material together. Don't press down on the tool as the base of the 'Vee' is very thin and can be pushed right through. As the tack weld is carried out, minor misalignment of the panel sides can be corrected by holding the sections in position until the weld has knitted and cooled.

SEAM WELDING

▲ WP12. If you run a bead of weld at right angles to the repair – this is the back of a bumper being repaired – the reinforcement weld will add greatly to the strength of the finished job. Add as many strengthening ribs as you wish.

▲ WP13. As with any type of welding, trim the welding rod to a pencil point to help the rod to fill the start of the Vee-groove progressively.

▲ WP14. This is a speed welding nozzle. Allow the heat gun to warm the nozzle for a couple of minutes before starting work.

▲ WP15. The welding rod is fed into the tube on top of the nozzle until approximately 5mm protrudes on the underside. Hold the tool so that the speed welding nozzle sole runs along the crack parallel to the component surface. The protruding rod must be held beyond the start of the Vee-groove so that heat is directed on to the start point for welding.

▲ WP16. When the surface plastic shows signs of slight 'wetting', move the welding nozzle along the groove. The nozzle toe should rest on the rod in the groove while under the heel there should be an air gap of 3mm. Feed the rod steadily into the nozzle with a downward hand pressure of about 2.5kg (5.5lb) – experiment with a set of kitchen scales to judge what this amount of pressure feels like – which will be sufficient to push the soft rod into the groove.

IMPORTANT
Do not apply downward force to the weld via the hot air tool itself.

Whenever possible, the weld should be completed in one continuous run along the contour of the crack.

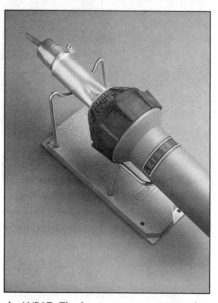

▲ WP17. The heat gun support stand supplied by Welwyn Tool Co. as part of the kit is useful for allowing the gun to cool down safely and can also be used to put the gun down while still running, if there is only going to be a minute or two between welds.

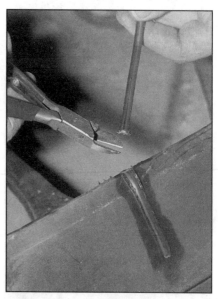

▲ WP18. As was pointed out earlier, the end of the weld must be completed by cutting off the welding rod.

PENDULUM WELDING

When welding in tight corners, it may be difficult to use the normal speed welding technique and in such cases, the technique of pendulum welding is preferable.

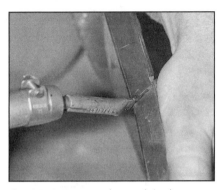

▲ WP19. Prepare the crack in the normal way and tack weld it – this is especially important for breaks in lightweight components such as this Golf radiator and headlight grille.

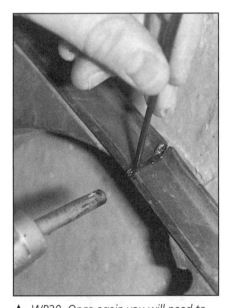

▲ WP20. Once again you will need to exert a downward force of about 2.5kg while playing the hot air tool fitted with the small nozzle on to both the base of the rod and into the Vee-groove in a constant pendulum action. You will need to put more or less heat on to the workpiece, depending on its thickness – a judgement that can only be made with experience, so you may wish to practice on a scrap piece from the breaker's yard first.

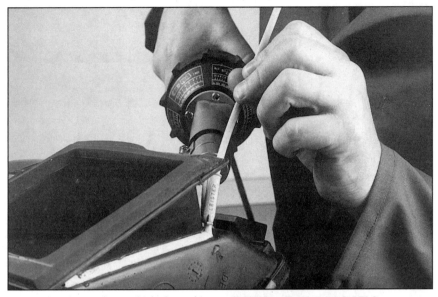

▲ WP21. The angle at which the rod is fed in can be varied according to how much penetration you want to achieve but in general, you should angle it away from the heat gun although it is being leaned in the opposite direction here to help get it round a corner in order to repair this heater component.

You really can save a lot of money by repairing your own plastic components or you can make your own custom trim items, adapting the manufacturer's grilles for instance to fit, say, extra spots where none were fitted to your model, or de-badging the grille.

CUSTOM-BUILT PLASTIC COMPONENTS

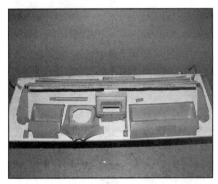

▲ WP22. The Citroën Mehari buggy-type vehicle was only built with left-hand drive – so I had to have a right-hand drive one! The mechanical components were all swapable but the main stumbling block was the plastic dashboard. I worked out that the centre portion of the dashboard – the bit that holds the ashtray – could be retained in position and the other components cut out and moved so that the steering wheel and speedo appear on the 'other' side.

◄ WP23. With an assembly as complex as this, I decided to reassemble it using strips of aluminium and self-tapping screws just to hold it all in position. You need the gaps to be as close as possible so it pays to use a knife or very thin bladed saw when cutting out components such as this.

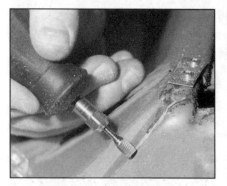

▲ WP24. There were extra splits, as always with this type of component, and Welwyn Tool Co.'s Clive used the Dremel to open them out as described earlier.

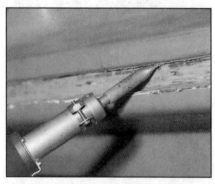

▲ WP25. He also tack welded each joint to give it extra strength, where necessary.

▲ WP26. The side cutters from the kit were used to cut the end of the welding rod to the required sharp angle . . .

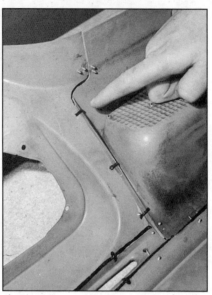

▲ WP27. . . . and the first welds were carried out as strengthening cross-welds on the rear of the panel where it seemed appropriate.

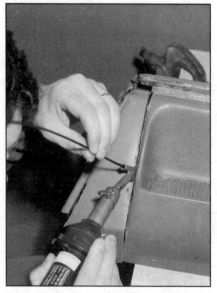

▲ WP28. Where he could, both for neatness and speed, Clive used the speed welding nozzle.

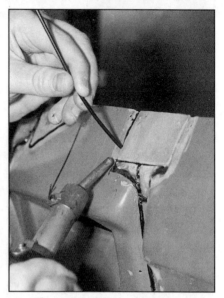

▲ WP29. Where the welding was trickier to carry out or the gaps larger, Clive chose to use the pendulum welding technique described earlier. Note the correct angle of the welding rod as it is pushed into the Vee-joint.

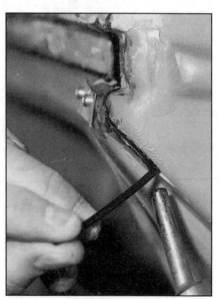

▲ WP30. Spot the deliberate mistake! Clive managed to weld this okay without cleaning the paint from either side of the joint and you can see it bubbling here. For those of us who are less experienced, it is strongly advisable to clean the paint away from the joint, as previously described.

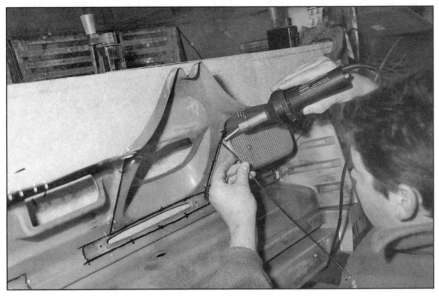

▲ WP31. The material used in this dashboard is thin and we decided that it would provide a stronger joint if the back of the weld was also welded up.

▲ WP32. After all the welding was complete, I cleaned off all the high spots using the sanding drum on the Dremel tool before turning to the UPOL plastic filling and painting system described earlier.

▶ WP34. The ideal tool for sanding down the raised beading is a random orbit sander, such as the Bosch electrically powered version. Start with a 120-grit abrasive disc, followed by 180 and 320 discs to obtain a smooth finish. Plastic sands quickly and easily, so beware of overflatting!

FAULTS AND FINISHING

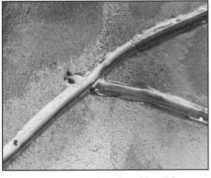

▲ WP33. A completed weld will have raised beading and a completely filled Vee-joint.

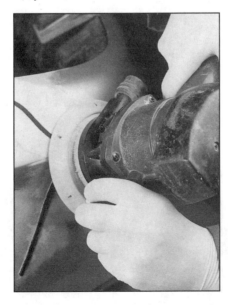

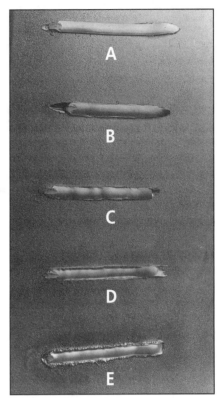

▲ WP35. This picture shows a number of weld defects:

A - the weld was started correctly but completed too quickly. No wash indicates haste or too low a temperature.

B - the hot air tool was not allowed to attain the correct operating temperature and the weld was finished too soon, leaving a hole.

C - uneven pressure has been applied to the rod or speed of movement has been varied, leaving a rippled finish and some undercutting.

D - too much pressure has been applied to the rod leaving a low and deformed bead. Filling may be necessary.

E - the welding temperature was too high, blistering the sides of the weld. The repair area may be brittle.

Chapter 6

Repairs on a shoestring

BODYWORK REPAIR AND IMPROVEMENTS FROM A CAN

Does your car look a disgrace to the neighbourhood? Or do you fancy buying a banger for a song and making it look presentable? Either way, this section shows a host of techniques and tricks for putting a shine on a car for which the spotlight has long gone out. Make no mistake the following tips won't make the car last a lot longer: they won't make it go faster or stop better, most important of all, they won't make it any safer. It is only worthwhile carrying out any of the cosmetic repairs that follow if the car's structure and running gear are safe. That is something that you must determine for yourself, if necessary with the aid of a professional tester. But it is surprising how even a basically sound car can be so badly knocked about and neglected that it looks far worse than it really is. So, if you are tired of punk rockers wanting to take your car home as a souvenir, or of patrol men pulling you up to count the rust bubbles, this chapter could be just what you have been waiting for. Read on! The author – with a little help from his father and friends – shows how it's done.

SIZING UP

▼ BC1. Well, this is it! I picked this one up with no MoT roadworthiness certificate, no Road Fund Licence, and a clutch that had rust-welded itself onto the flywheel. The owner was just about to chop off the rear axle and turn it into a trailer when I spotted the chariot's startling potential (!) and for around the cost of a dozen pints of Best Bitter, the deal was struck, leaving the ex-owner alcoholically ecstatic and the new owner stone cold sober at the realisation of what was to come. The car's underframe was sound, everything shone, tooted and flashed as it should and, by dramatic and distinctly unorthodox means, the clutch was freed in a trice.

▲ BC2. There were several places where rust was disturbing the surface of the paint and I knew that many of these would reveal gaping holes when they were prodded.

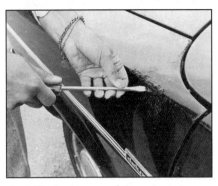

BC6. Even with a hubcap fitted, the wheel arch looked terrible when Michelle, a friend and neighbour, called around and said 'Oh, look how this comes apart when you touch it!' Who needs enemies ... But seriously, it just shows how weak rust is, and how filler applied some time ago will pop straight off again under the force of expanding rust beneath it.

BC3. At the rear of the same wing, the bubbling was even worse, and pushing a screwdriver into the corroded metal was as easy as breaking thin ice. Quite a big patch was going to be needed here.

BC7. Michelle tried the same trick with the front wing but this time the paint just flaked off revealing sound metal beneath. You never can tell just by looking.

BC4. This body scratch is typical of the sort of calling card that some morons leave behind to greet you on your return to the car park. It was worse than it looks in this picture and you could feel and see a shallow dent right along the line of the scratch.

BC8. This was NOT staged! It just goes to show how you can disregard an already battered looking car. I normally pride myself on being able to judge a car's dimensions but this time ...

BC9. ... Ouch! Just to make things equal, my wife clobbered the other side of the car the very next day. Now, believe it or not, denting cars is not something we make a habit of. It's just that there's a real psychological difference to the way you treat a car when it looks respectable.

BC5. The frame is worthy of the picture! Wheels look terrible without their trim but that was easily fixed. The rust on the wheel would have to be rubbed down and the wheel arch was of the back-to-nature variety; it was rapidly returning to its original metallurgical state!

▲ BC10. Michelle seems to be saying, 'How on earth d'you think you are going to repair this?' I didn't even try but simply visited the local breaker's yard and bought a more presentable seat along with the hub cap that replaced the one missing from the rear right-hand wheel.

▲ BC11. As well as the aerosol products described elsewhere, you'll need a glass-fibre repair kit of the type produced by David's of Isopon filler fame. You'll also need some zinc mesh, available from most auto accessory outlets.

PAINT BREAKDOWN – SOUND METAL

▲ BC12. I started off by nibbling away at a bubbling area with an old woodworking chisel. The paint scraped and flaked away quite easily and revealed metal that was pitted but which hadn't yet gone right through. The paint was scraped back beyond the obvious area of rust, out to shiny metal. That way you make sure that you don't miss any rust that might have started to creep under the paint without anything showing on the surface.

RUSTY REAR WING

▶ BC15. This wing hadn't been bumped (how did we miss it) so the corroded metal and flaking filler were cut away and the profile built back up with body filler. Although there's only one shot here of this being done, in truth the filling/sanding routine had to be carried out several times before the correct shape was sculptured. Unless you're **very** lucky don't expect to be able to get there with only one or two shots of filler.

▲ BC13. With this sort of repair, you'll need to apply a rust killer. This one, from Fertan, is the only one I've had success with. When I've tested Fertan, it's protected exposed surfaces for several months, but it obviously can't work on hidden rust that you can't get to.

▲ BC14. I've missed out all the filling and masking pictures (see the other sections for details) but note that once the filler was flatted it was sprayed with primer then with a light coat of finish paint straight away. Filler is absorbent and I didn't want it soaking up any moisture whilst the rest of the car was attended to. Incidentally, after using the Rust Eater but before applying the filler, the metal was sprayed with several coats of Holts Zinc Spray. Now, I know that zinc helps to hold back rust.

▲ BC16. Here I'm using a rubbing block with some medium grade production paper (dry sanding) wrapped around the flat part of the block. The outer flat lip of the rear wing is being sanded first.

▲ BC17. The back of the block gives a convex surface and this is handy for when you want to sand into concave surfaces.

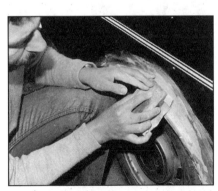

▲ BC18. The fairly strong curve of the rear wing is shown being sanded with left-to-right movements of paper and block. This is the sort of area that is impossible to machine sand both because of its shape and also because hand work allows finer judgement than a machine sander, which can rapidly remove more material than you intend.

▲ BC19. After achieving the correct shape it was found that there were lots of scratches and other small blemishes in the surface of the filler. I used a cellulose stopper which is air drying and can only be used for this purpose in a thin coat. It doesn't have the strength of filler and if used too liberally will shrink back as it dries, leaving you with an indifferent surface again. Ordinary filler can be pressed into service for this purpose provided that it is spread as thinly as this, but it doesn't possess the easy-flat properties of stopper.

▲ BC20. So little of the stopper has to be removed that a piece of fine grade production paper, hand held, will do the job perfectly well and should leave the surface ready for spraying primer.

PULLING OUT A DENT I

▲ BC21. If you recall, the deep scratch down the left-hand side panel was accompanied by a valley in the panel itself. There was no ready access to the rear of the panel without time consuming stripping-out of the trim panels. First, a hole was drilled in the centre of the dent, using a ⅛in drill.

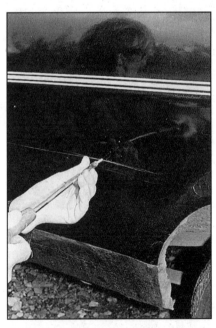

▲ BC22. Then a self-tapping screw with a flat head was screwed into the panel, making sure that it didn't go so far in that it damaged anything behind the panel but taking it in far enough to get a strong grip.

▲ BC23. The art of improvisation! A woodworker's claw hammer was used to grip the screw head while a strip of wood was used both as a fulcrum point and as a cushion to prevent the hammer marking the panel. The dent will come out really easily; the trick lies in not overdoing it.

▲ BC25. You can buy filler in pots right up to this size, which is made for commercial use but would be a more economical way of buying the stuff if you were going to use a lot. Try not to use the same surface twice for mixing your filler otherwise you will pick up hard pieces of filler from the previous mixing which will then drag across the surface as you attempt to spread the filler, leaving furrows which are infuriatingly difficult to get rid of.

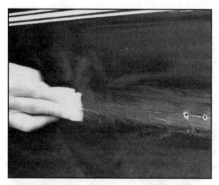

▲ BC24. When the dent had been pulled out all the way along its length (and actually, it was left just a little low, which is greatly preferable to creating a raised ridge) the paint was prepared for the application of filler by roughening the surface with medium grade production paper. If filler is applied over shiny paint, its adhesion is poor, it becomes prone to cracking out and it won't feather edge properly so its edges always show.

▲ BC26. Here a 'professional' sanding block is being used. It accepts ready made strips of self-adhesive backed production paper strips (any paint factor will stock them) and helps to create a true, flat surface. Attaining a flat surface is easier if you sand in more than one direction. Coarse production paper can be used at this stage.

▲ BC27. My father lent a hand here, using his power sander which really shifts the dust! That's why he was wearing a particle mask, and a hat to keep the dust out of his hair. While the power sander's quicker, it's not so easy to produce a flat surface over a large flat area.

▲ BC28. An excellent way of checking the 'trueness' of the surface is to hold a straightedge against it. This is a strip of Perspex (Plexiglass) which cost a song from a local supplier, bought as an offcut. Its machined edge is very straight; use it by looking for gaps between straight edge and panel. Use the straight edge at several different angles when checking for rippling. It is also very useful when held against convex panels as it can be held in a curve against the shape of the car's bodywork. Good tools need not always be expensive.

▲ BC29. Leaping ahead now to the time when the filling is almost finished a tin of spray paint was used to spray a very thin coat of paint called a 'guide coat' over the surface of the filler. The can was held further away than normal so that the paint landed as an almost dry, dusting coat.

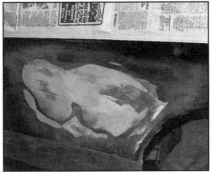

▲ BC30. When flatted off with a rubbing block and a fine grade production paper, the paint was removed from the high spots leaving the low areas standing out in stark relief. Depending on how deep these areas are, they can be brought out with filler or stopper, as already described. When using a guide coat, choose a colour that contrasts with the surrounding colours.

PULLING OUT A DENT II

▲ BC31. The dent on the front wing was in a very awkward place, just where the wing formed a fairly complex wheel arch extension. The DIY tools used here were an ordinary woodworker's G-cramp and the ubiquitous piece of wood again!

▲ BC32. The G-cramp was used right behind the worst part of the dent and then again each side of the first 'pull' to force the dented metal back to the line of the wood which was the same as the rest of the wheel arch. If the head of the G-cramp had not fitted so snugly inside the wheel arch, I would have used another, smaller piece of wood, shaped if necessary, to pull the metal to the correct shape.

▲ BC33. A small kink was left inside the wheel arch and this was easily knocked back into line using the panel beater's hammer.

▲ BC34. Well, all right, the G-cramp did leave a small mark. Unfortunately it had pushed a little of the concave curve out of line, but it was easily restored to the correct position with the cross-pein end of the panel beater's hammer.

▲ BC35. The repaired area was flatted with medium grade production paper, as were the scratches to the rear of the wing and the front of the door.

▲ BC36. The surfaces were filled, as shown and described earlier ...

▲ BC37. ... and the concave curve was flatted, this time using a slightly different technique. The production paper was rolled into a tube, the shape of which followed that of the concave part of the wing.

▲ BC38. The flatter areas were sanded as before, but this time the paper was wrapped round a flat piece of wood. Once again, the sanding was carried out in several different directions to ensure a flat surface.

▲ BC39. And finally, the filler was sprayed with primer to protect it from the elements.

CUTTING OUT CORROSION

▲ BC40. Rust frequently takes its strongest hold in the places where mud becomes lodged, and this area at the top of the wing is one of those places. When the surface was lightly tapped with the old wood chisel, the metal just fell into holes.

▲ BC41. I started off by cutting all the rusty steel away using a Monodex cutter, leaving only sound metal in place. A couple of fiddly bits wouldn't come out using the Monodex and they were finished off with a hammer and the trusty old wood chisel.

▲ BC42. Included in this body repair kit was a sheet of aluminium mesh. This can be bent and folded easier than card and can even be cut with scissors. It isn't intended to impart any strength to the job but just acts as a bridge for glass-fibre and filler while it goes off. You can't fill a gaping hole without putting in a support first and aluminium is ideal because it doesn't encourage the steel to start rusting again.

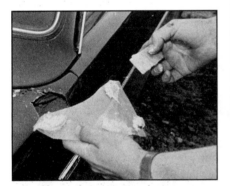

▲ BC43. The aluminium mesh was cut so that it covered the area of the holes and then a dollop of filler was placed on each corner of the mesh.

▶ BC46. The resin was left to go hard, then a scrape of filler was taken from the tin and mixed with the appropriate amount of hardener.

▲ BC44. You can't fully see what is going on here without having your X-ray specs on, but the mesh is being pushed into position from beneath the wing while the filler acts as a glue to hold it in position. Aluminium mesh is so soft that it can easily be pushed into the contours of the wing with light hand pressure.

▲ BC45. The kit provides resin (a thick liquid), hardener, and a spatula for stirring as well as a sheet of glass-fibre mat. The hardener was mixed with resin to the prescribed proportions and then resin was spread over the mesh and the edges of the steel. Then pieces of glass-fibre mat were cut to size, placed over the mesh and stippled down with resin until the mat became almost transparent. See the section on Getting to grips with GRP for more information.

▲ BC47. Filler was then spread over the depressed surface of the repair in the knowledge that there was a fairly sound foundation beneath. Note that the edges of surplus glass-fibre are treated as irrelevant at this stage.

▲ BC48. The whole lot was sanded flat using a medium grit disc fitted to a mini grinder. A rubber pad and disc fitted to an electric drill would have done the job just as well. It is extra important that you wear an efficient particle mask when carrying out this job because as well as particles of solidified polyester filler, there are also particles of glass-fibre floating around, and this can be extremely dangerous to health if inhaled.

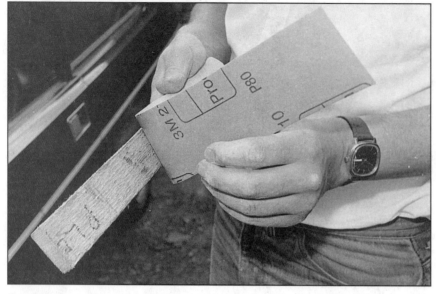

▲ BC49. As an alternative to using a professional sanding block, I used a sheet of P80 grade self-adhesive backed production paper and mounted it onto that piece of wood again!

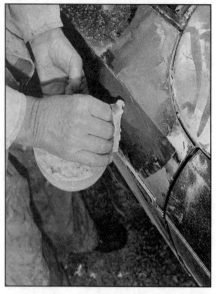

▲ BC52. Here, ordinary filler was used, finely spread, as a stopper. It works quite well but it really sets too hard for easy flatting and it also fails to spread as finely as cellulose stopper.

PAINTING THE PATCHES

▲ BC50. Remember to sand first in one direction ...

▲ BC53. There's no way with a job of this sort that you're going to want to remove the badges and sidestripes, so simply mask them. Take care in doing so because poor masking and overspray can look almost as bad as the rust you have spent so much time cutting out.

▲ BC51. ... and then the other, turning and turning about every six to ten strokes, to avoid the very real risk of rippling the surface.

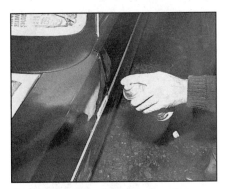

▲ BC54. Fortunately there is not so much power in an aerosol can that overspray is a real problem, so masking off to within a couple of feet of where you are spraying should be adequate. On the other hand, if you are working out of doors the ultra-light spray can carry on the wind. If it's windy, either transfer indoors, find a really sheltered spot or wait for a calmer day. Here, a coat of primer is being sprayed, working a strip at a time across the repair.

▲ BC56. As implied in the previous caption, the purpose of abrasive cutting compound is to remove some of the paint; you should polish until paint comes off and colours the cloth you are using like this.

▲ BC55. After priming the panel and allowing the paint to harden off thoroughly, rub the edges of the primer and the surrounding area with an abrasive paint polishing compound. This serves two purposes: it gives a very fine feather edge to the edge of the primer, so blending its thickness into that of its surrounds; and it polishes the oxides and traffic film off the surrounding colour which brings it back to its original colour and increases the chances of a good colour match with the paint you are spraying.

▲ BC57. Before starting to spray the finish coat, shake the can very very thoroughly to mix the paint. If you have ever seen the paint colours in a can separate themselves out, you will realise just how many times you have got to shake that ball bearing up and down the can to ensure that the right colour comes out of the nozzle. Then, spray some paint into thin air to clear the nozzle; there's nothing worse than to spend hours on preparation then start off with a big blob of paint right in the middle of the repair.

▲ BC58. Spray on a light first coat; don't even try to cover completely the colours beneath but spray on a coat which is light enough to let them show through. The paint should dry within a couple of minutes after which the second and later a third coat can be applied.

▲ BC59. Each coat should be sprayed as a series of horizontal or vertical strips, each coat half covering the one that went before. (If you get runs, you're passing too slowly or you're too close.) If you get a dull, dry finish, you're passing too quickly or you're holding the can too far away. Only trial and error can determine what will be exactly right for you and the conditions you are working in. Remember that a gust of wind will 'bend' the spray and spoil your aim and that damp air will cause blooming, ie the surface of the paint will go a milky colour. (Blooming can sometimes be polished out if it hasn't gone too deep.)

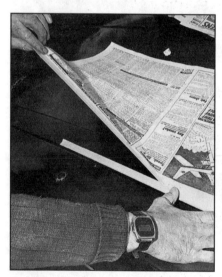

▲ BC60. Finally, here's a tip to remember when putting masking tape in place. Put a line of tape down the edge you want to protect taking care to place it accurately, then put a strip of tape half over the edge of a piece of newspaper before sticking that down to the first piece of masking tape. If you try to position the tape plus paper you will find it too cumbersome to handle easily.

FINISHING TOUCHES

▲ BC61. Stonechip or Stoneguard spray can serve two purposes. It saves you having to spend ages producing a good finish where it's going to be applied, such as sills and the inner flanges of wings, and it also does what it says on the can and protects against stone damage.

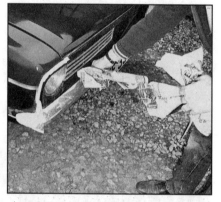

▲ BC62. Removing the masking tape can be quite exciting as it unwraps a 'new'car. Be sure not to fetch the masking off before the paint is dry and properly hard – it would be a shame to spoil it!

▲ BC63. Brush-on undershield should now be used beneath all of the repaired areas to keep out the damp and dirt from the especially vulnerable repair patches. If you don't underseal them, the patches will break through in no time at all.

▲ BC64. There were several small scratches and chips on this car and, while they certainly weren't bad enough to warrant spraying, they could only get worse if nothing was done. Here, some of the Holts finish paint is being sprayed into the cap from where it could be brushed on with a fine bristle kiddies paint brush. Paint for spraying is too thin for brushing; leave the cap to stand for a while to let the surplus solvent evaporate off before using it for painting.

▲ BC65. Don't forget to polish all the chromework – it can make an incredible difference to the appearance – and also clean all the windows to help to give the car a spring cleaned, fresh appearance.

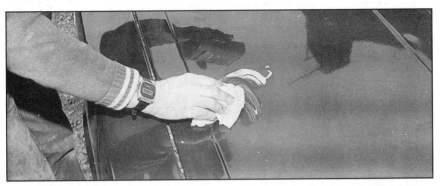

▲ BC66. After spraying random patches and panels the rest of the paintwork will look horribly dull by comparison. This car was polished with a light abrasive polish, a small area at a time, until it shone like the new paint. Then the whole car, chrome and all, was treated to a wax polishing to help to keep the shine in for a little longer.

▲ BC69. I knew that this car had leaked in from around the top corner of the windscreen. The only long-term cure for this problem is to remove and refit the windscreen but with a car of this sort, a good medium-term answer is to inject a good bead of windscreen sealer behind the rubber using the nozzle supplied with the tube. Cover a distance well to each side of the apparent source of the leak; water can creep disconcertingly before coming through.

◄ BC67. Tricks of the trade! You will never see a car in a showroom with anything but uniformly black tyres. The old Morris Marina was just about purring to itself as the tyrewall black was painted on.

▲ BC68. Next, the engine bay was cleaned up for what seemed like the first time ever. Aerosol degreaser was sprayed all over, allowed to soak in, worked in with a brush and then hosed off. Don't expect to use the car straight away if you try this, especially if you get water into the electrics.

▲ BC70. The old Morris Marina now had a real sparkle to it that it hadn't had for years. It seemed to sit an inch higher on its springs and certainly didn't look a candidate for being driven into the nearest gatepost. As I said right at the start, the car was only cosmetically improved but it was fit for a bit of fun classic car motoring until such time as a full restoration could be contemplated.

▲ BC71. If your car has untidy and stained velour pile seats, improve them by first scratching off any hard deposits with a blunt knife ...

▲ BC72. ... then squirt some velour upholstery foam cleaner onto the cloth or onto a rag and wipe the cloth clean, without actually soaking it.

▲ BC73. Black bumpers lose their crisp blackness really quickly and they can be perked up with a cleaner made just for the job – and so can black sunroof fabric, vinyl roof coverings and sportscar vinyl rag-tops, each of which seems to have a product made especially for the job.

▲ BC74. Just scrubbing deeply sculptured or wire wheels with soapy water and a stiff brush can make a real improvement to the general appearance. And don't forget to clean the window glass really thoroughly all the way around – your car contains a large area of glass and smears will detract from the brightest paintwork.

Smartening up an older car is one of the cheapest jobs you can carry out but with dramatic effect. Allow plenty of time and be prepared for some fairly hard work – more power to your elbow!

HOME SPRAYING WITH AEROSOL

Aerosol paint is the ideal way of spraying anything up to a single panel at a time. After all, you don't need to buy any expensive equipment, only the can that the paint comes in.

▲ HS2. The 'wet-or-dry' paper was used with water to feather out the filler, leaving no trace of a hard edge.

▲ HS1. As well as the aerosol paint itself, you'll need a whole range of ancillaries such as abrasive paper for rubbing down.

▲ HS3. Before starting to spray, the Spectra primer was taken outside, shaken vigorously, and the nozzle cleared.

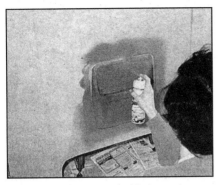

▲ HS4. The can was held about six inches away and red oxide primer sprayed onto the bare metal. When choosing your primer colour, go for red for dark shades of top coat, grey for lighter coats and grey or preferably white for white top coats and metallics.

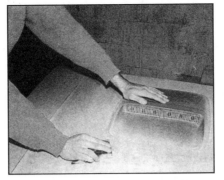

▲ HS7 Provided that the filler work was carried out properly, the use of High Build Spray Putty will allow you to remove every last blemish when you sand it out with fine wet-or-dry supported on a flat rubbing block.

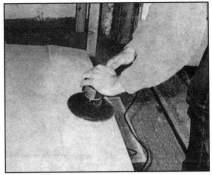

▲ HS10. To digress for a moment, the preparation of a large flat area can take quite a long time by hand. This is where the Black & Decker random orbit sander was particularly useful.

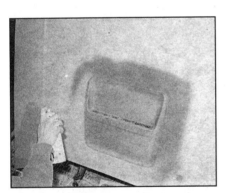

▲ HS5. This was magical (or at least, the results of sanding it later, were). High-build spray putty was sprayed onto the whole area ...

▲ HS8. By now, and for no apparent reason, we were working with the bonnet laid horizontally. We chose to spray on grey primer paint as a barrier colour between the yellow and the white top coat to follow. Red and yellow have a nasty habit of 'grinning through' white surface coats above them.

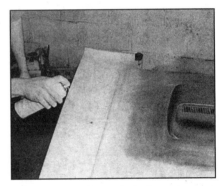

▲ HS11. Now here's a tip from the experts. Holding a tin of black spray paint about a foot or more away from the job, a light guide coat can be dusted onto the work.

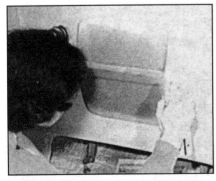

▲ HS6. ... and then, extending a little wider than the area of the original red oxide primer, a second coat of spray putty was applied after the first had dried.

▲ HS9. Plenty of water, a few spots of washing up liquid, and the finest grade of wet-or-dry and the final primer coat was prepared for finish painting.

▲ HS12. The idea is not to change the colour of the panel but just to put an even sprinkling of paint over the whole panel.

▲ HS13. Sand the entire panel all over once more with the finest grade of paper and the guide coat, as it is called, will be sanded off in all but the low areas. After you wipe off with a dry rag, any low spots and blemishes will stand out like a sore thumb!

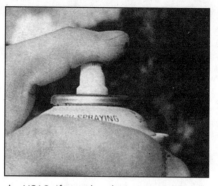

▲ HS16. If you do what comes naturally, the part of your finger sticking forwards catches the edge of the spray which builds up into a drip which is then shot forwards as a blob onto your lovely handiwork. Most annoying!

▲ HS18. The second coat, as already suggested, followed in a pattern which criss-crossed the first, and this time the colour beneath did disappear from view. Ideally, you may want to give another one or two coats. If any little bits of dust land in the surface, you may be able to polish them out with fine cutting compound, but be most careful not to go right through the paint and don't try it until the paint has had several days to dry really hard.

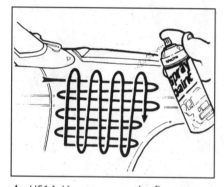

▲ HS14. You can spray the first two finish coats on in fairly quick succession, just leaving a few minutes between them for the first coat to 'flash off'.
The second coat should be at right angles to the first. (Drawing courtesy of Spectra.)

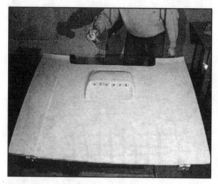

▲ HS17. The first coat was applied in regular strips up and down the bonnet, concentrating on obtaining an even coat without trying to blanket out the colour underneath. That's the way to achieve runs!

▲ HS19. Aerosol hammer finish paint gives an even hammer finish coat from an aerosol can without needing any primer beneath it. It also has good rust protection and easy-clean qualities.

▲ HS15. It might look uncomfortable but you should always hold the nozzle down with the very tip of your finger.

◄ HS20. A second coat sprayed at right angles to the first, gives a full, even coat. Do it within a few minutes of spraying the first coat but after the first coat's solvent has 'flashed off'.

▲ HS21. It's best to practise your spraying on a spare scrap of sheet steel. Hold the can too close and the paint will run; too far away and you'll have a 'dry' looking finish.

▲ HS22. Very slight runs may be polished out but most will have to be sanded out when the paint is dry using fine wet-or-dry paper.

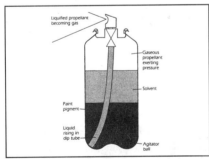

▲ HS23. How an aerosol works. If you tip the can upside down, the paint flow ceases. At the end of spraying, use this technique to clear the nozzle. You can see why it's essential to shake an aerosol paint can for several minutes before using it. The agitator ball has the job of mixing the paint pigment, which may be quite thick at the bottom; thoroughly with the solvent. In very cold weather you may also have to immerse the can in warm (not boiling) water for several minutes before use. Never puncture an aerosol can or expose it to direct heat.

USING SPECIAL PAINTS

As well as the paint types already shown, Spectra also produce Extra High Gloss chrome or gold paint for customising, black heat dispersant paint for cylinder blocks, engines and exhaust systems to aid cooling and improve efficiency, and clear acrylic lacquer called 'Wheel Protector', for preventing corrosion on alloy wheels. Spectra recommend that you don't use heat dispersant paint on manifolds; the extra heat found there being just too much for it!

[Illustration HS24]

▲ HS24 Spectra clear lacquer is a cellulose-based lacquered top seal for sealing styling stripes or for keeping the gloss on cellulose paint finishes.

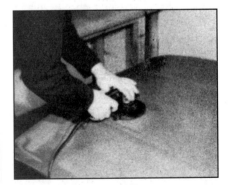

▲ HS25. Spectra wheel paints come in white, black, gold, silver and steel. You could mask off the tyre with masking tape and newspaper as shown in the drawing, or you could paint hand cleaner in a heavy layer on to the tyre before spraying on the wheel paint As soon as the wheel paint is dry the hand cleaner can be washed off leaving the tyre good as new. For a final finish, paint with tyre wall black.

HOME SPRAYING WITH A COMPRESSOR

Cellulose paint is not as durable as the 2-Pack paint which DIY enthusiasts must never use without the proper facilities (see manufacturer's instructions), but it has the virtue of being able to be sprayed on a DIY basis and it can also be polished to give the best shine of any paint.

SAFETY

All filler contains skin irritants, so you should wear gloves when handling it. When sanding paint or filler, particularly with a power sander, you must always wear an efficient particle mask otherwise the inhalation of sanding dust could damage your health. Nitro-cellulose paints, those made by Valentine for instance and shown here, are eminently suitable for DIY work. However, take full note of Valentine's own safety precautions and in particular, never spray in other than a well-ventilated work area. Also, bear in mind that paint, thinners and spray vapour are all highly flammable. Do not use near flames, sparks (including those created by central heating boilers and self-igniting gas cookers, etc), or any naked flames.

[Photograph]

▲ HS26. If many coats of paint have previously been applied, they will have to be stripped back to bare metal before being repainted. Sanding of any sort is far quicker with a random orbit sander, such as the Black & Decker electric unit shown here. This has the distinct advantage of not creating scratches which will show through the finished paintwork.

▲ HS27. Very minor blemishes such as pin holes or scratches in the paint should be filled with a thin scrape of stopper which can be sanded down after drying thoroughly.

▲ HS28. Hand sanding should always be carried out with the aid of a rubbing block, other than in the corners of fluted panels such as that shown here, where your fingers make an ideally shaped tool.

PREPARATION

Tools required: grinder, sander, P120 and P240 grit discs, P600 wet-or-dry paper, dust particle mask.

Materials required: 197-1005 degreasing fluid (this is essential for removing silicones which will most certainly ruin the finished paint surface if allowed to remain on the work), G112 stopper.

▲ HS29. With no attachment on the end of the hose, you can use the SIP Airmate compressor to blow any remaining sanding dust off the panel.

▲ HS30. Degreasing fluid should have been used before you started and should now be used again to remove any traces of silicones or other grease contamination. Silicones, which are contained in all domestic polishes, cause dreadful and irremovable 'fish eye' marks in the final paint.

▲ HS31. The Cordless drill was used with a paint stirrer in the chuck to stir the Primer Filler to an even consistency. Note the steel rule placed in the pot to aid accurate measurement when thinning the paint. Go initially for 50/50 thinning, but be prepared to readjust to suit the requirements of the SIP spray.

▲ HS32. The SIP gun has two adjustment screws at the rear. The top one is for the width of the spray pattern, while the lower one adjusts the quantity which comes out of the gun.

▲ HS33. Adjust the two spray gun screws so that the spray pattern and spray density are as you require. Test it out thoroughly upon a piece of scrap board or a cardboard box.

▲ HS34. The edge of this panel dipped away from the user so that part, the curved edge, was sprayed first. The SIP gun has a light triggering action and is easy to use.

▲ HS35. The whole panel was painted in consistent, even bands, each one half overlapping the previous one.

▲ HS36. The next day, after the two full coats of primer had thoroughly dried, a very light, heavily thinned coat of black paint was sprayed on with the SIP gun.

▲ HS39. Use an air line to blow any dust from around the top of the tin. SIP produce a trigger operated 'air duster' if you prefer.

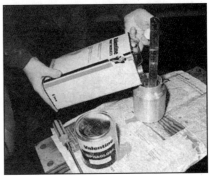

▲ HS42. Pour in an equal amount of thinner. Note: the supply of copious amounts of newspaper is essential.

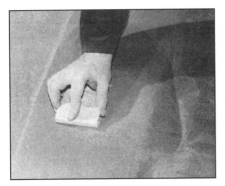

▲ HS37. When the primer was 'blocked' down with medium grit paper, the thin 'guide' coat, which was sprayed on with the SIP gun (although you could have used aerosol for greater speed), was sanded off as the primer filler coat was made smooth. It remained visible in the low spots, however, picking them out.

▲ HS40. The Cordless drill is again used for several minutes to mix the entire contents of the paint.

▲ HS43. After using the air line to blow off the panel once more, wipe it down yet again with spirit wipe ...

▲ HS38. Before spraying the top coat, wet the floor to lay the dust but take care to avoid electrical connections.

▲ HS41. Use a steel rule, if you haven't got the correct painter's measuring stick, to measure the correct amount of paint and thinners.

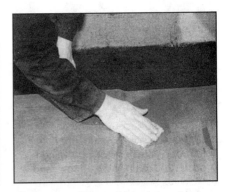

▲ HS44. ... followed by wiping down with a tack rag to remove every trace of dust or dirt.

▲ HS45. An accepted way of checking that the SIP gun is held the correct distance away is to use a hand span as a measure.

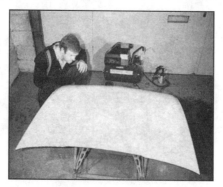

▲ HS48. Robert surveys the wonderful depth of gloss which four coats of Spragloss solid colour had given, and proves that the DIY SIP equipment can give fully professional results.

PRIMING

Tools required:
Masking tape, masking paper (such as newspaper), paint strainer, SIP spray gun, SIP compressor, spray mask, tack rag.

Materials required:
As well as those shown earlier and on these pages: cellulose thinner 199-207 for any additional thinning above 50/50 (don't use 199-6 thinner for more than 50/50), Red Oxide Primer.

▲ HS46. Robert started off by spraying a 'half coat'– a thin coat to aid adhesion without causing runs – sprayed in vertical, overlapping bands.

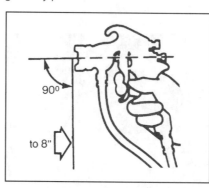

▲ HS49. Always hold the spray gun at right angles to the surface you are painting, keeping it between six and eight inches from the car. (Diagram courtesy of Glasurit.)

TOP COAT

Tools required:
The same SIP equipment and other 'hardware' as was used previously. Top coat paint must be strained. Add P1200 wet-or-dry paper and polishing compound for polishing out any dirt particles that may get into the final coat.

Materials required:
Solid colour paint and a compatible high-quality thinner. Consult your paint supplier.

▲ HS47. After this had 'flashed off' (ie, the thinners had evaporated) he sprayed a full coat in overlapping horizontal bands. The suspended panel reduces dirt contamination and an open door aids ventilation.

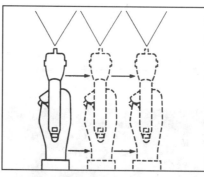

▲ HS50. Keep your wrists stiff and avoid swinging the gun in an arc from your elbow, to ensure even spraying. Always spray at a steady, even pace.

Before using primer check the existing paint to find out whether it is compatible with cellulose. Rub a small area of paint with cellulose thinner. If the paint film dissolves go ahead; if the paint wrinkles it is affected by cellulose and will have to be sprayed all over with isolating primer to seal it.

Chapter 7

Glass-fibre bodywork

REPAIRING GRP BODY DAMAGE

'Fibreglass', glass-fibre and Glass Reinforced Plastic are all names for a material that was once going to shake steel from its rust-ridden throne as king of the car panels. Although high-performance car manufacturers like Corvette in the USA, Lotus, TVR and many others in the UK and Renault-Alpine in France took to it, GRP has only ever been used on a small number of cars. Although GRP can split when put under stress, it has the great advantages that it *never* rots and it is one of the most suitable substances for DIY applications used in car bodywork. Thanks are due to the GRP experts, Smith & Deakin of Worcester, England and especially to Tom, who went to a great deal of trouble to help in the preparation of this section.

Materials: 1oz (25g) mat – meaning its weight per square foot – the heavier, the thicker. Pre-activated lay-up resin, sold by weight and nearly always sold complete with sufficient hardener. Barrier cream – strongly advisable. Resin stripper, for removing the resin from brushes on which it has gone hard, is useful for beginners. Ordinary washing powder is excellent and cheap for cleaning brushes provided it is used as a thick paste made

▼ *GFR1. The basic equipment you will need to carry out work with GRP, apart from the most basic workshop tools, includes a 1½ inch paintbrush, a pair of rubber or plastic gloves (ensuring that the plastic is not the type dissolved by resin), a container in which to mix the resin (again, some plastics are unsuitable), a mixing stick and plenty of newspaper on which to work. Very useful, but not essential is a roller which ensures absorption of the resin by the mat.*

with hot water and worked in really well before the resin goes hard. Acetone, though, is the recognised brush cleaner but brings its own hazards – check with your supplier.

Safety – The following points are strongly recommended:
a) the wearing of goggles and, b) the use of barrier cream and gloves when working with liquid resin, c) the use of gloves when working with 'raw' mat, ie handling or cutting it, and d) it is essential to wear an efficient respirator when sanding or cutting cured laminate, unless it is cut with a knife whilst in its soft, 'green', semi-cured state. In addition I would add that GRP should be cut or sanded away from children and pets and preferably, out of doors – breathing in the tiny air-borne particles is literally to inhale powdered glass. Not nice!

GRP – THE HOW AND WHY

'Fibreglass' is the trade name of the American company which markets the strands of silicone (or 'glass') which, when loosely bonded together make the familiar white coloured 'mat' with which we shall be dealing. The correct term for the substance is Glass Reinforced Plastic – quite literally a plastic of the thermo-setting type (ie it can't be re-softened by heating, unlike 'plastic' plastics) which, when reinforced by the glass, forms a material which weight for weight, is stronger than steel.

Within the glass-fibre mat itself, each strand is microscopically thin, thousands of these hair-like strands being drawn together to form the thicker fibres which

make up the visible strands of mat. Although the mat appears white, this is only the colour of the bonding agent which holds the strands together enabling the mat to be handled in sheet form. The behaviour of this bonding agent is important when it comes to impregnating the mat with resin as will be shown later.

The resin, technically known as Polyester Resin, is a long chain monomer. This is really a clever way of saying that all the molecules are linked together in long lines rather like the chain on a boat's anchor. While the resin is liquid, the chains are free to slip over one another, but the addition of hardener sets off a chemical reaction (confirmed by the fact that resin gets warm as it goes off) which bonds the lines of molecules in an extremely complex criss-crossed interlocking mesh.

If more than the maker's recommended quantity of hardener is added, the resin will go off more quickly and produce more heat. The reverse is also true. The greater the heat added, the more quickly will the resin go off. In hot weather less hardener should be added if you want to avoid the frustration of seeing your expensive resin turn in rapid succession from liquid to jelly to a solid lump, ruining your brush and temper in the process. Conversely, cold weather should be countered by the addition of extra hardener, or heat, which should only be applied generally to the work area and not directly to the job. Too much heat or too much hardener result in a weakened laminate. Confused? You won't be ...

By itself, the resin is very hard and brittle; combining it with the glass-fibre mat, however, transforms it almost miraculously into a substance that is far stronger than the sum of the two separate substances. This phenomenon is not restricted to GRP of course, reinforced concrete being another commonly used material which takes on additional strength in a somewhat similar way.

To be precise, hardener alone will not cause resin to go off in the way described. A further substance, Cobalt

Naphthenate (an unfriendly sounding substance if ever there was one), has to be mixed with the resin. This component of the mixture is known as 'accelerator'. Most resin manufacturers supply their product with the accelerator ready mixed in, though it is possible to buy it separately. As its name implies, the more accelerator added, the quicker the resin goes off. For various reasons it is far better to leave non pre-accelerated resin well alone. The most obvious reason is that when you buy ready-mixed resin you can be fairly sure that the manufacturers have added the optimum amount of accelerator for thorough and strong curing of the resin. Just be sure when you buy your resin (either from a specialist supplier to the public or from a boatyard or other specialist user) that the resin is pre-accelerated. If not, obtain accelerator too. **NB. Never mix neat accelerator with neat hardener. They react explosively!**

Basically, as far as resin for repairing GRP is concerned, that's it. There are in fact different types of resin, both chemically and practically speaking, such as gel-coat, flame retardant and casting resins and so on, as well as a range of 'accessory' materials to enable all sorts of jobs to be carried out. But really, it would take a book ...

GETTING DOWN TO IT

A golden rule for repairing local damage is, 'don't try to do too much at once'. Glass-fibre is awfully messy at the best of times and soggy feather edged patches of the stuff splodged all over your car will do your morale no good at all. Instead, be sensible and tackle a small part of a panel at a time, the smaller the better, until you have built up some experience of the materials you are using.

You should, however, strip off all the paint from the panel you are working on. With the paint off you will be able to see all of the stress damage developing in the painting process which might take months to show through. Even if you achieve a perfect feather edge between your repair, the existing panel and the old paint, the thinners in the new paint

will cause the existing paint to lift slightly, showing up some months later as a hollow around the repair.

Any paint stripper will remove the paint but unfortunately most types soften the gel coat of the existing bodywork. It will harden off again later but it is all too easy to cause extra work for yourself as your scraper digs in. Nitromors produce a stripper specially for GRP which takes a lot longer to work but gets there surely and rather more safely.

Once the old paint is off, the repair procedure to be followed will fall into a certain category depending upon the extent and type of damage found. The first item described is a general technique used in all GRP repair where more than surface blemishes are to be dealt with.

LAYING UP

1) Cut a piece of mat to fit the work to be carried out either by tearing against a straightedge or with scissors.
2) Pour the required amount of resin into a container (but *not* glass) and thoroughly stir in a measured amount of hardener. The manufacturer's literature will say how much, but remember to use more in cold weather, less in hot weather.
3) Paint resin liberally onto the surface on which the GRP is to be layed up.
4) Place the mat over the repair and stipple more resin briskly with a stiff, downward dabbing movement until the mat loses its whiteness and becomes translucent. Do not try to wet thoroughly the 'mat' a bit at a time. Get some resin over the whole surface then come back and start stippling from the place where you started, having given the resin a chance to soak in.
5) Consolidate the resin well into the mat by rolling it thoroughly in all directions. If resin hardens onto the roller, it can be burned off, but outdoors only, because it gives off dense, dangerous, choking fumes. Your hands and brush don't benefit from being coated in resin and should be cleaned off straight away with Swarfega (or other hand cleaner) and washing powder respectively.

STAR CRACKS

Star cracks and other surface crazing are the most common GRP faults. Often they seem to 'just happen' although flying stones or having the surface pushed in can also produce the same effects. The surface all around the cracks must be ground away, preferably by using a grinding disc on an electric drill, until the cracks themselves are no longer visible (wear a mask and goggles). Then a coat of lay-up resin should be applied to the whole surface followed, when set, by body filler applied in the normal way.

Really severe cracks, ones which can be accentuated by flexing the panel, should be treated as described but in addition the surface should be ground quite a lot more deeply and one layer, or two if possible, of 1oz (25g) mat should be layed-up over the repair before the filler is added. In severe cases of damage it would also be strongly advisable to add a couple of layers of mat to the back of the panel as well.

BITS MISSING

Apart from light star cracks, every other type of GRP damage must be repaired from the back so that sufficient strength can be restored to the panel without the repair being in any way evident. Cars which are constructed of double-skinned GRP *must* have a section cut out of their inner skin to enable the damaged outer skin to be repaired properly. The section can be fixed back in place later using a small modification of the basic repair technique shown for larger repairs.

Dealing with small repairs first of all, it is possible to place masking tape over the outside of the hole, clean up the inside of the damaged area for about 6 inches (150mm) around it using a sanding disc on an electric drill or angle grinder, and then lay up five or six layers of resin-impregnated mat across the hole and for an additional 6 inches (150mm) or so on each side.

When the resin has thoroughly gone-off turn your attention to the 'good' side and sand down any excess resin, which will have oozed under the edges of the masking tape, and also a margin of two to three inches around the patch to give

the filler something to grip on to.

Then apply a good layer of Plastic Padding or other 'fine' type of plastic filler over the patch and the sanded margin around it. If, when the desired level has been achieved imperfections are found, don't be tempted to try to sand them out. Nothing looks worse than a repair which is perfect except that it can be seen as a dip in the panel. Remember that inaccurate levelling is quite hard to spot on a matt section of filler but once it is painted, the gloss finish will always show up any mistakes. Pin holes, which are tiny craters left from cutting into air bubbles incorporated into the filler at the mixing stage can be simply dealt with by ignoring them. Until, that is, you have flatted the area and applied primer, when they can be filled by applying the thinnest smear of cellulose stopper before flatting down again in readiness for painting.

LARGER REPAIRS

Large repairs are no more difficult to deal with – just bigger. In much the same way as with steel panels, it is sometimes necessary to 'patch-in' a repair section, the main difference being that the patch does not have to be fitted quite as accurately as would be necessary with steel. Owners of Reliant Scimitars, TVRs and the like are in the fortunate position of being able to purchase replacement panels from which they can cut a suitable patch, keeping the edges as neat as possible. This can then be placed over the damaged area, drawn around and the damaged piece cut out.

Under impact, glass fibre bodywork tends to break up in much the same way as a broken eggshell and the pieces retain their original shape and dimensions so it is possible to pick up the wreckage and piece it together in best Humpty Dumpty fashion, bonding in one piece at a time. If a panel does suffer a mishap it makes repairs much more simple if the owner has the presence of mind or the opportunity to collect the bits from the scene of the misfortune.

Owners of rarer cars such as Rochdale or Berkeley may have to make their own mould either by using another complete

vehicle or by doing a 'bodge' repair on their own panel with filler which is finished as accurately as possible so that a mould can be taken from the repaired panel. A repair section can then be taken from the mould before cutting out the 'bodge' and repairing the panel properly.

Repair patches should be held in place using bridging pieces of aluminium screwed across the gaps in several places on the outer or the 'good' side. Hold them in place by drilling clearance holes in the pieces of aluminium (drill all holes before the aluminium is cut up into strips: it's easier and safer to grip that way) and drill pilot holes in the GRP before attaching the clips with self-tapping screws on the 'good' side of the panel.

If pop-rivets are used with the idea of later drilling them out, be sure not to use those with steel shafts since the bits left inside the repair, will eventually corrode causing a rare sight in GRP bodywork – rust bubbles!

Then masking tape must be stuck length-ways along the joint between the patch and the panel to prevent excess resin oozing through the crack and down onto good bodywork causing more cleaning-up work than is necessary.

Strips of mat, about 6 inches (150mm) wide and five or six layers thick should be layed-up over the length of the joint, after first cleaning up the inside of the panel in the way described for smaller repairs. The GRP should be given time to go off really thoroughly before the clips are removed – about a day should suffice; longer in really cold weather – and then the wisdom of placing your clips on the outside will manifest itself. If you had put them on the inside they would of course now be lost underneath six rock hard layers of GRP. It is possible to use filler to restore the surface. However, there will be more structural strength in the repair if the seams on the outer surface are now 'Vee'd', so that the edges of the panel and the replaced section gradually taper to meet each other. In effect the outer surface is tapered so that at the joint itself the panel is almost through to the supporting mat on the reverse side. The surface level should then be restored by applying layers of resin impregnated mat until the surface is slightly proud. When the mat has cured the repair is rubbed down level and any imperfections made good with conventional filler.

For safety's sake you must wear gloves when handling glass-fibre, even though the professional shown here chose not to. See also the 'Safety' section on P211.

LARGE-SCALE BODY REPAIR

▲ GFR2. This Reliant three-wheeler had received a bit of a punch on the cheek. As usual, the GRP had disintegrated under the shock of the crash.

▲ GFR3. No, this isn't an instant repair! It's a replacement panel from a scrap car placed over the top, although new panels can be bought in the normal way. Second-hand panels, provided they are not damaged, are as good as new ones, of course, in GRP.

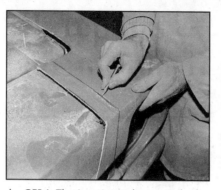

▲ GFR4. The 'new' panel was marked out, leaving in place most of the sound glass-fibre of the car being repaired, and the excess cut off from the repair panel. The damaged shell was marked out to suit.

▲ GFR5. Here, the old panel is cut out with a special GRP cutter blade fixed to a mini-grinder ...

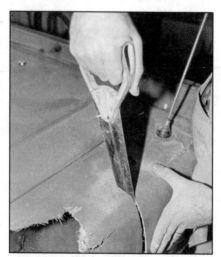

▲ GFR6. ... but it is almost as easy and far less dusty to use a panel saw, although GRP will quickly blunt a sharp saw. (You MUST wear adequate breathing protection because GRP dust can, quite literally, be lethal.)

▲ GFR7. More of the old panel was cut away ...

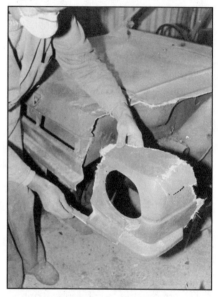

▲ GFR8. ... until all of the old, damaged portion was removed.

▲ GFR9. At this stage, it is essential to ensure that the repair section is correctly located. GRP is so easy to use that it's easy to get carried away and fit the panel without lining it up properly. Use a rule and check measurements from all directions using the undamaged side of the car as a reference point.

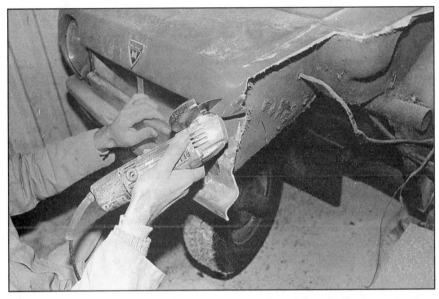

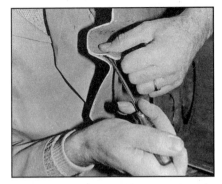

▲ GFR 13. Look inside the repair panel for any loose joints, strengtheners, or old repairs, and make sure that all joints are properly bonded. If they're not, roughen the surfaces and bond them together with extra layers of GRP.

▲ GFR10. Now, in the manner of manuals the world over, you were just told to cut the damage away and trim the repair panel to suit. Actually, in the real world, it's a bit slower than that! You should cut off the damage, then a little more and a little more until you reach a) sound GRP and b) a good position to join up the new panel.

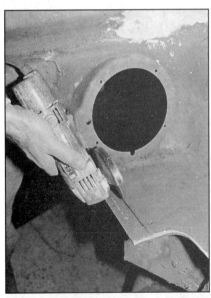

▲ GFR12. Here, part of the grille trim is being offered up as a double-check that the correct position of the new panel is being maintained.

▲ GFR11. Similarly, trim off enough of the repair panel to stop it being unwieldy but cut back to exact shape later, in conjunction with trimming the old panel.

▶ GFR 14. Roughen all the surfaces to be joined, using a mini-grinder and ...

215

▲ GFR15. ... clean off the inner surfaces of both existing and repair patches and wipe down with a spirit wipe – grease is a major enemy of successful GRP bonding.

▲ GFR18. ... and screw the strips across the joints to hold the two panels accurately together.

▲ GFR21. Place a piece of card on the floor and 'lay-up' three strips of mat. (Cut them out **before** you start, or the sticky resin will make it an almost impossible task.)

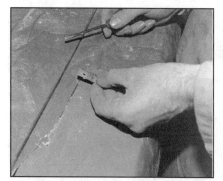

▲ GFR16. With all joints trimmed so that there is only a small gap between existing and repair panels, cut out some strips of thin steel or aluminium ...

▲ GFR19. Next, place a strip of masking tape firmly over the joint, pressing it down carefully around the joint strips.

▲ GFR22 Use suitable gloves or at the very least an effective barrier cream for this part of the work. Bear the section of mat on brush and hand, offering it up to the repair joint.

▲ GFR17. ... drill pilot holes ...

▲ GFR20. Mix up some ordinary lay-up resin with hardener, according to the supplier's instructions.

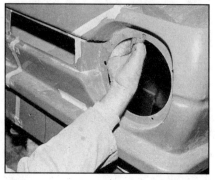

▲ GFR23. Press it firmly into place, trying not to pull it off again as you take your hand away.

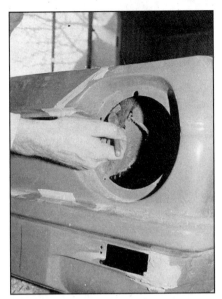

▲ GFR24. Then stipple the mat with the resin brush as thoroughly as you can to 'wet-out' the mat. Do the same with the next section of the repair, overlapping the second patch with the first to make a good bond.

▲ GFR27. ... and proceed to sand and flat the repair as you would any other.

REPAIRING A SMALL HOLE

▲ GFR25. Next, feather the edges of the repair inwards a little using the mini-grinder and a coarse sanding disc.

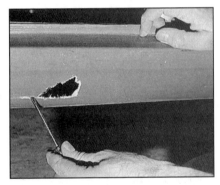

▲ GFR28. In the same crash, a small hole had been punched into the car's lower bodywork. The full extent of any cracks was investigated so that they too, could be repaired.

▲ GFR30. ... and wetted-out mat applied as in the previous section.

▲ GFR26. Spread filler into the shallow valley you have created ...

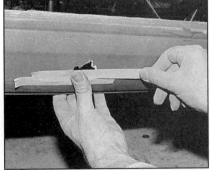

▲ GFR29. Masking tape was used to build up a temporary cover over the hole ...

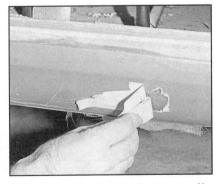

▲ GFR31. After the GRP has 'gone off' the tape can be removed ...

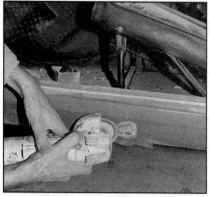

▲ GFR32. ... the proud surface of the GRP ground back...

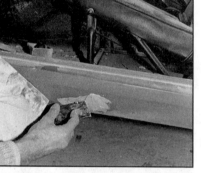

▲ GFR33. ... and the surface filled and finished in the usual way.

▲ GFR34. A useful tool for removing a larger area of filler without causing ripples is a large single-cut file (ie with one row of teeth, so it doesn't clog so easily). Work it half-a-dozen strokes in one direction, then the same number in another to help avoid rippling, which looks awful when the gloss paint goes on.

REPAIRING A TEAR

▲ GFR35. Edge damage in GRP frequently takes the form of a tear, like this. (You can prevent it by beefing up the edge of the panel with a flange or even just with extra layers.)

▲ GFR36. Repair the tear by screwing a clip or clips in place as in the earlier section ...

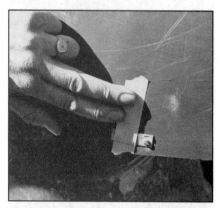

▲ GFR37. ... masking off the joint and then laying-up GRP on the inside before grinding and filling the outside of the tear in the normal way. If, as sometimes happens, the split is accompanied by delamination, the affected area should be ground away from the outside after the internal reinforcement is in place and then replaced by new layers of mat and resin.

▼ GFR38. You can carry out GRP repairs to plastic bumpers using the methods shown here, although with some kinds of plastic, the GRP may not bond and the repair could be no more than temporary. You should add a paint plasticiser to the paint before spraying it if the plastic is at all flexible. Far better to do the job properly – see 'Repairing plastics'.

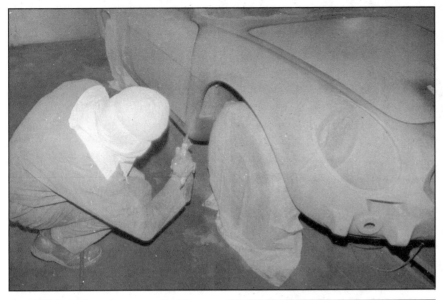

▲ GFR39. GRP can be sprayed with perfect success, but don't attempt to get rid of crazing in GRP just by filling over the top (see 'Star Cracks' earlier in this section) otherwise the cracks will, with absolute certainty, reappear through the paint in weeks or even days.

COPYING A GRP PANEL

▲ CP1. In the UK Mustang front spoilers are fairly easy to get hold of, but are outrageously expensive, and the same is true of most panels imported into one country from another. Because it is non-loadbearing, this is an ideal panel to copy, provided that the owner can get hold of one to copy from. First, a negative copy of the panel has to be made.

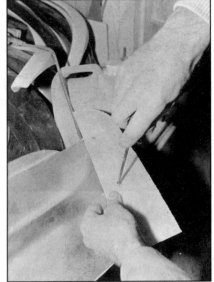

▲ CP2. This spoiler has a small internal flange. Obviously, if you laid glass-fibre over the outside of the panel and wrapped it round the flange, you wouldn't get the original panel out of the mould! A strip was screwed onto the flange ...

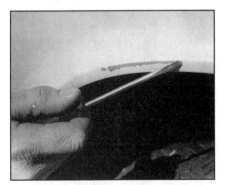

▲ GFR40. The surface of GRP must be well flatted, it must be wiped over with a degreasing spirit wipe and sprayed first in self-etch primer, which eats a key into the surface, otherwise paint will flake off like this.

▲ CP3. ... which stuck out beyond the edge of the panel. This is essential, but it is easier to explain what it does by showing it in the pictures to come.

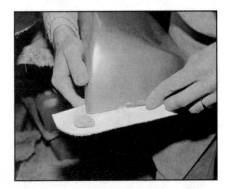

▶ CP4. The joint between spoiler and extension strip was sealed with modelling clay so that no resin could get in there.

▼ CP7. ... and paint the gel-coat on to the master shape; in this case, the spoiler. Aim to get a good, heavy, even coat, right up to the edges. Don't leave gaps or the mat will show through, and don't use ordinary resin for this job: gel-coat resin remains tacky even after hardening, which is ideal for bonding on the following layers.

▲ CP5. A release agent was wiped on to the surface of the panel, otherwise the GRP would bond itself to it, ruining the original panel. **Remember:** 1) Make sure you cover every inch with release agent. 2) Use only a wax polish **without** silicone additive. Most of them have it but your GRP supplier will be able to supply suitable wax if all else fails. 3) It may be best to operate a 'belts-and-braces' approach: apply wax release agent plus a paint-on PVA release agent. Ruining a good panel or mould can be expensive in terms of both time and money.

▲ CP6. Mix up some gel-coat resin to the supplier's recommended resin/hardener ratio ...

▲ CP8. Place a layer of mat all over the master shaft after the gel-coat has 'gone-off: Use gloves and, preferably, a heavy coat of barrier cream, even though this Smith & Deakin's worker doesn't go much on gloves.

▲ CP9. Then stipple on lay-up resin to which you have added hardener. 'Wet-out' the mat thoroughly until it loses most of its whiteness, goes thoroughly floppy and takes on a yellowed appearance.

◀ CP10. Make absolutely sure that the mat is down tight in all the corners because any gaps or air bubbles will severely weaken it.

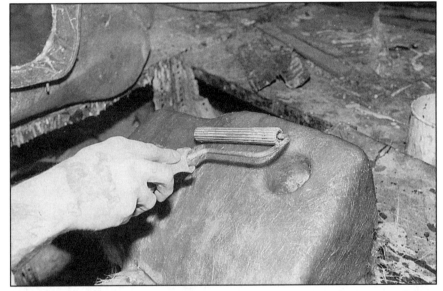

▲ CP11. You can make quite sure that all the air is out by using a special metal roller, sold by most GRP suppliers.

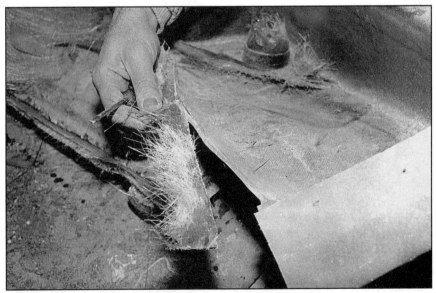

▲ CP12. You should have 'laid-up' right over the edge to be sure of getting a good thickness at the edge. If you can catch the resin just as it is 'green' you can cut it with a sharp knife. Otherwise, use a saw taking care not to damage the master, or mould.

▲ CP13. Remember the strip stuck over the flange? It has to be trimmed round and the screws undone then taken off. The surface made up of the original flange **plus** the extension now made up of fresh glass-fibre is treated thoroughly with release agent.

▲ CP14. Then, with the master spoiler still inside the mould, a pad of GRP is laid up across the whole flat surface, flange and all, but remember: there's release agent between this pad and the surface beneath.

▲ CP15. After the resin has gone off, but before removing the pad, it and the mould were drilled through in two places, so that later, when bolts and nuts are placed through these holes, the pad can be put back onto the mould in exactly the same place.

▲ CP19. Even with release agent, the two won't just fall apart. Hitting all the edges fairly hard with a rubber mallet helps them to start.

▲ CP16. The pad can now be removed from the mould and trimmed.

▲ CP22. ... hammering it all the way round.

▲ CP20. Protrusions like this are particularly bad sticking points. Just give it a few sharp cracks with the mallet and keep working at it.

▲ CP17. The whole mould is trimmed back to the master. Here, Tom is wearing a fully protective air-fed breathing set. See your local factor for something almost as good for mouth and nose only and take note of the safety advice regarding the potentially lethal glass dust mentioned earlier in this section.

▲ CP21. You can also try driving a smooth thin tapering piece of wood into the joint ...

▲ CP18. The surplus has also to be cut off the air vent...

▲ CP23. On the left is the negative or 'female' mould, while on the right is the original. To make a perfect copy, all you do is bolt the 'pads' of GRP back on to both ends, and lay up **inside** the mould; including inside the corners made by the two pads – they give the two flanges. To remove, take off the two pads, and hey presto! And not only will the copy be absolutely identical to the original, it could also be stronger!

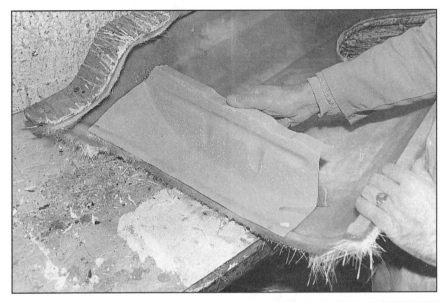

▲ CP24. Some pieces can't be cast-in even without removable pieces, as shown. This is the support on the inside of an MGB wing. Make it separately and, after putting ar least two coats of mat into the mould, put it in place and lay-up more mat over all the edges to hold it in place.

Incidentally, if you expect a mould to last a long time and provide many copies, make it with at least four layers of mat – but don't lay up more than four layers, *maximum* at one go, because the heat generated can cause problems. Also remember to leave the job on the master or in the mould for a couple of days: those nasty, rippled GRP panels you may have seen were probably caused by taking out the panel too soon.

With GRP work you are only restricted by your own imagination, and your ability to make a master of the shape you want, although you can use all sorts of materials to do it. But do remember that GRP copies everything – right down to blemishes and scratches, so spend time making sure that your master is as perfect as possible.

FITTING GRP PANELS IN PLACE OF STEEL

Glass-fibre panels must not be fitted to a car where the original panels form part of the vehicle's inherent strength. In many cases, the fitting of glass-fibre front wings, and occasionally rear wings, is perfectly acceptable as they do not significantly contribute to the car's overall rigidity. However, regulations on this issue can change over a period of time and also from country to country, so always check that a) the fitting of glass-fibre wings is legal in your area,

and b) that your car is going to be structurally sound after you have fitted them. The other drawback with glass-fibre panels, and in particular wings, is that they very rarely fit properly, often needing a lot of manipulation and ingenuity before they will go on: this is naturally very much more the case with cars which normally have welded-on wings rather than those which have bolt-on wings. There are many advantages however: they never corrode (although they do crack and craze), they are often quite a lot cheaper than steel equivalents and they provide the opportunity to substantially change the appearance and character of your car by the fitting of flared wings, wheel arches and spoilers.

SAFETY
Always wear an efficient particle mask when drilling or sanding glass-fibre; the glass fibres, if inhaled, can be injurious to health. Wear gloves and goggles when handling glass-fibre resin, hardener and mat. Follow the manufacturer's safety instructions.

▼ FP1. Peter Gorton's DIY Porsche Carrera look-alike is an excellent example of what can be achieved. By fitting a whole panoply of glass-fibre panels on a home-restored body shell he has created an extremely attractive car.

▲ FP2. The excellent fit of these panels reflects the hundreds of hours and huge sum of money that Peter put into his pet project. The dent he once put into the roof when driven mad with frustration at the difficulty of making panels fit properly in the early hours of one winter's night has since been panelbeaten out!

The following sequence shows the fitting of a range of glass-fibre panels to Porsches used in off-road racing.

▲ FP3. A glass-fibre wing is offered up to the restored Porsche 911 body shell prior to fitting.

▲ FP4. Before fitting the wing, the fuel filler flap is fitted in place.

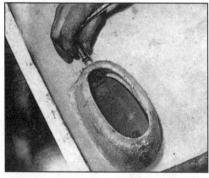

▲ FP5. Beware! This sort of thing takes time! You'll have to work out correct positions, drill holes in the panel in appropriate places and often use no little ingenuity in order to make the flap fit properly.

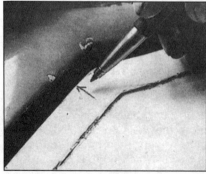

▲ FP6. With the wing held in place, mark the position of the mounting holes adjacent to the screen pillar.

▲ FP7. Take the wing back off and drill out the holes.

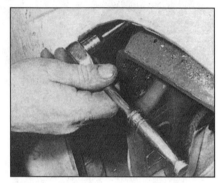

▲ FP8. Start fitting the wing by the screen pillar. To tighten this bolt up you'll need a socket with a universal joint extension on it.

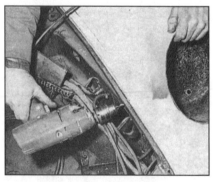

▲ FP9. Hold the front of the wing in place and drill through the holes in the flitch panel.

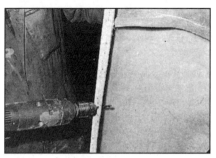

▲ FP10. Those you can't drill in situ, you'll have to drill after marking out carefully.

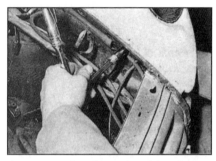

▲ FP11. Rather than using the spring washers used for steel wings, it is far better to use nuts and bolts with large flat washers between nut and glass-fibre, to spread the load.

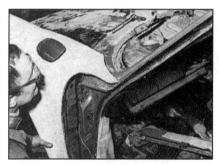

▲ FP12. The fit of the glass-fibre wing at this point, adjacent to the windscreen pillar, is quite often not particularly good although ...

▲ FP13. ... when the mounting bolts were tightened this panel was pulled nicely into position.

▲ FP14. However, the other side is quite a different story as this part of the panel is an extremely poor fit and some re-modelling is required to achieve the correct shape.

▲ FP15. The curvature of the wing where it meets the door is also all wrong.

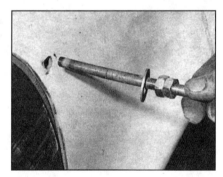

▲ FP16. A special bolt is made up to pull the panel into position whilst fixing at the top and bottom. When the bolt is removed the hole drilled in the wing can be filled. This is the kind of improvisation you almost expect to have to do with glass-fibre panels.

▶ FP20. Before finally tightening all the associated bolts, offer up the luggage bay cover and check the alignment of the panels. Adjust as necessary for an even gap between wings and luggage bay cover (bonnet).

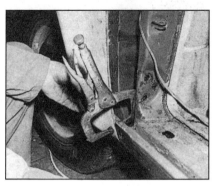

▲ FP17. The bottom of the wing was securely clamped in place ...

▲ FP18. ... while the A-post holes were marked in position ...

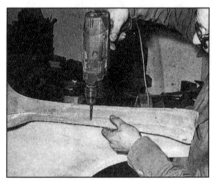

▲ FP19. ... and drilled out with the wing removed yet again!

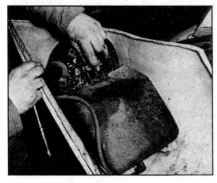

▲ FP21. At some stage, while the wing is off the car, it is necessary to fit the washer bottle brackets and the bottle itself.

FITTING GLASS-FIBRE REAR WINGS/FLARED WHEEL ARCHES

▲ FP22. Turning now to the rear wings, the glass-fibre panel is offered up to the steel wing and a line drawn around it. Don't worry that the car has miraculously turned into a 'Targa' model; the principle is exactly the same as on the fixed-head cars!

FP23. With the new panel taken away another line is drawn a couple of inches inside the other one.

▲ FP24. The steel panel is cut along the innermost line, here using a professional workshop air chisel although an electric jigsaw would be just as suitable.

▲ FP25. The steel wheel arch is then completely removed. The use of heavy duty leather gloves is strongly recommended here.

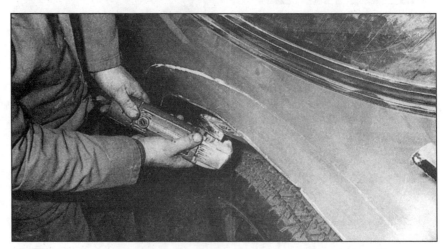

▲ FP26. The rough edge left on the steel is cleaned up using a grinder with a sanding disc fitted.

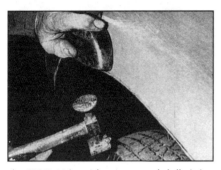

▲ FP27. Using a hammer and dolly it is necessary to make a 90° flange around the cut edge ...

▲ FP28. ... which is then turned right over and hammered flat to create a good strong seam.

▲ FP29. The glass-fibre flared wheelarch is offered up again ...

▲ FP30. ... and a few locating holes drilled right through the glass-fibre and steel.

▲ FP31. The panel can be held in place temporarily with pop-rivets.

▲ FP32. While the pop-rivets are fine for holding the panel on initially, they don't pull the panel really tight on to the steel wing.

▲ FP33. The replacement side skirt is then offered up and the new flared arch thoroughly checked for fitting. Now it is necessary to remove the wheel arch again by un-bolting and drilling out the pop-rivets.

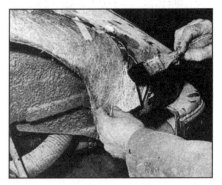

▲ FP34. Having sanded off all the paint, wipe the wing down with spirit-wipe to remove all traces of grease. Now start painting resin on to the edge of the steel panel, then place a strip of mat on the panel and stipple more resin into it.

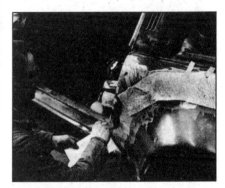

▲ FP35. Now bolt and rivet the wheelarch back on while the resin is still tacky underneath. Place some more mat stippled with resin over the top of the joint and also underneath to make a strong sealed band.

▲ FP36. The bolts can be undone once the resin has fully cured and any pop-rivets still in place drilled out.

▲ FP37. Apply some filler over all the holes left by the bolts and rivets and skim over the entire joint.

▲ FP38. Sand down all the obvious lumps and bumps and apply a further skim of filler ...

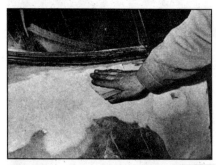

▲ FP39. ... followed by as much hand sanding and filling required to achieve a smooth blemish-free surface.

FITTING A GLASS-FIBRE FRONT SPOILER

▲ FP40. When offering up the new deeper front spoiler ...

▲ FP41. ... it was found that the mounting holes did not line up with the brackets on the spoiler. It was therefore necessary to fabricate some new mounting brackets as is often the case when fitting glass-fibre replacement panels.

FITTING SIDE SKIRTS

▲ FP42. First of all it is necessary to remove the old sill extensions.

GLOSSARY

GRP (Fibreglass, 'glass', glass-fibre) – a composite material consisting of matting woven from filaments of glass embedded in a chemically-hardened plastic bonding material.

Mat – fibres of glass bonded or woven together to form different types of weights of loose mat.

Resin – plastic liquid which is impregnated into mat and which goes hard after the addition of hardener. Actually starts life as a solid which has been dissolved in a Styrene solvent.

Gel-coat – the outer layer of GRP. A layer of plastic not impregnated into mat because it would show through its surface.

Gel-coat resin – A thixotropic (run-free) resin painted onto the mould first. Retains 'sticky' layer when exposed to air, thus facilitating adhesion of following layers.

▲ FP43. The new side skirts are then securely clamped in place and the hole positions marked for the fixing screws.

▲ FP44. Drill right through the new side skirt and the sill itself with a twist drill of a suitable size for the self-tapping screws provided.

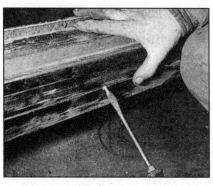

▲ FP45. The side skirt is now simply screwed into place.

Lay-up resin – doesn't leave a sticky outer layer. Stippled through mat.

Laying-up – the process of forming layers of resin impregnated mat.

Wet-out – to thoroughly impregnate mat with resin.

Green – newly gone off: firm but slightly rubbery and not completely hard.

Chapter 8

Doors, interiors, windows and soft-tops

STRIPPING OUT DOOR GEAR

Sometimes you have to take out door gear because the mechanism goes wrong and sometimes you have to remove it to repair a door. There are several different types of door gear and the main ones are shown here. There has been no attempt to cover every different make, however – that would clearly be impossible – but most types of door trim and window gear are shown here so there should be enough information contained in this chapter to apply to whatever car you are working upon. Before removing any type of window mechanism, remember to prop the glass up or have an assistant hold it there or it can crash down and cause a nasty injury.

When replacing glass channels and winder mechanisms, remember to replace everything without tightening up. Then make sure that everything operates smoothly before finally tightening nuts and bolts.

STRIPPING EARLY DOORS AND LATER VAN AND PICK-UP DOORS

▶ BDS1. Start by removing the trim rail at the top of the door (two crosshead screws at each end), then remove the single screw which holds the window winder in place.

▲ BDS2. Unscrew the two crosshead screws holding the door pull in place (lift the fold-down handle on earlier models).

▲ BDS3. Door catch bezels 'break' in the middle – they clip apart then slide out.

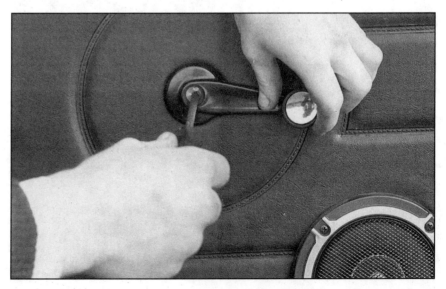

▲ BDS4. Remove door speakers if fitted.

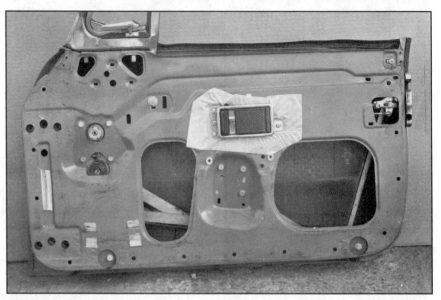

▲ BDS7. Open wide. This won't hurt! This now gives access to the door's internals.

▲ BDS5. The door trim clips forwards and off. Take care, if the trim is an old one, to lever near to the spring clips.

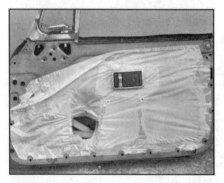

▲ BDS6. The protective plastic sheet should be carefully removed and reused later if not damaged.

▲ BDS8. Carefully prise off with a screwdriver, the spring clip which holds the latch release rods in place, leaving each rod connected at one end and make a note of where each one was taken from.

▲ BDS9. The more complete the assembly can be kept, the easier it will be to put it back together again.

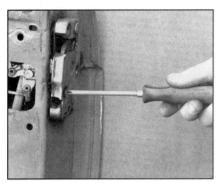

▲ BDS10. Take out the screws holding the latch unit in place and remove it.

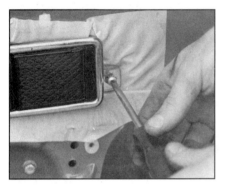

▲ BDS11. Remove the screws holding the interior latch pull in place ...

▲ BDS12. ... and remove it.

▲ BDS13. Locate the mounting screws (hex-head, Allen, screw-head or, sometimes, a 'special') for both a front and rear.

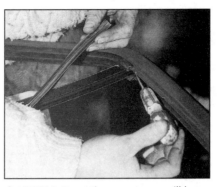

▲ BDS14. Sometimes, a screw will be concealed behind trim or a rubber seal.

▲ BDS15. Take out the window runner top screw.

▲ BDS16. Unbolt the bottom of the runner, either inside the door ...

▲ BDS17. ... or from outside, removing the bracket as well. Leave the runner loose, inside the door.

▲ BDS18. Occasionally, a runner will be held with a rivet; more often a thread will rust solid. In either case, drill through the head.

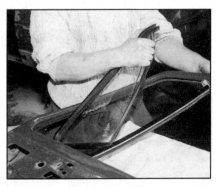

▲ BDS19. This glass and frame were held with the screw shown in BDS14 – detective work needed!

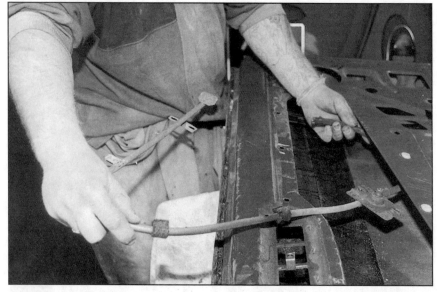

▲ BDS20. Sometimes, the glass regulator (operating gear) can be removed now.

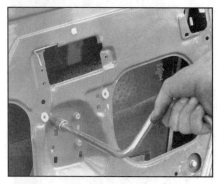

▲ BDS21. Remove the window regulator extension screws.

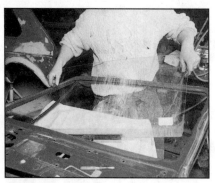

▲ BDS23. Lift the glass up and out of the door angling it to miss the door frame.

▲ BDS25. Where the regulator assembly is a large winding thing, you may now 'persuade' it out of the holes in the door.

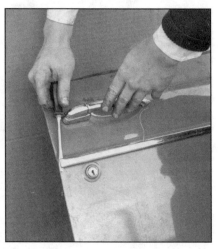

▲ BDS26. On this classic MGB, the chrome trim clips forwards and off (be very careful not to distort it), the door push is held by two nuts – two screw threads protrude from the handle, backwards through the door skin – and the lock is held by a spring clip which slides into a groove in the lock, tight against the inside of the door skin.

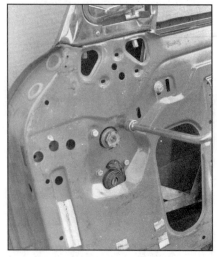

▲ BDS22. Remove the regulator securing screws. Slide the rollers out of the bottom of the channel fixed to the bottom of the window glass.

▲ BDS24. On some vehicles, the rear glass channel can only now be lifted out of the door.

▲ BDS27. Voila! The now denuded door shell is ready for whatever work is to be carried out.

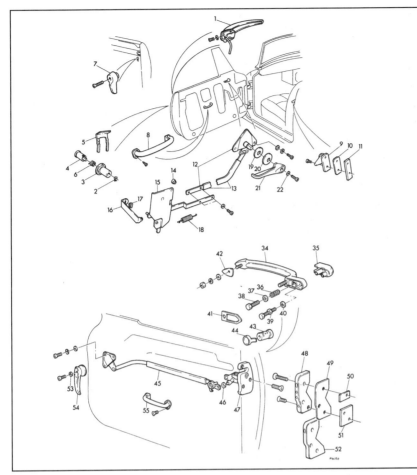

▲ Figure DS1. MGB door mechanism

The door mechanism shown here is typical of those fitted to many cars.

Items 1 to 22 apply to earlier sports-tourer only, with pull-out exterior door handles.

1 Outer door handle
2 Spring clip
3 Lock housing
4 Lock barrel
5 Lock retaining clip
6 Self-centring spring
7 Inner locking knob
8 Door pull
9 Striker
10 Packing
11 Tapping Plate
12 Remote control lock
13 Anti-rattle sleeve
14 Outside door handle buffer
15 Lock
16 Operating link
17 Spring clip
18 Tension spring
19 Fibre washer
20 Finisher
21 Inner door handle
22 Spring washer
34 Outer door handle

35 Pushbutton
36 Spring
37 Shakeproof washer
38 Set screw
39 Set screw with locknut
40 Shakeproof washer
41 Fibre washer
42 Fibre washer
43 Lock barrel
44 Retaining clip
45 Remote control link
46 Anti-rattle washer
47 Lock
48 Striker
49 Shim – 0.003in or 0.006in
   (0.08mm or 0.16mm)
50 Tapping plate (upper)
51 Tapping plate (lower)
52 Striker lock
53 Spring washer
54 Inner door handle
55 Door pull

STRIPPING MINI DOOR TRIM

Early type

▲ MDS1. Start by taking out the trim finishers which simply push into each end of the door pocket.

▲ MDS2. Take out the screws that hold the trim into the base of the door pocket.

▲ MDS3. Take out the card trim, being careful not to rip it.

▲ MDS4. Next ease your arm behind the main door trim and push it forwards in the centre so that it bows forwards and comes clear of the door frame at one end.

▲ MDS5. Lift that end upwards and lift out the main trim board as shown.

Later type

▲ MDS6. Take out the cross-headed screws that hold the window winder knob and the door catch handle (top right). Each handle then pulls off its square shaft.

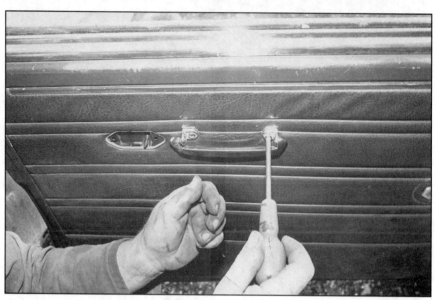

▲ MDS7. Next the door pull handle is removed by taking out the two screws which hold it in place.

◄ MDS8. The trim board is held to the door by a ring of clips which snap into holes in the door frame. Carefully ease a screwdriver behind the trim board and snap the clips out one at a time. Avoid snatching at the clips or they may pull out of the trim board, especially if it has started to age and lose its strength.

▼ Figure MDS1. Exploded view of Mini Van, Pick-up and early Saloon models' door lock and handle assembly.

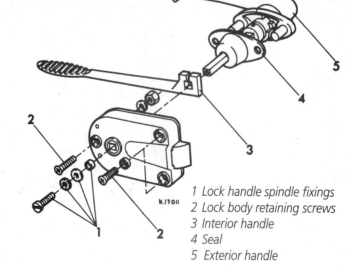

K.17011

1 Lock handle spindle fixings
2 Lock body retaining screws
3 Interior handle
4 Seal
5 Exterior handle

▲ MDS9. When the two sides and bottom of the trim panel have been snapped away, the top of the panel is eased downwards out of its retaining flap at the top of the door. There should be a waterproof covering behind the trim panel and if this has to be removed, re-glue it into place before refitting the trim panel.

STRIPPING EARLY DOORS AND LATER VAN AND PICK-UP DOORS

See Figure MDS1.

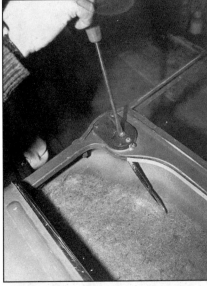

▲ MDS10. Start by taking off the screw which holds the lock handle spindle in place (Fig MDS1). Use a straight point screwdriver.

▲ MDS11. The exterior handle can now be removed, but not before ...

▲ MDS12. ... the interior handle (Fig 2, 3) has been eased off the spindle with a screwdriver. Some are held in place with a pinch screw and this is being undone in the photograph.

▲ MDS13. Keep the oddly sized, oddly threaded retaining screw and its washer safe by putting them straight back into the end of the spindle.

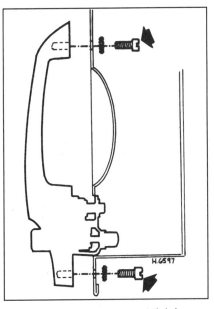

▲ Figure MDS2. Later type Mini door handle assembly.

▲ Figure MDS3. Front door lock removal.
A Remote control handle operating rod
B Interior lock operating rod
C Exterior handle lock link
D Latch lock rod

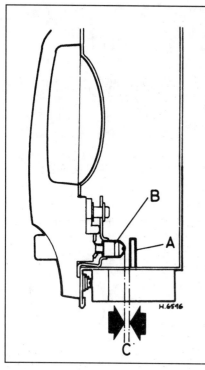

▲ *Figure MDS4. Door handle push button plunger adjustment.*

A Lock release lever
B Plunger cap
C = 0.031 to 0.062in
*   (1.0 to 7.5mm)*

See Figure MDS2. With door trim out of the way, later-type door handles are removed by unscrewing the two screws arrowed here. The screws holding the internal handle and lock in place are also clearly visible with the trim out of the way, while the latch assembly is screwed to the rear closing face of the door.

See Figure MDS3. Front door lock removal: note that clips at A and B have to be removed after all three mechanisms have been disconnected from the door. With the handle taken off, the lock barrel and push button can be dismantled as follows: 1) Prise off the retaining clip which holds the lock barrel to the handle. 2) Insert the key into the lock and use it to pull out the lock barrel. 3) Undo the screw that fixes the retaining plate to the exterior handle. 4) You can now take out the push button after lifting off the retaining plate, operating link, washer and spring.

See Figure MDS4. On earlier models the plunger cap (B) can be adjusted by screwing in or screwing out to give around 1mm to 1.5mm of free movement before the door lock release lever begins to move.

VOLVO DOOR STRIP

▲ *VDS1. The top of the door trim is held in place with self-tapping screws. Be sure to retain the cup washers.*

▲ *VDS2. Door handles push onto a splined shaft and are held in place with a spring 'hairgrip' clip.*

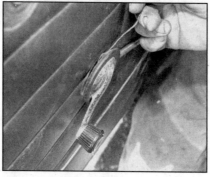

▲ *VDS3. This is best removed by 'fishing' for the loop end of it with a wire hook, whilst the door trim panel is pushed back far enough to give access.*

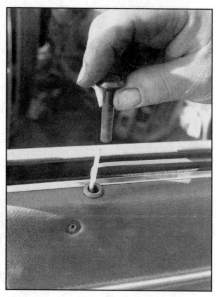

▲ *VDS4. The door lock button simply unscrews, leaving a threaded pin protruding.*

▲ *VDS5. Around the interior latch handle, the plastic bezel springs on – and off.*

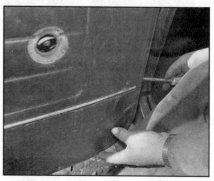

▲ *VDS6. Now, like most door trims, the concealed clips around sides and base are eased away ...*

▲ VDS12. Next the quarter light and door glass channel rubbers are eased out (use liquid soap to help ease them back in, using a blunt screwdriver for 'persuasion').

▲ VDS7. ... leaving the trim panel free to be lifted up over the door lock pin and away.

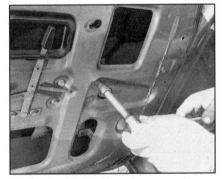

▲ VDS8. Next, the four bolts holding the mechanism to the door casing can be removed, but ensure that the glass is supported.

▲ VDS10. By feeling up inside the door casing, the spring clip has to be raised over the pin and pushed off ...

▲ VDS13. Take out the top screw holding the glass guide in place ...

▲ VDS9. Now, this is cheating! This clip is found on the assembly at the bottom of the glass, inside the door casing, facing away from you (ie facing the outside of the car), so there's no other way to photograph it!

▲ VDS11. ... followed by a spring and washers. All the while, the glass must be supported, preferably by an assistant.

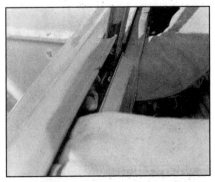

▲ VDS14. ... and the screws holding it just below the top of the door frame. This tightly-squeezed view is through the gap from whence the glass appears when wound upwards.

▲ VDS15. Then remove the bottom attachment screw ...

▲ VDS16. ... leaving the channel to be lifted upwards and clear.

▲ VDS17. Now the glass is free to be lifted up and away through the top of the door and the mechanism can be taken out through one of the bottom apertures.

CHEVROLET (FULL-SIZE MODELS) 1969 THROUGH 1981 DOOR STRIP

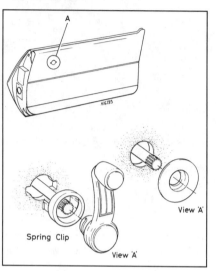

▲ Figure DS2. Chevrolet window handle installation.

On some models, the door handles are fitted as shown (see 'Volvo' section for removal details) while others are held on with screws. Door trim is screwed or clipped into place and the door pull handle and armrest are screwed on. After removing the trim panel, note the installation of the water seal beneath and ensure that it is refitted correctly later. When reinstalling the clip-type winder handles, first fit the clip to the handle, then hold the handle in place and strike it home with a sharp blow from the palm of the hand.

To remove the front door glass:
1) Remove the door trim as shown.
2) Take out the weatherstrip clips, the travel stops and the stabiliser guide assembly.
3) Half-lower the window and remove the lower sash channel nuts. Now raise the window glass completely and remove the other nuts.
4) Mark the position of the bolts and remove them, disengaging the guide from the roller, and rest the guide in the bottom of the door.
5) Tilt the top of the glass until the rear roller is clear of the inner panel and then lift the glass from the door.
6) You can remove the regulator by itself after propping the window in its fully open position. Mark the positions of the cam attaching bolts before removal. Disconnect the wiring harness from power-operated windows when fitted.

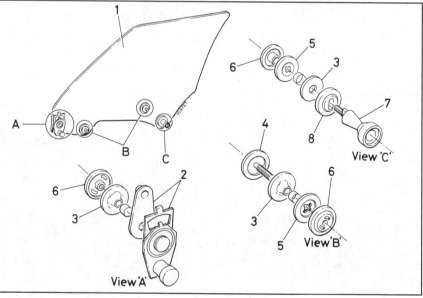

▲ Fig. DS3. Front door window components.

1 Window assembly
2 Window assembly (bell crank)
3 Spacer
4 Bolt inner panel cam
5 Washer (plastic)
6 Nut
7 Window roller
8 Washer (metal)

BUICK REGAL AND CENTURY DOOR STRIP

(Refer to Figure DS4 for door hardware and components).

1) Door trim and panels are removed in the normal way. Winder handles use the Chevrolet/Volvo-type attachment method. (See earlier sections).

2) Remove the decorative cover plate from around the inside door handle by prising away carefully with a screwdriver. Remove the screws which hold the handle in place, take off the remote control rod from the back of the handle and remove the handle.

3) Unscrew the locking knob from its shaft.

4) Remove the control escutcheon and control cable from the remote mirror control, where fitted.

5) Remove the armrest or armrest-cum-doorpull by unscrewing the retaining screws which are sometimes hidden beneath decorative plugs.

6) The trim panel unscrews and/or unclips in the conventional way.

7) If power windows are fitted, removal is not a DIY job and should be left to your dealer.

8) If manual windows are fitted, remove the inner water shield, then the up-travel stops at the front and rear of the door.

9) Loosen the front and rear belt trim support retainers located at the top of the door in the window channel.

10) With the glass three-quarters of the way down, remove the lower sash channel to glass attaching nuts through the special access holes in the inner door skin.

11) Lift the window straight up and out of the channel, aligning the rollers with the notches provided in the inner door skin.

12) If the regulator is to be removed, remove the window first, as described.

13) Disconnect the regulator from the inner door by undoing the nuts and bolts or if rivets have been used (later models) carefully drill them out with a ¼-inch drill bit. Remove the regulator through the large access hole.

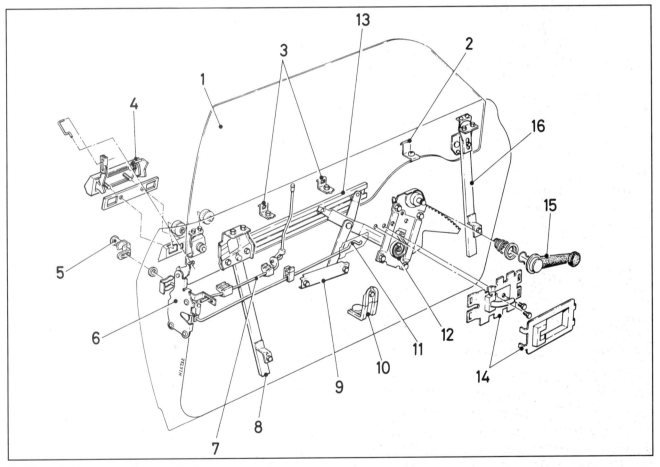

▲ *Figure DS4. Camaro door mechanism components.*

1 *Window assembly*
2 *Trim pad hanger plates*
3 *Trim pad hanger plate and stabiliser strip*
4 *Door outside handle*
5 *Lock cylinder*
6 *Lock assembly*
7 *Inside locking rod*
8 *Rear guide*
9 *Inner panel cam*
10 *Window down travel bumper support*
11 *Remote control to lock rod*
12 *Window regulator (manual)*
13 *Lower sash channel cam*
14 *Remote control handle assembly and escutcheon*
15 *Window regulator handle*
16 *Front guide*

14) If rivets were drilled out, replace the regulator using 20 x ½-inch screws and U-nuts on the regulator body.

Remove the door trim panel and also the door window glass and manually operated regulator following the instructions for Buick Regal and Century.

Power Windows: Note that if the following description of how to remove this type of power system is not followed, severe personal injury could be the result.

1. This system incorporates an electric motor and an independent control switch for each of the door windows. The driver's door has a master control switch permitting operation of all the windows.
2. The electric motor which powers the window regulator is a reversible direction motor and operates with 12 volts. It features an internal circuit breaker for protection. The motor is secured to the regulator with bolts.
3. The electrical motor can be removed from the regulator with the remainder of the window system intact only if the door glass is intact and attached to the regulator. If the door glass is broken or removed from the door, the motor must be separated after the regulator is removed from inside the door.

GLASS INTACT AND ATTACHED

4. Raise the window and remove the door trim panel and water shield as described in the previous sections.
5. Reach inside the door access cavity and disconnect the wiring harness at the motor.
6. It is imperative at this point that the window glass is taped or blocked in the up position. This will prevent the glass from falling into the door and possibly causing injury or damage.
7. Since the bolts used to secure the motor to the regulator are inaccessible, it is necessary to drill three large access holes in the metal door inner panel. The position of these holes is critical. Use the full-size template shown in Figure DS5. This template should be positioned on the door with tape after properly aligning

it with the regulator attaching rivets (late models) or bolts (early models).
8. Use a centre punch to dimple the panel at the centre of the template access holes and then drill the ¾-inch holes with a hole saw.
9. Reach through the access hole and support the motor as the attaching bolts are removed. Remove the motor through the access holes, being careful that the window glass is firmly supported in the up position.
10. Before installation, the motor drive gear and regulator sector teeth should be lubricated.
11. Upon positioning the motor, make sure that the drive gear engages properly with the regulator sector teeth. Install remaining components by reversing the removal order. Waterproof tape can be used to seal the three access holes drilled in the metal inner panel.

GLASS BROKEN OR NOT ATTACHED

12. Remove the window regulator as described. Make sure that the wiring harness to the motor is disconnected first.
13. It is imperative that the regulator sector gear be locked into position before removing the motor from the regulator. The control arms are under pressure and can cause serious injury if the motor is removed without performing the following operation.
14. Drill a hole through the regulator sector gear and backplate, install a bolt and nut to lock the gear in position. Do not drill closer than ½ inch to the edge of the sector gear or backplate.
15. Remove the three motor attaching bolts and remove the motor assembly from the regulator.
16. Prior to installation, the motor drive gear and regulator sector teeth should be lubricated. The lubricant should be cold weather approved to at least –20°F. Lubriplate Spray Lube 'A' is recommended by GM.
17. When installing the motor to the regulator make sure that the sector gear teeth and drive gear teeth properly mesh.
18. Once the motor attaching bolts are tightened, the locking nut and bolt can be removed. Install the regulator and don't forget to connect the motor wiring.

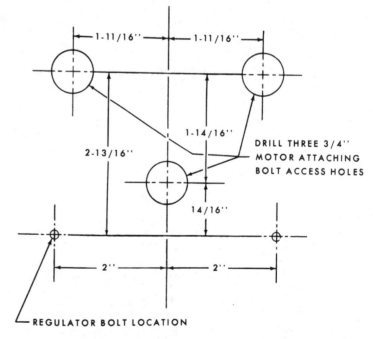

ALIGN TEMPLATE WITH APPROPRIATE REGULATOR LOWER ATTACHING BOLTS ON DOOR

1-11/16''   1-11/16''

1-14/16''

2-13/16''

DRILL THREE 3/4'' MOTOR ATTACHING BOLT ACCESS HOLES

14/16''

2''   2''

REGULATOR BOLT LOCATION

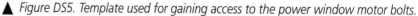

▲ *Figure DS5. Template used for gaining access to the power window motor bolts.*

FIAT DOOR STRIP

This is a cable type of winder system and is, if anything, easier to dismantle than any other because there are no bulky and mischevious mechanisms to handle.

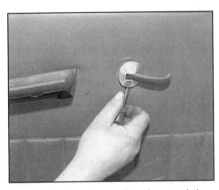

▲ FDS 1. The chrome bezel around the base of the door handle is carefully levered off.

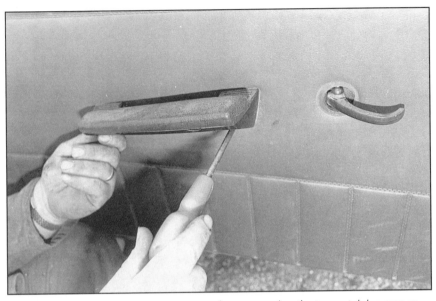

▲ FDS3. Door pull/armrest comes away after unscrewing the two retaining screws.

▲ FDS2. Once again, the handle is of the splined shaft/concealed spring clip variety.

▲ FDS4. The window channel is held at the top of the door frame by a screw ...

▲ FDS5. ... and at the bottom, inside the door casing, by a bolt.

◀ FDS6. The channel can be removed through the bottom of the door.

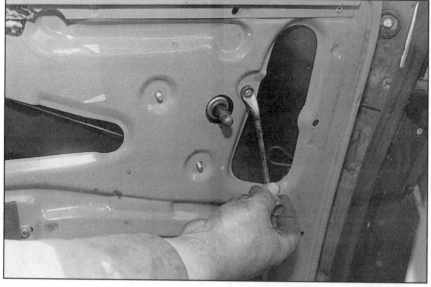

▲ FDS7. The winder regulator is held to the door frame by three nuts ...

▲ FDS12. Carefully lower the glass to the bottom of the door ...

▲ FDS13. ... and lift it over the bottom edge of the frame and out.

▲ FDS8. ... but when removing, be careful not to get the cable itself into a tangle.

▲ FDS10. ... and the window eased down far enough at least to expose the cable clamp. One of the screws must be taken out completely but the other need only be slackened.

▲ FDS9. The cable can be removed from the bottom pulley ...

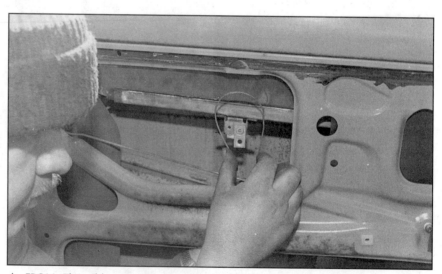

▲ FDS11. The cable comes clear of the clamp and can be removed from the concealed pulley up inside the door frame.

FORD DOOR STRIP

▲ FODS1. This particular Ford system is neither unconventional nor difficult to remove and it is common. Remove the three screws holding the regulator arm support from the door, after propping the glass in the ¾-down position.

▲ FODS2. Take out the screws holding the regulator winder mechanism to the door.

▲ FODS3. With the mechanism free inside the door casing, slide the rollers out of the channels on the bottom of the window glass.

▲ FODS4. Ease the mechanism out of the bottom of the door ...

▲ FODS5. ... and the glass out of the top as shown.

GENERAL

▶ GDS1. Remember that old doors will undoubtedly have had a good few gallons of water pass through them! Soak all fixing nuts, bolts and screws with a spray-on releasing fluid well before starting work.

▲ GDS2. On some older cars, quarter-light or vent assemblies were often attached to the glass runner so look out for screws holding the whole thing in place and not just the runner.

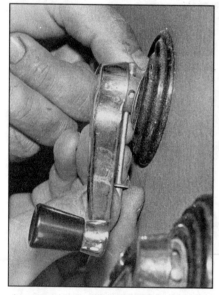

▲ GDS3. Some internal door handles are held on in a way that's a bit difficult to understand at first. Push the trim inwards and behind the bezel you may find that the shank of the handle and the squared shaft it pushes onto have a pin passing through them. It may or may not be a tapered pin, but if it is tapered, push from the narrow end, of course. Push the pin out with a thin punch or nail as shown – you may need to give it a tap with a hammer.

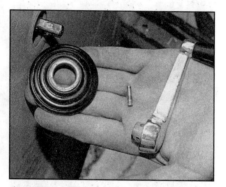

▲ GDS4. Then the handle and bezel just pull off. The trim may have a spring behind it placed around the squared shaft, to keep the assembly up tight.

'MOBILE' WINDSCREEN REPLACEMENT

Some fixing methods involve the use of an adhesive to hold the screen in place. Sometimes these are cold setting adhesives, applied and used like ordinary mastic (except that they are designed to set) and sometimes they are set by passing an electric current through a hot wire which passes through the adhesive. The heat softens the adhesive which sticks the glass in place then re-sets as it cools down.

Some cars have a great deal of trim around their windscreen rubbers which may or may not be simple to remove; much depends on the degree of competence and confidence of the individual. The first of the following sequences shows how to replace a simple rubber windscreen fitting system, and while others using this system may look more complicated, the principle will be the same.

WINDSCREENS HELD BY RUBBERS

Whenever I need a demonstration of how to change a windscreen, I call on our local branch of Autoglass – and here they are again! Mel talks us through the process of removing a windscreen and refitting it or fitting a new one. However, there are a certain points worth making, according to Alan:

A. Screen glass goes brittle with time and the chances of getting a screen out without breaking it are not high, unless you sacrifice the screen rubber. You might find that the cost of a replacement screen rubber is exorbitant or that it is not available, so check it out first!

B. Screen rubbers also go brittle and crack over a period of time and so you may have no option but to replace it. Your Autoglass supplier will usually be able to supply a replacement as close as possible to the original if that is no longer available.

C. If your windscreen needs replacing in an emergency or it has to come out because you are repairing a rusty windscreen surround (as in the case shown here) you'll have no choice but to call out the specialists. If you have a crack or chip and you can book the car in, you may be able to get a lower-priced deal by taking the car to the specialist rather than have them come out to you.

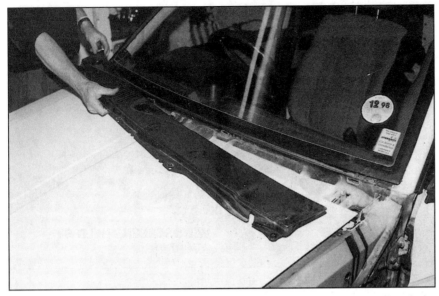

▲ MWR1. Your first job may be to remove any trim surrounds and also to detach the mirror or alarm sensor if either is bonded to the inside of the screen. Heat the bonded area gently with a hairdryer and push a spatula between the screen and bonded-on component, taking care not to scratch the glass if you want to reuse it.

▲ MWR4. The screen can then be eased free and lifted away from outside the car.

▲ MWR2. In Chapter 5, Repairing panels with adhesive, we show you how to carry out body repairs using adhesive. This technique is ideal for repairs in the region of the windscreen surround. Here, I have cut away all of the rusty metal, painted the whole area in rustproof primer and I'm getting the repair patch ready to glue into place. Plenty of body sealant was used around the repair to stop any further moisture from getting in.

▲ MWR3. This is a view from inside the car with Mel sitting on the front seat, easing the rubber away from around the screen surround while pushing gently on the glass with his hob-nailed boot. No, he didn't push too hard; he took a great deal of care. But nevertheless, the screen did crack and had to be replaced. Ah well!

▲ MWR5. If, as in this case, the screen rubber is to be reused, you will need to spend a good amount of time cleaning out all of the old sealant, fragments of rusted metal and other debris to make the rubber completely pristine, otherwise it will not seal properly when refitted. After scraping it as clean as possible, wash off thoroughly with ordinary household paint brush cleaner, such as white spirit.

► MWR6. Mel has his own purpose-made trestle for this part of the work. The rubber is fitted dry to the new screen ...

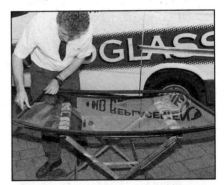

▲ MWR7. ... and is then prepared with a length of nylon cord pushed into the rubber where it fits over the screen aperture. In Mel's right hand is a plastic nozzle cut from the end of a dispenser of some sort through which the cord is passed. Once the middle of the cord is started, Mel runs the dispenser nozzle around the rubber, pushing the nozzle right into the gap as far as it will go, and inserting the cord into the rubber.

▲ MWR9. Mel places the screen and rubber into the aperture ...

▲ MWR10. ... and makes sure that the rubber is correctly aligned and correctly positioned.

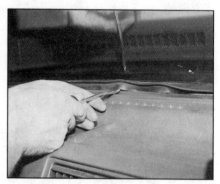

▲ MWR12. As he went along, Mel used a specially shaped lever, like a screwdriver with a bent end, to help to ease the rubber over the lip. This is necessary where the cord doesn't quite pull the rubber into place. It is more difficult with older, stiff rubbers – especially along the bottom of the screen where it is not so easy to get the right angle of pull on the cord.

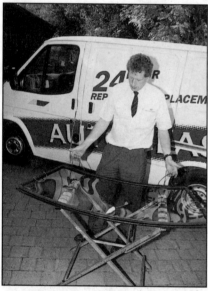

▲ MWR8. He goes all the way round, and back to the point where he started and then crosses so that the two ends of the cord come out as shown here.

▶ MWR11. By carefully pressing down on the screen and pulling on the cord, the rubber is eased over the lip of the windscreen aperture.

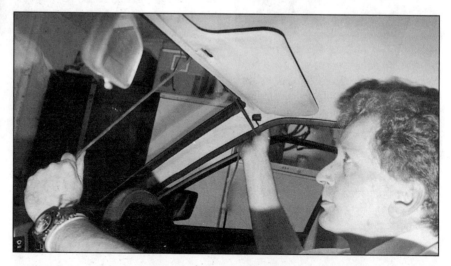

▶ MWR13. Mel assists the process by banging with the flat of his hand on the screen, all the way around. You need to use a mixture of all of these techniques – cord; levering; banging and pushing – to finally get the screen into place. Obviously, if the screen is an old one there is inevitably a higher risk of it cracking, but even a newer one can be cracked if too much twisting or local pressure is placed upon it.

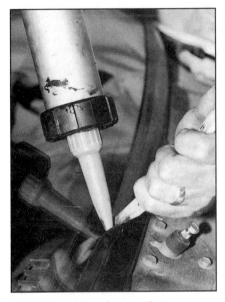

▲ MWR14. To make sure that everything was properly sealed, Mel ran a nylon stick between rubber and glass, and then rubber and bodywork, making a gap into which he gunned windscreen sealant.

◀ MWR16. ... followed this up with body wipe to get rid of all traces of the sealer. Note the gloves – it's tenacious stuff!

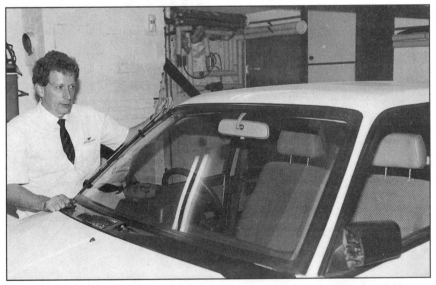

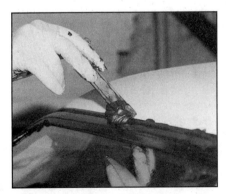

▲ MWR15. After letting the rubber settle down for a few minutes, he scraped away all the excess with a plastic spatula ...

▲ MWR17. The new screen, free of scratches and chips, actually improved the appearance of the car – after all, it comprises a large part of the car's total body area. Changing the screen is something that you can attempt to carry out at home, but on balance, I don't recommend it. Specialist like Autoglass are doing it all day, every day, sometimes in such inhospitable places as on the hard shoulder of a motorway in the pouring rain, so they're much more likely to get it right first time than the likes of you or me!

▲ MWR18. Last but by no means least, the windscreen wiper blades were minutely examined for trapped particles of glass and wiped off thoroughly with the paraffin dampened rag. There must be little that is more demoralising than to fit a brand new windscreen and then ruin it the first time the wipers switch on and score indelible scratches across the glass!

▲ MWR20. Quite often a windscreen will leak just because the rubber and the mastic inside it have dried out, allowing water through. This is how you can pipe in a bead of windscreen mastic, both sides of the rubber and preventing any further leaks.

SAFETY
If you replace a broken windscreen and the screen has smashed into small pieces before you can seal off all the vents, be sure to remove all heater and demister ducting to remove any fragments of glass which could so easily be blown into the face of an occupant of the car when the blower unit is next switched.

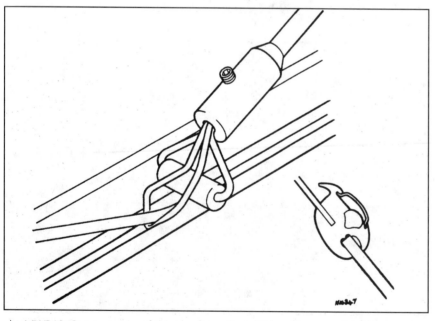

▲ MWR19. Some screens of this type have the additional feature of a rubber spreader strip which is let into yet another slit in the front of the windscreen rubber. This has the effect of pushing the rubber into closer contact with both screen and glass. It can be fitted using the special tool shown, or a more long-winded alternative is to use a pair of screwdrivers: one broad bladed to open up the rubber and one to push the filler strip down and into place. Wiping washing-up liquid over the filler strip makes it considerably easier to get into position.

SPORTS CAR WINDSCREEN
Many earlier sports cars have separate windscreen surrounds which are usually constructed of cast or extruded aluminium and which must first be removed from the car complete with windscreen glass before the glass can be changed. The method of holding the surround to the body varies from car to car but it is generally held in a pretty straightforward manner. This is especially so on older cars where the purists ideal was to whip off the screen and fit a pair of tiny aeroscreens. But we won't go into *that* particular form of masochism ...

The following sequence is based on the biggest-selling open top sports car of all time, the MGB, but the principles involved are applicable to many other cars.

▲ SCW1. The bottom bracket of the centre steady will have been disconnected when the screen was removed. Take off the domed nut which holds the top of the steady to the frame bracket.

▲ SCW2. Take out the two outer crosshead screws from each end of the top rail of the frame. Note the two rivets by the fitter's left hand – on later cars these are screws, too, which should be left in place.

▲ SCW3. It is not unusual to find an immovable screw. When this happens, the only recourse is to drill off the screw head, drill out the remainder of the screw after the frame has been disassembled and clean up the thread with a tap.

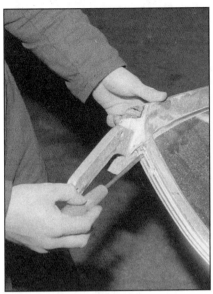

▲ SCW4. Bottom screws (two each side) are found beneath the rubber sealing strip which must first be pulled out of its seating and removed.

▲ SCW5. The side frame slots into the top and bottom rails and can be pulled off with all the screws removed. Top and bottom screws are of different lengths – make a note of where they come from!

▲ SCW6. Frame joints are often tight and have to be tapped apart with a wooden mallet.

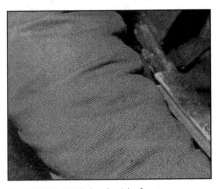

▲ SCW7. With both side frames removed, pull off the top rail, starting at one end and pulling the sealing rubber out of the frame as it is removed.

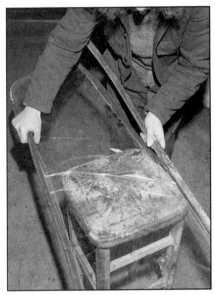

▲ SCW8. Remove the bottom rail in the same way. Note how a padded stool makes an ideal 'work surface'.

▲ SCW9. Take off the sealing rubber taking care not to be cut by any pieces of broken glass ...

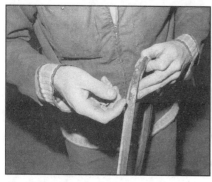

▲ SCW10. ... and clean all the old, hardened sealer from the rubber.

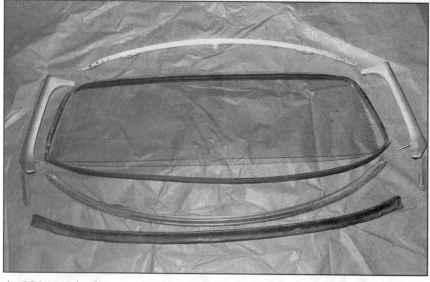

▲ SCW11. Take this opportunity to clean the frame and to grease threads before reassembly. Remember that care must be taken not to twist the screen and so cause it to crack.

▲ SCW12. Use a proprietary brand of screen sealer (available from motor factors) and inject a bead of sealer into each side of the rubber strip which has now been placed around the new screen.

◄ SCW13. Brush liquid detergent (washing-up liquid) around the outer edge of the rubber sealer.

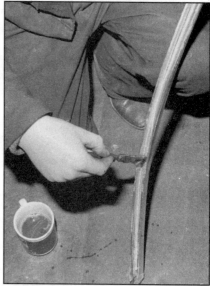

▲ SCW14. ... and also inside the top and bottom rail channels.

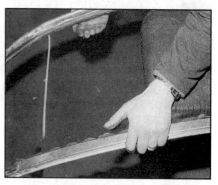

▲ SCW15. Push top and bottom rails on to the rubbers (ease them on slowly). They will push out the excess sealer as they go.

▲ SCW16. Slot the side rails into place.

▲ *SCW17. Ensure that the screw holes line up properly. Bang the side rails into place with the open hand if necessary.*

▲ *SCW20. Scrape off the excess sealer from around the screen. Paraffin (kerosene) used on a rag will remove what remains.*

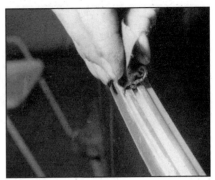

▲ *SCW23. Slide the leading edge of the rubber into the slot on the bottom of the frame and push it to the end.*

▲ *SCW18. If it is found difficult to pull the top and bottom rails sufficiently together, use a woodworker's sash cramp, but tighten SLOWLY – give the excess sealer time to ooze out.*

▲ *SCW21. The bottom rail to car body sealing rubber has to be fitted properly with the contours of the rubber fitting the contours of the bottom of the frame and the lip shown held open here, wrapped around the edge of the frame.*

▲ *SCW24. Work the rest of the rubber into place with a blunt screwdriver. You can see why Windscreen Services only employ fitters with four hands!*

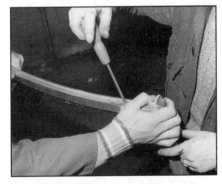

▲ *SCW19. Replace top and bottom screws. Make absolutely certain that the correct screw lengths are used in the corresponding holes.*

▲ *SCW22. Only apply liquid detergent to the frame if the rubber will not go in dry. If it goes in too easily, it will come out easily as well.*

▲ SCW25. Apply a good, heavy bead of screen sealer towards the front of the rubber ...

▲ SCW26. ... place the rubber corner seals in place and apply more sealer to the bottom of the corner rubber before refitting to the car.

GLASS 'BULLSEYE' DAMAGE

When a stone hits your windscreen, it often creates a 'bullseye' type of damage to the glass. If this damage occurs just ahead of the driver then the car will not pass the next MoT annual test, in the UK. But if it is caught early enough, this type of damage can be repaired at far lower cost than replacing the screen.

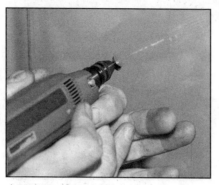

▲ WBR1. This windscreen, removed from an older car undergoing restoration, was out of the vehicle, but the principle remains the same. Tony Mousley from Paint Technik started by using the Dremel-type drill to make sure that there was a clear hole into the bullseye from the outer side of the screen.

▲ WBR2. He then fitted the Paint Technik's mirror assembly to the inside of the screen ...

▲ WBR3. ... and the repair fluid injector assembly to the outside of the screen. This creates a seal joint around the bullseye enabling Tony to use his syringe to inject the fluid.

▲ WBR4. The fluid was set off with a special ultra-violet light which means that the car can be back in use within a matter of minutes.

The damage to this screen had taken place several years earlier and there were some traces of dirt in the repair which meant that it was still visible. If the repair is carried out reasonably soon after the damage has taken place, it will be virtually invisible and certainly good enough for the screen to pass the MoT test.

You can buy off-the-shelf repair kits. They can't possibly be as effective as the professionally used units but then, the cost is so much lower.

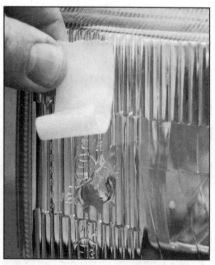

▲ WBR5. I also repaired a headlight in a similar sort of way, except that this time the glass on the inside of the 'bullseye' had dropped out leaving a tiny pin hole on the outside of the headlight. Luckily it was over the parking light area and was not the main part of the headlight itself. I covered the hole with a piece of masking tape . . .

▲ WBR6. ... then injected some of the Würth epoxy resin, with an injector nozzle, from the headlight bulb aperture at the back of the headlight. This left an unsightly yellow mark on the headlight, but when it was touched up with a little silver wheel paint, the repair was virtually invisible – and a lot better than the frightening cost of a replacement headlight unit.

PLASTIC INSTRUMENT PANEL REPAIR

▼ PIP1. This instrument panel was fine – except that the bodgers had been at it!

▲ PIP2. There were two areas of damage where screws had been overtightened, or wrong size screws fitted, breaking away the mounting points and, as shown here, the panel itself at one location.

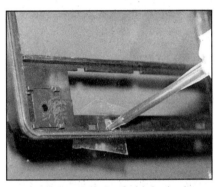

▲ PIP3. The trick is to hold the broken areas back together with tape and also to use tape to prevent adhesive from running away from the repair area. See Chapter 5, Bodywork repairs for information on how to choose which type of adhesive to use.

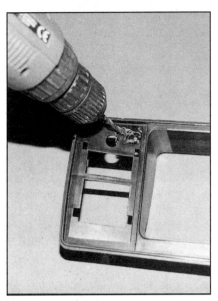

▲ PIP4. Each of the two fixing areas was filled solid with adhesive and then drilled out again afterwards.

PLASTIC DASHTOP REPAIR

▲ PDT1. Once again, Tony Mousley demonstrates how Paint Technik's mobile service can repair a range of plastic and other interiors, avoiding the high cost of replacement and, often without the need of any dismantling, although the parts being repaired in the following sections were already taken out of the vehicle.

▲ PDT2. Paint Technik use a range of products which they have developed to cover all types of plastic repair. See also the UPOL plastic repair products shown in Chapter 5, Bodywork repairs.

▲ PDT5. Tony starts the repair by carefully cutting away any excessively high areas with a knife and then he drips on some special primer ...

▲ PDT7. Once the hardener has gone off, a Dremel-type tool is used to sand the area down. The trick is not to use too much filler, so that there is as much as possible of the original textured surface left in place, but not to leave any low areas.

▲ PDT3. The majority of dash repairs Tony is called upon to carry out are to fill holes such as these shown here, that have been drilled to fit mobile phone holders or other accessories.

▲ PDT6. ... used prior to filling the damaged areas with plastic repair filler on a tiny spatula.

▲ PDT8. Tony then wipes the whole area down with pre-paint treatment ...

▲ PDT4. There are also other sundry marks, such as this one – (what on earth could it be?) – which destroy the appearance of an otherwise healthy looking dash. For repairs to splits, see the following section, Plastic door capping repair.

▲ PDT9. ... and uses a special texture-finish paint to replicate the original finish, as closely as possible.

▲ PDT10. After using a suitable polish ...

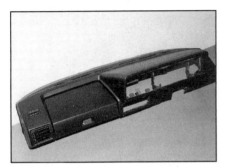

▲ PDT11. ... the dash looks superb and is certainly good enough to use again. It is possible to make out the repairs if you go looking for them but the damage no longer shouts at you, as it did before.

PLASTIC DOOR CAPPING REPAIR

Door cappings and dashtops have a nasty habit of splitting as the plastic hardens. The hotter the climate, the more likely this is to happen but it is inevitable almost anywhere. Replacement is usually prohibitively expensive and there can be an awful lot of work involved in replacing a dashtop.

▲ PDC1. If the crack is a very narrow one, it will need opening out. Tony Mousley uses the Dremel-type tool to run a cutting burr along the crack ...

▲ PDC2. ... so that two-pack filler/adhesive can be gunned into the crack. Use a tiny spatula to level it out. Once again, the trick is to use as little filler/adhesive as possible while leaving no low spots.

▲ PDC3. Tony uses a home-made wooden mini-sanding block with abrasive paper wrapped around it to sand down the repaired area ...

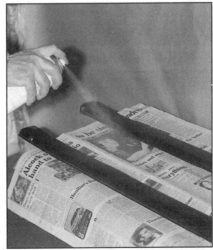

▲ PDC4. ... before spraying on primer, then textured finisher as described in the previous section on plastic dashtop repair.

▲ PDC5. As with all of these repairs, the cracks were not made invisible but the repair meant that the trim panels could be reused whereas before, they were virtually scrap.

'MOBILE' VELOUR SEAT BURN REPAIR

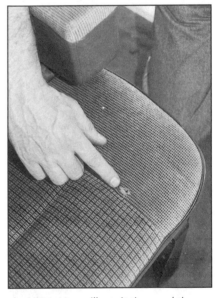

▲ VSB1. You will see it time and time again: a velour seat; a smoker in the car; a burn hole in the material. Once again, it's Paint Technik who demonstrate how they carry out this type of repair. The only way in which this kind of repair could be emulated on a DIY basis would be to cut a tiny piece of fabric from some hidden part of the seat and let it into the hole in place of the fibres shown here being blown in, but it would be extremely difficult to match the edges properly.

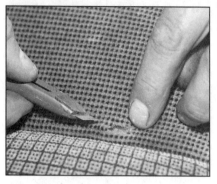

▲ VSB2. First, hardened, burned areas and loose strands of fabric have to be cut neatly away.

▲ VSB3. Small pieces of lint (although cotton wool would presumably do the trick) are pushed into the hole to build up to the level just below that of the seat fabric. The top surface of the lint is painted with clear adhesive which is also taken over the edges of the surrounding fabric.

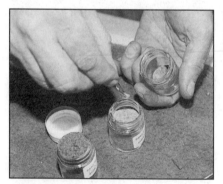

▲ VSB4. The Paint Technik van carries a wide range of velour fibres in different colours. The background pattern on this seat is a kind of check, which obviously cannot be matched perfectly. Tony pulls out fibres and mixes them to achieve an acceptable colour and when he is satisfied with the result, the pot is screwed onto the blower ...

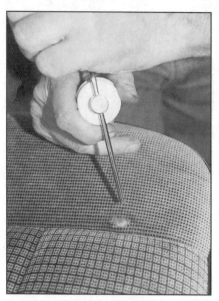

▲ VSB5. ... and velour fibres are puffed onto the repair. The first coating was not high enough and so Tony applied more adhesive and added more fibres.

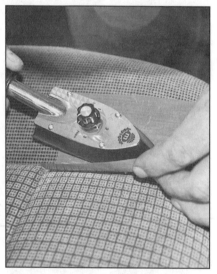

▲ VSB6. The whole thing was set off with a small iron used over a Teflon sheet.

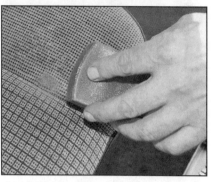

▲ VSB7. The Teflon helps to prevent the velour from being flattened by the iron but you do have to be extremely careful not to use too much heat otherwise some marking will take place. Tony brushes the surrounding area to try to bring back the pile on the velour. The finished repair, although once again not invisible – you can't achieve the impossible! – is a vast improvement over a gaping cigarette burn. On plain velour it should be possible to achieve an almost perfect match.

FOOTNOTE:
After a few weeks, this repair detached itself from the seat because (I suspect) too much wadding had been stuffed into the hole, preventing the repaired area from 'giving' when sat on. So beware!

FITTING A SOFT-TOP

Fitting a new soft-top (or hood, in Britain) to a sportscar can make all the difference in winter between continuing to enjoy the car and half freezing to death! In addition, elderly soft top rear windows tend to go cloudy and difficult to see through which is certainly inconvenient and unsafe, and quite possibly illegal too. The author visited the MGB Centre to see a hood or soft-top being fitted there.

Watching 'Smiling' Steve Langdell is a revelation! He makes fitting a hood to an MGB look like child's play – and it's not! But you CAN fit one yourself and avoid a nightmare of sags, draughts and flapping vinyl by working carefully and methodically, as shown in the following step-by-step instructions.

The first job and probably the most important one, is to buy the best hood that you can afford. If you can get an original factory hood the advantages are that it is very likely to fit much better than those made by outside concerns, it may be better made and it will be constructed of the correct material. The disadvantage of a factory fresh hood is that it is likely to cost a great deal. If you have to buy one from one of the hood specialists try, if you can, to avoid buying without seeing first (there are some horribly misshapen offerings) and get

yourself a hood with the clips and stud fastenings already fitted if possible. The small extra cost saves a lot of work – not to mention the risk of getting it wrong!

Do ensure that the hood is (a) the right one for your car, and (b) that it fits, before removing the old one or attempting to alter the new one. The fit can be checked by the simple expedient of draping and smoothing it over the old, erected hood and checking for shape and size. There will be some useful sized overlaps where the manufacturer has allowed for adjustment during fitting.

▲ *ST3. Lift away the aluminium channel being careful not to distort it.*

▲ *ST4. Unscrew the hood where it is folded and held down to the ends of the cant rail. Only a coat of adhesive stands between cant rail and removal of the front of the hood – peel them apart. Rub the cant rail down and repaint it to give a smooth finish under the new hood.*

▲ *ST1. Work methodically and – provided that the hood is a good one – there shouldn't be any problem. Choose a warm day so that the vinyl (if that type of hood is being fitted) is supple but avoid the heat of high summer for then the hood will be too soft and easily over-stretched. Laid out in the foreground here are all the materials necessary, plus the two earlier types of hood sticks used prior to the Michelotti design fitted to the subject car.*

◄ *ST2. First step is to open the doors, fold the hood back, remove the rubber cant rail sealing strip and drill off the pop-rivet heads found beneath.*

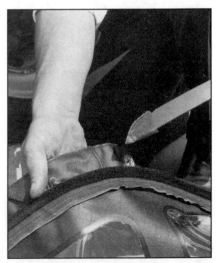

▲ *ST5. Slip the steel bar (which clips onto the two chrome 'claws' on the rear bodywork) out from the old hood and, right away slide it into the new hood – before you forget which way round it goes!*

◀ ST6. Refit the bare cant rail to the top of the screen frame.

◀ ST7. Clip the rear of the hood in place, after fitting the hood frame (if not Michelotti, in which case it will be attached to the cant rail) ...

◀ ST8. ... and after folding the front-most part of the hood back on itself, measure with a tape and mark the centre of the hood with chalk.

▲ ST9. Apply glue, with a brush, to the central third of the cant rail ...

▲ ST14. Stretch each corner forwards just enough to get rid of any sags or wrinkles – but not so much that you will need a team of three to close the hood on a cold day when the material has contracted!

▲ ST10. ... and to the corresponding part of the inside of the hood.

▲ ST12. Make absolutely certain that the sides of the hood line up with the closed door glasses.

▲ ST15. Fold the draught excluder corners down onto the cant rail, pierce them with an awl and fit them into place with the crosshead screw and cup washer removed earlier.

▲ ST11. Pull the hood forward, aligning the chalk mark with the windscreen steady bar and ensuring that the hood is taut.

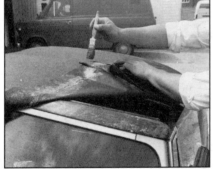

▲ ST13. Fold back each front corner, apply glue to it and the cant rail.

▶ ST16. Glue the flap at the front onto the face of the cant rail which sits on the top of the screen frame.

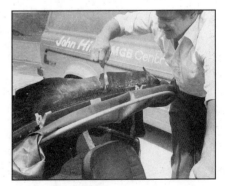

▲ ST17. Glue down the draught strip channel in order to prevent leaks behind the strip itself remembering to line up the holes with an awl before the glue dries.

▲ ST20. Snip the surplus hood material around the front frame clips ...

▲ ST23. ... have to be fitted to the tags provided one on each side, at the bottom of the window aperture. First, pierce with an awl ...

▲ ST18. Pop-rivet it back down then refit the draught excluder rubber ...

▲ ST21. ... then cut off the surplus with a craft knife.

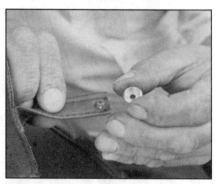

▲ ST24. ... push in the 'cock' from beneath, place the 'hen' on top and spread the hollow tube on the cock with a centre punch and hammer, using another hammer as an anvil beneath. Although fitting the press studs with the hood in place is awkward, it is the only way of ensuring that they align with the buttons on the car.

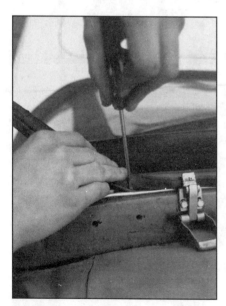

▲ ST19. ... carefully easing it into the channel with the aid of a screwdriver.

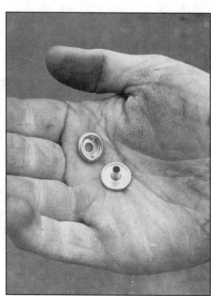

▲ ST22. Press-stud clips known in the trade as 'cocks and hens' ...

▲ *ST25. If at all possible, buy a hood with the rear clips already fitted. If this is not possible, pierce the cloth as shown on this sample and push the claw part of the clip into place through the material.*

▲ *ST26. Place the material on the bench with the claws sticking upwards through the material and locate the retaining plate over the claws before bending them inwards with a light hammer.*

FOUR SEATER SOFT-TOPS

The principles behind fitting a soft-top to a four-seater are just about the same as those for a two-seater except that sometimes, especially on older cars such as the Minor and 'Beetle' convertibles, the soft-top is pinned to a wooden body rail mounted at the rear and a wooden cant rail at the front. It is still normal practice to fit the rear of the hood first followed by careful stretching of the hood forwards before fixing the front of the hood to the cant rail. But it must be borne in mind that most four-seaters' hoods are rather more complex and certainly more cumbersome affairs and so require rather more time spent to ensure a good fit. For that reason a closer examination of the old hood as it comes off and, notes jotted down on any of its idiosyncracies will pay dividends when it comes to fitting the new hood properly.

WATCH THE WEATHER

Professional trimmers advise anyone fitting a hood to choose a mild, dry day or failing that, a reasonably warm garage. Vinyl is affected by temperature and in cold weather you just won't be able to tension the hood correctly – if you fit your hood on a very warm day the vinyl will stretch too easily and the result will be that the hood is dragged and may even be so tight that on a cold, wet day the seams will part, or you won't be able to raise the hood or fasten it down.

Fabrics such as 'double duck' or mohair should be fitted dry and will self-tension themselves to some degree once they get wet, but do tension them reasonably well in the first place. Because of the shrinkage factor the makers often leave these hoods a little wide. Don't try to compensate for this by applying uneven tension at the cant rail.

Chapter 9

Accessories and improvements

MIRRORS

First of all check that the mirrors are going to be in the right place by sitting in the driver's seat while someone else holds each mirror in turn and moves it to the best place. Too far away, and your rear vision will be restricted and the mirror will be difficult to see clearly in a hurry; too near or too low and your view of the mirror could be obstructed. Work out the correct position first, or your mirror will be no more than a showpiece.

▲ *SA1. Place several strips of masking tape on the panel in the area where you intend to fit the mirror. The tape is easy to mark as you measure out the exact position of the mirror and it protects the panel if you slip a little with drill or file.*

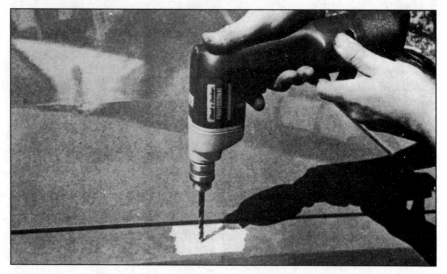

▶ *SA2. The Black & Decker cordless drill is ideal for outdoor uses like this. A small pilot hole was drilled first, then a larger one. Before the first hole was cut, the drill and chuck were turned by hand until the drill cut through paper and paint and started itself in the steel beneath. (You could use a centre punch, tapped lightly with a hammer). If you don't do either of these things, the drill will almost certainly skid across the panel, gouging the paint.*

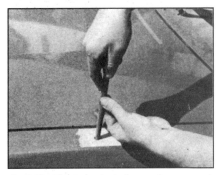

▲ SA3. Then the hole has to be opened out, if necessary using a round file.

▶ SA4. A good wing mirror should have a sealing rubber above and below the hole, a flat washer beneath the bottom rubber and a lock washer directly above the nut.

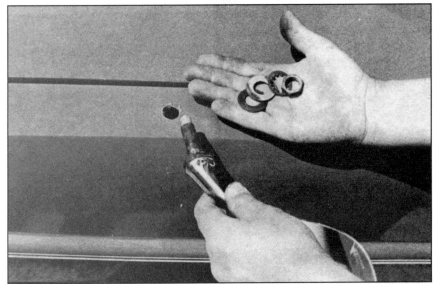

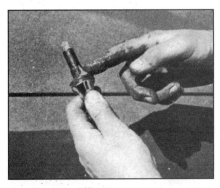

▲ SA5. It is difficult to get paint onto the edges of the new hole in the panel, but if you don't do something, it will certainly corrode. Waxoyl rust preventer or even grease could be spread around the hole and the mirror fixing.

WING-MOUNTED AERIAL

Position the aerial and cut out the hole as shown in the previous section. Make certain that there is room beneath the panel for the aerial body to fit and try to choose a place that won't be splashed with water and mud, particularly if you are fitting an electric aerial. Generally, place the aerial away from the car's electrical system to cut down on interference and make sure that its fixing clamp can earth (ground) onto bare metal.

▼ SA7. Work out the order in which the tilt/fixing clamps go together. The clamp held in the right hand here goes beneath the panel while all the others go above it.

▲ SA8. Fit the aerial into place, then extend it and adjust it to the angle you want.

▲ SA6. There's rarely a lot of room to get at the fixing nut. A ring spanner gives you smaller turns than an open-ender, but you may have to get hold of a long box-spanner. Remember to adjust the mirror accurately before final tightening-up.

▲ SA9. Finally, tighten up the fixing nut. In the case of electric aerials, it will be necessary to fit a supporting strap (supplied with the aerial) to locate the weighty base of the aerial. Screw, bolt or pop-rivet it into place against the car's inner bodywork.

▲ SA12. Mark the position of the lamp and drill a mounting hole. Use a rust preventer or grease around the hole to protect the bared metal from rust.

▲ SA13. With this lamp, the mounting bolt also tightened the lamp swivel. You can only set the lamp position really satisfactorily on the road.

FRONT AUXILIARY LAMPS

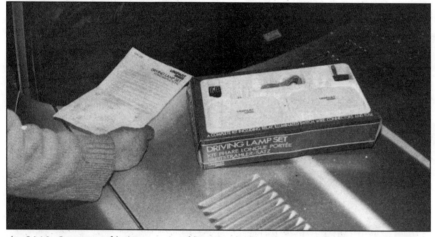

▲ SA10. One way of being certain of buying good quality parts is to buy those sold for your make of car. These Unipart lamps were chosen for that reason. The electrical side of things is detailed in the instructions and all the wire and wiring clips are supplied too.

▲ SA14. Fitted to this TR7, these driving lamps look the part and are useful in dull conditions for making the car's presence known to other road users and for lighting up the road for that time just before headlamps are really necessary.

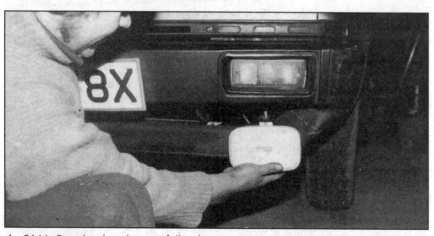

▲ SA11. Start by choosing carefully where you want your lamps to go. Try to make them compliment the existing features and lines of the car, but don't fit them as low as this if you want them to illuminate the road a long way ahead.

NEW NUMBER/LICENCE PLATES

▲ SA15. New plates make a car look terrific, especially after it has just been resprayed. Remove the old one and clean any loose rust or dirt from the supporting plate, using a wire brush or scraper.

▲ SA16. Paint it, or brush on a liberal coating of rust preventer so preventing dirt and moisture trapped there from causing any more problems.

▲ SA17. Place the old plate over the new one and drill the mounting holes, using the old plate as a template.

MUD FLAPS

▲ SA18. Then, just bolt your new plate in place. Special plastic nuts and bolts are also available to match the background colour of the plates.

▲ SA19. Mud flaps made specifically for one particular model of car will fit so much better than the 'universal' types freely available.

▶ SA20. The best way of finding where to drill is to clamp the mud flap in place. Here a Sykes-Pickavant body clamp is used. It's specially shaped, wide spread jaws make it ideal for clamping panels and parts together.

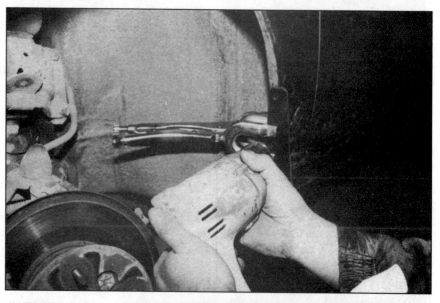

▶ SA21. The mud flaps are held in place with nylon bushes which push into the holes you drill and then act as anchors for the self-tapping screws screwed into them.

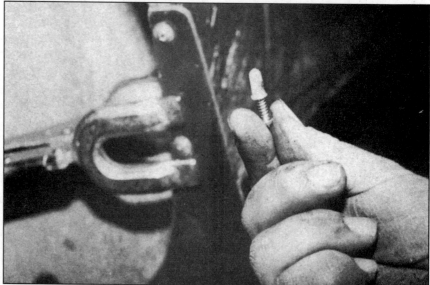

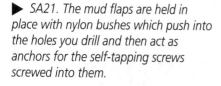

▶ SA22. Before inserting the nylon bushes, they were dipped in rust-preventer to protect the steel panel around them and the self-tapping screws from corrosion.

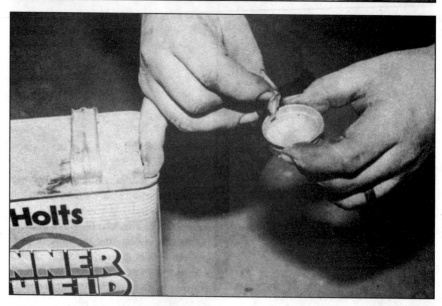

▶ SA23. Screwing the mud-flap into place is the easiest part of all!

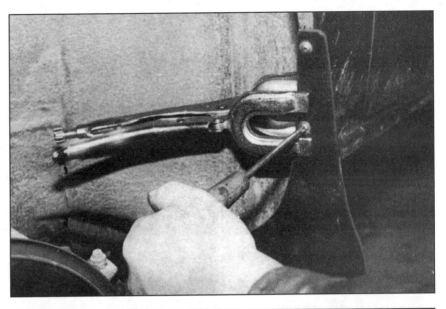

▶ SA24. 'Universal' type mud flaps are usually clamped in place with pinch clamps supplied as part of the kit.

▼ SA25. Here the mud flap has been supported on blocks of wood whilst clamped into place. The same blocks were then used at the other side of the car to ensure that both mud flaps were at the same height.

SOUNDPROOFING

You make a car less noisy by carrying out lots of small sound-deadening jobs rather than any big ones. One of the most fruitful areas to tackle is in the bulkhead/firewall and in the floor of the car, especially around the gear-change, where lots of small holes can let in a lot of noise. Use new grommets or mastic to block off any holes you may find.

▲ SA26. Flat panels exaggerate sound by resonating. You can damp that out by sticking on a self-adhesive sheet which reduces the vibrations in the panel. This is the Supra Dedsheet, having its protective layer pulled away from it.

▶ SA27. It's then a simple matter to stick the Dedsheet onto any large, flat panels where resonance can cause a noise problem.

▶ SA28. Another Supra product are these thick soundproofing mats which come in easy-handle large squares. They can be trimmed to fit the shape of the floor and inner bulkhead and glued into place beneath the carpet.

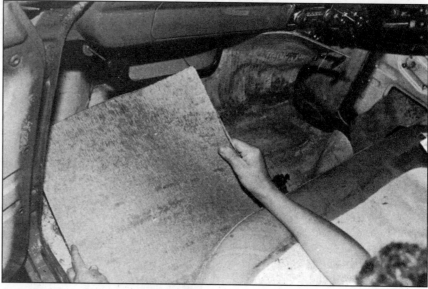

SPORTS CAR ROLL-OVER BAR

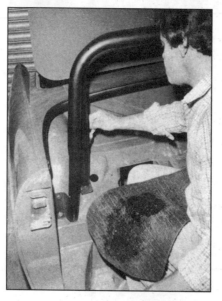

▶ SA29. A roll-over bar is a sensible safety accessory which also lends a 'macho' appearance to a sports car, if that is what you want! They almost always come complete with a fixing kit, so that they simply bolt through the sports car's bodywork. Make certain that the one you buy will fit beneath the soft-top when it's erected, because some versions made for use on the track don't.

FITTING A TOW BAR

Every vehicle is an individual when it comes to fitting a tow bar but there are a number of general points that can be made. The first, and the most important is that for cars in the UK registered after 1st August 1998, they have to be fitted with a Type-Approved tow bracket by law.

When you buy your tow bracket, if you choose a reputable manufacturer and state the model of vehicle you will be fitting the tow bracket to, they will ensure that the one supplied is the correct one for your car.

▶ SA30. We chose a Brink tow bracket to fit to our Volkswagen Transporter. You should start by laying all the parts out on the floor and checking that the instructions make sense and that all the parts are present and correct. With some cheaper tow brackets, you may have to file out holes and adjust the fit to make everything go together properly but we had no such trouble with this bracket.

▲ SA31. In almost every case, the rear bumper of the vehicle being fitted with the tow bracket will have to be removed temporarily. Apply plenty of releasing fluid on to all the bumper retaining bolts well in advance. It may be necessary to support the rear of the car well off the ground on ramps or axle stands to improve access.

▲ SA33. There was no drilling of any sort to carry out with the Brink unit it was just a matter of fitting the new bolts supplied through the chassis members and into the tow bracket arms. With many cars, not designed specifically to take a tow bracket, you may have to drill chassis or floor sections in the places prescribed by the tow bracket manufacturer before bolting through.

▲ SA34. Brink also supply all the necessary wiring connections. Their wiring instructions are comprehensive and include the information that the wiring relay must be fitted as close to the battery as possible. To comply with the UK law, there has to be a separate warning light and/or buzzer inside the vehicle to tell the driver when the trailer indicators are working. This is also supplied as part of the kit.

▲ SA32. With this particular model, the Volkswagen bumper brackets are removed and the Brink tow bracket is bolted to the chassis in place of them.

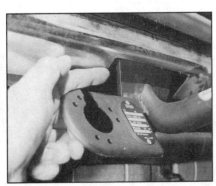

◀ SA35. You will be very fortunate if your tow bracket just bolts on without the need for any modifications whatsoever. In our case, we had to cut away part of the underneath of the bumper to allow the tow ball neck to protrude. This bracket only has a mounting for a single wiring socket but Brink also supplied a double-socket extension for those who want separate sockets for a caravan's lighting and interior accommodation.

FITTING AND MAINTAINING A SUNROOF

Sunroofs are becoming more and more popular as accessories fitted to cars of all ages, shapes and sizes. As well as making the car so much more pleasant to own they add extra light, fresh air and a breath of sunshine in the summer – and they also increase the car's value. Tudor Webasto, one of the leading suppliers and fitters of sunroofs, kindly showed how they fit one of the least expensive and popular sunroofs to an Austin Metro. This was quite a straightforward job but Tudor Webasto strongly recommend that DIY fitting be avoided. They say that some roof structures are quite complex and require expert attention, that headlinings can degenerate into a flapping nightmare if handled wrongly and that, if a mistake is made cutting out the roof ... it could all end in tears!

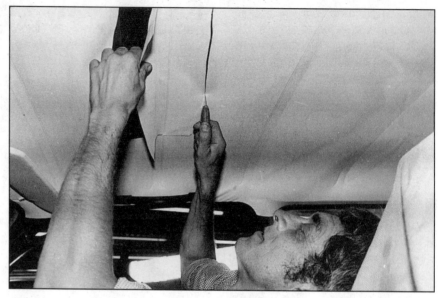

▲ SR1. First job for the Tudor Webasto fitter was to cut the headlining; just a small cut-out for access at this stage.

▲ SR2. Then he placed masking tape around the area where the sunroof was to be fitted, accurately marked out the area to be removed and (gulp!) drilled a hole into the roof panel.

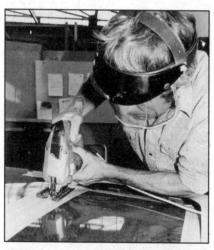

◀ SR3. Next (gulp, gulp!) he inserted a power jig saw blade into the hole and cut all around the line he had marked. A be-goggled assistant sat below holding the headlining out of the way and supporting the roof panel being removed so that it did not distort and trap the jigsaw blade.

▼ SR4. The roof panel was lowered and fitted into the accurately cut aperture.

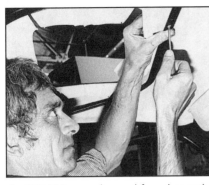

▲ SR5. This was clamped from beneath by a frame which has screws passing upwards and into the frame above. The two compress together to form a seal. The unwanted headlining was cut back and the headlining edges and screw heads hidden from view with trim strips.

▲ SR6. The smoked glass panel slotted into place via a pair of clips-cum-hinges. In use, the sunroof can be raised at the rear or, in hot weather, it can quickly be lifted right out – a reversal of the fitting process seen here and a work of moments.

▶ SR7. Last job for Tudor Webasto and just about the only piece of maintenance for the owner is to keep the glass clean. This type of sunroof should never leak (although a downpour after a long, hot, dry spell can temporarily catch the sealing rubbers out) but it must be said that cheap sunroofs are notorious for leaking with depressing regularity.

▲ SR8. From one end of the scale to the other. Tudor Webasto can fit a range of sunroofs from the simple opening glass light, through their luxurious 'off-the-peg' sliding roofs (definitely not for the amateur) ...

▲ SR9. ... through to bespoke tailored sunroofs made in a workshop pleasantly scented with beechwood shavings, and with wooden templates on the walls. This piece of wood is actually part of the sideframe of what Tudor Webasto claim to be the biggest sunroof in the world. It was made as a 'one-off' for a six-wheeled Range Rover for a certain Eastern gentleman who used it for shooting-parties. The roof, it was specified, had to be strong enough for the whole shooting-party to sit around it, sunroof open, with legs dangling inside!

▲ SR10. It's always pleasant to see a company taking care of their own products from years ago. This Volvo P1800 was in the process of receiving new fabric for its sliding roof, a step guaranteed to improve the appearance of any older car with a sliding sunroof.

▲ SR11. Sliding sunroofs don't need a great deal of maintenance but the sliding mechanism should be kept lubricated and clean. Periodically, wipe the slots out with a cloth and spray in some aerosol silicone lubricant; it's far more effective than anything else for this purpose and cleaner than oil.

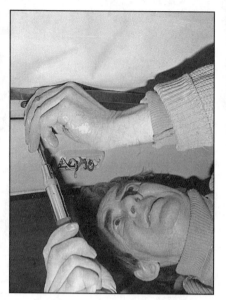

▲ SR12. Removing a sliding sunroof, either because the car is being resprayed or in order to replace the fabric section, is quite an easy job. Three or four screws will be found holding the rear of the roof in place from inside the car. Occasionally, on an older car, one will shear because of corrosion weakness. All you can do is to drill out the stud remains with the fabric off the car and re-tap the hole.

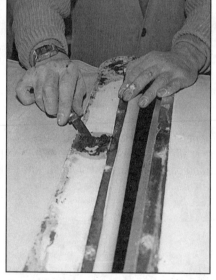

▲ SR13. From outside the car, fold the rear of the sunroof back and you will see a heavy encrustation of sealer which can be scraped off with a knife.

▲ SR14. Concertina all of the fabric together and turn the sunroof fabric so that it sits diagonally across the sunroof opening. One by one the rails can be eased out of their runners, leaving the fabric and rails free.

▲ SR15. Refitting is the reverse of this procedure. In this shot you can see the guides at the end of the front rail which have to be manoeuvred out as described.

▲ SR16. Before screwing down the back rail, but after all the runners have been fitted into place, fold the back rail over so that the base is uppermost and 'ice' it with mastic. Place a swirl of mastic around each of the screw holes and a double line across the edge where mastic had originally been placed by the manufacturer. All that remains is to re-insert the screws from inside the car.

POLISHING FADED PAINT

In time, paintwork of any sort is likely to lose the deep lustrous shine it had when sitting in the showroom, even though there is no corrosion in the panels beneath the paint and though the paint itself may be perfectly sound. Ordinary polishing may not bring it back to life, so this is the time to try something a little more vigorous. The results can be remarkable, transforming what previously looked like an old banger into a very respectable looking car – as any used car dealer can tell you!

Simply, paint fades when the top surface of the paint is affected by sunlight (which 'weakens' its colour – reds, oranges and yellows being particularly prone to sun bleaching) and it goes a dull, matt finish as it oxidises.

Many ordinary polishes contain a tiny amount of abrasive so that when you polish your car regularly, you will also be taking off a microscopically thin layer of paint – that's why the polishing cloth ends up the colour of the paintwork. There are, however, special compounds available which enable you to cope with the job of taking off a larger (though still microscopic) layer of paint when fading or bleaching is notably bad.

Rubbing compounds, as they are called, are like flatting papers; the coarser grades cut faster but produce deeper scratches and, like flatting paper, if you start with the coarser grade of compound, you must work through the grades and finish with a fine grade in order to produce a high quality shine. Beware if you are attempting to polish a thin coat of paint! The compound can break through and, with some colours, the result will be an apparent dark ring around the area that has broken through. Polishing compounds are generally only available through a trade paint factor (they almost all sell to whoever comes up to the counter). The DIY cutting compounds, such as T-cut, are too fine to remove anything but a very light amount of dull paint, unless you are prepared for a marathon, arm-aching rubbing session.

A third source of discoloration is so-called 'industrial fall-out' when chemical or particle discharge from industrial plant is carried by the wind, lands on a car's surface and causes discoloration. Such contamination is by no means restricted to immediately around industrial areas (indeed, some Scandanavian countries claim to be affected by 'acid rain' discharged from British factories). The results of such contamination must be polished out while the effects are still slight otherwise the damage can go deeply into the paint. If you suspect that heavy contamination has taken place, try to remove it by washing the panels affected in a solution of 10% oxalic acid. Remember to take the usual stringent precautions regarding skin and eye protection and safe storage of acids.

▶ *PFP1. Most people won't have access to a power tool and will therefore entrust the work to the power of their own arm. Bad cases of hazing or fading (and not forgetting that orange-peeled paint can be flatted using the same process) are best approached using a cutting compound. It is probably best to avoid the coarser grades of cutting compound – you can actually hear them roughing away at the paint surface – and go for a smooher grade. It might mean using a little more elbow grease, but that is preferable to overdoing it and rubbing straight through the paint. Rubbing through is most likely to happen on edges and raised body lines, so take it easy in those places.*

Use a clean cloth to rub the compound off and to polish the surface of the paint. Turn the cloth regularly to avoid too heavy a build-up of compound on any one part of the cloth. Try to keep the area being compounded at any one time relatively small. Hand polishing is quite hard work and fairly time consuming so approach it a section at a time. Polish ONLY in straight lines, following the line of the bodywork; rotary polishing will leave rotary marks.

▶ *PFP2. T-Cut or any other similar proprietary polishing compound is used last of all (remember the analogy with flatting papers?) to get rid of the minute scratches left by the cutting compound and to bring up a deep shine on the surface of the paint. Wet the soft cloth you use for polishing then wring it out very thoroughly to leave it damp; this stops the cloth soaking up the compound.*

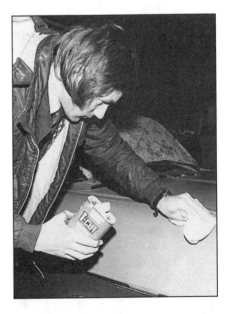

▲ PFP3. Here a 'pro' polishing mop is being used with cutting compound and of course this speeds the job up perhaps by as much as a factor of ten. Note that the use of a polishing mop requires a certain degree of skill to avoid cutting through the paint or burning the surface of the paint. Such polishing machines can be bought fairly cheaply to run from a compressed air source but their air consumption is massive, (at least in terms of workshop equipment output) and the great majority of DIY compressors come nowhere near having enough capacity to cope.

▲ PFP4. Electric machines are around 50 per cent more expensive, though they can usually be hired from tool hire stores. Alternatively an ordinary electric drill can be fitted with a soft backing pad and lambswool mop (you need a different mop for every grade of compound you use) but most professionals would consider that an electric drill spins too quickly for this purpose, even set at its slowest speed, so if you use this method avoid burning the paint by keeping the mop moving over the surface of the paint and apply only very light pressure; you'll also be doing a big favour to the bearings in your drill, which are not really intended for side pressure.

POLISHING HINTS

• When using compound either thin it with water or dampen the cloth or mop (take care where electrical components are involved) and apply even less pressure as the polish dries out.

• Take special care when machine polishing sharp curves and edges, perhaps leaving such areas for hand polishing along with the areas around door handles and accessories where the polishing mop can't reach.

• Always keep polishing mops clean. Excessive paint and polish residues in the mop increase friction at the point of contact and increase the tendency to burn the paint.

• Avoid all substitutes! Polishing compounds are specially formulated from materials which will not harm the paint. The same cannot be said of metal polish and other abrasive polishes designed for other uses.

• Take special care when compounding metallic finishes; only ever lightly compound them. If too much paint is removed, the metallic content will 'shear' and the finish will be ruined in a way that can only be cured by repainting.

• Finish off with a good quality wax polish to deepen the shine and protect the surface. **NEVER** wax polish paint that is less than four or five weeks old otherwise the paint can go dull (it absorbs the wax) or can develop a tendency to watermark.

• Cover the car windscreen and wear old clothes when machine compounding. The stuff tends to fly around a bit!

Thanks are due to Autotech Ltd of Belbroughton, Worcestershire, England and Village Detail, Thousand Oaks, California for their help with the photographs used here.

PINSTRIPING AND DECALS

Decal graphics are used on nearly all US cars nowadays and on a large number of European cars, too. Sometimes they are used where a chrome plated badge would have been fitted formerly, but often they are used to give stylish bodywork effects. Many owners may be interested in fitting pinstripes or decals to improve the appearance of a plain looking vehicle, but even when fitted from new the material gets damaged or discolours after a period of time and replacing it really improves the appearance of a car. The material is available from accessory shops when being applied as an additional feature, or from a dealer when it is being replaced; just order it like you would an engine part or door knob.

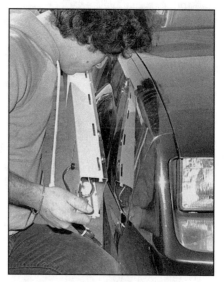

▲ P&D1. When replacing an old pinstripe or decal, the first job is getting the old one off without damaging the paintwork beneath. Start by heating the tape with a radiant heater (as shown here), or a professional air gun. Even a hand-held hairdryer at its hottest setting is better than nothing.

▲ P&D2. The idea is to soften the gum holding the pinstripe or decal in place. It helps if someone else can hold the heat source in place while you pick and peel the old tape away.

▲ P&D3. Here Ron Samuel is using a spirit solvent to wipe away the residual gum. Don't, obviously, use a solvent such as cellulose thinners which could react with and damage the paintwork.

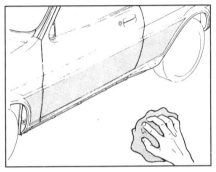

▲ P&D4. Before fitting a new decal or stripe, or after removing an old one, make sure that all traces of grease are removed using a spirit wipe. Methylated spirit would do the job equally well as a proprietary brand of wipe, and has the added advantage that it reacts with virtually no type of paint.

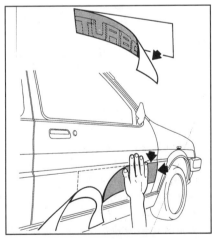

▲ P&D5. The new decal or stripe will have a protective sheet of paper on its reverse. Peel part of it back, locate the start of the decal or stripe accurately (it's not easy to remove again) and smooth out the decal or stripe, pulling the protective paper off as you go.

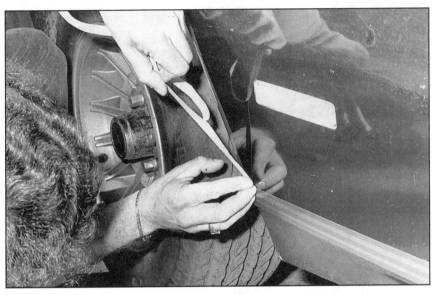

▲ P&D6. Treat a stripe in exactly the same way, but leave some overlap beyond where you want the stripe to fit.

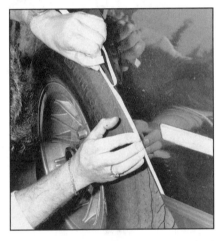

▶ P&D7. Carefully position the stripe as you go ...

▼ P&D8. ... easing it round any curves. If the stripe is to go straight down the side of a car, position 6 inches (300mm) or so, of one end, then peel back the tape for several feet before positioning the next part of the tape, say, where you come to the edge of a door. Pull it fairly tight before making the second point of contact so that the tape is bound to be straight. Do the same with the third and subsequent points of contact but get down on a level with the tape and sight along it to ensure its straightness. Then go along and smooth the whole tape down.

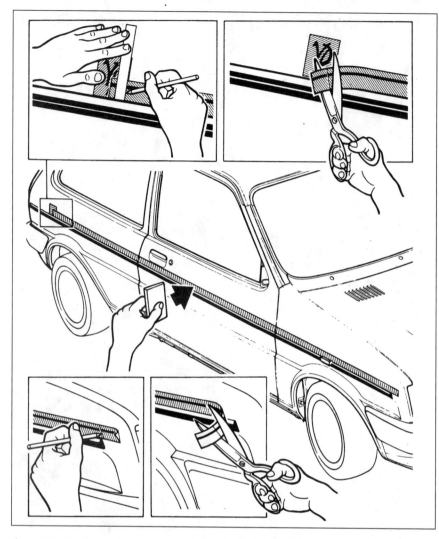

▲ P&D11. When fitting a decal, it's even more important to push out all the air, working from the centre outwards. Then, finally, peel back the top coating (which is sometimes clear plastic) starting from one corner.

▲ P&D9. As shown here, you must smooth all air out of the tape using a rubber, a clean cloth or just your hand. You can accurately pencil the correct position for cuts ...

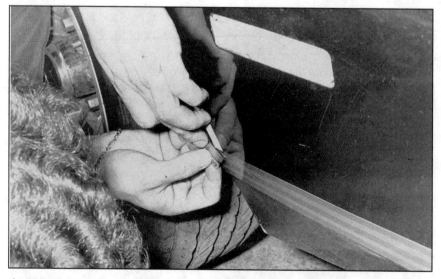

▲ P&D10. ... or do as Ron Samuel does and trim accurately in place with a sharp razor blade or craft knife.

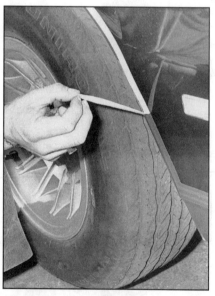

▲ P&D12. Sometimes a thin stripe will tend to lift up again with the top coating. If this happens, lift the first couple of inches, separate the two, push the stripe very carefully back down and continue to remove the top coating. If your strip bridges two or more panels, don't bother cutting to the length of each panel but take the stripe right over the panel gap. Trim it to fit afterwards.

◀ P&D13. Similarly, where a decal fits behind a side marker/flasher, take the unit off, cut the decal to suit the hole after it has been fitted, then refit the lamp.

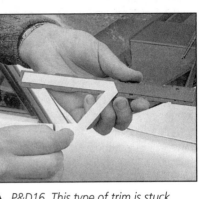

▲ P&D16. This type of trim is stuck down with double-sided tape. Factors sell it by the roll but it is obviously more economical if you can buy or cadge a short length from your friendly local body shop. Peel off one side of the protective covering, stick the tape down to the badge then expose the sticky surface on the other side of the tape as shown here.

FITTING SELF-ADHESIVE TRIM

▲ P&D14. Before attempting to replace stuck-on trim, make certain that there are no traces of grease or other contamination present on the surface of the panel. Here the author is using International Paints proprietary Spirit Wipe but methylated spirit would do the job just as well. Obviously, you can't use thinner on many paint types – unless you want to fetch the paint off as well!

◀ P&D15. Carefully measure and mark out the position of the trim or badge taking a look at the other side of the car or at another similar car if necessary. Use a water-based felt-tipped pen if you're worried about getting rid of any superfluous marks afterwards.

▲ P&D17. Position the badge or trim with very great care – you can't just lift it off and replace it or it wouldn't hold down well enough to do the job – and press it down well all over.

(All graphics in the preceding section are courtesy of Austin-Rover Ltd, and the picture sequence was carried out at Ron Samuel's body shop, Village Detail, Thousand Oaks, California.)

STEEL WHEEL APPEAL

Steel disc wheels can be one of the least obtrusive areas of the car but if they look good they will lift the whole appearance of the car while if they look shoddy and down at heel, so too, will the rest of the car.

Wheels are very vulnerable to damage from stone chips and are constantly subject to every destructive influence that the road can throw at them – and all from only a few inches away. For that reason, it is best to use paints that have been specially produced for use on wheels: although ordinary paint can be used, it simply won't last as long before it needs more attention.

▲ *SWA1. If you are painting wheels that consist of more than one colour, be prepared for an awful lot of fiddling around with masking tape.* **Don't**, *however, waste time in trying to follow every tricky little curve with masking tape. Instead, stick tape over the colour joint, rub it down really well so that the bit you want to stay in place actually does so during the next phase, and carefully cut along the joint line with a sharp craft knife. Then peel away the unwanted tape. Of course, to save having to do this twice, you can spray your first colour without having any masking in place, then just mask-up for the second colour.*

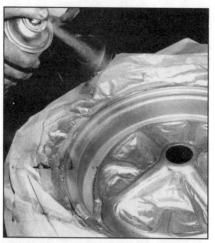

◀ *SWA2. The areas between the cutout masking tape are, naturally, much easier to mask-up in the normal way. Choose your colour carefully. Silver often looks too bright and garish but a steel colour (sold as such) usually suits steel disc wheels very much better.*

◀ *SWA3. The basic rules of preparation, flatting and priming, apply to wheels quite as much as to ordinary bodywork. Make sure that you sand off every trace of rust and also treat the afflicted areas with a rust killer to be certain, if you don't want it to break out again in double quick time.*

▲ *SWA4. An easy way to smarten up the wheels quickly when still on the car is to clean them up as recommended, then make an instant spraying mask with a piece of cardboard. To do this hold the card firmly against the wheel rim and press through the card to the edge of the wheel rim with your thumb to leave an indentation and a mark on the card. (If you've got a dirty 'workshop thumb', the mark will be all the clearer!)*

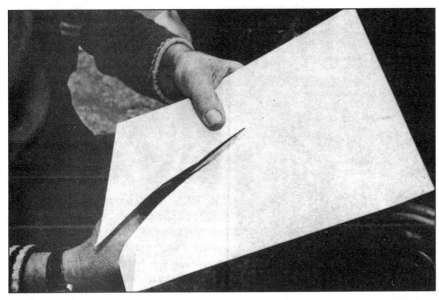

▲ SWA5. Then accurately cut around the curve you have marked on the card with a pair of scissors.

INTERIOR TRIM – RENOVATION AND REPAIR

Although interior trim is not strictly a part of bodywork, it is likely that the owner who wants to improve his car on the outside will welcome the chance to make the inside look a lot tidier, too, so here are a number of ways of improving seats, carpets and door trim.

Aluminium wheels can be protected by spraying a clear sealer onto their surface but if they are suffering from the all too common surface corrosion, they are best resuscitated by being taken to a specialist wheel polisher and then treated with sealer, which should be reapplied at regular intervals.

▲ SWA6. You can hold the card mask against the wheel rim while spraying the wheel and so prevent getting unsightly overspray onto the tyre sidewall, moving the mask around the wheel as you spray around the rim of the wheel. Of course, if you do slip up and get paint onto the tyre, nil desperandum! It's not recommended in top bodyshop circles, but you can simply paint over the overspray with tyrewall black. Then, as the black gets worn and rubbed away, so does the overspray!

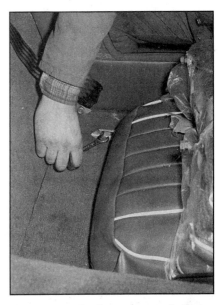

▲ IT1. Virtually all car seats are bolted down to the floor of the car. Some, such as sports car seats, can be a little hard to get at and you may have to slide the seat forwards to undo the rear bolts and back for the front ones. An even more common difficulty is that of seized nuts and bolts. Try soaking them in releasing fluid well before starting work, try applying heat, (but carefully, taking note of the promixity of fuel lines beneath the floor and flammable trim above it) but if all else fails, it may be necessary to drill out the bolts and replace them with new ones; preferably of the rust-resistant bright zinc-plated variety.

▲ IT2. Quite often the seat covering will go saggy without anything actually being wrong with the structure of the seat at all. Alternatively, the cover may have split and it may be possible to get hold of a new cover from a specialist supplier or a good second-hand one from a breaker's yard. (Slip-on, tie-on accessory covers are not shown here because they are just **too** easy to fit.) In this shot, the old cover has been removed and a layer of thin foam is being glued over the shoulders, back and base of the seat.

▲ IT3. Then, so that the new cover will slip on without binding on the surface of the foam, a plastic bag is split open and glued over the shoulders of the backrest.

▲ IT4. The cover is then pulled down on to the backrest and stretched down carefully, easing out any wrinkles or bunching as it is pulled on. The clips and method of fixing used by the manufacturer are reused to hold the cover down, if possible.

▲ IT5. The recovered seat will have all the smoothness and tautness of a new seat, especially if you took the opportunity to renew any worn springs or a rubber diaphragm while the seat was stripped down.

▲ IT6. A few cars have leather seats, these being aesthetically beautiful to see and smell and touch but painful to the pocket when they need repairing. You can invariably strip off the leather cover in the same way as for cloth covers and you can then restitch any broken stitching using the existing stitching holes in the leather. You could even let-in a repair patch yourself from a second-hand seat. Be sure to use strong, upholsterer's thread.

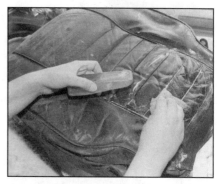

▲ IT7. Old leather can be cleaned up using saddle soap and then treated with hide food to stop it from splitting by making it supple again. Specialists such as Woolies and Connolly Brothers (see 'Classic' motoring press for addresses) can even supply recolouring kits which can bring leather seats back to almost-like-new.

◄ IT8. The far more common vinyl type of seat covering is also prone to splitting as the material age-hardens. Splits can be repaired using vinyl adhesive, available from motoring and DIY shops, after first roughening the edges of the split with fine sand paper.

▲ IT9. Really bad splits need support from behind, especially if they are unsupported by padding. The base of this seat was held on with claws which were bent open with a screwdriver, allowing the cover to be pulled loose.

▲ IT10. Then a piece of card was slid up behind the tear. This was used as a slipway for a piece of vinyl which was also slid up behind the tear – it would otherwise have dragged on the padding inside the seat.

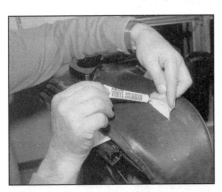

▲ IT11. After roughening the edges as before the flaps of vinyl were lifted and the vinyl glued down to the vinyl backing piece behind ...

▲ IT12 ... and the edges were pulled close together with masking tape and the tape left in place until the mend was completely dry.

▲ IT13. While the finished repair was far from invisible, it was vastly preferable to a gaping tear.

▲ IT14. Vinyl seating can become dull without you really noticing it, but a good clean-up can make a dramatic difference. Here Turtle Wax 'Vinyl Plus' has been rubbed onto the right-hand half of the seat. The extra shine it gave did not disappear even when the polish was completely dry – as indeed it was in this picture – and the vinyl actually felt more supple.

▲ IT15. Cloth upholstery can be a little more difficult to clean if only because it absorbs more dirt! Start by scraping off any clods of chocolate or dirt that might have embedded itself into the fabric, using a blunt table knife, then spray on an aerosol upholstery cleaner, taking care not to soak the fabric which could cause shrinking to take place.

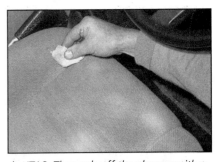

▲ IT16. Then rub off the cleaner with a clean cloth. You can fetch off a surprising amount of dirt in this way, but be prepared to have several goes at a really dirty seat allowing the cloth to dry out between each cleaning.

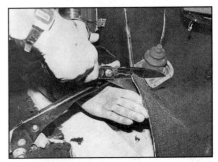

▲ IT17. It seems that with replacement carpets almost more than anything else, you get what you pay for – and no more! Top-quality carpets sold by a main agent or a specialist in your car should fit straight into place, but even only slightly down-market carpets may need a considerable amount of trimming to get them to fit properly.

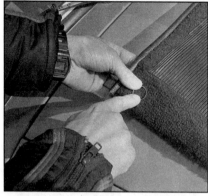

▲ IT18. Unless carpets are clipped down they will slip about, look untidy, and make a thorough nuisance of themselves. When you receive your new carpets and, if necessary, after you have trimmed them to shape, start by placing them in the car, feeling for the position of the stud and marking it with chalk. Press the clawed ring down onto the top of the carpet ...

▲ IT19. ... so that the claws protrude through the carpet.

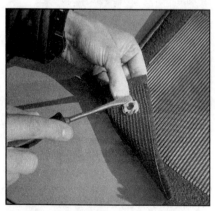

▲ IT20. Place the clip over the claws and fold the claws inwards with a screwdriver.

▲ IT21. It may be that the floor clips are missing for some reason in which case it is a simple matter to fix new ones in place using self-tapping screws or pop-rivets. If you fit sound-deadening materials beneath the carpets it will be necessary to raise the position of the studs using pieces of plywood placed beneath the stud, and longer screws.

▲ IT22. It is then simplicity itself to clip the carpets into place with the added bonus of being able to unclip them in a moment for cleaning out the car.

▲ IT23. Plasticised seat covers and door trim materials can be given a new lease of life by painting them with upholstery paint. Fumes from the paint could be dangerous if used in a confined area, by the way, so ventilate the work area thoroughly. The wrinkling you can see in the painted door panel at the rear disappeared after a day or two, presumably as all the solvent dried out. Strangely, this type of paint always seems to have covered properly when it is still wet only to look patchy when dry, so buy enough for two coats. Paint only in straight lines so that brush marks don't show.

Specialists and suppliers featured in this manual

The following addresses and telephone numbers were believed to be correct at the time of going to press. However, as these are subject to change, particularly telephone area codes, no guarantee can be given for their continued accuracy.

3M United Kingdom Plc,
PO Box 1,
Market Place, Bracknell,
Berks RG12 1JU
www.2m.com

A1 Wheel Renovation,
345 Bilston Road,
Wolverhampton.
Tel: 01902 871 422

AutoCare (Valeting),
65 Oakley Road,
Redditch B97 4EF
Tel: 0800 214 636

Autoglass
Autoglass operate the well-known, nationwide call-out service for both emergency and restoration-related glass and rubber removal and replacement. Ring Freephone 0800 363636 for details of your local branch or see www.autoglass.co.uk.

BOC Gases,
The Priestley Centre,
10 Priestley Road, Surrey Research Park,
Guildford,
Surrey GU2 7XY
Tel: 01483 579 857
www.boc-gases.com

Robert Bosch Ltd,
PO Box 98,
Broadwater Park, North Orbital Road,
Denham, Uxbridge,
Middx. UB9 5HJ
Tel: 01895 834 466
www.bosch.co.uk

Brink UK Ltd,
Unit 7, Centrovell Industrial Estate,
Calderwell Road, Nuneaton,
Warks CV11 4NG
Tel: 02476 352353
www.brink.eu

Clarke International,
Hemnall Street,
Epping, Essex CM16 4LG
Tel: 01992 565 300
www.clarkeinternational.com

David's Isopon,
See U-POL

Durafix (UK) Ltd,
41 Bowland Crescent,
Blackpool, Lancashire FY3 7TF
Tel: 0845 094 2131
www.durafix.co.uk

Fertan,
King and Queen House,
High Street,
Hamble, Hampshire SO31 4HA
Tel: 02380 456 600
www.fertan.co.uk

Hammerite Products Ltd,
Prudhoe,
Northumberland NE42 6LP
Tel: 01661 830 000
www.hammerite-automotive.com

Holt Lloyd International Ltd,
Oakhurst Drive,
Lawnhurst Trading Estate, Cheadle Heath,
Stockport SK3 0RZ
Tel: 0161 491 7391
www.holtsauto.com

ITW Finishing UK (De Vilbiss),
Ringwood Road, Bournemouth,
Dorset BH11 9LH
Tel: 01202 571 111
www.itwlfeuro.com

Murex Welding Products,
Hertford Road, Waltham,
Herts EN8 7RP
Tel: 01992 710 000
www.murexwelding.co.uk

Paint Technik,
PO Box 5066,
Leighton Buzzard,
Beds LU7 7YS
Tel: 01525 373 777

Ring Automotive,
Gelderd Road, Leeds, LS12 6NB
Tel: 0113 213 2000
www.ringautomotive.co.uk

Smith & Deakin Ltd,
75 Blackpole Trading Estate West,
Worcester WR3 8TJ
Tel: 01905 458 886
www.smithanddeakin.co.uk

Sykes-Pickavant Ltd
Full range of excellent DIY and professional panel beating tools. See local DIY and accessory shops.
www.sptools.co.uk

Unipart Group of Companies
Unipart House,
Garsington Road, Cowley, Oxon OX4 2PG
Tel: 01865 778 966
www.unipart.co.uk

U-POL,
Totteridge Lane, Whetstone,
London N20 0EY
Tel: 0870 8999 220

Welwyn Tool Group Ltd,
9 Blenheim Court,
Brownfields,
Welwyn Garden City,
Hertfordshire, AL7 1AD
Tel: 01707 331 111
www.welwyntoolgroup.com

Würth UK Ltd,
1 Centurion Way,
Erith, Kent DA18 4AF
Tel: 020 8319 6000
www.wurth.co.uk

Haynes
Restoration Manuals

Haynes
Restoration Manual
MGB (2nd Edition)

History   Mechanics
Buying   Interior
Specification   Electrics
Bodywork   Modifications

Lindsay Porter

For more information on books please contact: Customer Services,
Haynes Publishing, Sparkford, Yeovil, Somerset BA22 7JJ, UK
Tel. **01963 442030** Fax: **01963 440001**
Int. tel: **+44 1963 442030** Fax: **+44 1963 440001**
E-mail: **sales@haynes.co.uk** Website: **www.haynes.co.uk**